AQA Science
Additional Science

New GCSE

Jim Breithaupt
Ann Fullick
Lawrie Ryan
Bev Cox
Niva Miles
Gavin Reeder
John Scottow
Series Editor
Lawrie Ryan

Nelson Thornes

AQA examination questions are reproduced by permission of the
Assessment and Qualifications Alliance.

Published in 2011 by:
Nelson Thornes Ltd
Delta Place
27 Bath Road
CHELTENHAM
GL53 7TH
United Kingdom

11 12 13 14 15 / 10 9 8 7 6 5 4 3 2 1

A catalogue record for this book is available from the British
Library

ISBN 978 1 4085 0824 4

Cover photograph: Jack Peters/Getty Images

Illustrations include artwork drawn by Wearset Ltd and David
Russell Illustration

Page make-up by Wearset Ltd

Index created by Indexing Specialists (UK) Ltd

Printed and bound in Spain by GraphyCems

Photo acknowledgments

B1.1.4 iStockphoto; B1.1.1 Thomas Deerinck, NCMIR/Science
Photo Library; B1.2.1a Hybrid Medical Animation/Science Photo
Library; B1.2.1b Steve Gschmeissner/Science Photo Library;
B1.2.4 Eye Of Science/Science Photo Library; B1.4.3 Dr R.
Dourmashkin/Science Photo Library; B1.5.1 Eric Grave/Science
Photo Library; B2.1.1 Cordelia Molloy/Science Photo Library;
B2.3.1 iStockphoto; B2.3.2 Steve Gschmeissner/Science Photo
Library; B2.3.3 iStockphoto; B2.3.4 Cordelia Molloy/Science Photo
Library; B2.4.2 iStockphoto; B2.4.3 Noel Hendrickson/Getty;
B2.5.1 iStockphoto; B2.5.2 iStockphoto; B2.5.3 Roberto Danovaro;
B2.5.4 iStockphoto; B2.6.1 Edward Fullick; B2.6.4 Edward
Fullick; B2.7.1 iStockphoto; B2.7.2 Imagebroker/Imagebroker/
FLPA; B2.8.1 iStockphoto; B3.1.1 J.C. Revy, Ism/Science Photo
Library; B3.1.2 Martyn F. Chillmaid/Science Photo Library; B3.2.3
Darwin Dale/Science Photo Library; B3.4.1 Martyn F. Chillmaid/
Science Photo Library; B3.4.2 Dr P. Marazzi/Science Photo Library;
B3.5.1 iStockphoto; B3.5.2 iStockphoto; B3.5.3 Stuart Howells/
Rex; B3.6.1 allesalltag/Alamy; B3.6.2 Power And Syred/Science
Photo Library; B3.6.3 iStockphoto; B4.1.2 iStockphoto; B4.2.1
Eye Of Science/Science Photo Library; B4.3.1 iStockphoto; B4.3.2
iStockphoto; B5.1.2 Ed Reschke, Peter Arnold Inc./Science Photo
Library; B5.2.2 Eye Of Science/Science Photo Library; B5.3.2 Jan
Sochor/Alamy; B5.3.3 PA Photos; B5.4.1 Corbis; B5.5.1 CNRI/
Science Photo Library; B5.6.1 Zephyr/Science Photo Library;
B5.7 (left) Getty Images; B5.7 (right) Brand New Images; B5.8.1
iStockphoto; B6.1.1 Millard H. Sharp/Science Photo Library; B6.1.2
AFP/Getty Images; B6.2.1 Fotolia; B6.2.2 Desmond Dugan/FLPA;
B6.3.1 Norbert Wu/Minden Pictures/FLPA; B6.3.3 Martin Bond/
Science Photo Library; B6.4.1 iStockphoto; B6.4.2 Art Wolfe/
Science Photo Library; B6.4.3 Ulla Lohman.

C1.3.0 Fotolia; C1.3.1 Photolibrary; C1.4.1 Leonard Lee Rue/
Science Photo Library; C1.4.6 Dirk Wiersma/Science Photo
Library; C1.5.3 iStockphoto; C2.3.2 Fotolia; C2.4.1 Bloomberg/
Getty Images; C2.4.3a Fotolia; C2.4.3b iStockphoto; C2.4.4 Pascal
Goetgheluck/Science Photo Library; C2.5.1 Lawrence Lawry/
Science Photo Library; C2.5.2 Benelux Benelux/Photolibrary;
C2.5.5 Innershadows/Fotolia; C2.6.1 AFP/Getty Images; C2.6.2
Amaxim/Fotolia; C2.6.3a Pasieka/Science Photo Library; C2.6.3b
Laguna Design/Science Photo Library; C3.3.1 Bloomberg/Getty
Images; C3.4.1 iStockphoto; C3.6.1 Andrew Lambert Photography/
Science Photo Library; C3.6.2 Sciencephotos/Alamy; C3.7.1
Martyn F. Chillmaid; C3.7.2 Charles D. Winters/Science Photo
Library; C3.7.3 David Pearson/Alamy; C3.7.4a Mary Evans Picture
Library; C3.7.4b Noel Hendrickson/Photolibrary; C4.1.1 Colin
Marshall/FLPA; C4.2.1 Fotolia; C4.2.2 iStockphoto; C4.3.1 Age
Fotostock/Photolibrary; C4.3.2 iStockphoto; C4.4.1 Cordelia
Molloy/Science Photo Library; C4.5.1 Dr Keith Wheeler/Science
Photo Library; C4.5.2 Sheila Terry/Science Photo Library; C4.6.1
Sabine Lubnow FLPA; C4.6.2 Copyright 2009 American Chemical
Society; C4.7.1 iStockphoto; C4.7.2 iStockphoto; C4.7.3 Sian
Irvine/Photolibrary; C4.8.2 Martyn F. Chillmaid/Science Photo
Library; C4.8.3 Andrew Lambert Photography/Science Photo
Library; C4.9.1 Martyn F. Chillmaid; C4.9.3 Fuse/Getty Images;
C5.1.1a Martyn F. Chillmaid/Science Photo Library; C5.1.1b
Andrew Lambert Photography/Science Photo Library; C5.3.1
Adrian Sherratt/Alamy; C5.3.2 iStockphoto; C5.4.1 iStockphoto;
C5.6.1 iStockphoto; C5.7.2 iStockphoto; C5.8.1 iStockphoto,
C5.8.2 Aberenyi/Fotolia.

P1.1.1 Getty Images; P1.1.4 Martyn Chillmaid; P1.2.1 iStockphoto;
P1.2.3 Fotolia; P1.3.2a Data Harvest; P1.3.2b Martyn Chillmaid;
P2.3.3 Rob Melnychuk/Getty Images; P2.4.3 iStockphoto; P2.6.1
Martyn F. Chillmaid/Science Photo Library; P2.7.1 Martin Hospach/
Getty Images; P2.7.2 AFP/Getty Images; P2.7.3 iStockphoto;
P2.7.4 Cordelia Molloy/Science Photo Library; P3.1.1 iStockphoto;
P3.1.2 AFP/Getty Images; P3.3.2 iStockphoto; P3.4.1 Getty
Images; P3.5.3 AFP/Getty Images; P3.6.1 Photolibrary; P3.7.1
Fstop/Getty Images; P3.7.2 iStockphoto; P4.4.1a SSPL/Science
Museum; P5.1.1 Charles D. Winters/Science Photo Library; P5.2.3
iStockphoto; P5.3.1a Fotolia; P5.3.1b iStockphoto; P5.3.3 Fotolia;
P5.4.1 SSPL/Science Museum; P5.4.2 Cordelia Molloy/Science
Photo Library; P6.1.2 Popperfoto/Getty Images; P6.2.2 SSPL/
Science Museum; P6.6.3 Fotolia; P7.2.3 Photolibrary; P7.3.2
Getty Images; P7.3.3 Getty Images; P7.4.2 NOAO/AURA/NSF/T.
Rector and B.A. Wolpa; P7.4.3 Physics Today Collection/American
Institute Of Physics/Science Photo Library; P7.4.4 NASA Image
of the Day Collection; P7.5.3 X-ray: NASA/CXC/CfA/W. Forman et
al.; Optical: DSS; P7.6.1 NASA/ESA/JPL/Arizona State University;
P7.6.3 NASA/JPL/Cornell University.

Additional Science

Contents

Welcome to AQA GCSE Science!

This book has been written for you by the people who will be marking your exams, very experienced teachers and subject experts. It covers everything you need to know for your exams and is packed full of features to help you achieve the very best that you can.

Questions in yellow boxes check that you understand what you are learning as you go along. The answers are all within the text so if you don't know the answer, you can go back and reread the relevant section.

Figure 1 Many diagrams are as important for you to learn as the text, so make sure you revise them carefully.

Key words are highlighted in the text. You can look them up in the glossary at the back of the book if you are not sure what they mean.

 Where you see this icon, you will know that this part of the topic involves How Science Works – a really important part of your GCSE and an interesting way to understand 'how science works' in real life.

k Where you see this icon, there are supporting electronic resources in our Kerboodle online service.

Learning objectives

Each topic begins with key questions that you should be able to answer by the end of the lesson.

 Examiner's tip

Hints from the examiners who will mark your exams, giving you important advice on things to remember and what to watch out for.

Did you know ...?

There are lots of interesting, and often strange, facts about science. This feature tells you about many of them.

∞ links

Links will tell you where you can find more information about what you are learning.

Activity

An activity is linked to a main lesson and could be a discussion or task in pairs, groups or by yourself.

 Maths skills

This feature highlights the maths skills that you will need for your GCSE Science exams with short, visual explanations.

Practical

This feature helps you become familiar with key practicals. It may be a simple introduction, a reminder or the basis for a practical in the classroom.

Anything in the Higher Tier boxes must be learned by those sitting the Higher Tier exam. If you'll be sitting the Foundation Tier, these boxes can be missed out.

The same is true for any other places which are marked Higher or [H].

Higher

Summary questions

These questions give you the chance to test whether you have learned and understood everything in the topic. If you get any wrong, go back and have another look.

And at the end of each chapter you will find …

Summary questions

These will test you on what you have learned throughout the whole chapter, helping you to work out what you have understood and where you need to go back and revise.

Examination-style questions

These questions are examples of the types of questions you will answer in your actual GCSE exam, so you can get lots of practice during your course.

Key points

At the end of the topic are the important points that you must remember. They can be used to help with revision and summarising your knowledge.

B2 1.1 | Animal and plant cells ⓚ

Learning objectives

- What do the different parts of your cells do?
- Are human cells the same as other animal cells?
- How do plant and algal cells differ from animal cells?

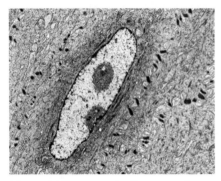

Figure 1 Diagrams of cells are much easier to understand than the real thing seen under a microscope. This picture shows a magnified animal cell.

The Earth is covered with a great variety of living things. However, they all have one thing in common – they are all made up of cells. Most cells are very small. You can only see them using a microscope.

The **light microscopes** in schools may magnify things several hundred times. Scientists have found out even more about cells using **electron microscopes**. These can magnify things more than a hundred thousand times!

Animal cells – structure and function

All cells have some features in common. We can see these clearly in animal cells. The cells of your body have these features, just like the cells of every other living thing.

- The **nucleus** – controls all the activities of the cell. It contains the genes on the chromosomes. They carry the instructions for making new cells or new organisms.
- The **cytoplasm** – a liquid gel in which most of the chemical reactions needed for life take place.
- The **cell membrane** – controls the passage of substances into and out of the cell.
- The **mitochondria** – structures in the cytoplasm where oxygen is used and most of the energy is released during respiration.
- **Ribosomes** – where **protein synthesis** takes place. All the proteins needed in the cell are made here.

Plant cells – structure and function

Plants are very different organisms from animals. They make their own food by photosynthesis. They stay in one place, and do not move their whole bodies about from one place to another.

Plant cells have all the features of a typical animal cell, but they also contain features that are needed for their very different way of life. Algae are simple aquatic organisms. They also make their own food and have many similar features to plant cells.

All plant and **algal cells** have:

- a **cell wall** made of **cellulose** that strengthens the cell and gives it support.

Many (but not all) plant cells also have these other features:

- **Chloroplasts** are found in all the green parts of the plant. They are green because they contain the green substance **chlorophyll**. Chlorophyll absorbs light energy to make food by photosynthesis. Root cells do not have chloroplast because they are underground and do not photosynthesise.
- A **permanent vacuole** is a space in the cytoplasm filled with cell sap. This is important for keeping the cells rigid to support the plant.

AQA *Examiner's tip*

Remember that not all plant cells have chloroplasts. Don't confuse chloroplasts and chlorophyll.

∞ links

For more information on photosynthesis, look at B2 2.1 Photosynthesis.

  a What are the main features found in all living cells?
  b How do plant cells differ from animal cells?

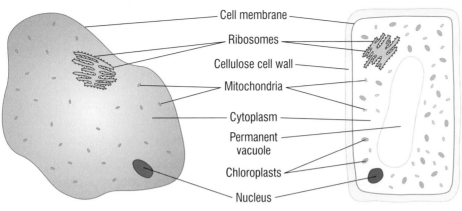

Figure 2 A simple **animal cell** like this shows the features which are common to all living cells – including human cells

Figure 3 A **plant cell** has many features in common with an animal cell, but others that are unique to plants

Practical

Looking at cells

Set up a microscope to look at plant cells, e.g. from onions and *Elodea*. You should see the cell wall, the cytoplasm and sometimes a vacuole but you won't see chloroplasts in the onion cells.

● Why won't you see any chloroplasts in the onion cells?

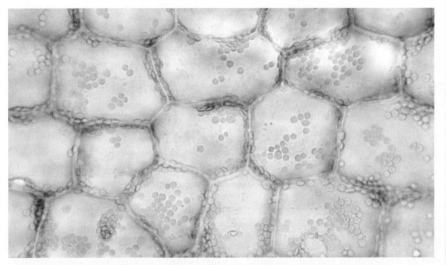

Figure 4 Microscopes can be used to look at the features of a plant cell

AQA Examiner's tip

Practise labelling an animal cell and a plant cell. You need to know the functions of each part of a cell. For example, chloroplasts contain chlorophyll, which absorbs light energy for photosynthesis. Write the functions of the parts on the diagram.

Summary questions

1 a List the main structures you would expect to find in an animal cell.

 b You would find all the things we have in animal cells also in a plant or algal cell. There are three extra features that are found in plant cells but not animal cells. What are they?

 c What are the main functions of these three extra structures?

2 Why are the nucleus and the mitochondria so important in all cells?

3 Chloroplasts are found in many plant cells but not all of them. Give an example of plant cells without chloroplasts and explain why they have none.

Key points

● Most human cells are like most other animal cells and contain a nucleus, cytoplasm, cell membrane, mitochondria and ribosomes.

● Plant and algal cells contain all the structures seen in animal cells as well as a cell wall. Many plant cells also contain chloroplasts and a permanent vacuole filled with sap.

B2 1.2

Bacteria and yeast ⓚ

Learning objectives

● What are bacterial cells like?

● How are yeast cells different from bacterial, plant and animal cells?

Bacteria are single-celled living organisms that are much smaller than animal and plant cells. Most bacteria are less than 1 µm in length. You could fit hundreds of thousands of bacteria on to the full stop at the end of this sentence. You can't see individual bacteria without a powerful microscope.

When you culture bacteria on an agar plate you grow many millions of bacteria. This enables you to see the **bacterial colony** with your naked eye.

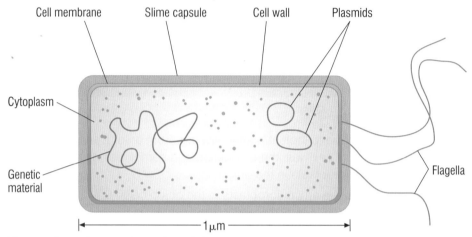

Figure 1 Bacteria come in a variety of shapes, but they all have the same basic structure

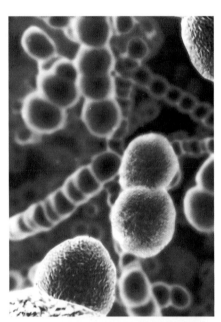

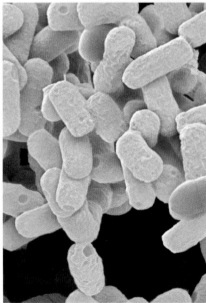

Figure 2 Bacteria come in several different shapes and sizes. This helps us to identify them under the microscope. *Streptococcus* causes sore throats and *E. coli* live in your gut.

Bacterial cells

Each bacterium is a single cell. It is made up of cytoplasm surrounded by a membrane and a cell wall. Inside the bacterial cell is the **genetic material**. Unlike animal, plant and algal cells, the genes are not contained in a nucleus. The long strand of DNA (the bacterial chromosome) is usually circular and found free in the cytoplasm.

Many bacterial cells also contain **plasmids**, which are small circular bits of DNA. These carry extra genetic information. Bacteria may have a slime capsule around the outside of the cell wall. Some types of bacterium have at least one flagellum (plural: flagella), a long protein strand that lashes about. These bacteria use their flagella to move themselves around.

Although some bacteria cause disease, many are harmless. Some are actually really useful to us. We use them to make food like yoghurt and cheese. Others are used in sewage treatment and to make medicines.

a How are bacteria different from animal and plant cells?

Yeast

Another type of microorganism that is very useful to people is yeast. Yeasts are single-celled organisms. Each yeast cell has a nucleus containing the genetic material, cytoplasm, and a membrane surrounded by a cell wall.

The cells vary in size but most are about 3–4 µm. This makes them bigger than bacteria but still very small.

The main way in which yeasts reproduce is by **asexual budding**. This involves a new yeast cell growing out from the original cell to form a new separate yeast organism.

b How do yeast cells differ from bacterial cells?

Yeast cells are specialised to be able to survive for a long time even when there is very little oxygen available. When yeast cells have plenty of oxygen they use **aerobic respiration**. They use oxygen to break down sugar to provide energy for the cell. During this process they produce water and carbon dioxide as waste products.

However, when there isn't much oxygen, yeast can use **anaerobic respiration**. When yeast cells break down sugar in the absence of oxygen, they produce **ethanol** and carbon dioxide.

Ethanol is commonly referred to as alcohol. The anaerobic respiration of yeast is sometimes called **fermentation**.

We have used yeast for making bread and alcoholic drinks almost as far back as human records go. We know yeast was used to make bread in Egypt 6000 years ago. Not only that, some ancient wine found in Iran is over 7000 years old.

Did you know ...?

In Ethiopia, natural yeast from the air is enough to make injera, the traditional bread. The dough is left for a couple of days before it is cooked for the yeast to produce carbon dioxide bubbles, which give injera its texture.

AQA Examiner's tip

Be clear about the similarities and differences between animal, plant, algal, bacterial and yeast cells.

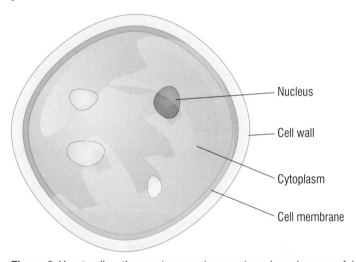

Figure 3 Yeast cells – these microscopic organisms have been useful to us for centuries

- Nucleus
- Cell wall
- Cytoplasm
- Cell membrane

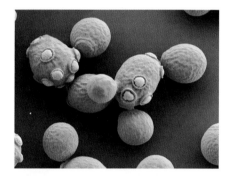

Figure 4 Brewers use the ethanol produced by yeast in their alcoholic drinks

Summary questions

1 Copy and complete using the words below:

   nucleus   bacteria   cell wall   microorganism   yeast   plasmids

   .... and .... are both types of .... Bacterial cells do not contain a .... but often have .... Bacteria and yeast cells both have a ....

2 **a** What is unusual about the genetic material in bacterial cells?
   b Which are bigger, bacterial cells or yeast cells?
   c What are flagella and what are they used for?

3 Make a table to compare the structures in animal, plant and algal, bacterial and yeast cells.

Key points

- A bacterial cell consists of cytoplasm and a membrane surrounded by a cell wall. The genes are not in a distinct nucleus.

- Yeast is a single-celled organism. Each cell has a nucleus, cytoplasm and a membrane surrounded by a cell wall.

B2 1.3

Specialised cells

Learning objectives

- What different types of cell are there?

- How is the structure of a specialised cell related to its function?

The smallest living organisms are single cells. They can carry out all of the functions of life. These range from feeding and respiration to excretion and reproduction. Most organisms are bigger and are made up of lots of cells. Some of these cells become **specialised** in order to carry out particular jobs.

When a cell becomes specialised its structure is adapted to suit the particular job it does. As a result, specialised cells often look very different to the 'typical' plant or animal cell. Sometimes cells become so specialised that they only have one function within the body. Examples of this include sperm, eggs, red blood cells and nerve cells.

Fat cells

If you eat more food than you need, your body makes fat and stores it in fat cells. These cells help animals, including us, to survive when food is in short supply. Fat cells have three main adaptations:

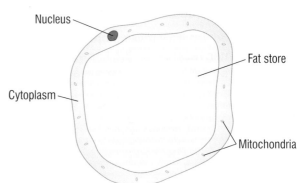

- Nucleus
- Fat store
- Cytoplasm
- Mitochondria

- They have a small amount of cytoplasm and large amounts of fat.

- They have few mitochondria as the cell needs very little energy.

- They can expand – a fat cell can end up 1000 times its original size as it fills up with fat.

Cone cells from human eye

Cone cells are in the light-sensitive layer of your eye (the retina). They make it possible for you to see in colour. Cone cells have three main adaptations:

- Outer segment – containing visual pigment
- Middle section – many mitochondria
- Nucleus
- Synapses – connections to nerve cells in optic nerve

- The outer segment contains a special chemical (a visual pigment). This changes chemically in coloured light. It needs energy to change it back to its original form.

- The middle segment is packed full of mitochondria. The mitochondria release the energy needed to reform the visual pigment. This lets you see continually in colour.

- The final part of the cone cell is a specialised synapse that connects to the **optic nerve**. When coloured light makes your visual pigment change, an impulse is triggered. The impulse crosses the synapse and travels along the optic nerve to your brain.

a In which part of the cone cell do we find mitochondria?

Root hair cells

You find root hair cells close to the tips of growing roots. Plants need to take in lots of water (and dissolved mineral ions). The root hair cells help them to take up water more efficiently. Root hair cells are always close to the xylem tissue. The xylem tissue carries water and mineral ions up into the rest of the plant.

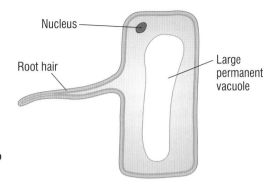

Root hair cells have two main adaptations:

- The root hairs increase the surface area for water to move into the cell.
- The root hair cells have a large permanent vacuole that speeds up the movement of water by osmosis from the soil across the root hair cell.

Sperm cells

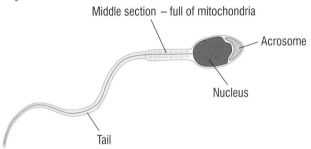

Sperm cells are usually released a long way from the egg they are going to fertilise. They contain the genetic information from the male parent. Depending on the type of animal, they need to move through water or through the female reproductive system to reach an egg. Then they have to break into the egg. Sperm cells have several adaptations to make all this possible:

- Long tail whips from side to side and helps move the sperm towards the egg.
- The middle section is full of mitochondria, which provide the energy for the tail to work.
- The acrosome stores digestive enzymes for breaking down the outer layers of the egg.
- A large nucleus contains the genetic information to be passed on.

b Why do sperm contain digestive enzymes?

Practical

Observing specialised cells

Try looking at different specialised cells under a microscope.

When you look at a specialised cell there are two useful questions you can ask yourself:

- How is this cell different in structure from a generalised cell?
- How does the difference in structure help it to carry out its function?

Summary questions

1 Make a table to explain how the structure of each cell on this spread is adapted to its function.

2 Think back to two other types of specialised cells you have met in biology, e.g. motor neurons, photosynthetic cells in plants, red or white blood cells.
Draw the cells you have chosen. Label them fully to show how the structures you can see are related to the function of the cells.

Key points

- Cells may be specialised to carry out a particular function.
- Examples of specialised cells are fat cells, cone cells, root hair cells and sperm cells.

B2 1.4

Diffusion

Learning objectives

- What is diffusion?
- What affects the rate of diffusion?

Your cells need to take in substances such as glucose and oxygen for respiration. Dissolved substances and gases can move into and out of your cells across the cell membrane. One of the main ways in which they move is by **diffusion.** Cells also need to get rid of waste products and chemicals that are needed elsewhere in your body.

Diffusion

Diffusion is the spreading out of the particles of a gas, or of any substance in solution (a solute). This results in the **net movement** (overall movement) of particles. The net movement is from an area of high concentration to an area of lower concentration. It takes place because of the random movement of the particles. All the particles are moving and bumping into each other and this moves them all around.

    a What is diffusion?

Imagine a room containing a group of boys and a group of girls. If everyone closes their eyes and moves around briskly but randomly, children will bump into each other. They will scatter until the room contains a mixture of boys and girls. This gives you a good model of diffusion.

 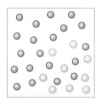

At the moment, when the blue particles are added to the red particles they are not mixed at all

As the particles move randomly, the blue ones begin to mix with the red ones

As the particles move and spread out, they bump into each other. This helps them to keep spreading randomly

Eventually, the particles are completely mixed and diffusion is complete

Figure 1 The random movement of particles results in substances spreading out or diffusing from an area of higher concentration to an area of lower concentration

Rates of diffusion

If there is a big difference in concentration between two areas, diffusion will take place quickly. Many particles will move randomly towards the area of low concentration. Only a few will move randomly in the other direction. However, if there is only a small difference in concentration between two areas, the net movement by diffusion will be quite slow. The number of particles moving into the area of lower concentration by random movement will only be slightly bigger than the number of particles that are leaving the area.

The net movement = particles moving in – particles moving out.

In general, the greater the difference in concentration, the faster the rate of diffusion. This difference between two areas of concentration is called the **concentration gradient**. The bigger the difference, the steeper the concentration gradient. The steeper the concentration gradient, the faster diffusion will take place. Diffusion occurs *down* a concentration gradient.

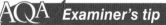
Examiner's tip

Particles diffuse randomly but the net movement is from a region of high concentration to a region of low concentration.

    b What is meant by the net movement of particles?

Both types of particles can pass through this membrane – it is freely permeable

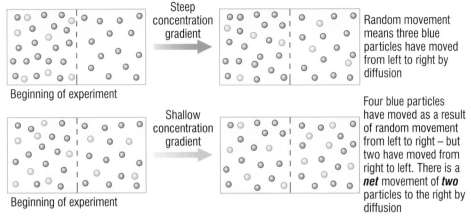

Steep concentration gradient

Random movement means three blue particles have moved from left to right by diffusion

Beginning of experiment

Shallow concentration gradient

Beginning of experiment

Four blue particles have moved as a result of random movement from left to right – but two have moved from right to left. There is a *net* movement of *two* particles to the right by diffusion

Figure 2 This diagram shows the effect of concentration on the rate of diffusion. This is why so many body systems are adapted to maintain steep concentration gradients.

Temperature also affects the rate of diffusion. An increase in temperature means the particles in a gas or a solution move more quickly. Diffusion takes place more rapidly as the random movement of the particles speeds up.

Diffusion in living organisms

Many important substances can move across your cell membranes by diffusion. Water is one, as well as simple sugars, such as glucose. The **amino acids** from the breakdown of proteins in your gut can also pass through cell membranes by diffusion.

The oxygen you need for respiration passes from the air into your lungs. From there it gets into your red blood cells through the cell membranes by diffusion. The oxygen moves along a concentration gradient from a region of high to low oxygen concentration.

Individual cells may be adapted to make diffusion easier and more rapid. The most common adaptation is to increase the surface area of the cell membrane. Increasing the surface area means there is more room for diffusion to take place. By folding up the membrane of a cell, or the tissue lining an organ, the area over which diffusion can take place is greatly increased. Therefore the rate of diffusion is also greatly increased. This means much more of a substance moves in a given time.

AQA Examiner's tip

Do not refer to movement *along* a gradient – this does not tell us whether it is from high to low or the other way!

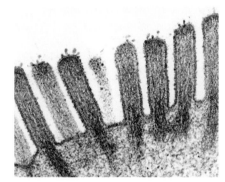

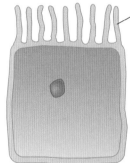

Infoldings of the cell membrane form microvilli, which increase the surface area of the cell

Figure 3 An increase in the surface area of a cell membrane means diffusion can take place more quickly. This is an intestinal cell.

Key points

- Dissolved substances and gases such as oxygen move in and out of cells by diffusion.

- Diffusion is the net movement of particles from an area where they are at a high concentration to an area where they are at a lower concentration.

- The greater the difference in concentration, the faster the rate of diffusion.

Summary questions

1 Copy and complete using the words below:

diffusion gas high lower random solute

.... is the net movement of particles of a .... or a .... from an area of .... concentration to an area of .... concentration as a result of the .... movement of the particles.

2 **a** Explain why diffusion takes place faster when there is an increase in temperature.

   b Explain in terms of diffusion why so many cells have folded membranes along at least one surface.

B2 1.5

Tissues and organs

Learning objectives

- What is a tissue?
- What is an organ?

⌒⌒ **links**

For more information on specialised cells, look back at B2 1.3 Specialised cells.

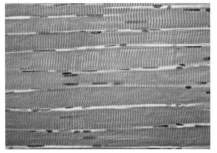

Figure 1 Muscle tissue like this contracts to move your skeleton around

Large **multicellular organisms** have to overcome the problems linked to their size. They develop different ways of exchanging materials. During the development of a multicellular organism, cells **differentiate**. They become specialised to carry out particular jobs. For example, in animals, muscle cells have a different structure to blood and nerve cells. In plants the cells where photosynthesis takes place are very different to root hair cells.

However, the adaptations of multicellular organisms go beyond specialised cells. Similar specialised cells are often found grouped together to form a tissue.

Tissues

A **tissue** is a group of cells with similar structure and function working together. **Muscular tissue** can contract to bring about movement. **Glandular tissue** contains secretory cells that can produce substances such as enzymes and hormones. **Epithelial tissue** covers the outside of your body as well as your internal organs.

Plants have tissues too. **Epidermal tissues** cover the surfaces and protect them. **Mesophyll tissues** contain lots of chloroplasts and can carry out photosynthesis. **Xylem** and **phloem** are the transport tissues in plants. They carry water and dissolved mineral ions from the roots up to the leaves and dissolved food from the leaves around the plant.

a What is a tissue?

Organs

Organs are made up of tissues. One organ can contain several tissues, all working together. For example, the stomach is an organ involved in the digestion of your food. It contains:

- muscular tissue to churn the food and **digestive juices** of the stomach together
- glandular tissue, to produce the digestive juices that break down food
- epithelial tissue, which covers the inside and the outside of the organ.

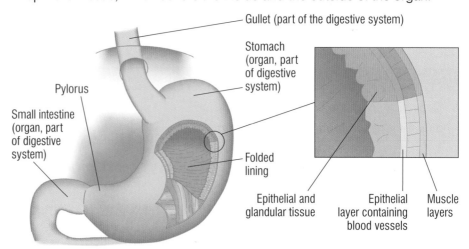

Figure 2 The stomach contains several different tissues, each with a different function in the organ

The pancreas is an organ that has two important functions. It makes hormones to control our blood sugar. It also makes some of the enzymes that digest our food. It contains two very different types of tissue to produce these different secretions.

To summarise, an organ is a collection of different tissues working together to carry out important functions in your body.

b What is an organ?

Different organs are combined in **organ systems** to carry out major functions in the body. These functions include transporting the blood or digesting food. The organ systems together make up your body.

Adaptations for exchange

Many of the organs of the body have developed to enable exchange to take place. For example:

● there is an exchange of gases in the lungs
● digested food moves from the **small intestine** into the blood
● many different dissolved substances are filtered out of the blood into the **kidney tubules**. Some of them then move back from the tubules into the blood.

These organs have adaptations that make the exchange of materials easier and more efficient.

Many of these adaptations increase the surface area over which materials are exchanged. The bigger the surface area, the more quickly diffusion can take place.

Other adaptations increase the concentration gradient across the membranes. The steeper the concentration gradient, the faster diffusion takes place. Many organs have a good blood supply, bringing substances in and taking them out. This helps to maintain the steep concentration gradient needed for diffusion to take place more rapidly.

Did you know ... ?

A human liver cell is about $10\,\mu m$ (1×10^{-5} m) in diameter. A human liver is about 22.5 cm (2.5×10^{-1} m) across. It contains a lot of liver cells!

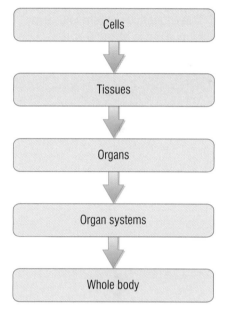

Figure 3 Larger living organisms have many levels of organisation

Summary questions

1 Copy and complete using the words below:

specialised tissue differentiated function multicellular

A .... organism is made up of many different cells. Some of these cells have .... and become .... to carry out a particular .... in the body. A group of these specialised cells working together forms a ....

2 For each of the following, state whether they are a specialised cell, a tissue or an organ. Explain your answer.
   a sperm
   b kidney
   c stomach

3 Find out and explain how the small intestine and the lungs are adapted to provide the biggest possible surface area for the exchange of materials within the organs.

Key points

● A tissue is a group of cells with similar structure and function.

● Organs are made of tissues. One organ may contain several types of tissue.

Organ systems

Learning objectives

- What are organ systems?
- What organs form the digestive system?
- What are plant organs?

?? Did you know ...?

The digestive system is 6–9 m long. That is about 9×10^6 times longer than an average human cell!

Organ systems are groups of organs that all work together to perform a particular function. The way one organ functions often depends on others in the system. The human digestive system is a good example of an organ system.

The digestive system

The digestive system of humans and other mammals exchanges substances with the environment. The food you take in and eat is made up of large **insoluble molecules**. Your body cannot absorb and use these molecules. They need to be broken down or digested to form smaller, soluble molecules. These can then be absorbed and used by your cells. This process of digestion takes place in your **digestive system**.

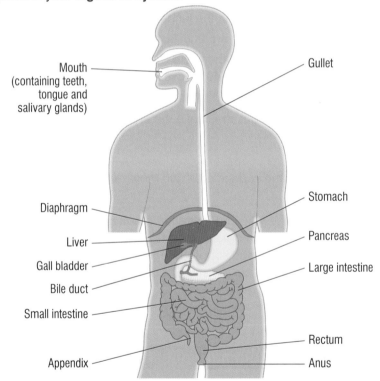

Mouth (containing teeth, tongue and salivary glands)

Gullet

Diaphragm

Stomach

Liver

Pancreas

Gall bladder

Large intestine

Bile duct

Small intestine

Rectum

Appendix

Anus

Figure 1 The main organs of the human digestive system

The digestive system is a **muscular tube** that squeezes your food through it. It starts at one end with your mouth, and finishes at the other with your anus. The digestive system contains many different organs. There are glands such as the pancreas and **salivary glands**. These glands make and release digestive juices containing enzymes to break down your food.

The stomach and the small intestine are the main organs where food is digested. Enzymes break down the large insoluble food molecules into smaller, soluble ones.

Your small intestine is also where the soluble food molecules are absorbed into your blood. Once there they get transported in the bloodstream around your body. The small intestine is adapted to have a very large surface area. This increases diffusion from the gut to the blood.

The muscular walls of the gut squeeze the undigested food onwards into your large intestine. This is where water is absorbed from the undigested food into your blood. The material left forms the faeces. Faeces are stored and then pass out of your body through the rectum and anus back into the environment.

a What is the digestive system and what does it do?

Plant organs

Animals are not the only organisms to have organs and organ systems – plants do too.

Plants have differentiated cells that form specialised tissues. These include mesophyll, xylem and phloem. Within the body of a plant, tissues such as these are arranged to form organs. Each organ carries out its own particular functions.

Plant organs include the leaves, stems and roots, each of which has a very specific job to do.

b What are the main organs in a plant?

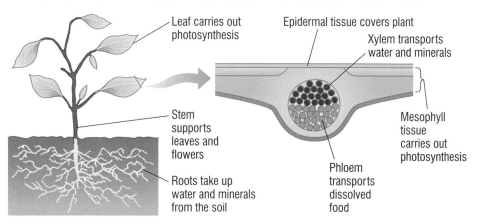

Leaf carries out photosynthesis

Epidermal tissue covers plant

Xylem transports water and minerals

Stem supports leaves and flowers

Mesophyll tissue carries out photosynthesis

Phloem transports dissolved food

Roots take up water and minerals from the soil

Figure 2 Plant organs and tissues

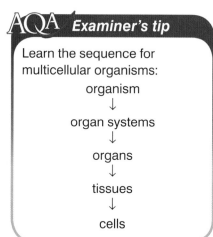

Did you know … ?

Some trees, like giant redwoods, have trunks over 40 m tall. A plant cell is about $100\,\mu m$ long. So the plant organ is 4×10^5 times bigger than the individual cells.

AQA Examiner's tip

Learn the sequence for multicellular organisms:

organism
↓
organ systems
↓
organs
↓
tissues
↓
cells

Summary questions

1 Match each of the following organs to its correct function.

A stem	**i** breaking down large insoluble molecules into smaller soluble molecules
B root	**ii** photosynthesising in plants
C small intestine for absorption	**iii** providing support in plants
D leaf	**iv** anchoring plants and obtaining water and minerals from soil

2 Explain the difference between organs and organ systems, giving two examples.

3 Using the human digestive system as an example, explain how the organs in an organ system rely on each other to function properly.

Key points

- Organ systems are groups of organs that perform a particular function.

- The digestive system in a mammal is an example of a system where substances are exchanged with the environment.

- Plant organs include stems, roots and leaves.

Summary questions 🄚

1 *Chlamydomonas* is a single-celled organism that lives under water. It can move itself to the light to photosynthesise, and stores excess food as starch.

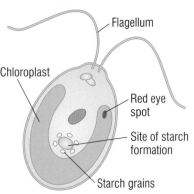

Flagellum
Chloroplast
Red eye spot
Site of starch formation
Starch grains

   a What features does it have in common with most plant cells?

   b What features are not like plant cells and what are they used for?

   c Would you class *Chlamydomonas* as a plant cell or an animal cell? Explain why.

2

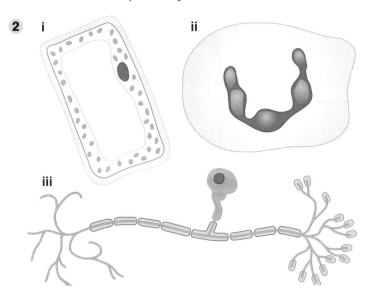

i   ii

iii

Each of these cells is specialised for a particular function in your body.

   a Copy each of these diagrams and label the cells carefully. Carry out some research if necessary.

   b Describe what you think is the function of each of these cells.

   c Explain how the structure of the cell is related to its function.

3 a Draw and label a bacterial cell and a yeast cell.

   b What are the common structures in all plant, algal and animal cells? Describe their functions.

4 a What is diffusion?

   b If you cut your hand and then put it in a bowl of water, it looks as if there is a lot of blood. Explain why this happens.

   c The scent of flowers in a garden is much more noticeable on a warm, still day than it is on a cold, still day. Explain this in terms of diffusion.

5 a What effect does surface area have on diffusion?

   b Describe one way in which the following can be adapted to increase the surface area available for diffusion:
     i individual cells
     ii body organs.

6 Plants have specialised cells, tissues and organs just as animals do.

   a Give three examples of plant tissues.

   b What are the main plant organs and what do they do?

   c Which plant tissues are found in all of the main plant organs and why?

7 It is possible to separate the different parts of a cell using a centrifuge which spins around rather like a very fast spin dryer. They are used to separate structures that might be mixed together in a liquid. One of their uses is to separate the different parts of a cell.

The cells are first broken open so that the contents spill out into the liquid. The mixture is then put into the centrifuge. The centrifuge starts to spin slowly and a pellet forms at the bottom of the tube. This is removed. The rest is put back into the centrifuge at a higher speed and the next pellet removed and so on.

Here are some results:

Centrifuge speed (rpm*)	Part of cell in pellet
3000	nuclei
10000	mitochondria
12000	ribosomes

*rpm = revolutions per minute

   a From these observations can you suggest a link between the speed of the centrifuge and the size of the part of the cell found in the pellet?

   b What apparatus would you need to test your suggestion?

   c If your suggestion is correct, what results would you expect?

   d What would be the easiest measurement to make to show the size of the mitochondria?

   e Suggest how many mitochondria you might measure.

   f How would you calculate the mean for the measurements you have taken?

AQA Examination-style questions 🄚

1 The diagram shows a plant cell.

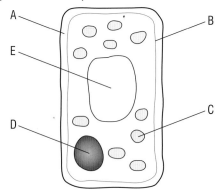

a Identify the structures listed. Choose the correct letter A, B, C, D or E for each structure.
  i nucleus (1)
  ii chloroplast (1)
  iii cell wall (1)

b Animal cells are different from plant cells.
Give the letters of the two parts that are also found in animal cells. (2)

c What is a tissue? (2)

2 The parts of plant cells have important functions. **List A** contains names of cell parts. **List B** lists some functions of cell parts.

Match each cell part to its correct function.

List A	List B
nucleus	controls entry of materials into cell
mitochondria	produce protein
chloroplasts	release energy
ribosomes	controls cell activities
	absorb light for photosynthesis

(4)

3 Plant and animal organs contain tissues.

a Name one example of a plant tissue and describe its function. (2)

b **i** Name one example of an animal tissue. (1)
  ii Give an example of an organ where this tissue would be found. (1)
  iii What is the function of the tissue you have named? (1)

4 The diagram shows four ways in which molecules may move into and out of a cell. The dots show the concentration of molecules.

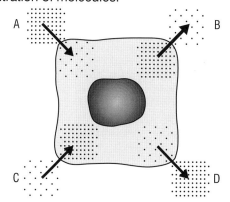

a Name the cell structure that controls the movement of materials into or out of cells. (1)

b **i** Name the process illustrated by A and B. (1)
  ii Explain the direction of the arrows in A and B. (2)

5 The diagram shows a yeast cell.

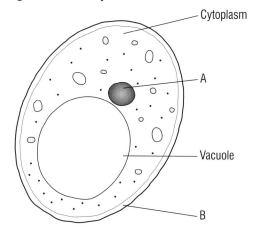

a Identify the parts labelled A and B. (2)

b The cytoplasm also contains mitochondria and ribosomes.
What is the function of these structures? (2)

c Suggest what is found in the vacuole. (1)

6 *In this question you will be assessed on using good English, organising information clearly and using specialist terms where appropriate.*

The digestive system is a group of organs which changes food from insoluble into soluble molecules. Soluble molecules can be absorbed into the blood stream. Some food cannot be digested.

Describe the functions (jobs) of the organs in the digestive system. (6)

B2 2.1

Photosynthesis

Learning objectives

- What is photosynthesis?
- What are the raw materials for photosynthesis?
- Where does the energy for photosynthesis come from and how do plants absorb it?

Like all living organisms, plants and algae need food. It provides them with the energy for respiration, growth and reproduction. But plants don't need to eat – they can make their own food. They do it by photosynthesis. This takes place in the green parts of plants (especially the leaves) when it is light. Algae can also carry out photosynthesis.

The process of photosynthesis

Photosynthesis can be summed up in the following equation:

$$\text{carbon dioxide} + \text{water} \xrightarrow{\text{(+ light energy)}} \text{glucose} + \text{oxygen}$$

The cells in algae and the leaves of a plant are full of small green parts called chloroplasts. They contain a green substance called chlorophyll.

During photosynthesis, light energy is absorbed by the chlorophyll in the chloroplasts. This energy is then used to convert carbon dioxide from the air plus water from the soil into a simple sugar called **glucose**. The chemical reaction also produces oxygen gas as a by-product. The gas is released into the air, which we can then use when we breathe it in.

a Write the word equation for photosynthesis.

Some of the glucose produced during photosynthesis is used immediately by the cells of the plant. However, a lot of the glucose made is converted into insoluble starch and stored.

Iodine solution is a yellow-brown liquid. It turns dark blue when it reacts with starch. You can use this iodine test for starch to show that photosynthesis has taken place in a plant.

Practical

Producing oxygen

You can show that a plant is photosynthesising by the oxygen given off as a by-product. Oxygen is a colourless gas, but if you use water plants you can see and collect the bubbles of gas they give off when they are photosynthesising. The gas will relight a glowing splint, showing that it is oxygen.

Practical

Testing for starch

To show that light is vital for photosynthesis to take place:

Take a leaf from a plant kept in the light and a plant kept in the dark for at least 24 hours. Leaves have to be specially prepared so the iodine solution can reach the cells. Just adding iodine to a leaf is not enough, because the waterproof cuticle keeps the iodine out so it can't react with the starch. The green chlorophyll would mask any colour changes if the iodine did react with the starch. You need to treat the leaves by boiling them in ethanol first to destroy the waxy cuticle and remove the colour. The leaves are then rinsed in hot water to soften them. After treating the leaves, use iodine solution to show how important light is (see Figure 1).

- What happens in the test? Explain your observations.

Safety: Take care when using ethanol. It is volatile, flammable, and harmful. Always wear eye protection.

Figure 1 These **variegated** leaves came from a plant which has been kept in the light for several hours. The one on the right has been tested for starch, using iodine solution.

b What is chlorophyll?

Leaf adaptations

The leaves of plants are perfectly adapted because:

- most leaves are broad, giving them a big surface area for light to fall on
- they contain chlorophyll in the chloroplasts to absorb the light energy
- they have air spaces that allow carbon dioxide to get to the cells, and oxygen to leave them by diffusion
- they have veins, which bring plenty of water to the cells of the leaves.

These adaptations mean the plant can photosynthesise as much as possible whenever there is light available.

Algae are aquatic so they are adapted to photosynthesising in water. They absorb carbon dioxide dissolved in the water around them.

c How does the broad shape of leaves help photosynthesis to take place?

AQA *Examiner's tip*

- Learn the word equation for photosynthesis.
- Be able to explain the results of experiments on photosynthesis.

Practical

Observing leaves

Look at a whole plant leaf and then a section of a leaf under a microscope. You can see how well adapted it is. Compare what you can see with Figure 2.

- What magnification did you use?

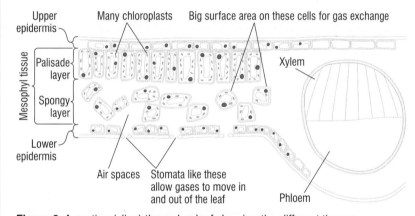

Figure 2 A section (slice) through a leaf showing the different tissues

?? Did you know ...?

Every year plants produce about 368 000 000 000 tonnes of oxygen, so there is plenty to go round!

Summary questions

1 Copy and complete using the words below:

   carbon dioxide   chlorophyll   energy   gas   glucose   light   oxygen   water

   During photosynthesis .... energy is absorbed by ...., a substance found in the chloroplasts. This .... is then used to convert .... from the air and .... from the soil into a simple sugar called .... is also produced and released as a ....

2 a Where does a plant get the carbon dioxide and water that it needs for photosynthesis, and how does it get the light it needs?
   b Where do algae get the same things from?
   c Work out the path taken by a carbon atom as it moves from being part of the carbon dioxide in the air to being part of a starch molecule in a plant

Key points

- Photosynthesis can be summed up by the equation:

  (+ light energy)
  carbon dioxide + water ⟶ glucose + oxygen.

- During photosynthesis light energy is absorbed by chlorophyll in the chloroplasts of the green parts of the plant. It is used to convert carbon dioxide and water into sugar (glucose). Oxygen is released as a by-product.

- Leaves are well adapted to allow the maximum amount of photosynthesis to take place.

B2 2.2 Limiting factors

Learning objectives

- What factors limit the rate of photosynthesis in plants?
- How can we use what we know about limiting factors to grow more food?

AQA *Examiner's tip*

Make sure you can explain limiting factors.
Learn to interpret graphs that show the effect of limiting factors on photosynthesis.

You may have noticed that plants grow quickly in the summer, yet they hardly grow at all in the winter. Plants need certain things to grow quickly. They need light, warmth and carbon dioxide if they are going to photosynthesise as fast as they can.

Sometimes any one or more of these things can be in short supply. Then they may limit the amount of photosynthesis a plant can manage. This is why they are known as **limiting factors**.

a Why do you think plants grow faster in the summer than in the winter?

Light

The most obvious factor affecting the rate of photosynthesis is light. If there is plenty of light, lots of photosynthesis can take place. If there is very little or no light, photosynthesis will stop. It doesn't matter what other conditions are like around the plant. For most plants, the brighter the light, the faster the rate of photosynthesis.

Practical

How does the intensity of light affect the rate of photosynthesis?

We can look at this experimentally (see Figure 1). At the start, the rate of photosynthesis goes up as the light intensity increases. This tells us that light intensity is a limiting factor.

When the light is moved away from this water plant, the rate of photosynthesis falls – shown by a slowing in the stream of oxygen bubbles being produced. If the light is moved closer (keeping the water temperature constant) the stream of bubbles becomes faster, showing an increased rate of photosynthesis.

However, we reach a point when no matter how bright the light, the rate of photosynthesis stays the same. At this point, light is no longer limiting the rate of photosynthesis. Something else has become the limiting factor.

The results can be plotted on a graph, which shows the effect of light intensity on the rate of photosynthesis.

- Why is light a limiting factor for photosynthesis?
- Name the **independent** and the **dependent variables** in this investigation.

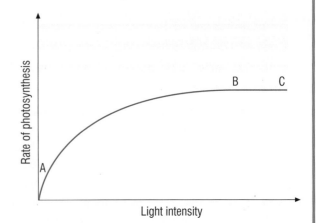

Figure 1 Investigating the effect of light intensity on the rate of photosynthesis

Temperature

Temperature affects all chemical reactions, including photosynthesis. As the temperature rises, the rate of photosynthesis increases as the reaction speeds up. However, photosynthesis is controlled by enzymes. Most enzymes are destroyed (denatured) once the temperature rises to around 40–50°C. So if the temperature gets too high, the enzymes controlling photosynthesis are denatured. Therefore the rate of photosynthesis will fall (see Figure 2).

b Why does temperature affect photosynthesis?

Carbon dioxide levels

Plants need carbon dioxide to make glucose. The atmosphere only contains about 0.04% carbon dioxide. This means that carbon dioxide levels often limit the rate of photosynthesis. Increasing the carbon dioxide levels will increase the rate of photosynthesis.

On a sunny day, carbon dioxide levels are the most common limiting factor for plants. The carbon dioxide levels around a plant tend to rise at night. That's because in the dark a plant respires but doesn't photosynthesise. Then, as the light and temperature levels increase in the morning, the carbon dioxide all gets used up.

However, in a science lab or greenhouse the levels of carbon dioxide can be increased artificially. This means they are no longer limiting. Then the rate of photosynthesis increases with the rise in carbon dioxide.

In a garden, woodland or field rather than a lab, light, temperature and carbon dioxide levels interact and any one of them might be the factor that limits photosynthesis.

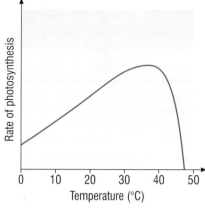

Figure 2 The effect of increasing temperature on the rate of photosynthesis

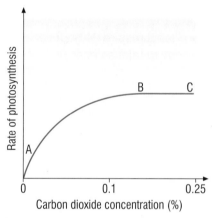

Figure 3 This graph shows the effect of increasing carbon dioxide levels on the rate of photosynthesis at a given light level and temperature

Summary questions

1 a What is photosynthesis?
  b What are the three main limiting factors that affect the rate of photosynthesis in a plant?

2 a In each of these situations *one* factor in particular is most likely to be limiting photosynthesis. In *each* case listed below, suggest which factor this is and explain why the rate of photosynthesis is limited.
  i a wheat field first thing in the morning
  ii the same field later on in the day
  iii plants growing on a woodland floor in winter
  iv plants growing on a woodland floor in summer.
  b Why is it impossible to be certain which factor is involved in each of these cases?

3 Look at the graph in Figure 1.
  a Explain what is happening between points A and B on the graph.
  b Explain what is happening between points B and C on the graph.
  c Look at Figure 2. Explain why it is a different shape to the other two graphs shown in Figures 1 and 0.

Key points

- The rate of photosynthesis may be limited by shortage of light, low temperature and shortage of carbon dioxide.

- We can manipulate the levels of light, temperature and carbon dioxide artificially to increase the rate of photosynthesis in food crops.

B2 2.3 How plants use glucose

Learning objectives

- What do plants do with the glucose they make?
- How do plants store food?
- What other materials do plant and algal cells need to produce proteins?

Examiner's tip

Two important points to remember:

- Plants respire 24 hours a day to release energy.
- Glucose is soluble in water, but starch is insoluble.

Figure 2 Algal cells contain a nucleus and chloroplasts so they can photosynthesise

Plants and algae make glucose when they photosynthesise. This glucose is vital for their survival. Some of the glucose produced during photosynthesis is used immediately by the cells. They use it for respiration to provide energy for cell functions such as growth and reproduction.

Using glucose

Plants cells and algal cells, like any other living cells, respire all the time. They use some of the glucose produced during photosynthesis as they respire. The glucose is broken down using oxygen to provide energy for the cells. Carbon dioxide and water are the waste products of the reaction.

Figure 1 Worldwide, algae produce more oxygen and biomass by photosynthesis than plants do – but we often forget all about them

The energy released in respiration is used to build up smaller molecules into bigger molecules. Some of the glucose is changed into starch for storage. Plants and algae also build up glucose into more complex carbohydrates like cellulose. They use this to strengthen the cell walls.

Plants use some of the glucose from photosynthesis to make amino acids. They do this by combining sugars with **nitrate ions** and other **mineral ions** from the soil. These amino acids are then built up into proteins to be used in the cells. This uses energy from respiration.

Algae also make amino acids. They do this by taking the nitrate ions and other materials they need from the water they live in.

Plants and algae also use glucose from photosynthesis and energy from respiration to build up fats and oils. These may be used in the cells as an energy store. They are sometimes used in the cell walls to make them stronger. In addition, plants often use fats or oils as an energy store in their seeds. They provide lots of energy for the new plant as it germinates.

Some algal cells are very rich in oils. They are even being considered as a possible source of biofuels for the future.

a Why do plants respire?

Starch for storage

Plants make food by photosynthesis in their leaves and other green parts. However, the food is needed all over the plant. It is moved around the plant in the phloem.

Plants convert some of the glucose produced in photosynthesis into starch to be stored. Glucose is soluble in water. If it were stored in plant cells it could affect the way water moves into and out of the cells. Lots of glucose stored in plant cells could affect the water balance of the whole plant.

Figure 3 Oilseed rape plants use energy from respiration and glucose from photosynthesis to produce oil to store in their seeds. We use this to make oil for cooking and as a source of biofuels.

Starch is insoluble in water. It will have no effect on the water balance of the plant. This means that plants can store large amounts of starch in their cells.

So, the main energy store in plants is starch and it is found all over a plant. It is stored in the cells of the leaves. The starch provides an energy store for when it is dark or when light levels are low.

Insoluble starch is also kept in special storage areas of a plant. Many plants produce **tubers** and bulbs. These help them to survive through the winter. They are full of stored starch. We often take advantage of these starch stores and eat them ourselves. Potatoes and onions are all full of starch to keep a plant going until spring comes again.

b What is the main storage substance in plants?

Summary questions

1 Copy and complete using the words below:

energy glucose growth photosynthesise respiration reproduction starch storage 24

Plants make .... when they .... Some of the glucose produced is used by the cells of the plant for ...., which goes on .... hours a day. It provides .... for cell functions, ... and .... Some glucose is converted to .... for ....

2 List as many ways as possible in which a plant uses the glucose produced by photosynthesis.

3 a Why is some of the glucose made by photosynthesis converted to starch to be stored in the plant?
 b Where might you find starch in a plant?
 c How could you show that a potato is a store of starch?

Practical

Making starch

The presence of starch in a leaf is evidence that photosynthesis has taken place. You can test for starch using the iodine test. See B2 2.1 Photosynthesis for details of how to treat the leaves so they will absorb the iodine. After this treatment, adding iodine will show you clearly if the leaf has been photosynthesising or not.

Figure 4 The leaf on the right has been kept in the dark. Its starch stores have been used for respiration or moved to other parts of the plant. The leaf on the left has been in the light and been able to photosynthesise. The glucose has been converted to starch, which is clearly visible when it reacts with iodine and turns blue-black.

Key points

- Plant and algal cells use the soluble glucose they produce during photosynthesis in several different ways:
 – for respiration
 – to convert into insoluble starch for storage
 – to produce fats or oils for storage
 – to produce fats, proteins or cellulose for use in the cells and cell walls.

- Plants and algal cells need other materials including nitrate ions to make the amino acids which make up proteins.

B2 2.4

Making the most of photosynthesis

The more a plant photosynthesises, the more biomass it makes and the faster it grows. It's not surprising that farmers want their plants to grow as fast and as big as possible. It helps them to make a profit.

In theory, if you give plants a warm environment with plenty of light, carbon dioxide and water, they should grow as fast as possible. Out in the fields it is almost impossible to influence any of these factors. However, people have found ways in which they can artificially control the environment of their plants.

The garden greenhouse

Lots of people have glass or perspex greenhouses in their gardens. Farmers use the same idea in huge plastic '**polytunnels**'. They are used for growing crops ranging from tomatoes to strawberries and potatoes.

So how does a greenhouse affect the rate of photosynthesis? Within the glass or plastic structure the environment is much more controllable than outside. Most importantly, the atmosphere is warmer inside than out. This affects the rate of photosynthesis, speeding it up so plants grow faster. They will flower and fruit earlier and produce higher yields. We can also use greenhouses to grow fruit like peaches, lemons and oranges, which don't normally grow well outside in the UK.

Did you know ...?

The first recorded greenhouse was built in about 30 AD for Tiberius Caesar, a Roman emperor who wanted to eat cucumbers out of season.

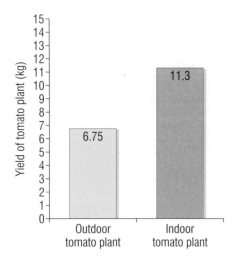

Figure 1 One piece of American research showed that the crop yield inside a greenhouse was almost double that of crops grown outdoors

Figure 2 Tomatoes certainly grow better in a greenhouse

a Why do plants grow faster in a greenhouse than outside?

Controlling a crop's environment

In a science lab you can change one factor at a time while keeping the others constant. Then you can judge how each one limits the rate of photosynthesis.

Outside, most plants are affected by a mixture of these factors. Early in the morning, light levels and temperature may limit the rate of photosynthesis. As light levels and temperature rise, carbon dioxide levels become limiting. On a bright, cold day, temperature might be the limiting factor. So there is a continuous interaction between the different factors.

Control through technology

Companies using big commercial greenhouses take advantage of what we know about limiting factors. They control the temperature and the levels of light and carbon dioxide. The levels are varied to get the fastest possible rates of photosynthesis. As a result the plants grow increasingly quickly.

The plants can even be grown in water with a perfect balance of mineral ions instead of soil, so nothing slows down their growth. This type of system is known as **hydroponics**.

The greenhouses are huge and conditions are controlled using computer software. It costs a lot of money but controlling the environment has many benefits. Turnover is fast, which means profits can be high. The crops are clean and unspoilt. There is no ploughing or preparing the land and in these systems crops can be grown where the land is poor.

b What are hydroponics?

It takes a lot of energy to keep conditions in the greenhouses just right – but fewer staff are needed. Monitoring systems and alarms are vital in case things go wrong, but for plants grown hydroponically, limiting factors are a thing of the past!

Figure 3 By controlling the temperature, light and carbon dioxide levels in a greenhouse like this you can produce the biggest possible crops – fast!

Summary questions

1 What are the main differences between a garden greenhouse and a hydroponics growing system?

2 What are the main benefits of artificially controlling the environment in which we grow our food plants?

B2 2.5 Organisms in their environment

Learning objectives

- What factors affect the distribution of organisms in their natural environment?
- Are animals as well as plants affected by physical factors?

??? Did you know ... ?

Reindeer live in cold environments where most of the plants are small because temperature limits growth. They eat grass, moss and lichen. Reindeer travel thousands of miles as they feed. They cannot get enough food to survive in just one area.

In any habitat you will find different distributions of living organisms. These organisms form communities, with the different animals and plants often dependent on each other.

Factors affecting living organisms

A number of factors affect how living organisms are distributed in the environment. They include the following.

Temperature

You have seen that temperature is a limiting factor on photosynthesis and therefore growth in plants. In cold climates temperature is always a limiting factor. For example, Arctic plants are all small. This in turn affects the numbers of herbivores that can survive in the area.

Figure 1 Reindeer distribution depends on temperature, which affects the rate of photosynthesis and growth of their food

Nutrients

The level of mineral ions (e.g. nitrate ions) available has a big impact on the distribution of plants. Carnivorous plants such as Venus flytraps thrive where nitrate levels are very low because they can trap and digest animal prey. The nitrates they need are provided when they break down the animal protein. Most other plants struggle to grow in these areas with low levels of mineral ions.

a How do nutrient levels affect the distribution of plants like the Venus fly trap?

Figure 2 The distribution of plants like these Venus flytraps depends heavily on nutrient levels

Amount of light

Light limits photosynthesis, so it also affects the distribution of plants and animals. Some plants are adapted to living in low light levels. They may have more chlorophyll or bigger leaves. However, most plants need plenty of light to grow well.

The breeding cycles of many animal and plant species are linked to the day length. They only live and breed in regions where day length and light intensity are right for them.

Availability of water

The availability of water is important in the distribution of plants and animals in a desert. As a rule plants and animals are relatively rare in a desert. However, the distribution changes after it rains. A large number of plants grow, flower and set seeds very quickly while the water is available. These plants are eaten by many animals that move into the area to take advantage of them. If there is no water, there will be little or no life.

Availability of oxygen and carbon dioxide

The availability of oxygen has a big impact on water-living organisms. Some invertebrates can survive in water with very low oxygen levels. However, most fish need a high level of dissolved oxygen. The distribution of land organisms is not affected by oxygen levels as there is plenty of oxygen in the air and levels vary very little.

Carbon dioxide levels act as a limiting factor on photosynthesis and plant growth. They can also affect the distribution of organisms. For example, mosquitoes are attracted to the animals on whose blood they feed by high carbon dioxide levels. Plants are also more vulnerable to insect attacks in an area with high carbon dioxide levels.

b How do carbon dioxide levels affect the distribution of plants?

The physical factors that affect the distribution of living organisms do not work in isolation. They interact to create unique environments where different animals and plants can live.

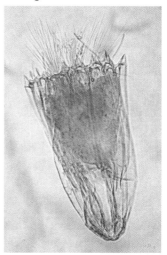

Figure 4 Mosquitoes are attracted to us by the carbon dioxide we breathe out

Key points

- Physical factors that may affect the distribution of living organisms include:
  - temperature
  - nutrients
  - the amount of light
  - the availability of water
  - the availability oxygen and carbon dioxide.

Summary questions

1 What are the physical factors most likely to affect living organisms?

2 How do carnivorous plants survive in areas with very low levels of nitrate ions whilst other plants cannot grow there?

3 Explain how the limiting factors for photosynthesis – light, temperature and carbon dioxide levels – also affect the distribution of animals directly and indirectly.

B2 2.6

Measuring the distribution of organisms ⓚ

Learning objectives

- How can you measure the distribution of living things in their natural environment?

- What are mean, median and mode? How do they help you understand your data?

It is often important to show how a physical factor (or changes in a physical factor) affects the distribution of living organisms. To do this you must be able to measure how those organisms are distributed in the first place.

Quadrats

The simplest way to sample an area (to count the number of organisms there) is to use a **quadrat.** A quadrat is usually a square frame made of wood or metal that you lay on the ground. This outlines your sample area.

A quadrat with sides 0.5 m long gives you a 0.25 m² sample area. Quadrats are used to investigate the size of a population of plants. They can also be used for animals that move very slowly, e.g. snails, sea anemones.

   a What is a quadrat?

You use the same size quadrat every time and sample as many areas as you can. This makes your results as valid as possible. **Sample size** is very important. You must choose your sample areas *at random*. This ensures that your results reflect the true distribution of the organisms. So any findings you make will be valid. There are a number of ways to make sure that the samples you take are random. For example, the person with the quadrat closes their eyes, spins round, opens their eyes and walks 10 paces before dropping the quadrat. A random number generator is a more scientific way of deciding where to drop your quadrat.

Figure 1 Using a quadrat to measure barnacles on a rocky shore

You need to take a number of random readings and then find the **mean** number of organisms per m². This technique is known as **quantitative sampling**. You can use quantitative sampling to compare the distribution of the same organism in different habitats. You can use it to compare the variety of organisms in a number of different habitats.

 Maths skills

Finding the range, the mean, the median and the mode

A student takes 10 random 1 m² quadrat readings looking at the number of snails in a garden. The results are:

4	4	3	4	5	2	6	5	4	3

The **range** of the data is the range between the minimum and maximum values – in this case from **2–6 snails per m².**

To find the **mean** distribution of snails in the garden, add all the readings together and divide by 10:

4 + 4 + 3 + 4 + 5 + 2 + 6 + 5 + 4 + 3/10 = 40/10 = **4 snails per m²**

The **median** is the middle value of the range – in this case, the range is 2–6 snails per m² so the median is **4 snails per m².**

The **mode** is the most frequently occurring value – in this case , **4 snails per m².**

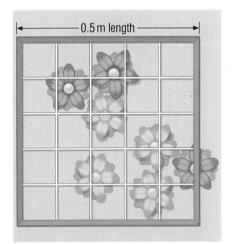

Figure 2 It doesn't matter if organisms partly covered by a quadrat are counted as in or out as long as you decide and stick to it. In this diagram of a quadrat, you have six or seven plants per 0.25 m² (that's 24 or 28 plants per square metre), depending on the way you count.

Sampling is also used to measure changes in the distribution of organisms over time. You do this by repeating your measurements at regular time intervals. Finding the **range** of distribution and the **median** and **mode** of your data can also give you useful information (see Examiner's tip).

Counting along a transect

Sampling along a **transect** is another useful way of measuring the distribution of organisms. There are different types of transect. A line transect is most commonly used.

Transects are not random. You stretch a tape between two points. You sample the organisms along that line at regular intervals using a quadrat. This shows you how the distribution of organisms changes along that line. You can also measure some of the physical factors, such as, light levels and soil pH, that might affect the growth of the plants along the transect.

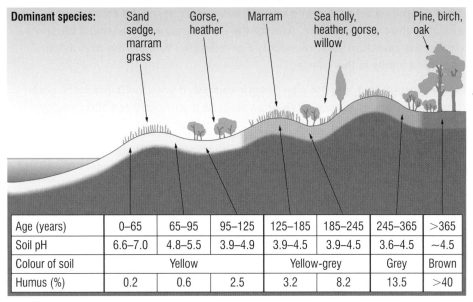

Dominant species:	Sand sedge, marram grass	Gorse, heather	Marram	Sea holly, heather, gorse, willow		Pine, birch, oak
Age (years)	0–65	65–95	95–125	125–185	185–245	245–365	>365
Soil pH	6.6–7.0	4.8–5.5	3.9–4.9	3.9–4.5	3.9–4.5	3.6–4.5	~4.5
Colour of soil	Yellow			Yellow-grey		Grey	Brown
Humus (%)	0.2	0.6	2.5	3.2	8.2	13.5	>40

Figure 3 In this transect of some sand dunes at Gibraltar Point you can clearly see the effect of changes in the physical factors on the distribution of the plants

Figure 4 Carrying out a transect of a rocky shore

Summary questions

1 Copy and complete using the words below:

transects habitat organisms environment quadrats distribution

Physical factors in the .... affect the .... of living .... Ways to measure the numbers of animals and plants in a .... include .... and ....

2 a How can you make sure your sampling with a quadrat is random?
  b Why is it so important for samples to be random?
  c In a series of 10 random 1 m² quadrats, a class found the following numbers of dandelions: 6, 3, 7, 8, 4, 6, 5, 7, 9, 8. What is the mean density of dandelions per m² on the school field?

3 Explain the ways in which the information you get from quadrats and transects is similar and how it differs.

B2 2.7

How valid is the data?

Environments are changing naturally all the time. But people also have an effect on the environment. This can be locally, e.g. dropping litter or building a new road, or on a worldwide scale with possible global warming and climate change. A change in the distribution of living organisms can be evidence of a change in the environment. However, if you want to use this type of data as evidence for environmental change it is important to use **reproducible** and **valid** methods to collect your results.

Reproducible, valid data

When you measure the distribution of living organisms you want your investigation to be reproducible and valid. In a reproducible investigation, other people can do the same investigation and get results that are very similar or the same as yours. And for the investigation to be valid it must answer the question you are asking. For example: What is the population density of snails in this garden?

One important factor is the size of your sample. If you do 10 quadrats, your data will not be as reproducible or as valid as if you carry out 100 quadrats.

Your method of sampling must be appropriate. If you want to measure the distribution of plants in an area, random quadrats work well. If you want to measure change in distribution over a range of habitats, a transect is a better technique to use.

If you are trying to measure change over time, you must be able to replicate your method every time you repeat your readings.

Changes in the distribution of a species are often used as evidence of environmental change. You must use a method of measuring that works regardless of who is collecting the data.

Figure 1 If you are trying to find evidence of environmental change in an area as big as this, it is important to use a method that is as valid as possible

Controlling variables

When you are working in a lab you can control as many of the **variables** as possible. Then other scientists can carry out the investigation under the same conditions. This increases the likelihood that your results will be reproducible.

In fieldwork, it is not possible to control all the variables of the natural environment, but you can control some. For example, you can always measure at the same time of day. However, you cannot control the weather or the arrival of different organisms.

You must be clear about the problems of collecting data if you want to use them as evidence of environmental change.

A penguin case study

In the early 1980s Dee Boersma noticed that the numbers of penguins in a breeding colony in Argentina were falling. In 1987 she set up a research project making a transect of the colony with 47 permanent stakes, 100 metres apart.

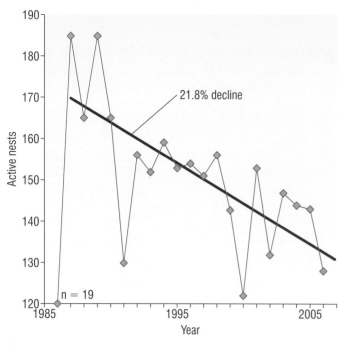

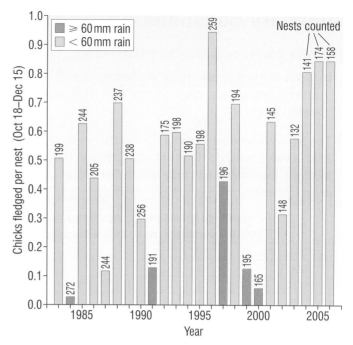

Figure 2 Patagonian penguins reflect environmental change in a very sensitive way. This graph shows clearly the effect of heavy rain on chick survival.

Every year Dee counted the active nests within a 100 m² circle around 19 of the stakes. She surveyed the remaining sites less regularly. However, Dee found the same pattern everywhere – numbers were falling.

What is causing these changes? Climate change seems to be significant:

● There have been several breeding seasons where unusually heavy rainfall has occurred. This has destroyed many nests and killed many chicks (see Figure 2).

● There have been changes in the numbers of small fish that the penguins eat. This is in response to changes in the water temperature. So there has been less food available in some years.

However, in biology things are rarely simple. The penguins are also affected by oil and waste from nearby shipping lanes. Around 20 000 penguins were killed by one major oil spill in 1991 alone. People catch the same small fish that the penguins feed on. Thousands of tourists visit the colony every year. They trample the area and cause stress to the birds.

Many factors, probably including climate change, are involved in the distribution changes of the penguins.

Figure 3 The penguin population at Punta Tombo fell by almost 22% between 1987 and 2006

Summary questions

1 What is meant by the terms: **a** reproducible and **b** valid, when you are talking about scientific data?

2 Look at Figure 2 and Figure 3 and the text above to help you answer this question.
   a When was the penguin population at Punta Tombo at its peak?
   b When was the population at its lowest? Suggest a reason for this.
   c How could Professor Boersma's data be used as evidence for environmental change?

3 Professor Boersma is widely respected in the scientific community. In what ways can you see that her data are both reproducible and valid?

Key points

● Different methods can be used to collect environmental data.

● Validity and reproducibility must be considered carefully as it is difficult to control variables in fieldwork.

● Sample size is an important factor in both reproducibility and validity of data.

Summary questions ⓚ

1 a Write the word equation for photosynthesis.

  b Much of the glucose made in photosynthesis is turned into an insoluble storage compound. What is this compound?

2 The figures in the table show the mean growth of two sets of oak seedlings. One set was grown in 85% full sunlight, the other set in only 35% full sunlight.

Year	Mean height of seedlings grown in 85% full sunlight (cm)	Mean height of seedlings grown in 35% full sunlight (cm)
2005	12	10
2006	16	12.5
2007	18	14
2008	21	17
2009	28	20
2010	35	21
2011	36	23

The figures in the table show the mean growth of two sets of oak seedlings. One set was grown in 85% full sunlight, the other set in only 35% full sunlight.

  a Plot a graph to show the growth of both sets of oak seedlings.

  b Using what you know about photosynthesis and limiting factors, explain the difference in the growth of the two sets of seedlings.

3 More of the biomass and oxygen produced by photosynthesis comes from algae than from plants.

  a Where do you find most algae?

  b How do algal cells use the products of photosynthesis?

4 Palm oil is made from the fruit of oil palms. Large areas of tropical rainforests have been destroyed to make space to plant these oil palms, which grow rapidly.

  a Why do you think that oil palms grow rapidly in the conditions that support a tropical rainforest?

  b Where does the oil in the oil palm fruit come from?

  c What is it used for in the plant?

  d How else is glucose used in the plant?

5 Here are the yields of some different plants grown in Bengal, India. The yields per acre when grown normally in the field and when grown hydroponically are compared.

Name of crop	Hydroponic crop per acre (kg)	Ordinary soil crop per acre (kg)
wheat	3629	2540
rice	5443	408
potatoes	70760	8164
cabbage	8164	5896
peas	63503	11340
tomatoes	181437	9072
lettuce	9525	4080
cucumber	12700	3175

  a Why are yields always higher when the crops are grown hydroponically?

  b Which crops would it be most economically sensible to grow hydroponically? Explain your choice.

  c Which crops would it be least sensible to grow hydroponically? Explain your choice.

  d What are the benefits and problems of growing crops:

   i in their natural environment

   ii in an artificially manipulated environment?

AQA Examination-style questions *k*

1 The picture shows a snail. Snails feed on plants.

Some students wanted to investigate the distribution of snails in the hedges on two sides of their school field. All the hedges were trimmed to a height of 1.5 metres. One side of the field was very open but the opposite side was shaded by trees. The students thought there would be more snails in the hedges on the open side because birds living in the trees would eat the snails. In the investigation they:

● measured a transect of 50 metres along the hedge on the open side of the field
● leaned a 1 m² quadrat against the hedge every 5 metres
● counted all the snails they could see in the quadrat
● recorded the data in a table
● repeated the investigation with the hedge that was shaded by trees.

a Choose the correct answer to complete each sentence.

i The idea that birds in the trees eat the snails is a .... (1)

conclusion   hypothesis   test

ii A transect is a .... (1)

line   square   triangle

iii One thing that was controlled in this investigation was the .... (1)

light intensity   number of trees   size of quadrat

b The data recorded by the students can be seen in the table.

	Number of snails									
Quadrat number	1	2	3	4	5	6	7	8	9	10
Open hedge	3	3	5	3	2	3	6	3	6	2
Hedge shaded by trees	2	3	4	3	5	2	1	4	1	5

Use the data to answer the questions. Choose the correct answer.

i The mean for the number of snails in the open hedge is [3 / 3.6 / 5]. (1)

ii The median for the number of snails in the shaded hedge is [2 / 3 / 4]. (1)

c One student said he didn't think the results would be valid. Suggest **one** reason why. (1)

2 A farmer has decided to grow strawberry plants in polytunnels, similar to the one shown in the diagram.

The tunnels are enclosed spaces with walls made of plastic sheeting. The farmer decides to set up several small polytunnels, as models, so he can work out the best conditions for the strawberry plants to grow. He needs help from a plant biologist who provides some data.

The data is shown in the graph.

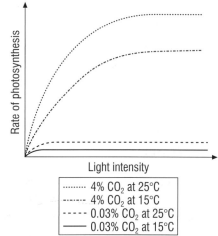

Rate of photosynthesis (y-axis) *Light intensity* (x-axis)

.... 4% CO₂ at 25°C
------- 4% CO₂ at 15°C
- - - - 0.03% CO₂ at 25°C
——— 0.03% CO₂ at 15°C

a *In this question you will be assessed on using good English, organising information clearly and using specialist terms where appropriate.*

You are advising the farmer.

Using all the information given, describe the factors the farmer should consider when building his model tunnels so he can calculate the optimal conditions for growing strawberry plants. (6)

b Biologists often use models in their research. Suggest **one** reason why. (1)

AQA, 2007

B2 3.1 Proteins, catalysts and enzymes

Learning objectives

- What is a protein?
- What do proteins do?
- What is an enzyme and how do they work?

 Did you know ...?

15–16% of your body mass is protein – second only to water, unless you are overweight. Protein is found in tissues ranging from your hair and nails to the muscles that move you around and the enzymes that control your body chemistry.

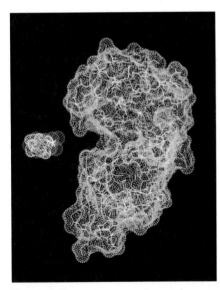

Figure 1 Enzymes are made up of chains of amino acids folded together, as you can see in this computer-generated image

AQA *Examiner's tip*

Remember that the way an enzyme works depends on the shape of the active site that allows it to bind with the substrate.

Protein molecules are very important in your body. A protein molecule is made up of long chains of small units called amino acids. Different arrangements of amino acids give you different proteins.

Proteins carry out many different functions in your body. They act as:

- structural components such as muscles and tendons
- hormones such as insulin
- antibodies, which destroy pathogens
- catalysts in the form of enzymes.

a What is an amino acid?

Controlling the rate of reactions

In everyday life we control the rates of chemical reactions all the time. You increase the temperature of your oven to speed up chemical reactions when you cook. You lower the temperature in your fridge to slow down reactions in stored food. Sometimes we use special chemicals known as **catalysts** to speed up reactions for us. A catalyst speeds up a chemical reaction, but it is not used up in the reaction. You can use a catalyst over and over again.

b What is a catalyst?

Enzymes – biological catalysts

In your body, chemical reaction rates are controlled by **enzymes**. These are special **biological catalysts** that speed up reactions.

Enzymes are large protein molecules. The long chains of amino acids are folded to produce a molecule with a specific shape. This special shape allows other molecules (substrates) to fit into the enzyme protein. We call this the **active site**. The shape of an enzyme is vital for the way it works.

Enzymes are involved in:

- building large molecules from lots of smaller ones
- changing one molecule into another
- breaking down large molecules into smaller ones.

Enzymes do not change a reaction in any way – they just make it happen faster. Different enzymes catalyse (speed up) specific types of reaction. In your body you need to build large molecules from smaller ones, e.g. making glycogen from glucose or proteins from amino acids. You need to change certain molecules into different ones, e.g. one sugar into another, such as glucose to fructose, and to break down large molecules into smaller ones, e.g. breaking down insoluble food molecules into small soluble molecules, such as glucose. All these reactions are speeded up using enzymes.

Practical

Breaking down hydrogen peroxide

Investigate the effect of:

a manganese(ɪᴠ) oxide, and **b** raw liver,

on the breakdown of hydrogen peroxide solution.

● Describe your observations and interpret the graph (see Figure 2).

Safety: Wear eye protection.

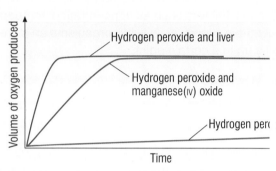

Figure 2 The decomposition of hydrogen peroxide to oxygen and water goes much faster using a catalyst like manganese(ɪᴠ) oxide. Raw liver contains the enzyme catalase, which speeds up the same reaction.

How do enzymes work?

The **substrate** (reactant) of the reaction fits into the active site of the enzyme. You can think of it like a lock and key. Once it is in place the enzyme and the substrate bind together.

The reaction then takes place rapidly and the products are released from the surface of the enzyme (see Figure 3). Remember that enzymes can join small molecules together as well as break up large ones.

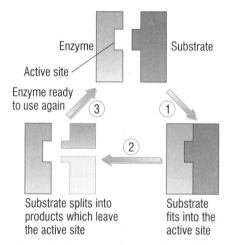

Figure 3 Enzymes act as catalysts using the 'lock-and-key' mechanism shown here

Summary questions

1 Match each word with its correct definition:

A	catalyst	i	the special part in the structure of an enzyme where the substrate binds
B	enzyme	ii	a substance that speeds up a chemical reaction without being changed itself
C	active site	iii	a biological catalyst made of protein

2 **a** What is a protein?
   b How are proteins used in the body?

3 **a** What is an enzyme?
   b What are enzymes made of?
   c How do enzymes act to speed up reactions in your body?

Key points

● Protein molecules are made up of long chains of amino acids.

● Proteins act as structural components of tissues, as hormones, as antibodies and as catalysts.

● Catalysts increase the rate of chemical reactions without changing themselves. Enzymes are biological catalysts.

● Enzymes are proteins. The amino acid chains are folded to form the active site.

B2 3.2 Factors affecting enzyme action

Learning objectives

● How does increasing the temperature affect your enzymes?

● Why does a change in pH affect your enzymes?

A container of milk left at the back of your fridge for a week or two will be disgusting. The milk will go off as enzymes in bacteria break down the protein structure.

Leave your milk in the sun for a day and the same thing happens – but much faster. Temperature affects the rate at which chemical reactions take place even when they are controlled by biological catalysts.

Biological reactions are affected by the same factors as any other chemical reactions. Factors such as concentration, temperature and surface area all affect them. However, in living organisms an increase in temperature only works up to a certain point.

a Why does milk left in the sun go off quickly?

The effect of temperature on enzyme action

The reactions that take place in cells happen at relatively low temperatures. Like other reactions, the rate of enzyme-controlled reactions increases as the temperature increases.

However, this is only true up to temperatures of about 40 °C. After this the protein structure of the enzyme is affected by the high temperature. The long amino acid chains begin to unravel. As a result, the shape of the active site changes. We say the enzyme has been **denatured**. It can no longer act as a catalyst, so the rate of the reaction drops dramatically. Most human enzymes work best at 37 °C.

b What does it mean if an enzyme is denatured?

Practical

Investigating the effect of temperature on enzymes

You can show the effect of temperature on the rate of enzyme action using simple practical procedures.

The enzyme amylase (found in your saliva) breaks down starch into simple sugars. You can mix starch solution and amylase together and keep them at different temperatures. Then you test samples from each temperature with iodine solution at regular intervals.

● How does iodine solution show you if starch is present?

● Why do we test starch solution without any amylase added?

● What conclusion can you draw from the results?

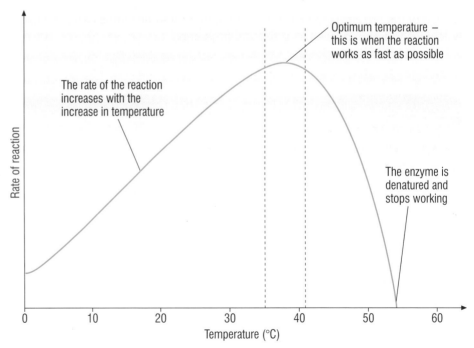

Figure 1 The rate of an enzyme-controlled reaction increases as the temperature rises – but only until the protein structure of the enzyme breaks down

Effect of pH on enzyme action

The shape of the active site of an enzyme comes from forces between the different parts of the protein molecule. These forces hold the folded chains in place. A change in the pH affects these forces. That's why it changes the shape of the molecule. As a result, the active site is lost, so the enzyme no longer acts as a catalyst.

Different enzymes have different pH levels at which they work best. A change in the pH can stop them working completely.

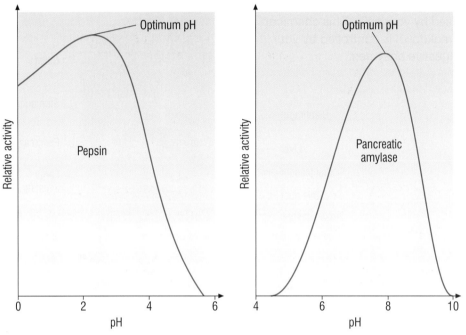

Figure 2 These two digestive enzymes need very different pH levels to work at their maximum rate. Pepsin is found in the stomach, along with hydrochloric acid, while pancreatic amylase is in the small intestine along with alkaline bile.

Without enzymes, none of the reactions in your body would happen fast enough to keep you alive. This is why it is so dangerous if your temperature goes too high when you are ill. Once your body temperature reaches about 41 °C, your enzymes start to be denatured and you will soon die.

Summary questions

1 Copy and complete using the words below:

   active site   cells   denatured   enzyme   increase   protein
   reactions   shape   temperatures   40 °C

   The chemical .... that take place in living .... happen at relatively low .... The rate of these ....-controlled reactions .... with an increase in temperature. However, this is only true up to temperatures of about .... After this the .... structure of the enzyme is affected and the .... of the .... is changed. The enzyme has been ....

2 Look at Figure 2.
   a At which pH does pepsin work best?
   b At which pH does amylase work best?
   c What happens to the activity of the enzymes as the pH increases?
   d Explain why this change in activity happens.

Did you know ...?

Not all enzymes work best at around 40 °C. Bacteria living in hot springs survive at temperatures up to 80 °C and higher. On the other hand, some bacteria that live in the very cold, deep seas have enzymes that work effectively at 0 °C and below.

Figure 3 The magical light display of a firefly is caused by the action of an enzyme called luciferase

AQA Examiner's tip

Enzymes aren't killed (they are molecules, not living things themselves) – use the term 'denatured'.

Key points

- Enzyme activity is affected by temperature and pH.
- High temperatures and the wrong pH can affect the shape of the active site of an enzyme and stop it working.

B2 3.3 Enzymes in digestion

Learning objectives

- Where are your digestive enzymes made?
- How are enzymes involved in the digestion of your food?

Your food is made up of large, insoluble molecules that your body cannot absorb. They need to be broken down or **digested** to form smaller, soluble molecules. These can then be absorbed and used by your cells. This chemical breakdown is controlled by your digestive enzymes.

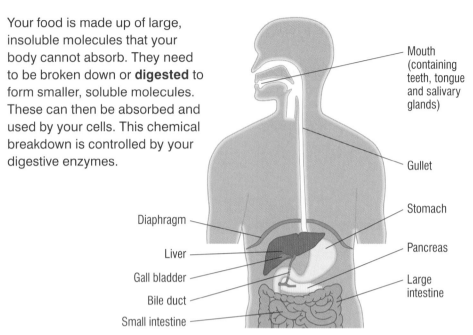

Figure 1 The human digestive system is a collection of organs all working together to digest your food

Most of your enzymes work *inside* the cells of your body, controlling the rate of the chemical reactions. Your digestive enzymes are different. They work *outside* your cells. They are produced by specialised cells in glands (like your salivary glands and your pancreas), and in the lining of your gut.

The enzymes then pass out of these cells into the gut itself. Your gut is a hollow, muscular tube that squeezes your food. It helps to break up your food into small pieces with a large surface area for your enzymes to work on. It mixes your food with your digestive juices so that the enzymes come into contact with as much of the food as possible. The muscles of the gut move your food along from one area to the next.

a How do your digestive enzymes differ from most of your other enzymes?

Digesting carbohydrates

Enzymes that break down carbohydrates are called **carbohydrases**. Starch is one of the most common carbohydrates that you eat. It is broken down into sugars in your mouth and small intestine. This reaction is catalysed by an enzyme called **amylase**.

Amylase is produced in your salivary glands. So the digestion of starch starts in your mouth. Amylase is also made in your pancreas and your small intestine. No digestion takes place inside the pancreas. All the enzymes made there flow into your small intestine, where most of the starch you eat is digested.

b What is the name of the enzyme that breaks down starch in your gut?

Digesting proteins

The breakdown of protein food like meat, fish and cheese into amino acids is catalysed by **protease** enzymes. Proteases are produced by your stomach, your pancreas and your small intestine. The breakdown of proteins into **amino acids** takes place in your stomach and small intestine.

c Which enzymes break down protein in your gut?

Digesting fats

The **lipids** (fats and oils) that you eat are broken down into **fatty acids** and **glycerol** in your small intestine. The reaction is catalysed by **lipase** enzymes. These are made in your pancreas and your small intestine. Again, the enzymes made in the pancreas are passed into the small intestine.

Once your food molecules have been completely digested into soluble glucose, amino acids, fatty acids and glycerol, they leave your small intestine. They pass into your bloodstream to be carried around the body to the cells that need them.

d Which enzymes break down fats in your gut?

Practical

Investigating digestion

You can make a model gut using a special bag containing starch and amylase enzymes. When the enzyme has catalysed the breakdown of the starch, you can no longer detect the presence of starch inside the 'gut'.

● How can you test for starch?

Smaller molecules of sugar diffuse out of the gut. Test the water in the beaker for (reducing) sugar.

● How can you test for this?

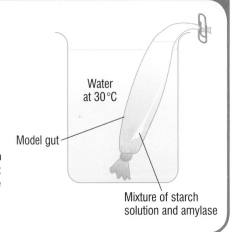

Figure 2 This apparatus provides you with a model of the gut. You can use it to investigate the effects of factors like temperature and pH on how the gut enzymes work.

Water at 30 °C

Model gut

Mixture of starch solution and amylase

Summary questions

1 Copy and complete using the words below:

   *absorbed   broken down   cells   digestive   food
   insoluble   soluble*

   The .... you eat is made up of large .... molecules that need to be .... to form smaller, ... molecules. These can be .... by your body and used by your .... This chemical breakdown is controlled by your .... enzymes.

2 Make a table that describes amylase, protease and lipase. For each enzyme show where it is made, which reaction it catalyses and where it works in the gut.

3 Why is digestion of your food so important? Explain your answer in terms of the molecules involved.

Key points

● Digestive enzymes are produced by specialised cells in glands and in the lining of the gut. They work outside of the body cells in the gut itself.

● Different enzymes catalyse the breakdown of carbohydrates, proteins and fats into smaller, soluble molecules during digestion.

B2 3.4

Speeding up digestion

Learning objectives

- Why does your stomach contain hydrochloric acid?

- What is bile and why is it so important in digestion?

∞ links

For information on the sensitivity of enzymes to temperature and pH, look back at B2 3.2 Factors affecting enzyme action.

Your digestive system produces many enzymes that speed up the breakdown of the food you eat. As your body is kept at a fairly steady 37°C, your enzymes have an ideal temperature that allows them to work as fast as possible.

Keeping the pH in your gut at ideal levels isn't that easy because different enzymes work best at different pH levels. For example, the protease enzyme found in your stomach works best in acidic conditions.

On the other hand, the proteases made in your pancreas need alkaline conditions to work at their best

So, your body makes a variety of different chemicals that help to keep conditions ideal for your enzymes all the way through your gut.

a Why do your enzymes almost always have the right temperature to work at their best?

Changing pH in the gut

You have around 35 million glands in the lining of your stomach. These secrete protease enzymes to digest the protein you eat. The enzymes work best in an acid pH. So your stomach also produces a concentrated solution of hydrochloric acid from the same glands. In fact, your stomach produces around 3 litres of acid a day! This acid allows your stomach protease enzymes to work very effectively. It also kills most of the bacteria that you take in with your food.

Finally, your stomach also produces a thick layer of mucus. This coats your stomach walls and protects them from being digested by the acid and the enzymes.

b How does your stomach avoid digesting itself?

Practical

Breaking down protein

You can see the effect of acid on pepsin, the protease found in the stomach, quite simply. Set up three test tubes: one containing pepsin, one containing hydrochloric acid and one containing a mixture of the two. Keep them at body temperature in a water bath. Add a similar-sized chunk of meat to all three of them. Set up a webcam and watch for a few hours to see what happens.

- What conclusions can you make?

Figure 1 These test tubes show clearly the importance of protein-digesting enzymes and hydrochloric acid in your stomach. Meat was added to each tube at the same time.

After a few hours – depending on the size and type of the meal you have eaten – your food leaves your stomach. It moves on into your small intestine. Some of the enzymes that catalyse digestion in your small intestine are made in your pancreas. Some are also made in the small intestine itself. They all work best in an alkaline environment.

The acidic liquid coming from your stomach needs to become an alkaline mix in your small intestine. So how does it happen?

Your liver makes a greenish-yellow alkaline liquid called **bile**. Bile is stored in your gall bladder until it is needed.

As food comes into the small intestine from the stomach, bile is squirted onto it. The bile neutralises the acid from the stomach and then makes the semi-digested food alkaline. This provides the ideal conditions needed for the enzymes in the small intestine.

c Why does the food coming into your small intestine need neutralising?

Altering the surface area

It is very important for the enzymes of the gut to have the largest possible surface area of food to work on. This is not a problem with carbohydrates and proteins. However, the fats that you eat do not mix with all the watery liquids in your gut. They stay as large globules (like oil in water) that make it difficult for the lipase enzymes to act.

This is the second important function of the bile. It **emulsifies** the fats in your food. This means bile physically breaks up large drops of fat into smaller droplets. This provides a much bigger surface area for the lipase enzymes to act on. The larger surface area helps the lipase chemically break down the fats more quickly into fatty acids and glycerol.

 Did you know ...?

Sometimes gall stones block the gall bladder and bile duct. The stones can range from a few millimetres to several centimetres long and can cause terrible pain.

Figure 2 Gall stones

AQA **Examiner's tip**

Remember, food is not digested in the liver or the pancreas.
Bile is *not* an enzyme and it does *not* break down fat molecules.
Bile emulsifies fat droplets to increase the surface area, which in turn increases the rate of fat digestion by lipase.

Summary questions

1 Copy and complete using the words below:

alkaline emulsifies gall bladder liver neutralises small intestine

Bile is an .... liquid produced by your .... It is stored in the .... and released onto food as it enters the .... It .... the acidic food from the stomach and makes it alkaline. It also .... fats.

2 Look at Figure 1.
 a In what conditions does the protease from the stomach work best?
 b How does your body create the right pH in the stomach for this enzyme?
 c In what conditions does the proteases in the small intestine work best?
 d How does your body create the right pH in the small intestine for this enzyme?

3 Draw a diagram to explain how bile produces a big surface area for lipase to work on and explain why this is important

Key points

● The enzymes of the stomach work best in acid conditions.

● The enzymes made in the pancreas and the small intestine work best in alkaline conditions.

● Bile produced by the liver neutralises acid and emulsifies fats.

B2 3.5 Making use of enzymes

Figure 1 Many people now have a dishwasher. Dishwasher detergents contain enzymes that digest cooked-on proteins like eggs, which are often hard to remove.

Figure 2 Learning to eat solid food isn't easy. Having some of it predigested by protease enzymes can make it easier to get the amino acids you need to grow.

Enzymes were first isolated from living cells in the 19th century. Ever since then, we have found more and more ways of using them in industry. Some microorganisms produce enzymes that pass out of the cells and are easy for us to use. In other cases we use the whole microorganism.

Enzymes in the home

In the past, people boiled and scrubbed their clothes to get them clean – by hand! Now we have washing machines and enzymes ready and waiting to digest the stains.

Many people use **biological detergents** to remove stains such as grass, sweat and food from their clothes. Biological washing powders contain proteases and lipases. These enzymes break down the proteins and fats in the stains. They help to give you a cleaner wash. Biological detergents work better than non-biological detergents at lower temperatures. This is because the enzymes work best at lower temperatures – they are denatured if the water is too hot. This means you use less electricity too.

a What is a biological washing powder?

Practical

Investigating biological washing powder

Weigh a chunk of cooked egg white and leave it in a strong solution of biological washing powder.

- What do you think will happen to the egg white?
- How can you measure just how effective the protease enzymes are?
- How could you investigate the effect of surface area on enzyme action?

Enzymes in industry

Pure enzymes have many uses in industry.

Proteases are used to make baby foods. They 'predigest' some of the protein in the food. When babies first begin to eat solid foods they are not very good at digesting it. Treating the food with protease enzymes makes it easier for a baby's digestive system to cope with it. It is easier for them to get the amino acids they need from their food.

Carbohydrases are used to convert starch into sugar (glucose) syrup. We use huge quantities of sugar syrup in food production. You will see it on the ingredients labels on all sorts of foods.

Starch is made by plants like corn and it is very cheap. Using enzymes to convert this plant starch into sweet sugar provides a cheap source of sweetness for food manufacturers.

It is also important for the process of making fuel (ethanol) from plants.

b Why does starch need to be converted to sugar before it is used to make ethanol?

Sometimes the glucose syrup made from starch is passed through another process that uses a different set of enzymes. The enzyme **isomerase** is used to change glucose syrup into **fructose syrup**.

Glucose and fructose contain exactly the same amount of energy (1700 kJ or 400 kcal per 100 g). However, fructose is much sweeter than glucose. Much smaller amounts are needed to make food taste sweet. Fructose is widely used in 'slimming' foods – the food tastes sweet but contains fewer calories.

The advantages and disadvantages of using enzymes

In industrial processes, many of the reactions need high temperatures and pressures to make them go fast enough to produce the products needed. This needs expensive equipment and requires a lot of energy.

Enzymes can solve industrial problems like these. They catalyse reactions at relatively low temperatures and normal pressures. Enzyme-based processes are therefore often fairly cheap to run.

One problem with enzymes is that they are denatured at high temperatures, so the temperature must be kept down (usually below 45 °C). The pH also needs to be kept within carefully controlled limits that suit the enzyme. It costs money to control these conditions.

Many enzymes are also expensive to produce. Whole microbes are relatively cheap, but need to be supplied with food and oxygen and their waste products removed. They use some of the substrate to grow more microbes. Pure enzymes use the substrate more efficiently, but they are also more expensive to produce.

Figure 3 Some people are always trying to lose weight. Enzyme technology is used to convert more and more glucose syrup into fructose syrup to make so-called 'slimming' foods.

AQA Examiner's tip

Remember that most enzyme names end in '-ase'.

Some enzymes used in industry work at quite high temperatures – so don't be put off if a graph shows an optimum temperature well above 45 °C!

Summary questions

1 List three enzymes and the ways in which we use them in the food industry.

2 Biological washing powders contain enzymes in tiny capsules. Explain why:
   a they are more effective than non-biological powders at lower temperatures
   b they are not more effective at high temperatures.

3 Make a table to show the advantages and disadvantages of using enzymes in industry.

Key points

- Some microorganisms produce enzymes that pass out of the cells and can be used in different ways.
- Biological detergents may contain proteases and lipases.
- Proteases, carbohydrases and isomerase are all used in the food industry.

B2 3.6

High-tech enzymes

Learning objectives

- What are the advantages and disadvantages of using enzymes in detergents?
- Can doctors use enzymes to help keep you healthy?

The pros and cons of biological detergents

For many people, biological washing powders have lots of benefits. Children can be messy eaters and their clothes get lots of mud and grass stains as well. Many of the stains that adults get on their clothes – sweat, food and drink – are biological too. So these enzyme-based washing powders are effective and therefore widely used.

Biological powders have another advantage. They are very effective at cleaning at low temperatures. Therefore they use a lot less electricity than non-biological detergents. That's good for the environment and cheaper for the consumer.

Figure 1 Biological detergents come in many different forms

Figure 2 The enzymes in biological detergents are held in tiny capsules – these are seen under an electron microscope

Practical

Plan and carry out an investigation to compare the effectiveness of a biological detergent with a non-biological detergent at 40 °C.

However, when biological detergent was first manufactured many factory staff developed allergies. They were reacting to enzyme dust in the air – proteins often trigger allergies. Some people using the powders were affected in the same way. But there was a solution – the enzymes were put in tiny capsules and then most of the allergy problems stopped.

Unfortunately, it got bad publicity, which some people still remember. However, research (based on 44 different studies) was published by the British Journal of Dermatology in 2008. This showed that biological detergents do not seem to be a major cause of skin problems.

Some people worry about all the enzymes going into our rivers and seas from biological detergents. The waste water from washing machines goes into the sewage system. Also, the low temperatures used to wash with biological detergents may not be as good at killing pathogens on the clothes.

Enzymes and medicine

Some of the ways in which enzymes are used in medicine

TO DIAGNOSE DISEASE

If your liver is damaged or diseased, some of your liver enzymes may leak out into your bloodstream. If your symptoms suggest your liver isn't working properly, doctors can test your blood for these enzymes. This will tell them if your liver really is damaged.

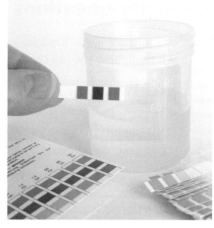

Figure 3 Enzymes are vital in the human body, so it is not surprising that they are widely used in the world of medicine as well

TO DIAGNOSE AND CONTROL DISEASE

People who have diabetes have too much glucose in their blood. As a result, they also get glucose in their urine. One commonly used test for sugar in the urine relies on a colour change on a test strip. The test strip contains a chemical indicator and an enzyme. It is placed in a urine sample. The enzyme catalyses the breakdown of any glucose found in the urine. The strip changes colour if the products of this reaction are present. This shows that glucose was present in the original sample.

TO CURE DISEASE

- If your pancreas is damaged or diseased it cannot make enzymes. So, you have to take extra enzymes – particularly lipase – to allow you to digest your food. The enzymes are in special capsules to stop them being digested in your stomach.
- If you have a heart attack, an enzyme called streptokinase will be injected into your blood as soon as possible. It dissolves clots in the arteries of the heart wall and reduces the amount of damage done to your heart muscle.
- An enzyme is being used to treat a type of blood cancer in children. The cancer cells cannot make one particular amino acid. They need to take it from your body fluids. The enzyme speeds up the breakdown of this amino acid. The cancer cells cannot get any and they die. Your normal cells can make the amino acid so they are not affected.

Activity

Make a poster with the title 'Enzymes in medicine' which could be displayed on the walls of the science department to inform and interest students in KS3 and/or KS4. Use this material as a starting point and do some more research about the way enzymes are used, to help you make your poster as interesting as possible.

Key points

- Enzymes in detergents break down biological stains such as sweat. They work at low temperatures so use less electricity, which is cheaper and environmentally friendly. They originally caused problems with allergies, but this has been solved now. The lower-temperature washes are less good at killing pathogens; but higher temperatures can denature the enzymes.
- Enzymes can be produced industrially, both to diagnose and to treat disease.

Summary questions

1 Some people think that biological detergents are better for the environment than non-biological detergents. Why is this?

2 Write a short report in the use of one enzyme in industry or medicine. Explain things such as where the enzyme comes from, what it does, why it is an advantage to use it and what disadvantages there might be.

Summary questions

1 a Copy and complete the following sentences, matching each beginning with its correct ending.

A	A catalyst will speed up a reaction	i	.... could not occur without enzymes.
B	Living organisms make very efficient catalysts	ii	.... made of protein.
C	All enzymes are	iii	.... binds to the active site.
D	The reactions that keep you alive	iv	.... known as enzymes.
E	The substrate of an enzyme	v	.... a specific type of molecule.
F	Each type of enzyme affects	vi	.... but is not changed itself.

b Explain how an enzyme catalyses a reaction. Use diagrams if they make your explanation clearer.

2 The table gives some data about the relative activity levels of an enzyme at different pH levels.

pH	Relative activity
4	0
6	3
8	10
10	1

a Plot a graph of this data.

b Does this enzyme work best in an acid or an alkaline environment?

c This is a protein-digesting enzyme. Where in the gut do you think it might be found? Explain your answer.

3 The results in these tables come from a student who was investigating the breakdown of hydrogen peroxide using manganese(IV) oxide and mashed raw potato.

Table 1 Manganese(IV) oxide

Temperature (°C)	Time taken (s)
20	106
30	51
40	26
50	12

Table 2 Raw mashed potato

Temperature (°C)	Time taken (s)
20	114
30	96
40	80
50	120
60	no reaction

a Draw a graph of the results using manganese(IV) oxide.

b What do these results tell you about the effect of temperature on a catalysed reaction? Explain your observation.

c Draw a graph of the results when raw mashed potato was added to the hydrogen peroxide.

d What is the name of the enzyme found in living cells that catalyses the breakdown of hydrogen peroxide?

e What does this graph tell you about the effect of temperature on an enzyme-catalysed reaction?

f Why does temperature have this effect on the enzyme-catalysed reaction but not on the reaction catalysed by manganese(IV) oxide?

g How could you change the second investigation to find the temperature at which the enzyme works best?

AQA Examination-style questions

1 Enzymes are chemicals produced in living cells.

a Copy and complete the following sentences, using some of the words below.

amylase   bile   catalysts   fats   lipase   protease
protein   sugars

  i   Enzymes are described as biological .... (1)

  ii Enzyme molecules are made of .... (1)

  iii The enzyme that digests starch is called .... (1)

  iv The substance that neutralises stomach acid is called .... (1)

  v Glycerol is one of the products of the digestion of .... (1)

b An enzyme works well in pH 7.

  i   What happens to this enzyme when it is placed in an acid solution? (1)

  ii Give **one** other factor that will affect the activity of the enzyme. (1)

c Explain what happens to starch when it is digested. (2)

AQA, 2002

2 Enzymes have many uses in the home and in industry.

a Which type of organisms are used to produce these enzymes?

Choose the correct answer from the following options:

mammals   microorganisms   plants (1)

b Babies may have difficulty digesting proteins in their food. Baby-food manufacturers use enzymes to 'pre-digest' the protein in baby food to overcome this difficulty.

Copy and complete the following sentences, using some of the words below.

amino acids   amylases   proteases   sugars

  i   Proteins are 'pre-digested' using enzymes called .... (1)

  ii This pre-digestion produces .... (1)

c A baby-food manufacturer uses enzyme **V** to predigest protein.

He tries four new enzymes, **W**, **X**, **Y** and **Z**, to see if he can reduce the time taken to predigest the protein. The graph shows the time taken for the enzymes to completely predigest the protein.

The manufacturer uses the same concentration of enzyme and the same mass of protein in each experiment.

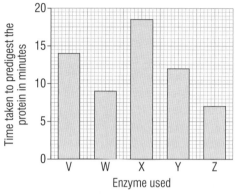

  i   How long did it take enzyme **V** to predigest the protein? (1)

  ii Which enzyme would you advise the baby food manufacturer to use?

Choose the correct answer from the following options:

enzyme V   enzyme W   enzyme X   enzyme Y
enzyme Z

Give a reason for your answer. (2)

  iii Give **two** factors which should be controlled in the baby-food manufacturer's investigations.

Choose the correct answer from the following options:

oxygen concentration   temperature
light intensity   pH (2)

3 *In this question you will be assessed on using good English, organising information clearly and using specialist terms where appropriate.*

Describe the roles of the liver and pancreas in the digestion of fats. (6)

B2 4.1

Aerobic respiration ⓚ

Learning objectives

- What is aerobic respiration?
- Where in your cells does respiration take place?

?? Did you know ... ?

The average energy needs of a teenage boy are 11 510 kJ of energy every day – but teenage girls only need 8830 kJ a day. This is partly because on average girls are smaller than boys, but also because boys have more muscle cells, which means more mitochondria demanding fuel for aerobic respiration.

One of the most important enzyme-controlled processes in living things is aerobic respiration. It takes place all the time in plant and animal cells.

Your digestive system, lungs and circulation all work to provide your cells with the glucose and oxygen they need for respiration.

During aerobic respiration, glucose reacts with oxygen. This reaction releases energy that your cells can use. This energy is vital for everything that goes on in your body.

Carbon dioxide and water are produced as waste products of the reaction. We call the process aerobic respiration because it uses oxygen from the air.

Aerobic respiration can be summed up by the equation:

$$\text{glucose} + \text{oxygen} \rightarrow \text{carbon dioxide} + \text{water} (+ \text{energy})$$

a Why is aerobic respiration so important?

⚙ Practical

Investigating respiration

Animals, plants and microorganisms all respire. It is possible to show that cellular respiration is taking place. You can either deprive a living organism of the things it needs to respire, or show that waste products are produced from the reaction.

Depriving a living thing of food and/or oxygen would kill it. This would be unethical. So we concentrate on the products of respiration. Carbon dioxide is the easiest to identify. We can also measure the energy released to the surroundings.

Limewater goes cloudy when carbon dioxide bubbles through it. The higher the concentration of carbon dioxide, the quicker the limewater goes cloudy. This gives us an easy way of showing that carbon dioxide has been produced. We can also look for a rise in temperature to show that energy is being released during respiration.

- Plan an ethical investigation into aerobic respiration in living organisms.

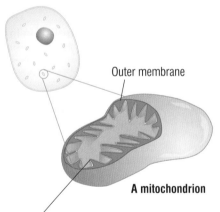

Outer membrane

A mitochondrion

Folded inner membrane gives a large surface area where the enzymes which release cellular respiration are found

Figure 1 Mitochrondria are the powerhouses that provide energy for all the functions of your cells

Mitochondria – the site of respiration

Aerobic respiration involves lots of chemical reactions. Each reaction is controlled by a different enzyme. Most of these reactions take place in the mitochondria of your cells.

Mitochondria are tiny rod-shaped parts (organelles) that are found in almost all plant and animal cells. They have a folded inner membrane. This provides a large surface area for the enzymes involved in aerobic respiration.

The number of mitochondria in a cell shows you how active the cell is.

b Why do mitochondria have folded inner membranes?

Reasons for respiration

Respiration releases energy from the food we eat so that our cells can use it.

● Living cells need energy to carry out the basic functions of life. They build up large molecules from smaller ones to make new cell material. Much of the energy released in respiration is used for these 'building' activities (synthesis reactions). For example, in plants the sugars, nitrates and other nutrients are built up into amino acids. The amino acids are then built up into proteins.

● In animals, energy from respiration is used to make muscles contract. Muscles are working all the time in your body. Even when you sleep your heart beats, you breathe and your gut churns. All muscular activities use energy.

● Finally, mammals and birds keep their bodies at a constant temperature inside almost regardless of the temperature of their surroundings. So on cold days you will use energy to keep warm, while on hot days you use energy to sweat and keep your body cool.

Figure 2 When the weather is cold, birds like this robin use up a lot of energy from respiration just to keep warm. Giving them extra food supplies can mean the difference between life and death.

Summary questions

1 Copy and complete using the words below:

aerobic respiration mitochondria glucose waste products energy water

.... is released from .... in a reaction with oxygen by a process known as .... This takes place in the .... of the cells. Carbon dioxide and .... are formed as ....

2 Why do muscle cells have many mitochondria but fat cells very few?

3 You need a regular supply of food to provide energy for your cells. If you don't get enough to eat you become thin and stop growing. You don't want to move around and you start to feel cold.
   a What are the three main uses of the energy released in your body during aerobic respiration?
   b How does this explain the symptoms of starvation described above?

4 Suggest an experiment to show that: **a** oxygen is taken up, and **b** carbon dioxide is released, during aerobic respiration.

Key points

● Aerobic respiration involves chemical reactions that use oxygen and sugar and release energy. The reaction is summed up as:

glucose + oxygen → carbon dioxide + water (+ energy)

● Most of the reactions in aerobic respiration take place inside the mitochondria.

● The energy released during respiration is used to build large molecules from smaller ones. This allows muscles to contract. In mammals and birds, it enables them to maintain a steady body temperature.

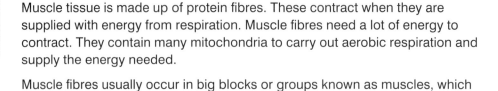

B2 4.2

The effect of exercise on the body

Learning objectives

- How does your body respond to the increased demands for oxygen during exercise?
- What is glycogen and how is it used in the body?

Your muscles use a lot of energy. They move you around and help support your body against gravity. Your heart is made of muscle and pumps blood around your body. The movement of food along your gut depends on muscles too.

Muscle tissue is made up of protein fibres. These contract when they are supplied with energy from respiration. Muscle fibres need a lot of energy to contract. They contain many mitochondria to carry out aerobic respiration and supply the energy needed.

Muscle fibres usually occur in big blocks or groups known as muscles, which contract to cause movement. They then relax, which allows other muscles to work.

Your muscles also store glucose as the carbohydrate **glycogen**. Glycogen can be converted rapidly back to glucose to use during exercise. The glucose is used in aerobic respiration to provide the energy to make your muscles contract:

$$\text{glucose} + \text{oxygen} \rightarrow \text{carbon dioxide} + \text{water} \; (+ \text{ energy})$$

a What is aerobic respiration?

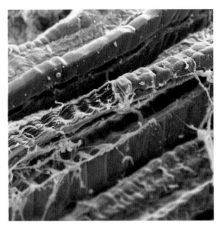

Figure 1 All the work done by the muscles is based on these special protein fibres, which contract when they work and relax afterwards

The response to exercise

Even when you are not moving about your muscles use up a certain amount of oxygen and glucose. However, when you begin to exercise, many muscles start contracting harder and faster. As a result they need more glucose and oxygen to supply their energy needs. During exercise the muscles also produce increased amounts of carbon dioxide. This needs to be removed for muscles to keep working effectively.

b Why do you need more energy when you exercise?

So during exercise, when muscular activity increases, several changes take place in your body:

- Your heart rate increases and the arteries supplying blood to your muscles dilate (widen). These changes increase the blood flow to your exercising muscles. This in turn increases the supply of oxygen and glucose to the muscles. It also increases the rate that carbon dioxide is removed from the muscles.

- Your breathing rate increases and you breathe more deeply. So you breathe more often and also bring more air into your lungs each time you breathe in. More oxygen is brought into your body and picked up by your red blood cells. This oxygen is carried to your exercising muscles. It also means that more carbon dioxide can be removed from the blood in the lungs and breathed out.

c Why do you produce more carbon dioxide when you are exercising hard?

The benefits of exercise

Your heart and lungs benefit from regular exercise. Both the heart and the lungs become larger. They both develop a bigger and more efficient blood supply. This means they function as effectively as possible, whether you are exercising or not. Look at the table below.

Table 1 A comparison of heart and lung functions before and after getting fit

	Before getting fit	After getting fit
Amount of blood pumped out of the heart during each beat at rest (cm³)	64	80
Volume of the heart at rest (cm³)	120	140
Resting breathing rate at rest (breaths/min)	14	12
Resting pulse rate (beats/min)	72	63
Maximum lung volume (cm³)	1000	1200

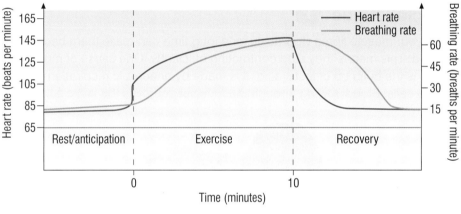

Figure 2 During exercise the heart rate and breathing rate increase to supply the muscles with what they need and remove the extra waste produced. The maximum rate to which you should push your heart is usually calculated as approximately 220 beats per minute minus your age. When you exercise, you should ideally get your heart rate into the range between 60 per cent and 90 per cent of your maximum.

Practical

Testing fitness

A good way of telling how fit you are is to measure your resting heart rate and breathing rate. The fitter you are, the lower they will be. Then see what happens when you exercise. The increase in your heart rate and breathing rate and how fast they return to normal is another way of finding out how fit you are – or aren't!

Summary questions

1 Using Figure 2, describe the effect of exercise on the heart rate and the breathing rate of a fit person and explain why these changes happen.

2 Plan an investigation into the fitness levels of your classmates. Describe how you might carry out this investigation and explain what you would expect the results to be.

Key points

- The energy that is released during respiration is used to enable muscles to contract.

- When you use your muscles you need more glucose and oxygen and produce more carbon dioxide.

- Body responses to exercise include:
  - an increase in heart rate, in breathing rate and in depth of breathing
  - glycogen stores in the muscle are converted to glucose for cellular respiration
  - the blood flow to the muscles increases.

- These act to increase the supply of glucose and oxygen to the muscle and remove more carbon dioxide.

B2 4.3 Anaerobic respiration

Learning objectives

- Why do muscles use anaerobic respiration to obtain energy?

- Why is less energy released by anaerobic respiration than aerobic respiration? **[H]**

- What is an oxygen debt? **[H]**

Figure 1 Training hard is the simplest way to avoid anaerobic respiration. When you are fit you can get oxygen to your muscles and remove carbon dioxide more efficiently.

Your everyday muscle movements use energy released by aerobic respiration. However, when you exercise hard your muscle cells may become short of oxygen. Although you increase your heart and breathing rates, sometimes the blood cannot supply oxygen to the muscles fast enough. When this happens the muscle cells can still get energy from glucose. They use **anaerobic respiration**, which takes place without oxygen.

In anaerobic respiration the glucose is not broken down completely. It produces **lactic acid** instead of carbon dioxide and water.

If you are fit, your heart and lungs will be able to keep a good supply of oxygen going to your muscles while you exercise. If you are unfit, your muscles will run short of oxygen much sooner.

a How does anaerobic respiration differ from aerobic respiration?

Muscle fatigue

Using your muscle fibres vigorously for a long time can make them become fatigued. This means they stop contracting efficiently. One cause of muscle fatigue is the build up of lactic acid. It is made by anaerobic respiration in the muscle cells. Blood flowing through the muscles removes the lactic acid.

Figure 2 Repeated movements can soon lead to anaerobic respiration in your muscles – particularly if you're not used to it

Anaerobic respiration is not as efficient as aerobic respiration. This is because the glucose molecules are not broken down completely. So far less energy is released than during aerobic respiration.

The end product of anaerobic respiration is lactic acid and this leads to the release of a small amount of energy, instead of the carbon dioxide and water plus lots of energy released by aerobic respiration.

Anaerobic respiration:

$$glucose \rightarrow lactic\ acid\ (+ energy)$$

Higher

Oxygen debt

If you have been exercising hard, you often carry on puffing and panting for some time after you stop. The length of time you remain out of breath depends on how fit you are. But why do you keeping breathing faster and more deeply when you have stopped using your muscles?

The waste lactic acid you produce during anaerobic respiration is a problem. You cannot simply get rid of lactic acid by breathing it out as you can with carbon dioxide. As a result, when the exercise is over lactic acid has to be broken down to produce carbon dioxide and water. This needs oxygen.

The amount of oxygen needed to break down the lactic acid to carbon dioxide and water is known as the **oxygen debt**.

After a race, your heart rate and breathing rate stay high to supply the extra oxygen needed to pay off the oxygen debt. The bigger the debt (the larger the amount of lactic acid), the longer you will puff and pant!

Oxygen debt repayment:

$$lactic\ acid + oxygen \rightarrow carbon\ dioxide + water$$

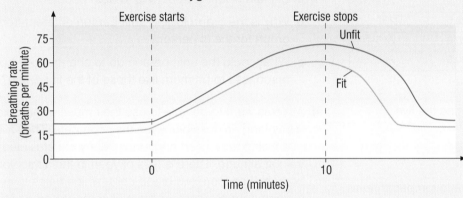

b What is an oxygen debt?

Figure 3 Everyone gets an oxygen debt if they exercise hard, but if you are fit you can pay it off faster

Practical

Making lactic acid

Carry out a single repetitive action such as stepping up and down or lifting a weight or a book from the bench to your shoulder time after time or even just clenching and unclenching your fist. You will soon feel the effect of a build up of lactic acid in your muscles.

● How can you tell when your muscles have started to respire anaerobically?

Summary questions

1 Define the following terms:

aerobic respiration   anaerobic respiration   lactic acid

2 If you exercise very hard or for a long time, your muscles begin to ache and do not work so effectively. Explain why.

3 If you exercise very hard, you often puff and pant for some time after you stop. Explain what is happening.   [H]

Key points

● If muscles work hard for a long time they become fatigued and don't contract efficiently. If they don't get enough oxygen they will respire anaerobically.

● Anaerobic respiration is respiration without oxygen. Glucose is incompletely broken down to form lactic acid.

● The anaerobic breakdown of glucose releases less energy than aerobic respiration.   [H]

● After exercise, oxygen is still needed to break down the lactic acid which has built up. The amount of oxygen needed is known as the oxygen debt.   [H]

Higher

Summary questions 🄺

1 Edward and Jess wanted to investigate the process of cellular respiration. They set up three vacuum flasks. One contained live, soaked peas. One contained dry peas. One contained peas which had been soaked and then boiled. They took daily observations of the temperature in each flask for a week. The results are shown in the table.

Day	Room temperature (°C)	Temperature in flask A containing live, soaked peas (°C)	Temperature in flask B containing dry peas (°C)	Temperature in flask C containing soaked, boiled peas (°C)
1	20.0	20.0	20.0	20.0
2	20.0	20.5	20.0	20.0
3	20.0	21.0	20.0	20.0
4	20.0	21.5	20.0	20.0
5	20.0	22.0	20.0	20.0
6	20.0	22.2	20.0	20.5
7	20.0	22.5	20.0	21.0

a Plot a graph to show these results.

b Explain the results in flask A containing the live, soaked peas.

c Why were the results in flask B the same as the room temperature readings?

d Why did Edward and Jess record room temperature in the lab every day?

e How would you explain the results seen in flask C? Why is the temperature at 20 °C for the first five days? Give two possible explanations why the temperature then increases.

2 It is often said that taking regular exercise and getting fit is good for your heart and your lungs.

	Before getting fit	After getting fit
Amount of blood pumped out of the heart during each beat (cm³)	64	80
Heart volume (cm³)	120	140
Breathing rate (breaths/ min)	14	12
Pulse rate (beats/min)	72	63

a The table shows the effect of getting fit on the heart and lungs of one person. Display this data in four bar charts.

b Use the information on your bar charts to explain exactly what effect increased fitness has on:
   i your heart
   ii your lungs.

3 Look at the graph that shows the difference between a fit and unfit person and the time taken to repay oxygen debt.

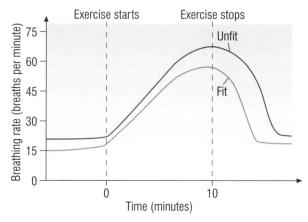

a Explain what is happening to both people.

b Why is the graph for the unfit person different from the graph for the fit person?

c What could the unfit person do to change their body responses to be more like those of the fit person? **[H]**

4 Athletes want to be able to use their muscles aerobically for as long as possible when they compete. They train to develop their heart and lungs. Many athletes also train at altitude. There is less oxygen in the air so your body makes more red blood cells, which helps to avoid oxygen debt. Sometimes athletes remove some of their own blood, store it and then just before a competition transfuse it back into their system. This is called blood doping and it is illegal. Other athletes use hormones to stimulate the growth of extra red blood cells. This is also illegal.

a What is aerobic respiration?

b Why do athletes want to be able to use their muscles aerobically for as long as possible?

c How does developing more red blood cells by training at altitude help athletic performance?

d How does blood doping help performance?

e Explain in detail what happens to the muscles if the body cannot supply enough glucose and oxygen when they are working hard. **[H]**

f It is legal to train at altitude but illegal to carry out blood doping or to take hormones that stimulate the development of red blood cells. What do you think about this situation?

AQA Examination-style questions

1 The diagram shows a group of muscle cells from the wall of the intestine.

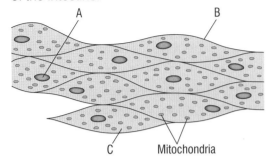

a Choose the correct words to name the structures labelled **A**, **B** and **C**.

cell membrane   cell wall   chloroplast   cytoplasm
nucleus (3)

b Suggest **two** ways that these muscle cells are adapted to release a lot of energy? (2)

2 Respiration is a chemical process.

a Where does respiration take place? Choose the correct answer.

chloroplasts   mitochondria   nuclei   ribosomes (1)

b Which food material is used in respiration? (1)

c Name the **two** waste materials that are produced in respiration. (2)

d Respiration is important in muscle contraction. Explain why. (2)

3 a Copy and complete the word equation for aerobic respiration.
oxygen + ... → water + ... (+ energy) (2)

b i Which substance is missing in anaerobic respiration? (1)
ii What is made during anaerobic respiration? (1)
iii Muscles get tired during anaerobic respiration. Explain why. (1)

4 An athlete started a fitness programme. He was advised to eat a diet containing 18000 kJ per day.

a The athlete was told that 80% of this energy was needed to keep his body temperature at normal levels. Calculate the remaining number of kilojoules available to the athlete. Show your working. (2)

b The athlete decided to double his amount of exercise and assumed he should increase the number of kilojoules in his diet.
Using only the information available to the athlete, calculate the extra energy is he likely to need. (1)

c The energy supplied in the diet must be transferred to the muscles.
Explain in detail this process of energy transfer to the muscles. (4)

5 *In this question you will be assessed on using good English, organising information clearly and using specialist terms where appropriate.*

The bar charts show what happens in an athlete's muscles when running in two races of different distances.

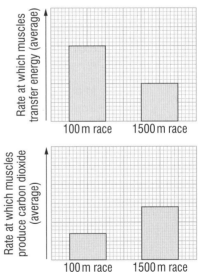

The equations show two processes that occur in muscle cells.

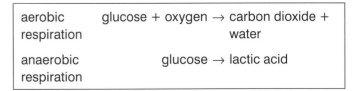

| aerobic respiration | glucose + oxygen → carbon dioxide + water |
| anaerobic respiration | glucose → lactic acid |

Use all the information to explain what happens in the athlete's muscles when running in the two races. (6)

B2 5.1

Cell division and growth ⓚ

Learning objectives

- How are chromosomes arranged in body cells?
- What is mitosis?
- What is cell differentiation and how does it differ in animals and plants?

⬭⬭ links

For more information on alleles, look at B2 5.5 Inheritance in action.

New cells are needed for an organism, or part of an organism, to grow. They are also needed to replace cells which become worn out and to repair damaged tissue. However, the new cells must have the same genetic information as the originals. Then they can do the same job.

Each of your cells has a nucleus containing the instructions for making both new cells and all the tissues and organs needed to make an entire new you. These instructions are carried in the form of genes.

A gene is a small packet of information that controls a characteristic or part of a characteristic, of your body. It is a section of DNA. Different forms of the same gene are known as **alleles**. The genes are grouped together on chromosomes. A chromosome may carry several hundred or even thousands of genes.

You have 46 chromosomes in the nucleus of your body cells. They are arranged in 23 pairs. One of each pair is inherited from your father and one from your mother. Your sex cells (gametes) have only one of each pair of chromosomes.

a Why are new cells needed?

Mitosis

The cell division in normal body cells produces two identical cells and is called **mitosis**. As a result of mitosis all your body cells have the same chromosomes. This means they have the same genetic information.

In asexual reproduction, the cells of the offspring are produced by mitosis from the cells of their parent. This is why they contain exactly the same alleles as their parent with no genetic variation.

How does mitosis work? Before a cell divides it produces new copies of the chromosomes in the nucleus. Then the cell divides once to form two genetically identical cells.

In some parts of an animal or plant, cell division like this carries on rapidly all the time. Your skin is a good example. You constantly lose cells from the skin's surface, and make new cells to replace them. In fact about 300 million body cells die every minute so mitosis is very important.

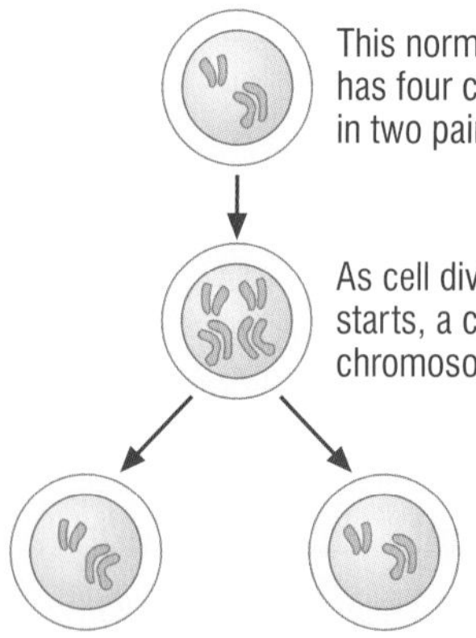

This normal body cell has four chromosomes in two pairs

As cell division starts, a copy of each chromosome is made

The cell divides in two to form two daughter cells. Each daughter cell has a nucleus containing four chromosomes identical to the ones in the original parent cell.

Figure 1 Two identical cells are formed by the simple division that takes place during mitosis. For simplicity this cell is shown with only two pairs (not 23).

Practical

Observing mitosis

View a special preparation of a growing root tip under a microscope. You should be able to see the different stages of mitosis as they are taking place. Use Figure 2 for reference.

- Describe your observations of mitosis.

---

b What is mitosis?

Differentiation

In the early development of animal and plant embryos the cells are unspecialised. Each one of them (known as a **stem cell**) can become any type of cell that is needed.

In many animals, the cells become specialised very early in life. By the time a human baby is born most of its cells are specialised. They will all do a particular job, such as liver cells, skin cells or muscle cells. They have differentiated. Some of their genes have been switched on and others have been switched off.

This means that when, for example, a muscle cell divides by mitosis it can only form more muscle cells. So in a mature (adult) animal, cell division is mainly restricted. It is needed for the repair of damaged tissue and to replace worn out cells. This is because in most adult cells differentiation has already occurred. Specialised cells can divide by mitosis, but they only form the same sort of cell. Therefore growth stops once the animal is mature.

In contrast, most plant cells are able to differentiate all through their life. Undifferentiated cells are formed at active regions of the stems and roots. In these areas mitosis takes place almost continuously.

Plants keep growing all through their lives at these 'growing points'. The plant cells produced don't differentiate until they are in their final position in the plant. Even then the differentiation isn't permanent. You can move a plant cell from one part of a plant to another. There it can redifferentiate and become a completely different type of cell. You can't do that with animal cells – once a muscle cell, always a muscle cell.

We can produce huge numbers of identical plant clones from a tiny piece of leaf tissue. This is because in the right conditions, a plant cell will become unspecialised and undergo mitosis many times. Each of these undifferentiated cells will produce more cells by mitosis. Given different conditions, these will then differentiate to form a tiny new plant. The new plant will be identical to the original parent.

It is difficult to clone animals because animal cells differentiate permanently, early in embryo development. The cells can't change back. Animal clones can only be made by cloning embryos in one way or another, although adult cells can be used to make an embryo.

∞ links

For information on cell differentiation, look back to B2 1.5 Tissues and organs.

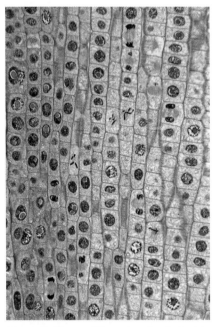

Figure 2 The undifferentiated cells in this onion root tip are dividing rapidly. You can see mitosis taking place, with the chromosomes in different positions as the cells divide.

AQA Examiner's tip

Cells produced by mitosis are genetically identical.

Summary questions

1 Copy and complete using the words below:

*chromosomes   genetic information   genes   growth
mitosis   nucleus   replace*

New cells are needed for .... and to .... worn out cells. The new cells must have the same .... in them as the originals. Each cell has a .... containing the .... grouped together on .... The type of cell division that produces identical cells is known as ....

2 a Explain why the chromosome number must stay the same when the cells divide to make other normal body cells.

b Why is mitosis so important?

3 a What is differentiation?

b How does differentiation differ in animal and plant cells?

c How does this difference affect the cloning of plants and animals?

Key points

● In body cells, chromosomes are found in pairs.

● Body cells divide by mitosis to produce more identical cells for growth, repair and replacement, or in some cases asexual reproduction.

● Most types of animal cell differentiate at an early stage of development. Many plant cells can differentiate throughout their life.

B2 5.2 Cell division in sexual reproduction

Learning objectives

- What is meiosis?
- What happens to your chromosomes when your gametes are formed? [H]
- How does sexual reproduction give rise to variation?

Mitosis is taking place all the time, in tissues all over your body. But there is another type of cell division that takes place only in the reproductive organs of animals and plants. In humans this is the ovaries and the testes. **Meiosis** results in sex cells, called gametes, with only half the original number of chromosomes.

Meiosis

The female gametes or **ova** are made in the ovaries. The male gametes or sperm are made in the testes.

The gametes are formed by meiosis – cell division where the chromosome number is reduced by half. When a cell divides to form gametes, the chromosomes (the genetic information) are copied so there are four sets of chromosomes. The cell then divides twice in quick succession to form four gametes, each with a single set of chromosomes.

Each gamete that is produced is slightly different from all the others. They contain random mixtures of the original chromosomes pairs. This introduces variety.

a What are the names of the male and female gametes in animals? How do they differ from normal body cells?

Did you know ... ?

The testes can produce around 400 million sperm by meiosis every 24 hours between them. Only one sperm is needed to fertilise an egg but each sperm needs to travel 100 000 times its own length to reach the ovum and less than one in a million make it!

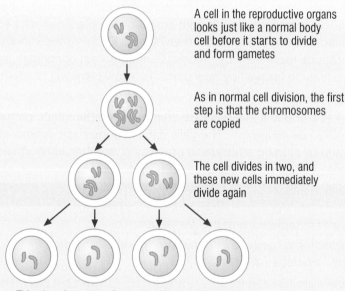

A cell in the reproductive organs looks just like a normal body cell before it starts to divide and form gametes

As in normal cell division, the first step is that the chromosomes are copied

The cell divides in two, and these new cells immediately divide again

This gives four sex cells, each with a single set of chromosomes – in this case two instead of the original four

Figure 1 The formation of sex cells in the ovaries and testes involves meiosis to halve the chromosome number. The original cell is shown with only two pairs of chromosomes to make it easier to follow what is happening.

b What type of cell division is needed to produce the gametes?

Fertilisation

More variety is added when fertilisation takes place. Each sex cell has a single set of chromosomes. When two sex cells join during fertilisation the single new cell formed has a full set of chromosomes. In humans, the egg cell (ovum) has 23 chromosomes and so does the sperm. When they join together they produce a single new body cell with the body human number of 46 chromosomes in 23 pairs.

The combination of genes on the chromosomes of every newly fertilised ovum is unique. Once fertilisation is complete, the unique new cell begins to divide by mitosis to form a new individual. This will continue long after the foetus is fully developed and the baby is born.

In fact about 80% of fertilised eggs never make it to become a live baby – about 50% never even implant into the lining of the womb.

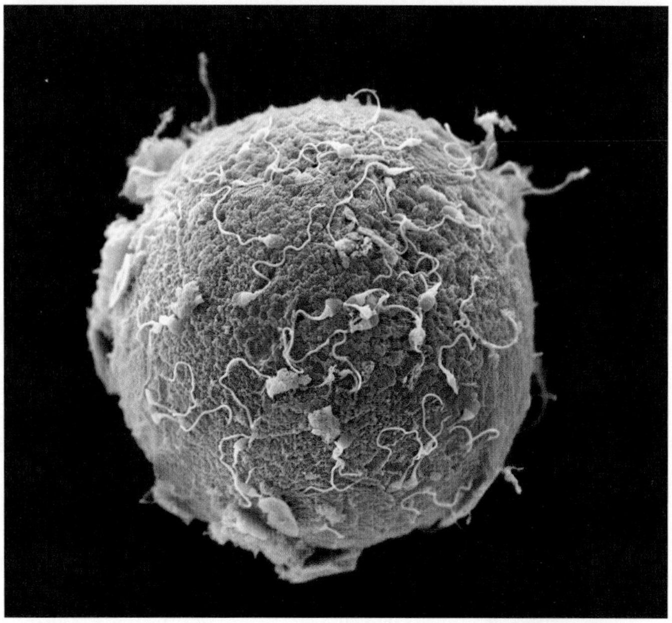

Figure 2 At the moment of fertilisation the chromosomes in the two gametes are combined. The new cell has a complete set of chromosomes, like any other body cell. This new cell will then grow and reproduce by mitosis to form a new individual.

Variation

The differences between asexual and sexual reproduction are reflected in the different types of cell division involved.

In asexual reproduction the offspring are produced as a result of mitosis from the parent cells. So they contain exactly the same chromosomes and the same genes as their parents. There is no variation in the genetic material.

In sexual reproduction the gametes are produced by meiosis in the sex organs of the parents. This introduces variety as each gamete is different. Then when the gametes fuse, one of each pair of chromosomes, and so one of each pair of genes, comes from each parent.

The combination of genes in the new pair of chromosomes will contain alleles from each parent. This also helps to produce variation in the characteristics of the offspring.

AQA Examiner's tip

Learn to spell mitosis and meiosis.
Remember their meanings:
Mitosis – **m**aking **i**dentical **t**wo.
Meiosis – **m**aking **e**ggs (and sperm).

Key points

- Cells in the reproductive organs divide by meiosis to form the gametes (sex cells).

- Body cells have two sets of chromosomes; gametes have only one set.

- In meiosis the genetic material is copied and then the cell divides twice to form four gametes, each with a single set of chromosomes [H]

- Sexual reproduction gives rise to variety because genetic information from two parents is combined.

Summary questions

1 a How many pairs of chromosomes are there in a normal human body cell?
  b How many chromosomes are there in a human sperm cell?
  c How many chromosomes are there in a fertilised human egg cell?

2 Sexual reproduction results in variety. Explain how.

3 a What is the name of the special type of cell division that produces gametes from ordinary body cells? Describe what happens to the chromosomes in this process.
  b Where in your body would this type of cell division take place?
  c Why is this type of cell division so important in sexual reproduction?
  [H]

B2 5.3

Stem cells

Early human embryo

Stem cells removed

Stem cells cultured

Stem cells made to differentiate into different tissues

Spinal cord   Heart   Kidney   Insulin-producing cells

Organs or tissues transplanted into a patient to cure them

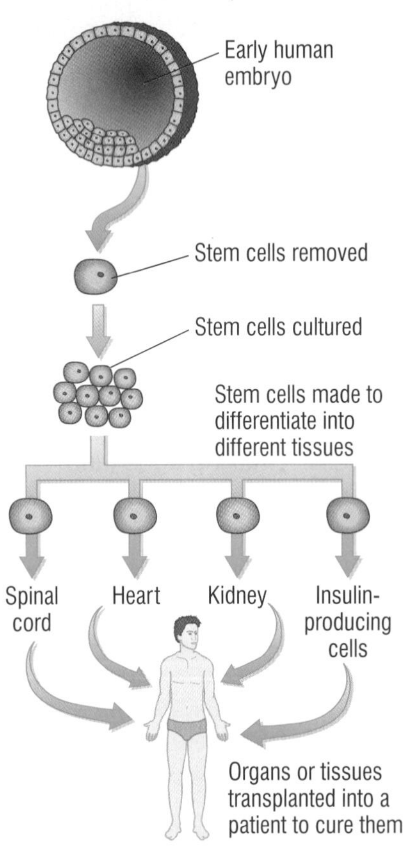

Figure 1 This shows how scientists hope embryonic stem cells might be formed into adult cells and used as human treatments in the future

The function of stem cells

An egg and sperm cell fuse to form a zygote, a single new cell. That cell divides and becomes a hollow ball of cells – the embryo. The inner cells of this ball are the stem cells. Stem cells differentiate to form the specialised cells of your body that make up your various tissues and organs. They will eventually produce every type of cell in your body.

Even when you are an adult, some of your stem cells remain. Your bone marrow is a good source of stem cells. Scientists now think there may be a tiny number of stem cells in most of the different tissues in your body. This includes your blood, brain, muscle and liver.

The stem cells can stay in the different tissues for many years. They are only needed if your tissues are injured or affected by disease. Then they start dividing to replace the different types of damaged cell.

    a What are stem cells?

Using stem cells 🅚

Many people suffer and even die because parts of their body stop working properly. For example, spinal injuries can cause paralysis. That's because the spinal nerves do not repair themselves. Millions of people would benefit if we could replace damaged body parts.

In 1998, there was a breakthrough. Two American scientists managed to culture human embryonic stem cells. These were capable of forming other types of cell.

Scientists hope that the embryonic stem cells can be encouraged to grow into almost any different type of cell needed in the body. For example, scientists in the US have grown nerve cells from embryonic stem cells. In rats, these have been used to reconnect damaged spinal nerves. The rats regained some movement of their legs. In 2010 the first trials using nerve cells grown from embryonic stem cells in humans were carried out. The nerve cells were injected into the spinal cords of patients with new, severe spinal cord injuries. These first trials were to make sure that the technique is safe. The scientists and doctors hope it will not be long before they can use stem cells to help people who have been paralysed walk again.

We might also be able to grow whole new organs from embryonic stem cells. These organs could be used in transplant surgery. Conditions from infertility to dementia could eventually be treated using stem cells. Doctors in the UK hope to begin using embryonic stem cells to treat a common cause of blindness in 2011.

    b What was the big scientific breakthrough by American scientists in 1998?

Problems with stem cells

Many embryonic stem cells come from aborted embryos. Others come from spare embryos in fertility treatment. This raises ethical issues. There are people, including many religious groups, who feel this is wrong. They question the use of a potential human being as a source of cells, even to cure others.

Some people feel that as the embryo cannot give permission, using it is a violation of its human rights. As well as this, progress with stem cells is slow. There is some concern that embryonic stem cells might cause cancer if they are used to treat sick people. This has certainly been seen in mice. Making stem cells is slow, difficult, expensive and hard to control.

c What is the biggest ethical concern with the use of embryonic stem cells?

The future of stem cell research

Scientists have found embryonic stem cells in the umbilical cord blood of newborn babies. These may help to overcome some of the ethical concerns.

Scientists are also finding ways of growing the adult stem cells found in bone marrow and some other tissues. So far they can only develop into a limited range of cell types. However, this is another possible way of avoiding the controversial use of embryonic tissue. Adult stem cells have been used successfully to treat some forms of heart disease and to grow some new organs such as tracheas (windpipes).

The area of stem cell research known as **therapeutic cloning** could be very useful. However, it is proving very difficult. It involves using cells from an adult to produce a cloned early embryo of themselves. This would provide a source of perfectly matched embryonic stem cells. In theory these could then be used to grow new organs for the original donor. The new organs would not be rejected by the body because they have been made from the body's own cells.

Most people remain excited by the possibilities of embryonic stem cell use in treating many diseases. At the moment, after years of relatively slow progress, hopes are high again that stem cells will change the future of medicine. We don't know how many of these hopes will be fulfilled; only time will tell.

Figure 2 For years, funding for stem cell research in the US was blocked by the government. In 2009 President Obama changed that ruling so US research could move forward. However, the battle continues in the courts.

Figure 3 In 2010 Ciaran Finn-Lynch was the first child to be given a life-saving new windpipe grown using his own stem cells

Summary questions

1 Copy and complete using the words below:

bone marrow   differentiate   embryos   hollow   inner   stem cells

Unspecialised cells known as .... can .... (divide and change) into many different types of cell when they are needed. Human stem cells are found in .... and in adult .... The embryo forms a .... ball of cells and the .... cells of this ball are the stem cells.

2 **a** What are the advantages of using stem cells to treat diseases?
  b What are the difficulties with stem cell research?
  c How are scientists hoping to overcome the ethical objections to using embryonic stem cells in their research?

Key points

● Embryonic stem cells (from human embryos) and adult stem cells (from adult bone marrow) can be made to differentiate into many different types of cell.

● Stem cells have the potential to treat previously incurable conditions. We may be able to grow nerve cells or whole new organs for people who need them.

B2 5.4

From Mendel to DNA

Learning objectives

- What did Mendel's experiments teach us about inheritance?
- What is DNA?
- How are specific proteins made in the body? [H]

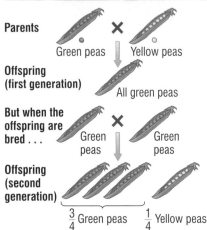

Parents — Green peas **×** Yellow peas

Offspring (first generation) — All green peas

But when the offspring are bred ... Green peas **×** Green peas

Offspring (second generation) — $\frac{3}{4}$ Green peas $\frac{1}{4}$ Yellow peas

Figure 1 Gregor Mendel, the father of modern genetics. His work was not recognised in his lifetime but now we know just how right he was!

Until about 150 years ago people had no idea how information was passed from one generation to the next. Today we can identify people by the genetic information in their cells.

Mendel's discoveries

Gregor Mendel was born in 1822 in Austrian Silesia. He was clever but poor, so he became a monk to get an education.

He worked in the monastery gardens and became fascinated by the peas growing there. He carried out some breeding experiments using peas. He used smooth peas, wrinkled peas, green peas and yellow peas for his work. Mendel cross-bred the peas and counted the different offspring carefully. He found that characteristics were inherited in clear and predictable patterns.

Mendel explained his results by suggesting there were separate units of inherited material. He realised that some characteristics were dominant over others and that they never mixed together. This was an amazing idea for the time.

a Why did Gregor Mendel become a monk?

Mendel kept records of everything he did, and analysed his results. This was almost unheard of in those days. Eventually in 1866 Mendel published his findings.

He had never seen chromosomes nor heard of genes. Yet he explained some of the basic laws of genetics using mathematical models in ways that we still use today.

Mendel was ahead of his time. As no one knew about genes or chromosomes, people simply didn't understand his theories. He died 20 years later with his ideas still ignored – but convinced that he was right.

b What was unusual about Mendel's scientific technique at the time?

Sixteen years after Mendel's death, his work was finally recognised. By 1900, people had seen chromosomes through a microscope. Other scientists discovered Mendel's papers and repeated his experiments. When they published their results, they gave Mendel the credit for what they observed.

From then on ideas about genetics developed rapidly. It was suggested that Mendel's units of inheritance might be carried on the chromosomes seen under the microscope. And so the science of genetics as we know it today was born.

DNA – the molecule of inheritance

The work of Gregor Mendel was just the start of our understanding of inheritance. Today, we know that our features are inherited on genes carried on the chromosomes found in the nuclei of our cells.

These chromosomes are made up of long molecules of a chemical known as DNA (deoxyribonucleic acid). This has a double helix structure. Your genes are small sections of this DNA. The DNA carries the instructions to make the proteins that form most of your cell structures. These proteins also include the enzymes that control your cell chemistry. This is how the relationship between the genes and the whole organism builds up. The genes make up the chromosomes in the nucleus of the cell. They control the proteins, which make up the different specialised cells that form tissues. These tissues then form organs and organ systems that make up the whole body.

The genetic code

The long strands of your DNA are made up of combinations of four different chemical bases (see Figure 2). These are grouped into threes and each group of three codes for an amino acid.

Each gene is made up of hundreds or thousands of these bases. The order of the bases controls the order in which the amino acids are put together so that they make a particular protein for use in your body cells. Each gene codes for a particular combination of amino acids, which make a specific protein.

A change or mutation in a single group of bases can be enough to change or disrupt the whole protein structure and the way it works.

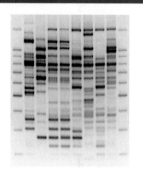

A section of three bases like this codes for one amino acid

Figure 2 DNA codes for the amino acids that make up the proteins that make up the enzymes that make each individual

DNA fingerprinting

Unless you have an identical twin, your DNA is unique to you. Other members of your family will have strong similarities in their DNA. However, each individual has their own unique pattern. Only identical twins have the same DNA. That's because they have both developed from the same original cell.

The unique patterns in your DNA can be used to identify you. A technique known as 'DNA fingerprinting' can be applied to make the patterns known as **DNA fingerprints**.

These patterns are more similar between people who are related than between total strangers. They can be produced from very tiny samples of DNA from body fluids such as blood, saliva and semen.

The likelihood of two identical samples coming from different people (apart from identical twins) is millions to one. As a result, DNA fingerprinting is very useful in solving crimes. It can also be used to find the biological father of a child when there is doubt.

??? Did you know ... ?

The first time DNA fingerprinting was used to solve a crime, it identified Colin Pitchfork as the murderer of two teenage girls and cleared an innocent man of the same crimes.

Figure 3 A DNA fingerprint

Summary questions

1 a How did Mendel's experiments with peas convince him that there were distinct 'units of inheritance' that were not blended together in offspring?

 b Why didn't people accept his ideas?

 c The development of the microscope played an important part in helping to convince people that Mendel was right. How?

2 Two men claim to be the father of the same child. Explain how DNA fingerprinting could be used to find out which one is the real father.

3 Explain the saying 'One gene, one protein'. [H]

Key points

- Gregor Mendel was the first person to suggest separately inherited factors, which we now call genes.

- Chromosomes are made up of large molecules of DNA.

- A gene is a small section of DNA that codes for a particular combination of amino acids, which make a specific protein. [H]

- Everyone (except identical twins) has unique DNA that can be used to identify them using DNA fingerprinting

B2 5.5

Inheritance in action

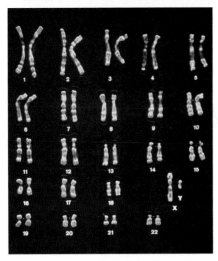

Figure 1 This special photo shows the 23 pairs of human chromosomes. You can see the XY chromosomes, which tell you they are from a male.

The way features are passed from one generation to another follows some clear patterns. We can use these to predict what may be passed on.

How inheritance works

Scientists have built on the work of Gregor Mendel. We now understand how genetic information is passed from parent to offspring.

Humans have 23 pairs of chromosomes. In 22 cases, each chromosome in the pair is a similar shape. Each one has genes carrying information about the same things. One pair of chromosomes is different – these are the **sex chromosomes**. Two X chromosomes mean you are female; one X chromosome and a much smaller one, known as the Y chromosome, mean you are male.

a Twins are born. Twin A is XY and twin B is XX. What sex are the two babies?

The chromosomes we inherit carry our genetic information in the form of genes. Many of these genes have different forms or alleles. Each allele will result in a different protein.

Picture a gene as a position on a chromosome. An allele is the particular form of information in that position on an individual chromosome. For example, the gene for dimples may have the dimple (D) or the no-dimple (d) allele in place.

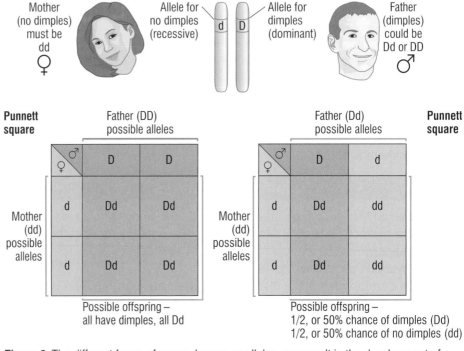

Figure 2 The different forms of genes, known as alleles, can result in the development of quite different characteristics. Genetic diagrams like these Punnett squares help you explain what is happening and predict what the offspring might be like.

Most of your characteristics, like your eye colour and nose shape, are controlled by a number of genes. However, some characteristics, like dimples or having attached earlobes, are controlled by a single gene. Often there are only two possible alleles for a particular feature. However, sometimes you can inherit one from a number of different possibilities. We can use biological models like the Punnett square in Figure 2 to predict the outcome of different genetic crosses.

Some alleles control the development of a characteristic even when they are only present on one of your chromosomes. These alleles are **dominant**, e.g. dimples and dangly earlobes. We use a capital letter to represent them, e.g. D.

Some alleles only control the development of a characteristic if they are present on both chromosomes – in other words, no dominant allele is present. These alleles are **recessive**, e.g. no dimples and attached earlobes. We use a lower case letter to represent them, e.g. d.

Higher

Genetic terms

Some words are useful when you are working with biological models such as Punnett squares or family trees:

● **Homozygous** – an individual with two identical alleles for a characteristic, e.g. **DD**, **dd**.
● **Heterozygous** – an individual with different alleles for a characteristic, e.g. **Dd**.
● **Genotype** – this describes the genetic makeup of an individual regarding a particular characteristic, e.g. **Dd**, **dd**.
● **Phenotype** – this describes the physical appearance of an individual regarding a particular characteristic, e.g. dimples, no dimples.

Family trees

You can trace genetic characteristics through a family by drawing a family tree. Family trees show males and females and can be useful for tracing family likenesses. They can also be used for tracking inherited diseases, showing a physical characteristic or showing the different alleles people have inherited.

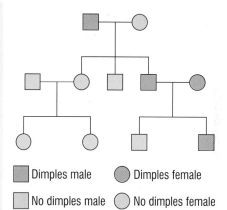

AQA **Examiner's tip**

When you choose a letter as a genetic symbol, try and use a letter that looks different in upper and lower case. Whatever you choose, be very careful to make the upper and lower case symbols clear. **[H]**

☐ Dimples male   ○ Dimples female

☐ No dimples male   ○ No dimples female

Figure 3 A family tree to show the inheritance of dimples

Summary questions

1 Copy and complete using the words below:

male   sex chromosomes   23   22   X   XX   Y

Humans have .... pairs of chromosomes. In .... pairs the chromosomes are always the same. The final pair are known as .... If you inherit .... you will be female, while an .... and a .... chromosome make you ....

2 a What is meant by the term 'dominant allele'?
  b What is meant by the term 'recessive allele'?
  c Try and discover as many human characteristics as you can that are inherited on a single gene. Which alleles are dominant and which are recessive?

3 Draw a Punnett square like the ones in Figure 2 to show the possible offspring from a cross between two people who both have dimples and the genotype Dd. **[H]**

Key points

● In human body cells the sex chromosomes determine whether you are female (XX) or male (XY).

● Some features are controlled by a single gene.

● Genes can have different forms called alleles.

● Some alleles are dominant and some are recessive.

● We can construct genetic diagrams to predict characteristics **[H]**

B2 5.6
Inherited conditions in humans

Learning objectives

- How are human genetic disorders inherited?

- How can we use a genetic diagram to predict whether a child will inherit a genetic disorder?

- Can you construct a genetic diagram to make predictions about the likelihood of inheriting a genetic disorder? **[H]**

Not all diseases are infectious. Sometimes diseases are the result of a problem in our genes and can be passed on from parent to child. They are known as **genetic or inherited disorders**.

We can use our knowledge of dominant and recessive alleles to work out the risk of inheriting a **genetic disorder**.

a How is an inherited disorder different from an infectious disease?

Polydactyly

Sometimes babies are born with extra fingers or toes. This is called **polydactyly**. The most common form of polydactyly is caused by a dominant allele. It can be inherited from one parent who has the condition. People often have their extra digit removed, but some live quite happily with them.

If one of your parents has polydactyly and is heterozygous, you have a 50% chance of inheriting the disorder. That's because half of their gametes will contain the faulty allele. If they are homozygous, you will definitely have the condition.

Higher

Cystic fibrosis

Cystic fibrosis is a genetic disorder that affects many organs of the body, particularly the lungs and the pancreas. Over 8500 people in the UK have cystic fibrosis.

Organs become clogged up by thick, sticky mucus, which stops them working properly. The reproductive system is also affected, so many people with cystic fibrosis are infertile.

Treatment for cystic fibrosis includes physiotherapy and antibiotics. These help keep the lungs clear of mucus and infections. Enzymes are used to replace the ones the pancreas cannot produce and to thin the mucus.

However, although treatments are getting better all the time, there is still no cure.

Cystic fibrosis is caused by a recessive allele so it must be inherited from both parents. Children affected by cystic fibrosis are usually born to parents who do not suffer from the disorder. They have a dominant healthy allele, which means their bodies work normally. However, they also carry the recessive cystic fibrosis allele. Because it gives them no symptoms, they have no idea it is there. They are known as **carriers**.

In the UK, one person in 25 carries the cystic fibrosis allele. Most of them will never be aware of it. They only realise when they have children with a partner who also carries the allele. Then there is a 25% (one in four) chance that any child they have will be affected.

b You will only inherit cystic fibrosis if you get the cystic fibrosis allele from both parents. Why?

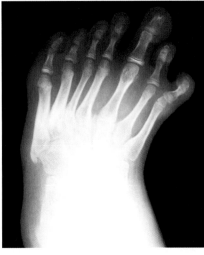

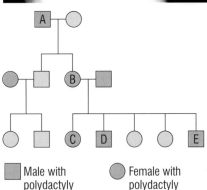

■ Male with polydactyly
● Female with polydactyly
□ Unaffected male
○ Unaffected female

Figure 1 Polydactyly is passed through a family tree by a dominant allele

The genetic lottery

When the genes from parents are combined, it is called a genetic cross. We can show this using a genetic diagram (see Figures 2 and 3). A genetic diagram shows us:

- the alleles for a characteristic carried by the parents (the genotype of the parents)
- the possible gametes which can be formed from these
- how these could combine to form the characteristic in their offspring. The genotype of the offspring allows you to work out the possible phenotypes too.

When looking at the possibility of inheriting genetic disorders, it is important to remember that every time an egg and a sperm fuse it is down to chance which alleles combine. So if two parents who are heterozygous for the cystic fibrosis allele have four children, there is a 25% chance (one in four) that each child might have the disorder.

But in fact all four children could have cystic fibrosis, or none of them might be affected. They might all be carriers, or none of them might inherit the faulty alleles at all. It's all down to chance!

Figure 3 A genetic diagram for cystic fibrosis

	P	p
p	Pp	pp
p	Pp	pp

50% chance polydactyly, PP or Pp, 50% chance normal pp

Pp = Parent with polydactyly
pp = Normal parent

Figure 2 A genetic diagram for polydactyly

Both parents are carriers, so Cc

	C	c
C	CC	Cc
c	Cc	cc

Genotype:
25% normal (CC)
50% carriers (Cc)
25% affected by cystic fibrosis (cc)

Phenotype:
3/4, or 75% chance normal
1/4, or 25% chance cystic fibrosis

Curing genetic diseases

So far we have no way of curing genetic disorders. Scientists hope that genetic engineering could be the answer. It should be possible to cut out faulty alleles and replace them with healthy ones. They have tried this in people affected by cystic fibrosis. Unfortunately, so far they have not managed to cure anyone.

Genetic tests are available that can show people if they carry the faulty allele. This allows them to make choices such as whether or not to have a family. It is possible to screen fetuses or embryos during pregnancy for the alleles which cause inherited disorders. You can also screen embryos before they are implanted in the mother during IVF treatment. These tests are very useful but raise many ethical issues.

Summary questions

1 a What is polydactyly?
  b Why can one parent with the allele for polydactyly pass the condition on to their children even though the other parent is not affected?
  c Look at the family tree in Figure 1. For each of the five people labelled A to E affected by polydactyly, give their possible alleles and explain your answers.

2 a Why are carriers of cystic fibrosis not affected by the disorder themselves?
  b Why must both of your parents be carriers of the allele for cystic fibrosis before you can inherit the disease?

3 A couple have a baby who has cystic fibrosis. Neither the couple, nor their parents, have any signs of the disorder.
  Draw genetic diagrams showing the possible genotypes of the grandparents and the parents to show how this could happen. [H]

Key points

- Some disorders are inherited.

- Polydactyly is caused by a dominant allele of a gene and can be inherited from only one parent.

- Cystic fibrosis is caused by a recessive allele of a gene and so must be inherited from both parents.

- You can use genetic diagrams to predict how genetic disorders might be inherited.

- You can construct genetic diagrams to predict the inheritance of genetic disease. [H]

B2 5.7

Stem cells and embryos – science and ethics

Learning objectives

- Does everyone agree with the use of embryonic stem cells?

- Are there any problems related to embryo screening?

The stem cell dilemma

Doctors have treated people with adult stem cells for many years by giving bone marrow transplants. Now scientists are moving ever closer to treating very ill people using embryonic stem cells. This area of medicine raises many issues. People have strong opinions about using embryonic stem cells – here are some of them:

In favour of using embryonic stem cells in medical research and possible treatments

- Embryonic stem cells offer one of the best chances of finding treatments for many different and often very serious conditions, including paralysis from spinal injury, Alzheimer's and diabetes.
- The embryos used are generally spare embryos from infertility treatment which would be destroyed anyway.
- Embryos are being created from adult cells for use in research and therapy – they would never become babies.
- It may be possible to use embryonic stem cells from the umbilical cord of newborn babies, so that no embryos need to be destroyed for the research and treatments to go ahead.
- Embryonic stem cells could be used to grow new tissues and organs for transplants.

Against using embryonic stem cells in medical research and possible treatments

- Embryonic stem cell treatments are very experimental and there is a risk that they may cause further problems such as the development of cancers.
- All embryos have the potential to become babies. It is therefore wrong to experiment on them or destroy them.
- Embryos cannot give permission to be used in experiments or treatments, so it is unethical.
- It is taking a long time to develop any therapy that works – the money and research time would be better spent on other possible treatments such as new drugs or using adult stem cells.

Activity 1

Your class is going to produce a large wall display covered with articles both for and against stem cell research. Your display is aimed at students in Years 10–11. Make sure the level of content is right for your target group.

Try and carry out a survey or a vote with your target group before the display is put up to assess attitudes to the use of embryonic stem cells. Record your findings.

Work on your own or in a small group to produce one piece of display material either in favour of stem cell research or against it. Use a variety of resources to help you – the material in this chapter is a good starting point. Make sure that your ideas are backed up with as much scientific evidence as possible.

Once the material has been displayed for a week or two, repeat your initial survey or vote. Analyse the data to see if easy access to information has changed people's views.

The ethics of screening

Today we not only understand the causes of many genetic disorders, we can also test for them. However, being able to test for a genetic disorder doesn't necessarily mean we should always do it.

- Huntington's disease is inherited through a dominant allele. It causes death in middle age. People in affected families can take a genetic test for the faulty allele. Some people in affected families take the test and use it to help them decide whether to marry or have a family. Others prefer not to know.

- Some couples with an inherited disorder in their family have any developing embryos tested during pregnancy. Cells from the embryo are checked. If it is affected, the parents have a choice. They may decide to keep the baby, knowing that it will have a genetic disorder when it is born. On the other hand, they may decide to have an abortion. This prevents the birth of a child with serious problems. Then they can try again to have a healthy baby.

- Some couples with an inherited disorder in the family have their embryos screened before they are implanted in the mother. Embryos are produced by IVF (*in vitro* fertilisation). Doctors remove a single cell from each embryo and screen it for inherited disorders. Only healthy embryos free from genetic disorders are implanted back into their mother, so only babies without that disorder are born.

	H	h
h	Hh	hh
h	Hh	hh

H = dominant, Huntington's disease
h = recessive, no Huntington's disease

Offspring genotype: 50% Hh, 50% hh

Phenotype: 50% Huntington's disease
50% healthy

Figure 1 A genetic diagram for Huntington's disease

Activity 2

Genetic counsellors help families affected by particular genetic disorders to understand the problems and the choices available. Plan a role play of an interview between a genetic counsellor and a couple who already have one child with cystic fibrosis, and would like to have another child.

Either: Plan the role of the counsellor. Make sure you have all the information you need to be able to explain the chances of another child being affected and the choices that are open to the parents.

Or: Plan the role of a parent or work in pairs to give the views of a couple. Think carefully about the factors that will affect your decision, e.g. can you cope with another sick child? Are you prepared to have an abortion? Do you have religious views on the matter? What is fairest to the unborn child, and the child you already have? Is it ethical to choose embryos to implant?

Summary questions

1 What are the main ethical issues associated with the use of embryonic stem cells?

2 It would cost a lot of money to screen all embryos for genetic conditions. Put forward two arguments for, and two against, this process.

Key points

- It is important that people make informed judgements about the use of embryonic stem cells in medical research and treatment.

- There are a number of economic, social and ethical issues surrounding the screening of embryos.

Summary questions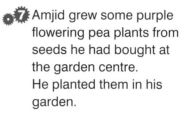

1 a What is mitosis?

b Explain, using diagrams, what takes place when a cell divides by mitosis.

c Mitosis is very important during the development of a baby from a fertilised egg. It is also important all through life. Why?

2 What is meiosis and where does it take place?

3 a Why is meiosis so important?

b Explain, using labelled diagrams, what takes place when a cell divides by meiosis. **[H]**

4 a What are stem cells?

b It is hoped that many different medical problems may be cured using stem cells. Explain how this might work.

c There are some ethical issues associated with the use of embryonic stem cells. Explain the arguments both for and against their use.

5 Hugo de Vries is one of the scientists who made the same discoveries as Mendel several years after Mendel's death. Write a letter from Hugo to one of his friends after he has found Mendel's writings. Explain what Mendel did, why no one took any notice of him and how the situation has changed so that you (Hugo) can come up with a clear explanation for the results of your own experiments. Explain your attitude to Mendel.

6 Whether you have a straight thumb or a curved one is decided by a single gene with two alleles. The allele for a straight thumb, S, is dominant to the curved allele, s. Use this information to help you answer these questions.

Josh has straight thumbs but Sami has curved thumbs. They are expecting a baby.

a We know exactly what Sami's thumb alleles are. What are they and how do you know?

b If the baby has curved thumbs, what does this tell you about Josh's thumb alleles? Draw and complete a Punnett square to show the genetics of your explanation.

c If the baby has straight thumbs, what does this tell us about Josh's thumb alleles? Draw and complete a Punnett square to show the genetics of your explanation. **[H]**

7 Amjid grew some purple flowering pea plants from seeds he had bought at the garden centre. He planted them in his garden.

Here are his results.

Seeds planted	247
Purple-flowered plants	242
White-flowered plants	1
Seeds not growing	4

a Is the white-flowered plant an anomaly? Why?

b Are the seeds that did not grow anomalies? Why?

c Suggest other investigations Amjid could carry out into the cause of the colour of the white-flowered plant.

Amjid was interested in these plants, so he collected the seed from some of the purple-flowered plants and used them in the garden the following year. He made a careful note of what happened.

Here are his results:

Seeds planted	406
Purple-flowered plants	295
White-flowered plants	102
Seeds not growing	6

Amjid was slightly surprised. He did not expect to find that a third of his flowers would be white.

d i The purple allele (P) is dominant and the allele for white flowers (p) is recessive. Draw a genetic diagram that explains Amjid's numbers of purple and white flowers.

ii How accurate were Amjid's results compared with the expected ratio?

e How could Amjid have improved his method of growing the peas to make his results more valid? **[H]**

AQA Examination-style questions

1 Copy and complete the following sentences using the words or symbols below:

characteristics cytoplasm fitness genes nucleus proteins tissue

2 23 46 X XX XY Y

In the body cells of a boy there are .... chromosomes that are found in the .... The boy's cells can be identified as male by the .... chromosome. On all the chromosomes there are sections called .... that determine the .... of the boy. (5)

2 The drawing shows some of the stages of reproduction in horses.

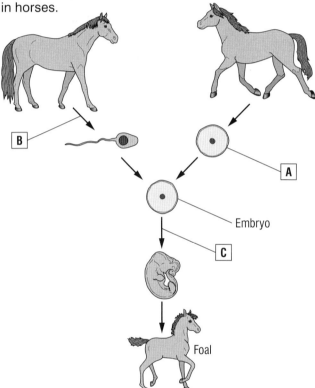

Embryo

Foal

a i Name this type of reproduction (1)
  ii Name the type of cell labelled **A**. (1)

b Name the type of cell division taking place at the stages labelled:
  i **B** (1)
  ii **C**. (1)

c How does the number of chromosomes in each cell of the embryo compare with the number of chromosomes in cell **A**? (1)

d When the foal grows up it will look similar to its parents but it will **not** be identical to either parent.
  i Explain why it will look similar to its parents. (1)
  ii Suggest **two** reasons why it will **not** be identical to either of its parents. (2)

AQA, 2001

3 When an embryo is formed, the cells divide and start to differentiate. Some adult cells are still able to differentiate.

a What is meant by the term *differentiation*? (1)

b What name do we give to cells which have not differentiated? (1)

c Give an example of adult cells that can differentiate. (1)

d Some of the embryo cells may be used in the future to treat conditions such as paralysis.
There are people who do not think we should use embryos in this way. What is an ethical reason for objecting to the use of embryos? (1)

4 *In this question you will be assessed on using good English, organising information clearly and using specialist terms where appropriate.*

Doctors all over the world are investigating the use of stem cells to treat a wide variety of disorders.

Many doctors use adult stem cells but some use embryonic stem cells. There is evidence that adult stem cells do not cause cancer tumours if they are transferred soon after being removed from the body. Embryonic stem cells multiply very quickly and there is a risk of cancer developing after treatment with them.

Bone marrow cells are stem cells which continually replace your blood cells every day of your life.

Adult stem cells from bone marrow have been used successfully to treat leukaemia for over 40 years. Many patients with damage to the nervous system have reported improvements in movement following treatment with adult stem cells, but more research is needed before widespread use of the treatment.

One doctor said, 'It is safer to use adult stem cells. Using embryonic stem cells is not ethical.'

Using the information and your own knowledge explain the statement made by the doctor. (6)

B2 6.1

The origins of life on Earth

Learning objectives

- What is the evidence for the origins of life on Earth?
- What are fossils?
- What can we learn from fossils?

There is no record of the origins of life on Earth. It is a puzzle that can never be completely solved. There is not much valid evidence for what happened – no one was there to see it! We don't even know exactly when life on Earth began. However, most scientists think it was somewhere between 3 to 4 billion years ago.

There are some interesting ideas and well-respected theories that explain most of what you can see around you. The biggest problem we have is finding the evidence to support the ideas.

a When do scientists think life on Earth began?

What can we learn from fossils?

Some of the best evidence we have about the history of life on Earth comes from **fossils**. Fossils are the remains of organisms from many thousands or millions of years ago that are found preserved in rocks, ice and other places. For example, fossils have revealed the world of the dinosaurs. These lizards dominated the Earth at one stage and died out millions of years before humans came to dominate the Earth.

Maths skills

Time scales for the evolution of life are big:

- A thousand years is 10^3 years.
- A million years is 10^6 years.
- A billion years is 10^9 years.

You have probably seen a fossil in a museum or on TV, or maybe even found one yourself. Fossils can be formed in a number of ways:

- They may be formed from the hard parts of an animal. These are the bits that do not decay easily, such as the bones, teeth, claws or shells.
- Another type of fossil is formed when an animal or plant does not decay after it has died. This happens when one or more of the conditions needed for decay are not there. This may be because there is little or no oxygen present. It could be because poisonous gases kill off the bacteria that cause decay. Sometimes the temperature is too low for decay to take place. Then the animals and plants are preserved in ice. These ice fossils are rare, but they give a clear insight into what an animal looked like. They can also tell us what an animal had been eating or the colour of a long-extinct flower. We can even extract the DNA and compare it to modern organisms.
- Many fossils are formed when harder parts of the animal or plant are replaced by other minerals. This takes place over long periods of time. These are the most common fossils (see Figure 3).
- Some of the fossils we find are not of actual animals or plants, but of traces they have left behind. Fossil footprints, burrows, rootlet traces and droppings are all formed. These help us to build up a picture of life on Earth long ago.

b Which is the most common type of fossil?

 Did you know …?

The biggest herbivore found so far is *Argentinosaurus huinculensis.* It was nearly 40 metres long and probably weighed about 80–100 tonnes! The biggest carnivore found, *Giganotosaurus,* was about 14 metres long. It had a brain the size of a banana and 20 cm long serrated teeth. By comparison, the biggest modern lizard, the Komodo dragon, is about 3 metres long and weighs around 140 kg.

Figure 1 A fossil of *Tyrannosaurus rex*

An incomplete record

The fossil record is not complete for several reasons. Many of the very earliest forms of life were soft-bodied organisms. This means they have left little fossil trace. It is partly why there is so little valid evidence of how life began. There is no fossil record of the earliest life forms on Earth.

Most organisms that died did not become fossilised – the right conditions for fossil formation were rare. Also, many of the fossils that were formed in the rocks have been destroyed by geological activity. Huge amounts of rock have been broken down, worn away, buried or melted over the years. As this happens the fossil record is lost too. Finally, there are many fossils that are still to be found.

In spite of all these limitations, the fossils we have found can still give us a 'snapshot' of life millions of years ago.

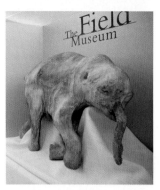

Figure 2 This baby mammoth was preserved in ice for at least 10 000 years. Examining this kind of evidence helps scientists check the accuracy of ideas based on fossil skeletons alone.

1 The reptile dies and falls to the ground

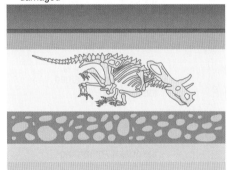

2 The flesh rots, leaving the skeleton to be covered in sand or soil and clay before it is damaged

3 Protected, over millions of years, the skeleton becomes mineralised and turns to rock. The rocks shift in the earth with the fossil trapped inside.

4 Eventually, the fossil emerges as the rocks move and erosion takes place

Figure 3 It takes a very long time for fossils to form, but they provide us with invaluable evidence of how life on Earth has developed

Summary questions

1 Copy and complete using the words below:

animal   decay   evidence   fossils   ice fossils   minerals   plant

One important piece of .... for how life has developed on Earth are .... The most common type are formed when parts of the .... or .... are replaced by .... as it decays. Some fossils are formed when an organism does not .... after it dies. An example is ...., which are very rare.

2 There are several theories about how life on Earth began.
   a Why is it impossible to know for sure?
   b Why are fossils such important evidence for the way life has developed?

3 How do ice fossils help scientists check the evidence provided by the main fossil record?

Key points

● Fossils are the remains of organisms from many years ago that are found in rocks.

● Fossils may be formed in different ways.

● Fossils give us information about organisms that lived millions of years ago.

● It is very difficult for scientists to know exactly how life on Earth began because there is little evidence that is valid.

B2 6.2

Exploring the fossil evidence

⦾ links

For information on fossil records, look back at B2 6.1 The origins of life on Earth.

Using the fossil record

The fossil record helps us to understand how much organisms have changed since life developed on Earth. However, this understanding is often limited. Only small bits of skeletons or little bits of shells have been found. Luckily we have a very complete fossil record for a few animals, including the horse. These relatively complete fossil records can show us how some organisms have changed and developed over time.

Fossils also show us that not all animals have changed very much. For example, fossil sharks from millions of years ago look very like modern sharks. They evolved early into a form that was almost perfectly adapted for their environment and their way of life. Their environment has not changed much for millions of years so sharks have also remained the same.

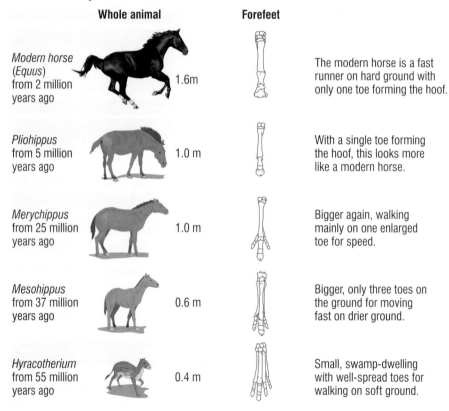

Whole animal		Forefeet	
Modern horse (*Equus*) from 2 million years ago	1.6 m		The modern horse is a fast runner on hard ground with only one toe forming the hoof.
Pliohippus from 5 million years ago	1.0 m		With a single toe forming the hoof, this looks more like a modern horse.
Merychippus from 25 million years ago	1.0 m		Bigger again, walking mainly on one enlarged toe for speed.
Mesohippus from 37 million years ago	0.6 m		Bigger, only three toes on the ground for moving fast on drier ground.
Hyracotherium from 55 million years ago	0.4 m		Small, swamp-dwelling with well-spread toes for walking on soft ground.

Figure 1 The evolutionary history of the horse based on the fossil record

Extinction

Throughout the history of life on Earth, scientists estimate that about 4 billion different species have existed. Yet only a few million species of living organisms are alive today. The rest have become extinct. **Extinction** is the permanent loss of all the members of a species.

As conditions change, new species evolve that are better suited to survive the new conditions. The older species that cannot cope with the changes gradually die out. This is because they are not able to compete so well for food and other resources. This is how evolution takes place and the number of species on Earth slowly changes. Some of the species that have become extinct are lost forever or only exist in the fossil record. Others have left living relatives.

a What is extinction?
b How many species of living organisms are thought to have existed on Earth over the years?

There are many different causes of extinction. They always involve a change in the environment such as new **predators**, new diseases or new, more successful competitors.

The gradual change of the climate over millions of years has also caused changes in the species that are adapted for a particular area. This is still happening today.

Organisms that cause extinction

Living organisms can change an environment and cause extinction in several different ways:

● New predators can wipe out unsuspecting prey animals very quickly. This is because the prey animals do not have adaptations to avoid them. New predators may evolve, or an existing species might simply move into new territory. Sometimes this can be due to human intervention. People accidentally brought the brown tree snake from Australia to the island of Guam after World War II. This caused the rapid extinction of many bird species on Guam. They were being eaten by the snakes. The birds had no time to evolve a defence against this new predator.

● New diseases (caused by microorganisms) can bring a species to the point of extinction. They are most likely to cause extinctions on islands, where the whole population of an animal or plant are close together. The Australian Tasmanian devil is one example of this. These rare animals are dying from a new form of infectious cancer. It attacks and kills them very quickly.

● Finally, one species can cause another to become extinct by successful competition. New mutations can give one type of organism a real advantage over another. Sometimes new species are introduced into an environment by mistake. This means that a new, more successful competitor can take over from the original animal or plant and make it extinct. In Australia, the introduction of rabbits has caused severe problems. They eat so much and breed so fast that the other native Australian animals are dying out because they cannot compete.

Did you know …?

The Scottish island of North Uist has a similar problem to Guam. Hedgehogs were brought to the island to combat the problem of garden slugs. Unfortunately, the hedgehogs bred rapidly and are eating the eggs and chicks of the many rare sea birds that breed on the island. Now people are trying to kill or remove the hedgehogs to save the birds.

AQA Examiner's tip

Always mention a *change* when you suggest reasons for extinction.

Summary questions

1 Copy and complete using the words below:

climate competitors diseases Earth environment extinction predators species

.... is the permanent loss of all the members of a .... from the .... It may be caused by new ...., new .... or new, successful .... It can also be caused by changes in the .... or the ....

2 Look at the evolution of the horse shown in Figure 1. Explain how the fossil evidence of the legs helps us to understand what the animals were like and how they lived.

3 Explain how each of the following situations might cause a species of animal or plant to become extinct.

  a Mouse Island has a rare species of black-tailed mice. They are preyed on by hawks and owls, but there are no mammals that eat them. A new family bring their pregnant pet cat to the island.

  b English primroses have quite small leaves. Several people bring home packets of seeds from a European primrose, which has bigger leaves and flowers very early in the spring.

Key points

● We can learn from fossils how much or how little organisms have changed as life has developed on Earth.

● Extinction may be caused by new predators, new diseases or new, more successful competitors.

B2 6.3

More about extinction

Learning objectives

- How does environmental change over long time scales affect living organisms?

- What caused the mass extinctions of the past?

It isn't just changes in living organisms that bring about extinctions. The biggest influences on survival are changes in the environment.

Environmental changes

Throughout history, the climate and environment of the Earth has been changing. At times the Earth has been very hot. At other times, temperatures have fallen and the Earth has been in the grip of an Ice Age. These changes take place over millions and even billions of years.

Organisms that do well in the heat of a tropical climate won't do well in the icy conditions of an Ice Age. Many of them will become extinct through lack of food or being too cold to breed. However, species that cope well in cold climates will evolve and thrive by natural selection.

Changes to the climate or the environment have been the main cause of extinction throughout history. There have been five occasions during the history of the Earth when big climate changes have led to extinction on an enormous scale (see Figure 2).

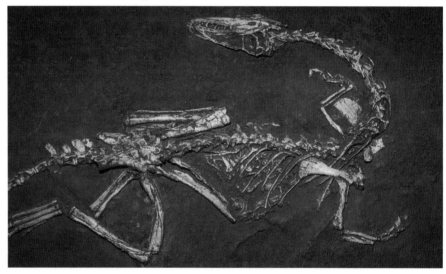

Figure 1 The dinosaurs ruled the Earth for millions of years, but when the whole environment changed, they could not adapt and most of them died out. Mammals, which could control their own body temperature, had an advantage and became dominant.

a Why are Ice Ages often linked to extinctions?

Extinction on a large scale

Fossil evidence shows that at times there have been mass extinctions on a global scale. During these events many (or even most) of the species on Earth die out. This usually happens over a relatively short time period of several million years. Huge numbers of species disappear from the fossil record.

The evidence suggests that a single catastrophic event is often the cause of these mass extinctions. This could be a massive volcanic eruption or the collision of giant asteroids with the surface of the Earth.

b What is a mass extinction?

NOW

	Approx. time years ago
50–70% species lost	
Dinosaurs died out	65 million
50% marine invertebrates lost	205 million
80% land quadrupeds lost	
80–95% marine species lost	251 million
70% species lost	360–75 million
60% species lost	440 million
ORIGINS OF LIFE	3500 million years ago

Figure 2 The five main extinction events so far in the evolutionary history of the Earth

What destroyed the dinosaurs?

The most recent mass extinction was when the dinosaurs became extinct around 65 million years ago. In 2010 an international team of scientists published a review of all the evidence put together over the last 20 years. They agreed that around 65 million years ago a giant asteroid collided with the Earth in Chicxulub in Mexico.

We can see a huge crater (180 km in diameter) there. Scientists have identified a layer of rock formed from crater debris in countries across the world. The further you move away from the crater, the thinner the layer of crater debris in the rock. Also, deep below the crater, scientists found lots of a mineral only formed when a rock is hit with a massive force such as an asteroid strike.

Figure 3 This layer of debris from the asteroid crater appears in rocks that are 65 million years old – the time the dinosaurs died out

The asteroid impact would have caused huge fires, earthquakes, landslides and tsunamis. Enormous amounts of material would have been blasted into the atmosphere. The accepted theory is that the dust in the atmosphere made everywhere almost dark. Plants struggled to survive and the drop in temperatures caused a global winter. Between 50–70% of all living species, including the dinosaurs, became extinct.

No sooner had this work been published than a group of UK scientists published different ideas and evidence. They suggest that the extinction of the dinosaurs started sooner (137 million years ago) and was much slower than previously thought.

Their idea is that the melting of the sea ice (caused by global warming) flooded the seas and oceans with very cold water. A drop in the sea temperature of about 9 °C triggered the mass extinction. Their evidence is based on an unexpected change in fossils and minerals that they found in areas of Norway.

As you can see, building up a valid, evidence-based history of events so long ago is not easy to do. Events can always be interpreted in different ways.

AQA Examiner's tip

Remember that the time scales in forming new species and mass extinctions are huge.

Try to develop an understanding of time in millions and billions of years.

Summary questions

1 a Give four causes of extinction in species of living organisms.
  b Give two possible causes of mass extinction events.

2 Why do you think extinction is an important part of evolution?

3 a Summarise the evidence for a giant asteroid impact as the cause of the mass extinction event that resulted in the death of the dinosaurs.
  b Explain why scientists think that low light levels and low temperatures would have followed a massive asteroid strike. Why would these have caused mass extinctions?

Key points

- Extinction can be caused by environmental change over geological time.

- Mass extinctions may be caused by single catastrophic events such as volcanoes or asteroid strikes.

B2 6.4

Isolation and the evolution of new species

Learning objectives

- How do new species arise?
- How do populations become isolated?
- Do new species always form at the same rate?
- How does speciation take place in an isolated population? **[H]**

??? Did you know ... ?

Sometimes the organisms are separated by **environmental isolation**. This is when the climate changes in one area where an organism lives but not in others. For example, if the climate becomes warmer in one area plants will flower at a different time of year. The breeding times of the plants and the animals linked with them will change and new species emerge.

Figure 1 Both the marsupial koala and the eucalyptus tree have evolved in geographical isolation in Australia

After a mass extinction, scientists have noticed that huge numbers of new species appear in the fossil record. This is evolution in action. Natural selection takes place and new organisms adapted to the different conditions evolve. But evolution is happening all the time. There is a natural cycle of new species appearing and others becoming extinct.

Isolation and evolution

You have already learnt about the role of genetic variation and natural selection in evolution. Any population of living organisms contains genetic variety. If one population becomes isolated from another, the conditions they are living in are likely to be different. This means that different characteristics will be selected for. The two populations might change so much over time that they cannot interbreed successfully. Then a new species evolves.

How do populations become isolated?

The most common way is by **geographical isolation**. This is when two populations become physically isolated by a geographical feature. This might be a new mountain range, a new river or an area of land becoming an island.

There are some well-known examples of this. Australia separated from the other continents over 5 million years ago. That's when the Australian populations of marsupial mammals that carry their babies in pouches became geographically isolated.

As a result of natural selection, many different species of marsupials evolved. Organisms as varied as kangaroos and koala bears appeared. Across the rest of the world, competition resulted in the evolution of other mammals with more efficient reproductive systems. In Australia, marsupials remain dominant.

a What is geographical isolation?

Organisms in isolation

Organisms on islands are geographically isolated from the rest of the world. The closely related but very different species on the Galapagos Islands helped Darwin form his ideas about evolution.

When a species evolves in isolation and is found in only one place in the world, it is said to be **endemic** to that area. An area where scientists are finding many new endemic species is Borneo. It is one of the largest islands in the world. Borneo still contains huge areas of tropical rainforest.

Between 1994 and 2006 scientists discovered over 400 new species in the Borneo rainforest. There are more than 25 species of mammals found only on the island. All of these organisms have evolved through geographical isolation.

Speciation

Any population will contain natural genetic variety. This means it will contain a wide range of alleles controlling its characteristics, that result from sexual reproduction and mutation. In each population, the alleles which are selected will control characteristics which help the organism to survive and breed successfully. This is natural selection. Sometimes part of a population becomes isolated with new environmental conditions. Alleles for characteristics that enable organisms to survive and breed successfully in the new conditions will be selected. These are likely to be different from the alleles that gave success in the original environment. As a result of the selection of these different alleles, the characteristic features of the isolated organisms will change. Eventually they can no longer interbreed with the original organisms and a new species forms. This is known as **speciation.**

This is what has happened on the island of Borneo, in Australia and on the Galapagos Islands. If conditions in these isolated places are changed or the habitat is lost, the species that have evolved to survive within it could easily become extinct.

Figure 2 Orang-utans like these are just one example of the many endemic species that have evolved in isolation in Borneo

b What is an endemic organism?

Geographical isolation may involve very large areas like Borneo or very small regions. Mount Bosavi is the crater of an extinct volcano in Papua New Guinea. It is only 4 km wide and the walls of the crater are 1 km high. The animals and plants trapped within the crater have evolved in different ways to those outside.

Very few people have been inside the crater. During a 3-week expedition in 2009 scientists discovered around 40 new species. These included mammals, fish, birds, reptiles, amphibians, insects and plants. All of these species are the result of natural selection caused by the specialised environment of the isolated crater. They include an enormous 82 cm long rat that weighs 1.5 kg!

Figure 3 Mount Bosavi in Papua New Guinea – a small, geographically isolated environment where many new species have evolved

Summary questions

1 Copy and complete using the words below:

   geographically interbreeding populations evolution species selection

   When two .... become .... isolated .... may take place. Natural .... in each area means the populations become so different that successful .... can no longer take place. New .... have evolved.

2 **a** How might populations become isolated?
   b Why does this isolation lead to the evolution of new species?

3 Explain how genetic variation and natural selection result in the formation of new species in isolated populations. [H]

Key points

- New species arise when two populations become isolated.

- Populations become isolated when they are separated geographically, e.g. on islands.

- There are natural cycles linked to environmental change when species form and when species die out.

- In an isolated population alleles are selected that increase successful breeding in the new environment. [H]

- Speciation takes place when an isolated population becomes so different from the original population that successful interbreeding can no long take place. [H]

Summary questions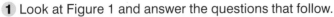

1 Look at Figure 1 and answer the questions that follow.

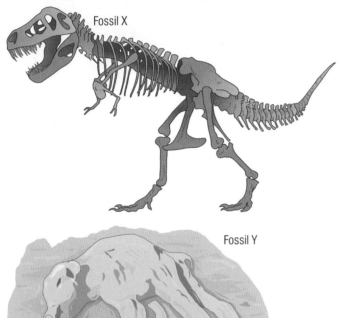

Fossil X

Fossil Y

Figure 1

a What is a fossil?

b Explain fully how fossil X and fossil Y were formed.

c How can fossils like these be used as evidence for the development of life on Earth and what are their limitations?

d Why are fossils of little use in helping us understand how life on Earth began?

2 a What is extinction?

b How does mass extinction differ from species extinction?

c What is the evidence for the occurrence of mass extinctions throughout the history of life on Earth?

d Suggest at least two theories about the possible causes of mass extinctions and explain the sort of evidence that is used to support these ideas.

e What important part have mass extinctions played in the evolution of life on Earth and why?

3

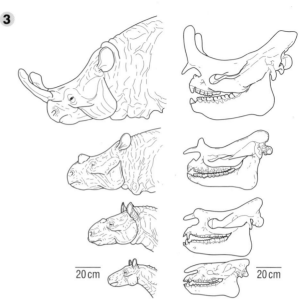

20 cm   20 cm

Figure 2

a This sequence of skulls comes from the fossil record of a group of animals known as perissodactyls. Suggest a possible living relative of these animals.

b How do you think these organisms changed as they evolved, based on the evidence of the diagram above?

c What are the limitations of this type of evidence?

d What other fossil remains would you want to see to understand more about the lives of these extinct organisms?

4 How does evolution take place?

5 Describe how evolution takes place in terms of speciation. Explain the roles of isolation and genetic variation in the process of speciation. Use as many examples and as much evidence as you can in your answer. **[H]**

AQA Examination-style questions

1 The diagram shows a timeline for the evolution of some groups of animals. The earliest forms of the animals shown below the line for **Present day** are extinct.

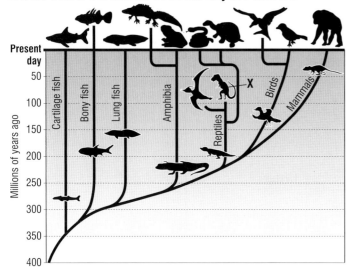

Use information from the diagram to answer these questions.

a Name the **four** groups of animals that developed legs. (1)

b Which group of animals shown in the diagram evolved first? (1)

c The animal labelled **X** has been extinct for over 50 million years.

How do scientists know that it once lived? (1)

d Copy and complete the sentence by choosing the correct words from below.

diseases enzymes hormones plants predators rocks

Animals may become extinct because of new .... and new .... (2)

AQA, 2003

2 a What is meant by the term 'extinction'? (2)

b The bar charts show the population of the world from the 17th to the 20th century and the number of animal extinctions that have taken place over the same period.

Use the information in the bar charts to answer the questions.

i What was the world population in the 19th century? (1)

ii How many animals became extinct in the 18th century? (1)

iii What is the relationship between the population of humans and the number of animal extinctions? (2)

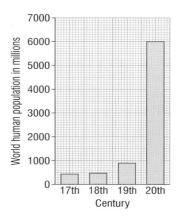
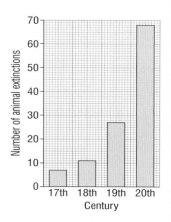

c Between 1900 and 1960 (20th century) 64 animals became extinct.

i How many animals became extinct from 1960–2000?
Show your working. (2)

ii Suggest a reason for the difference in numbers between the beginning and the end of the 20th century. (2)

3 The diagram shows how the number of groups of animals has changed during the history of life on Earth.

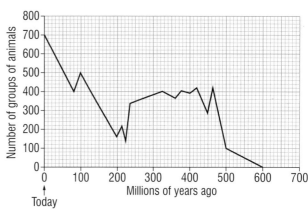

a i How long ago did the first living animals appear on Earth? Give your answer in millions of years. (1)

ii How long did it take for the number of groups to rise to 400? Give your answer in millions of years. (1)

b i Calculate the proportion of groups that disappeared between 100 million years and 80 million years ago. Show your working. (2)

ii Give **two** reasons why some groups of animals disappeared during the history of life on Earth (2)

AQA, 2008

4 *In this question you will be assessed on using good English, organising information clearly and using specialist terms where appropriate.*

Describe how new species may arise by isolation. [H] (6)

1 a i Put the following structures into the correct order from the smallest to the largest. (1)

    cell   chromosome   gene   nucleus

    smallest   largest

    -----------   -----------   -----------   -----------

  ii What is the function of the nucleus? (1)

b Plant cells contain chloroplasts.

  i What is the role of chloroplasts in photosynthesis? (1)

  ii Name the gas produced in photosynthesis. (1)

2 The diagrams show three processes.

Match the correct letter to the process.

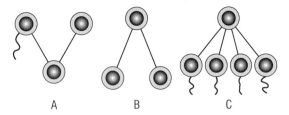

A   B   C

Process	Letter
Fertilisation	
Meiosis	
Mitosis	

(3)

3 The diagram shows two villi in the small intestine of a healthy person.

The small intestine is an organ in the digestive system.

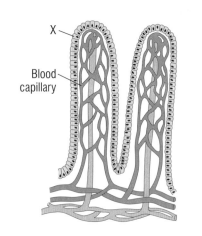

X

Blood capillary

  a i Name another organ in the digestive system. (1)

  ii Name tissue X. (1)

  b The villi are surrounded by digested food materials which must enter the blood capillaries.

  Explain how these materials enter the blood. (4)

4 The graph shows the effect of temperature on photosynthesis.

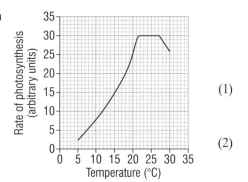

  a i Between which temperatures is the rate of photosynthesis fastest?

  .... and .... °C (1)

  ii Suggest why the rate of photosynthesis stays the same between these two temperatures. (2)

  b A greenhouse owner wants to grow lettuces as quickly and cheaply as possible in winter.

  At what temperature should he keep his greenhouse in order to grow the lettuces as quickly and cheaply as possible? .... °C

  Explain your answer. (3)

5 The picture shows a model of a protein.

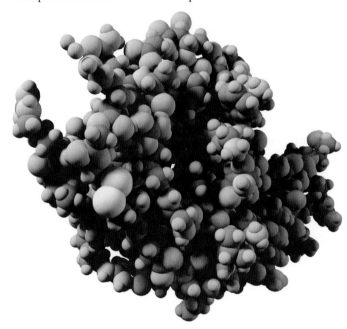

Some proteins are enzymes but proteins also have other functions.

a i Give two other functions of proteins.

1 ....

2 .... (2)

ii What is the function of an enzyme? (1)

b This protein is normally found in neutral conditions. What would happen to the protein if it was placed in acid conditions? (2)

c When the model protein is put together the scientists use smaller molecules to make the specific shape.

i Choose the correct answer to complete the sentence.

amino acids   fatty acids   lactic acid

The smaller molecules used to make the model protein are .... (1)

ii Cells are able to put the smaller molecules together in the correct order.

Explain how the cell does this. (1)

6 Some cattle are affected by an inherited condition called glycogen storage disease.

a i Where is glycogen stored? (1)

ii Cattle with this disease become tired easily.

Explain why. (2)

b Glycogen storage disease can be inherited by a calf whose parents do not have the disease.

i Use the symbols G and g and a genetic diagram to explain how this is possible. (4)

ii If the same parents have another calf, what is the probability that it will not have glycogen storage disease? (1)

7 *In this question you will be assessed on using good English, organising information clearly and using specialist terms where appropriate.*

Describe the changes which take place in the human body during exercise to ensure that the muscles receive enough oxygen and what happens if oxygen is in short supply.

(6)

AQA *Examiner's tip*

Q7 requires a description in a logical order. Think about your answer before writing. Make a brief list of the key words and number them in the correct sequence. Rehearse your answer in your head and change the numbers if necessary. Now write your answer using the numbered words as a guide.

Do not forget to cross out any notes which are not intended for marking

C2 1.1

Chemical bonding

Learning objectives

● How do elements form compounds?

● How do the elements in Group 1 bond with the elements in Group 7?

You already know that we can mix two substances together without either of them changing. For example, we can mix sand and salt together and then separate them again. No change will have taken place. But in chemical reactions the situation is very different.

When the atoms of two or more elements react they make a compound.

A compound contains two or more elements which are chemically combined.

The compound formed is different from the elements and we cannot get the elements back again easily. We can also react compounds together to form other compounds. However, the reaction of elements is easier to understand as a starting point.

a What is the difference between mixing two substances and reacting them?

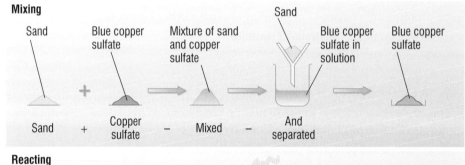
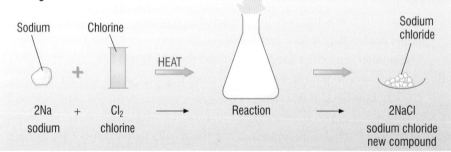

Figure 1 The difference between mixing and reacting. Separating mixtures is usually quite easy, but separating substances once they have reacted can be quite difficult. Why do atoms react?

When an atom has an arrangement of electrons like a noble gas in Group 0, it is stable and unreactive. However, most atoms do not have this **electronic structure**. When atoms react they take part in changes which give them a stable arrangement of electrons. They may do this by either:

● sharing electrons, which we call **covalent bonding**

● transferring electrons, which we call **ionic bonding**.

Losing electrons to form positive ions

In ionic bonding the atoms involved lose or gain electrons to form charged particles called ions. The ions have the electronic structure of a noble gas. So, for example, if sodium (2,8,1) loses one electron it is left with the stable electronic structure of neon (2,8).

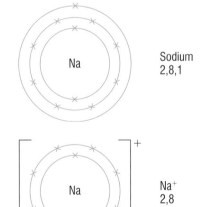

Sodium
2,8,1

Na+
2,8

Figure 2 A positive sodium ion (Na+) is formed when a sodium atom loses an electron during ionic bonding

However, it is also left with one more **proton** in its **nucleus** than there are electrons around the nucleus. The proton has a positive charge so the sodium atom has now become a positively charged **ion**. The sodium ion has a single positive charge. We write the formula of a sodium ion as Na^+. The electronic structure of the Na^+ ion is 2,8. This is shown in Figure 2.

Gaining electrons to form negative ions

When non-metals react with metals, the non-metal atoms gain electrons to achieve a stable noble gas structure. Chlorine, for example, has the electronic structure 2,8,7. By gaining a single electron, it gets the stable electronic structure of argon (2,8,8).

In this case there is now one more electron than there are positive protons in the nucleus. So the chlorine atom becomes a negatively charged ion. This carries a single negative charge. We write the formula of the chloride ion as Cl^-. Its electronic structure is 2,8,8. This is shown in Figure 3.

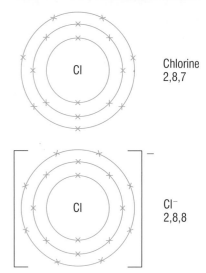

Chlorine
2,8,7

Cl^-
2,8,8

Figure 3 A negative chloride ion (Cl^-) is formed when a chlorine atom gains an electron during ionic bonding

b When atoms join together by *sharing* electrons, what type of bond is formed?

c When ions join together as a result of *gaining* or *losing* electrons, what type of bond is this?

Representing ionic bonding

Metal atoms, which need to lose electrons, react with non-metal atoms, which need to gain electrons. So when sodium reacts with chlorine, each sodium atom loses an electron and each chlorine atom gains that electron. They both form stable ions. The electrostatic attraction between the oppositely charged Na^+ ions and Cl^- ions is called ionic bonding.

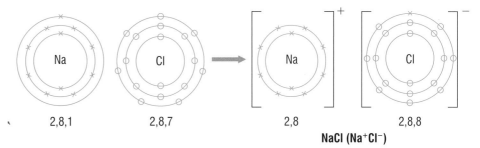

2,8,1   2,8,7   2,8   2,8,8

NaCl (Na^+Cl^-)

Figure 4 The formation of sodium chloride (NaCl) – an example of ion formation by transferring an electron

We can show what happens in a diagram. The electrons of one atom are represented by dots, and the electrons of the other atom are represented by crosses. This is shown in Figure 4.

Key points

● Elements react together to form compounds by gaining or losing electrons or by sharing electrons.

● The elements in Group 1 react with the elements in Group 7. As they react, atoms of Group 1 elements can each lose one electron to gain the stable electronic structure of a noble gas. This electron can be given to an atom from Group 7, which then also achieves the stable electronic structure of a noble gas.

Summary questions

1 Copy and complete using the words below:

covalent difficult compound gaining ionic losing new noble

When two elements react together they make a .... substance called a .... It is .... to separate the elements after the reaction. Some atoms react by sharing electrons. We call this .... bonding. Other atoms react by .... or .... electrons. We call this .... bonding. When atoms react in this way they get the electronic structure of a .... gas.

2 Draw diagrams to show the ions that would be formed when the following atoms are involved in ionic bonding. For each one, state how many electrons have been lost or gained and show the charge on the ions formed.

a aluminium (Al)   **b** fluorine (F)   **c** potassium (K)   **d** oxygen (O)

C2 1.2

Ionic bonding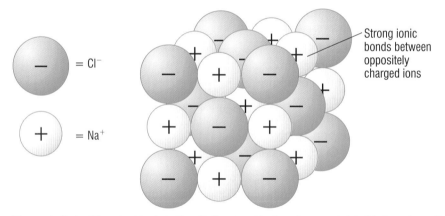

Learning objectives

- How are ionic compounds held together?
- Which elements, other than those in Groups 1 and 7, form ions?

You have seen how positive and negative ions form during some reactions. Ionic compounds are usually formed when metals react with non-metals.

The ions formed are held next to each other by very strong forces of attraction between the oppositely charged ions. This electrostatic force of attraction, which acts in all directions, is called **ionic bonding**.

The ionic bonds between the charged particles result in an arrangement of ions that we call a **giant structure** (or a **giant lattice**). If we could stand among the ions they would seem to go on in all directions forever.

The force exerted by an ion on the other ions in the lattice acts equally in all directions. This is why the ions in a giant structure are held so strongly together.

The giant structure of ionic compounds is very regular. This is because the ions all pack together neatly, like marbles in a box.

    a What name do we give to the arrangement of ions in an ionic compound?

    b What holds the ions together in this structure?

$-$ = Cl^-

$+$ = Na^+

Strong ionic bonds between oppositely charged ions

Figure 1 Part of the giant ionic lattice (3-D network) of sodium and chloride ions in sodium chloride

Sometimes the atoms reacting need to gain or lose two electrons to gain a stable noble gas structure. An example is when magnesium (2,8,2) reacts with oxygen (2,6). When these two elements react they form magnesium oxide (MgO). This is made up of magnesium ions with a double positive charge (Mg^{2+}) and oxide ions with a double negative charge (O^{2-}).

We can represent the atoms and ions involved in forming ionic bonds by **dot and cross diagrams**. In these diagrams we only show the electrons in the outermost shell of each atom or ion. This makes them quicker to draw than the diagrams on the previous page. Figure 2 on the next page shows an example.

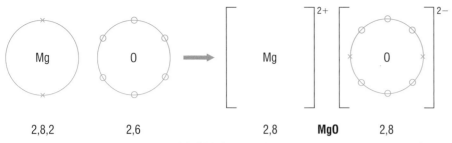

2,8,2   2,6   2,8   **MgO**   2,8

Figure 2 When magnesium oxide (MgO) is formed, the reacting magnesium atoms lose two electrons and the oxygen atoms gain two electrons

Another example of an ionic compound is calcium chloride. Each calcium atom (2,8,8,2) needs to lose two electrons but each chlorine atom (2,8,7) needs to gain only one electron. This means that two chlorine atoms react with every one calcium atom to form calcium chloride. So the formula of calcium chloride is $CaCl_2$.

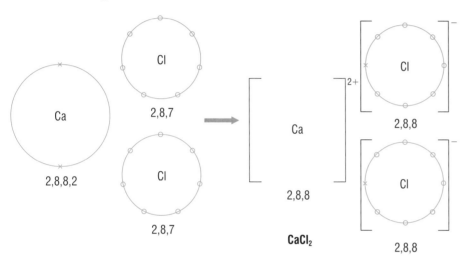

Figure 3 The formation of calcium chloride ($CaCl_2$)

Summary questions

1 a Copy and complete the table:

Atomic number	Atom	Electronic structure of atom	Ion	Electronic structure of ion
8	O			$[2,8]^{2-}$
19		2,8,8,1	K+	
17	Cl		Cl−	
20		2,8,8,2		

b Explain why potassium chloride is KCl but potassium oxide is K_2O.

c Explain why calcium oxide is CaO but calcium chloride is $CaCl_2$.

2 Draw dot and cross diagrams to show how you would expect the following elements to form ions together:

a lithium and chlorine

b calcium and oxygen

c aluminium and fluorine.

Key points

- Ionic compounds are held together by strong forces of attraction between the oppositely charged ions. This is called ionic bonding.

- Besides the elements in Groups 1 and 7, other elements that can form ionic compounds include those from Groups 2 and 0.

C2 1.3   Formulae of ionic compounds

Learning objectives

- How can we write the formula of an ionic compound, given its ions?

In this chapter we have seen how three different ionic compounds are formed. You should understand how atoms turn to ions when sodium chloride, magnesium oxide and calcium chloride are formed from their elements.

The overall charge on any ionic compound is zero. The compounds are neutral. Therefore we do not have to draw dot and cross diagrams to work out each ionic formula. As long as we know or are given the charge on the ions in a compound we can work out its formula.

  a What is the overall charge on an ionic compound?

If we look at the three examples above, we can see how the charges on the ions in a compound cancel out:

Ionic compound	Ratio of ions in compound	Formula of compound
sodium chloride	$Na^+ : Cl^-$ 1:1	NaCl
magnesium oxide	$Mg^{2+} : O^{2-}$ 1:1	MgO
calcium chloride	$Ca^{2+} : Cl^-$ 1:2	$CaCl_2$

  b What is the formula of magnesium chloride?

We can work out the formula of some ions given a copy of the periodic table. Remember that in your exams you will have a Data Sheet which includes a periodic table and a table showing the charges of common ions.

> **Groups of metals**
> - The atoms of Group 1 elements form 1+ ions, e.g. Li^+.
> - The atoms of Group 2 elements form 2+ ions, e.g. Ca^{2+}.
>
> **Groups of non-metals**
> - The atoms of Group 7 elements form 1− ions, e.g. F^-.
> - The atoms of Group 6 elements form 2− ions, e.g. S^{2-}.

The names of compounds of transition metals contain the charge on their ions in brackets in roman numerals. This is because they can form ions carrying different sizes of positive charge. For example, iron can form 2+ and 3+ ions. So the name iron(III) oxide tells us that the iron is present as Fe^{3+} ions in this compound.

  c What is the formula of lithium sulfide?
  d What is the formula of iron(III) oxide?

Did you know ...?

Common salt is sodium chloride. In just 58.5 g of salt there are over 600 000 000 000 000 000 000 000 ions of Na^+ and the same number of Cl^- ions.

More complicated ions

Some ions are made up of more than one element. When you studied limestone, you learned that the formula of calcium carbonate is $CaCO_3$. It contains calcium ions, Ca^{2+}, and carbonate ions, CO_3^{2-}. The carbonate ions contain carbon and oxygen. However, the rule about cancelling out charges still applies as in one-element ions. Calcium carbonate is $CaCO_3$ as the 2+ and 2− ions in the ionic compound cancel out in the ratio 1 : 1.

Two-element ions you might come across are shown in the table below:

Name of ion	Formula of ion	Example of compound
hydroxide	OH^-	calcium hydroxide, $Ca(OH)_2$
nitrate	NO_3^-	magnesium nitrate, $Mg(NO_3)_2$
carbonate	CO_3^{2-}	sodium carbonate, Na_2CO_3
sulfate	SO_4^{2-}	calcium sulfate, $CaSO_4$

Notice how the formula of a compound containing a two-element ion sometimes contains brackets. To write calcium hydroxide as $CaOH_2$ would be misleading. It would tell us the ratio of Ca : O : H ions was 1 : 1 : 2. However, as there are twice as many hydroxide ions as calcium ions, the ratio should be 1 : 2 : 2. This is why we write the formula as $Ca(OH)_2$.

e What is the formula of calcium nitrate?

Figure 1 Haematite is an ore of iron. It is mined (as here) and used as a source of iron(III) oxide for the blast furnace in the extraction of iron.

Summary questions

1 Using the charges on the ions given on this spread, give the formula of:
   a calcium oxide
   b lithium oxide
   c magnesium chloride

2 Draw a table with K^+, Mg^{2+} and Fe^{3+} down the side and Br^-, OH^-, NO_3^- and SO_4^{2-} across the top. Then fill in the formula of the compound in each cell of the table.

3 **a** The formula of strontium nitrate is $Sr(NO_3)_2$. What is the charge on a strontium ion?
   b The formula of aluminium sulfate is $Al_2(SO_4)_3$. What is the charge on an aluminium ion?

Key points

- The charges on the ions in an ionic compound always cancel each other out.

- The formula of an ionic compound shows the ratio of ions present in the compound.

- Sometimes we need brackets to show the ratio of ions in a compound, e.g. magnesium hydroxide, $Mg(OH)_2$.

C2 1.4

Covalent bonding

Learning objectives

- How are covalent bonds formed?

- What types of substance have covalent bonds?

Figure 1 Most of the molecules in substances which make up living things are held together by covalent bonds between non-metal atoms

Hydrogen chloride HCl

Water H₂O

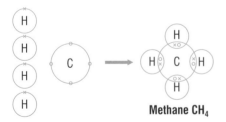

Methane CH₄

Figure 3 The principles of covalent bonding remain the same however many atoms are involved

Reactions between metals and non-metals usually result in ionic bonding. However, many, many compounds are formed in a very different way. When non-metals react together their atoms share pairs of electrons to form molecules. We call this **covalent bonding**.

Simple molecules

The atoms of non-metals generally need to gain electrons to achieve stable outer energy levels. When they react together neither atom can give away electrons. So they get the electronic structure of a noble gas by sharing electrons. The atoms in the molecules are then held together by the shared pairs of electrons. We call these strong bonds between the atoms covalent bonds.

a What is the bond called when two atoms share a pair of electrons?

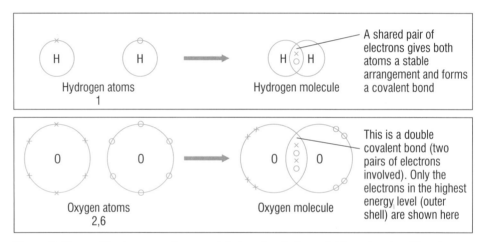

Figure 2 Atoms of hydrogen and oxygen join together to form stable molecules. The atoms in H_2 and O_2 molecules are held together by strong covalent bonds.

Sometimes in covalent bonding each atom brings the same number of electrons to share. But this is not always the case. Sometimes the atoms of one element will need several electrons, while the other element only needs one more electron for each atom to get a stable arrangement. In this case, more atoms become involved in forming the molecule.

We can represent the covalent bonds in substances such as water, ammonia and methane in a number of ways. Each way represents the same thing. The method chosen depends on what we want to show.

Figure 4 We can represent a covalent compound by showing **a** the highest energy levels (or outer shells), **b** the outer electrons in a dot and cross diagram or **c** the number of covalent bonds

Giant covalent structures

Many substances containing covalent bonds consist of small molecules, for example, H_2O. However, some covalently bonded substances are very different. They have giant structures where huge numbers of atoms are held together by a network of covalent bonds. These are sometimes referred to as macromolecules.

Diamond has a giant covalent structure. In diamond, each carbon atom forms four covalent bonds with its neighbours. This results in a rigid giant covalent lattice.

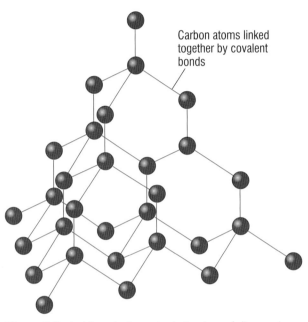

Carbon atoms linked together by covalent bonds

Figure 5 Part of the giant covalent structure of diamond

Figure 6 Diamonds owe their hardness to the way the carbon atoms are arranged in a giant covalent structure

Silicon dioxide (silica) is another substance with a giant covalent structure.

b What do we call the structure of a substance held together by a network of covalent bonds?

Summary questions

1 Copy and complete using the words below:

covalent giant molecules macromolecules shared

When non-metal atoms react together they make .... bonds. The atoms in these bonds are held together by .... electrons. Most substances held together by covalent bonds consist of ...., but some have .... covalent structures, sometimes called ....

2 Draw diagrams, showing all the electrons, to represent the covalent bonding between the following atoms.
   a two hydrogen atoms
   b two chlorine atoms
   c a hydrogen atom and a fluorine atom

3 Draw dot and cross diagrams to show the covalent bonds when:
   a a nitrogen atom bonds with three hydrogen atoms
   b a carbon atom bonds with two oxygen atoms.

Key points

● Covalent bonds are formed when atoms share pairs of electrons.

● Many substances containing covalent bonds consist of simple molecules, but some have giant covalent structures.

C2 1.5 Metals

Learning objectives

- How are the atoms in metals arranged?
- How are the atoms in metals held together? [H]

Metal crystals

The atoms in metals are built up layer upon layer in a regular pattern (see Figure 1).

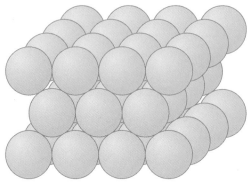

Figure 1 The close-packed arrangement of copper atoms in copper metal

This means that they form crystals. These are not always obvious to the naked eye. However, sometimes we can see them. You can see zinc crystals on the surface of some steel. Steel can be dipped into molten zinc to prevent it from rusting. For example, look at galvanised lamp posts and wheelie bins.

a Why do metals form crystals?

Practical

Growing silver crystals

You can grow crystals of silver metal by suspending a length of copper wire in silver nitrate solution. The crystals of silver will appear on the wire quite quickly. However, for the best results they need to be left for several hours.

- Explain your observations.

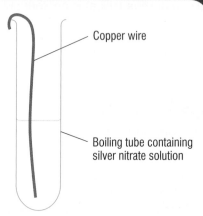

Figure 2 Growing silver crystals

Practical

Survey of metallic crystals

Take a look round your school to see if you can find any galvanised steel. See if you can spot the metal crystals. You can also look for crystals on brass fittings that have been left outside and not polished.

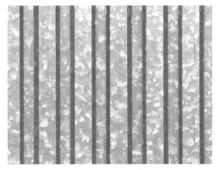

Figure 3 Metal crystals, such as the zinc ones shown on this wheelie bin, give us evidence that metals are made up of atoms arranged in regular patterns

Metallic bonding

Metals are another example of giant structures. You can think of a metal as a lattice of positively charged ions. The metal ions are arranged in regular layers, one on top of another.

The outer electrons from each metal atom can easily move throughout the giant structure. The outer electrons (in the highest occupied energy level) form a 'sea' of free electrons surrounding positively charged metal ions. Strong electrostatic attraction between the negatively charged electrons and positively charged ions bond the metal ions to each other. The electrons act a bit like a glue.

b Which electrons do metal atoms use to form metallic bonds?

The 'sea' of free electrons are called **delocalised electrons**. They are no longer linked with any particular ion in the giant metallic structure. These electrons help us explain the properties of metals. (See C2, 2.4 Giant metallic structures.)

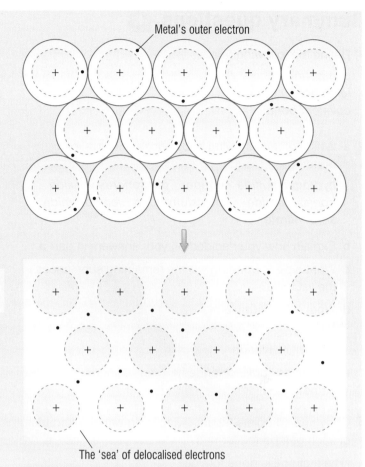

Metal's outer electron

The 'sea' of delocalised electrons

Figure 4 A metal consists of positively charged metal ions surrounded by a 'sea' of delocalised electrons. This diagram shows us a model of metallic bonding.

Summary questions

1 Copy and complete using the words below:

atoms   regular   crystals   giant

Metals have .... structures. They are made up of metal .... which are closely packed and arranged in .... patterns. There is evidence of this in the .... we can sometimes see at the surface of a metal.

2 Copy and complete using the words below:

electrons   electrostatic   free   outermost   positive

In metallic bonding, the metal ions are held together by .... from the .... shell (highest energy level) of the metal atoms. The .... ions that this produces are held together by strong .... forces. The electrons in metals are .... to move throughout the structure.   [H]

3 Use the theory of metallic bonding to explain the bonding in magnesium metal. Make sure you mention delocalised electrons. (Magnesium atoms have 12 protons.)   [H]

4 Explain why the bonding electrons in a metal act both like a glue and not like a glue.   [H]

⬤⬤ links

For more information about explaining the properties of metals, see C2 2.4 Giant metallic structures.

Key points

● The atoms in metals are closely packed together and arranged in regular layers.

● We can think of metallic bonding as positively charged metal ions which are held together by electrons from the outermost shell of each metal atom. These delocalised electrons are free to move throughout the giant metallic lattice.   [H]

Summary questions

1 Define the following terms:

compound
ionic bonding
covalent bond

2 a Which of the following substances will have ionic bonding?

hydrogen sulfide   copper   phosphorus(v) oxide
iron(II) chloride   potassium oxide   lead bromide
silver nitrate

b Explain how you decided on your answers in part **a**.

c What type of bonding will the remaining substances in the list have?

d What is the formula of:

i hydrogen sulfide
ii iron(II) chloride.

e Why does iron(II) chloride have roman numerals in its name?

3 Copy and complete the following table with the formula of each compound formed.

(The first one is done for you).

	fluoride, F^-	oxide, O^{2-}	carbonate, CO_3^{2-}	phosphate(V), PO_4^{3-}
lithium, Li^+	LiF			
barium, Ba^{2+}				
copper, Cu^{2+}				
aluminium, Al^{3+}				

4 a Which of the following substances are made up of small molecules and which have a giant covalent structure?

methane, CH_4
silicon dioxide, SiO_2
diamond, C
ammonia, NH_3

b Draw a dot and cross diagram to show the bonding in ammonia.

5 The diagrams show the arrangement of electrons in energy levels in three atoms:

(The letters are NOT the chemical symbols.)

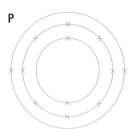
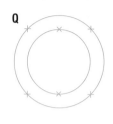

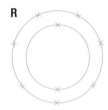

a Which atom belongs to Group 2 of the periodic table?

b To which group does atom R belong?

c i Atom Q bonds with four atoms of hydrogen. Draw a dot and cross diagram to show the compound that is formed.

ii What do we call the type of bonding between the atom of Q and the hydrogen atoms?

d i Draw dot and cross diagrams to show how atom P bonds with R atoms.

ii What do we call the type of bonding in the compound formed by P and R?

iii What is the formula of the compound formed by P and R?

6 Describe, with diagrams, how the particles are held together in the following substances:

a a molecule of fluorine (F_2)

b a salt crystal (NaCl).

7 Draw a diagram which shows how the atoms in carbon dioxide, O=C=O, bond to each other.   **[H]**

AQA Examination-style questions

Use a periodic table and a table of charges on ions to help you to answer these questions.

1 Choose a word from the list to complete each sentence.
   a When metals react with non-metals electrons are .... (1)

   combined   shared   transferred

   b When non-metal elements combine their atoms are held together by .... bonds. (1)

   covalent   ionic   metallic

2 Choose a description from the list for each of the substances.

   giant covalent   giant ionic   metal   simple molecule

   a ammonia, NH_3 c lithium, Li
   b diamond, C   d sodium oxide, Na_2O (4)

3 Choose a number from the list to complete each sentence.

   0   1   2   3   4   6   7

   a The elements in Group .... in the periodic table all form ions with a charge of 1+. (1)
   b The elements in Group .... in the periodic table all form ions with a charge of 2−. (1)
   c The elements in Group 4 in the periodic table all form .... covalent bonds. (1)
   d The aluminium ion has a charge of .... + (1)

4 a Choose the correct formula from the list for iron(III) chloride.

   FeCl Fe_3Cl $FeCl_3$ Fe_3Cl_3   (1)

   b Choose the formula from the list for each of these ionic compounds.

   NaS $NaSO_4$ $Na(SO_4)_2$ Na_2S NaS_2 Na_2SO_4

   i sodium sulfide (1)
   ii sodium sulfate (1)

5 Calcium hydroxide, $Ca(OH)_2$, is an ionic compound.

   Which of these ions in the list are the ions in calcium hydroxide?
   Ca^+ Ca^{2+} Ca^{4+} OH^- OH_2^- OH^{2-} (2)

6 Sodium reacts with chlorine. The reaction forms sodium chloride.

   a Use words from the list to answer the questions.

   compound   element   hydrocarbon   mixture

   Which word best describes:
   i sodium (1)
   ii sodium chloride? (1)

b When sodium reacts with chlorine the sodium atoms change into sodium ions. The diagrams represent a sodium atom and a sodium ion.

Sodium atom (Na)   Sodium ion (Na⁺)

Use the diagrams to help you explain how a sodium atom turns into a sodium ion. (2)

c i The diagram below represents a chlorine atom. When chlorine reacts with sodium the chlorine forms negative chloride ions.

   Copy and complete the diagram below to show how the outer electrons are arranged in a chloride ion (Cl^-). (1)

   ii Chloride ions are strongly attracted to sodium ions in sodium chloride.

   Explain why. (1)
   AQA, 2010

7 Chlorine can form compounds with ionic or covalent bonds.

   a Potassium chloride, KCl, has ionic bonds. Draw dot and cross diagrams to show what happens to potassium atoms and chlorine atoms when they react to form potassium chloride. You only need to show the outer electrons in your diagrams. (4)

   b Hydrogen chloride, HCl, has covalent bonds. Draw a dot and cross diagram to show the bonding in hydrogen chloride. (2)

8 Sodium metal is a giant structure of sodium atoms.

Explain how the atoms are held together in sodium metal. [H] (3)

Giant ionic structures

- Why do ionic compounds have high melting points?

- Why do ionic compounds conduct electricity when we melt them or dissolve them in water?

AQA *Examiner's tip*

Remember that every ionic compound has a giant structure. The oppositely charged ions in these structures are held together by strong electrostatic forces of attraction. These act in all directions.

We have already seen that an ionic compound consists of a giant structure of ions arranged in a lattice. The attractive electrostatic forces between the oppositely charged ions act in all directions and are very strong. This holds the ions in the lattice together very tightly.

a What type of force holds the ions together in an ionic compound?

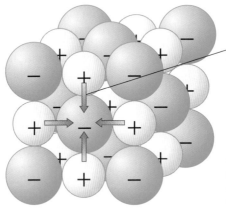

Strong electrostatic forces of attraction called ionic bonds

Figure 1 The attractive forces between the oppositely charged ions in an ionic compound are very strong. The regular arrangement of ions in the giant lattice enables ionic compounds to form crystals.

It takes a lot of energy to break up a giant ionic lattice. There are lots of strong ionic bonds to break. To separate the ions we have to overcome all those electrostatic forces of attraction. This means that ionic compounds have high melting points and boiling points. Look at the graph in Figure 2.

b Why do ionic compounds have high melting points and boiling points?

Once we have supplied enough energy to separate the ions from the lattice, they are free to move around. That's when the ionic solid melts and becomes a liquid. The ions are free to move anywhere in this liquid. Therefore they can carry their electrical charge through the molten liquid. A solid ionic compound cannot conduct electricity. That's because its ions are held in a fixed position in the lattice. They cannot move around. They can only vibrate 'on the spot' when solid.

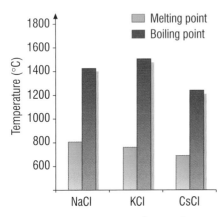

Figure 2 The many strong forces of attraction in a lattice of ions mean that ionic compounds have high melting points and boiling points

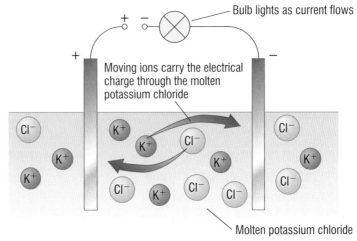

Bulb lights as current flows

Moving ions carry the electrical charge through the molten potassium chloride

Molten potassium chloride

Figure 3 Because the ions are free to move, a molten ionic compound can conduct electricity

Many ionic compounds will dissolve in water. When we dissolve an ionic compound in water, the lattice is split up by the water molecules. Then the ions are free to move around in the solution formed. Just as molten ionic compounds will conduct electricity, solutions of ionic compounds will also conduct electricity. The ions are able to move to an oppositely charged electrode dipped in the solution (See Figure 3).

c   Why can ionic compounds conduct electricity when they are molten or dissolved in water?

Ionic solid	Molten ionic compound	Ionic compound in solution
Ions are fixed in a lattice. They vibrate but cannot move around – it does not conduct electricity.	High temperature provides enough energy to overcome the many strong attractive forces between ions. Ions are free to move around within the molten compound – it does conduct electricity.	Water molecules separate ions from the lattice. Ions are free to move around within the solution – it does conduct electricity.

Practical

Testing conductivity

Using a circuit as shown in Figure 3, dip a pair of electrodes into a 1 cm depth of sodium chloride crystals. What happens?

Now slowly add water.

● What happens to the bulb?

Repeat the experiment using potassium chloride.

● Explain your observations.

Key points

● It takes a lot of energy to break the many strong ionic bonds which hold a giant ionic lattice together. So ionic compounds have high melting points. They are all solids at room temperature.

● Ionic compounds will conduct electricity when we melt them or dissolve them in water. That's because their ions can then move freely around and can carry charge through the liquid.

Summary questions

1   Copy and complete using the words below:

attraction   conduct   high   lattice   molten   move oppositely   solution

Ionic compounds have .... melting points and boiling points because of the many strong electrostatic forces of .... between .... charged ions in the giant .... Ionic compounds will .... electricity when .... or in .... because the ions are able to .... freely around in the liquids.

2   Why is seawater a better conductor of electricity than water from a freshwater lake?

C2 2.2 — Simple molecules

Learning objectives

- Which type of substances has low melting points and boiling points?
- Why do these substances have low melting points and boiling points? [H]
- Why don't these substances conduct electricity?

When the atoms of non-metal elements react to form compounds, they share electrons in their outer shells. In this way each atom gains the electron arrangement of a noble gas. The bonds formed like this are called covalent bonds.

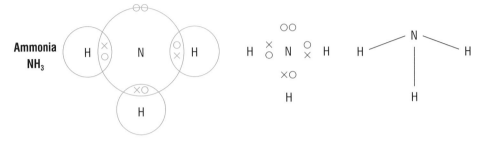

Ammonia
NH₃

Figure 1 Covalent bonds hold the atoms found within molecules tightly together

a How are covalent bonds formed?

Many substances made up of covalently bonded molecules have low melting points and boiling points. Look at the graph in Figure 2.

These substances have low melting points and boiling points. This means that many substances made up of simple molecules are liquids or gases at room temperature. Others are solids with quite low melting points, such as iodine (I_2) and sulfur (S_8).

b Do the compounds shown on the graph exist as solids, liquids or gases at 20°C?

c You have a sample of ammonia (NH_3) at −120°C. Describe the changes that you would see as the temperature of the ammonia rises to 20°C (approximately room temperature).

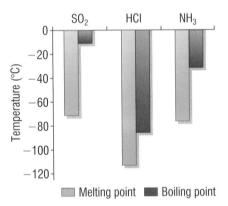

Figure 2 Substances made of simple molecules usually have low melting points and boiling points

Intermolecular forces

Covalent bonds are very strong. So the atoms within each molecule are held very tightly together. However, each molecule tends to be quite separate from its neighbouring molecules. The attraction between the individual molecules in a covalent substance is relatively small. We say that there are weak **intermolecular forces** between molecules. Overcoming these forces does not take much energy.

Look at the molecules in a sample of chlorine gas:

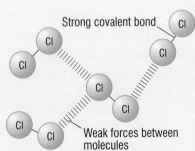

Figure 3 Covalent bonds and the weak forces between molecules in chlorine gas. It is the weak intermolecular forces that are overcome when substances made of simple molecules melt or boil. The covalent bonds are not broken.

d How strong are the forces between the atoms in a covalently bonded molecule?

e How strong are the forces between molecules in a covalent substance? [H]

We have seen that ionic compounds will conduct electricity when they are liquids. But although a substance that is made up of simple molecules may be a liquid at room temperature, it will not conduct electricity. Look at the demonstration below.

There is no overall charge on the simple molecules in a compound like ethanol. So their molecules cannot carry electrical charge. This makes it impossible for substances made up of simple molecules to conduct electricity.

f Why don't simple molecular substances conduct electricity?

⚭ links

For information on ionic compounds conducting electricity, look back at C2 2.1 Giant ionic structures.

Demonstration

Conductivity

● What happens?

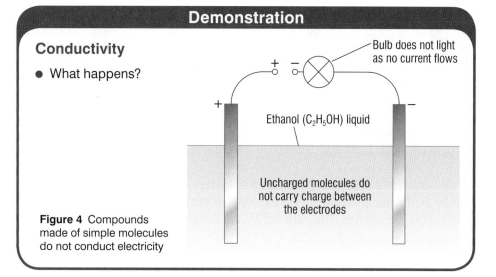

Bulb does not light as no current flows

Ethanol (C_2H_5OH) liquid

Uncharged molecules do not carry charge between the electrodes

Figure 4 Compounds made of simple molecules do not conduct electricity

Summary questions

1 Copy and complete using the words below:

boiling   solids   covalent   melting   molecules   strongly   liquids

Non-metals react together to form .... which are held together by .... bonds. These hold the atoms together very .... If these substances are made of simple molecules, they have low .... points and .... points. So at room temperature they often exist as gases and .... or as .... which melt relatively easily.

2 A compound called sulfur hexafluoride (SF_6) is used to stop sparks forming inside electrical switches designed to control large currents. Explain why the properties of this compound make it particularly useful in electrical switches.

3 The melting point of hydrogen chloride is –115 °C, whereas sodium chloride melts at 801 °C. Explain why. [H]

Key points

● Substances made up of simple molecules have low melting points and boiling points.

● The forces between simple molecules are weak. These weak intermolecular forces explain why substances made of simple molecules have low melting points and boiling points. [H]

● Simple molecules have no overall charge, so they cannot carry electrical charge. Therefore substances made of simple molecules do not conduct electricity.

C2 2.3 Giant covalent structures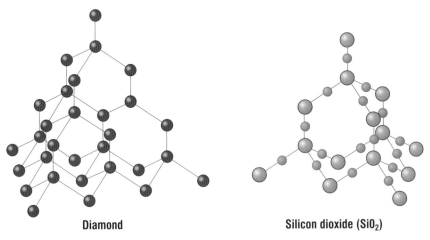

(k)

AQA Examiner's tip

Giant covalent structures are held together by covalent bonds throughout the lattice.

Most covalently bonded substances are made up of individual molecules. However, a few form very different structures. These do not have a relatively small number of atoms in simple molecules. They form huge networks of atoms held together by covalent bonds. We call these **giant covalent structures**. They are sometimes called **macromolecules.**

Substances such as diamond, graphite and silicon dioxide (silica) have giant covalent structures.

Diamond   **Silicon dioxide (SiO_2)**

Figure 1 The structures of diamond and silicon dioxide (silica) continue in all directions

All the atoms in these giant lattices are held in position by strong covalent bonds. Both diamond and silicon dioxide are examples. This gives them some very special properties. They are very hard, have high melting points and boiling points, and are insoluble in water. Diamond is exceptionally hard. All its carbon atoms each form four strong covalent bonds.

a What do we call the structures which contain many millions of atoms joined together by a network of covalent bonds?

b What kind of physical properties do these substances have?

Figure 2 Hard, shiny and transparent – diamonds make beautiful jewellery

?? Did you know …?

Diamond is the hardest natural substance that we know. Artificial diamonds can be made by heating pure carbon to very high temperatures under enormous pressures. 'Industrial diamonds' made like this are used in the drill bits oil companies use when drilling for oil.

We don't always find carbon as diamonds. Another form is graphite (well known for its use in pencil 'lead'). In graphite, carbon atoms are only bonded to three other carbon atoms. They form hexagons which are arranged in giant layers. There are no covalent bonds between the layers. So the layers can slide over each other easily. It's a bit like playing cards sliding off a pack of cards. This makes graphite a soft material that feels slippery.

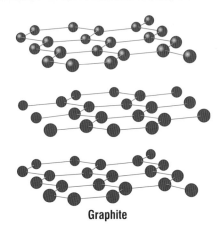

Graphite

Figure 3 The giant structure of graphite. When you write with a pencil, some layers of carbon atoms slide off the 'lead' and are left on the paper.

Bonding in graphite

There are only relatively weak intermolecular forces between the layers in graphite, so they can slide over each other quite easily. The carbon atoms in graphite's layers are arranged in hexagons. So each carbon atom forms three strong covalent bonds (see Figure 3). Carbon atoms have four electrons in their outer shell available for bonding. This leaves one spare outer electron on each carbon atom.

This electron is free to move along the layers of carbon atoms. We call the free electrons found in graphite **delocalised electrons**. They behave rather like the electrons in a metallic structure.

These free electrons allow graphite to conduct electricity. Diamond – and most other covalent substances – cannot conduct electricity.

> **c** What type of electrons enable graphite to conduct electricity?

Fullerenes

Apart from diamond and graphite, there are other different structures that carbon atoms can form. In these structures the carbon atoms join together to make large cages which can have all sorts of shapes. Chemists have made shapes looking like balls, onions, tubes, doughnuts, corkscrews and cones! They are all built up of hexagonal rings of carbon atoms.

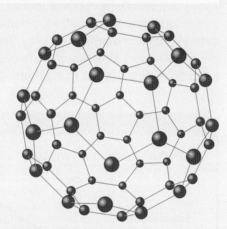

Figure 4 The first fullerene to be discovered contained 60 carbon atoms, but chemists can now make giant fullerenes which contain many thousands of carbon atoms

Chemists discovered carbon's ability to behave like this in 1985. We call the large carbon molecules containing these cage-like structures **fullerenes**. Scientists can now place other molecules inside these carbon cages. This has exciting possibilities, including the delivery of drugs to specific parts of the body. They are sure to become very important in nanoscience applications, for example as catalysts and lubricants.

∞ **links**

For information about delocalised electrons, look back at C2 1.5 Metals.

∞ **links**

For more information on nanoscience, see C2 2.6 Nanoscience.

Key points

- Some covalently bonded substances have giant structures. These substances have high melting points and boiling points.

- Graphite contains giant layers of covalently bonded carbon atoms. However, there are no covalent bonds between the layers. This means they can slide over each other, making graphite soft and slippery. The atoms in diamond have a different structure and cannot slide like this. So diamond is a very hard substance.

- Graphite can conduct electricity because of the delocalised electrons along its layers. **[H]**

- As well as diamond and graphite, carbon also exists as fullerenes which can form large cage-like structures based on hexagonal rings of carbon atoms. **[H]**

Summary questions

1 Copy and complete using the words below:

   atoms boiling carbon hard high covalent layers slide soft

   Giant covalent structures contain many .... joined by covalent bonds. They have .... melting points and .... points. Diamond is a very .... substance because the .... atoms in it are held strongly to each other. However, graphite is .... because there are .... of atoms which can .... over each other. They can do this because there are no .... bonds between its layers.

2 Graphite is sometimes used to reduce the friction between two surfaces that are rubbing together. How does it do this?

3 Explain in detail why graphite can conduct electricity but diamond cannot. **[H]**

C2 2.4 Giant metallic structures ⓚ

Learning objectives

- Why can we bend and shape metals?
- Why are alloys harder than pure metals?
- Why do metals allow electricity and energy pass through them? [H]
- What are shape memory alloys?

Figure 1 Drawing copper out into wires depends on being able to make the layers of metal atoms slide easily over each other

Iron

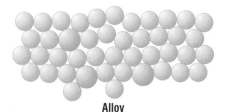

Alloy

Figure 2 The atoms in pure iron are arranged in layers which can easily slide over each other. In alloys the layers cannot slide so easily because atoms of other elements change the regular structure.

We can hammer and bend metals into different shapes, and draw them out into wires. This is because the layers of atoms in a pure metal are able to slide easily over each other.

The atoms in a pure metal, such as iron, are held together in giant metallic structures. The atoms are arranged in closely-packed layers. Because of this regular arrangement, the atoms can slide over one another quite easily. This is why pure iron is soft and easily shaped.

a Why can metals be bent, shaped and pulled out into wires when forces are applied?

Alloys are usually mixtures of metals. However, most steels contain iron with controlled amounts of carbon, a non-metal, mixed in its structure. So there are different sizes of atoms in an alloy. This makes it more difficult for the layers in the metal's giant structure to slide over each other. So alloys are harder than the pure metals used to make them. This is shown in Figure 2.

Practical

Making models of metals

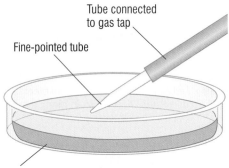

Tube connected to gas tap

Fine-pointed tube

Plastic container with soap solution

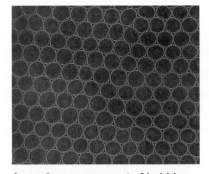

A regular arrangement of bubble 'atoms'

We can make a model of the structure of a metal by blowing small bubbles on the surface of soap solution to represent atoms.

- Why are models useful in science?

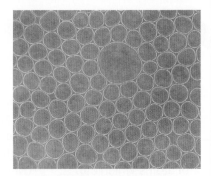

A larger bubble 'atom' has a big effect on the arrangement around it

Metal cooking utensils are used all over the world, because metals are good conductors of heat. Wherever we generate electricity, it passes through metal wires to where it is needed. That's because metals are also good conductors of electricity.

Higher

Explaining the properties of metals

The positive ions in a metal's giant structure are held together by a sea of delocalised electrons. These electrons are a bit like 'glue'. Their negative charge between the positively charged ions holds the ions in position.

However, unlike glue, the electrons are able to move throughout the whole giant lattice. Because they can move around and hold the metal ions together at the same time, the delocalised electrons enable the lattice to distort. When struck, the metal atoms can slip past one another without breaking up the metal's structure.

b How are metal atoms held together?

Metals are good conductors of heat and electricity because the delocalised electrons can flow through the giant metallic lattice. The electrical current and heat are transferred quickly through the metal by the free electrons.

c Why do metals conduct electricity and heat so well?

Figure 3 Metals are essential in our lives – the delocalised electrons mean that they are good conductors of both energy and electricity

Shape memory alloys

Some alloys have a very special property. Like all metals they can be bent (or **deformed**) into different shapes. The difference comes when you heat them up. They then return to their original shape all by themselves.

We call these metals **shape memory alloys**, which describes the way they behave. They seem to 'remember' their original shape!

We can use the properties of shape memory alloys in many ways, for example in health care. Doctors treating a badly broken bone can use alloys to hold the bones in place while they heal. They cool the alloy before it is wrapped around the broken bone. When it heats up again the alloy goes back to its original shape. This pulls the bones together and holds them while they heal.

Dentists have also made braces to pull teeth into the right position using this technique.

⬭⬭ **links**

For more about the bonding in metals, look back at C2 1.5 Metals.

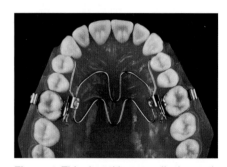

Figure 4 This dental brace pulls the teeth into the right position as it warms up. It is made of a shape memory alloy called nitinol. It is an alloy of nickel and titanium.

Summary questions

1 Copy and complete using the words below:

delocalised electricity energy heat shape slide

The positively charged .... in metals are held together by .... electrons. These also allow the layers to .... over each other so that the metal's .... can be changed. They also allow the metal to conduct .... and .... **[H]**

2 **a** Use your knowledge of metal structures to explain how adding larger metal atoms to a metallic lattice can make the metal harder.
   b What is a shape memory alloy?

3 Explain how a dental brace made out of nitinol is more effective than a brace made out of a traditional alloy.

4 Explain why metals are good conductors of heat and electricity **[H]**

Key points

- We can bend and shape metals because the layers of atoms (or ions) in a giant metallic structure can slide over each other.

- Delocalised electrons in metals enable electricity and heat to pass through the metal easily. **[H]**

- If a shape memory alloy is deformed, it can return to its original shape on heating.

C2 2.5 | The properties of polymers

Learning objectives

Learning objectives

- Do the properties of polymers depend on the monomers we use?

- Can changing reaction conditions modify the polymers that are made?

- What are thermosetting and thermosoftening polymers?

Figure 1 The forces between the molecules in poly(ethene) are relatively weak as there are no strong covalent bonds (cross links) between the molecules. This means that this plastic softens fairly easily when heated.

Figure 2 Nylon is very much stronger than poly(ethene). This climber's life depends on nylon's high-tensile strength. Nylon can withstand large forces without snapping.

As you know, we can make **polymers** from chemicals made from crude oil. Small molecules called monomers join together to make much bigger molecules called polymers. As the monomers join together they produce a tangled web of very long chain molecules. Poly(ethene) is an example.

The properties of a polymer depend on:

- the monomers used to make it, and

- the conditions we choose to carry out the reaction.

  a How are polymer chains arranged in poly(ethene)?

Different monomers

The polymer chains in nylon are made from two different monomers. One monomer has acidic groups at each end. The other has basic groups at each end. The polymer they make is very different from the polymer chains made from hydrocarbon monomers, such as ethene. So the monomers used make a big difference to the properties of the polymer made. (See Figures 1 and 2.)

Different reaction conditions

There are two types of poly(ethene). One is called high density (HD) and the other low density (LD) poly(ethene). Both are made from ethene monomers but they are formed under different conditions.

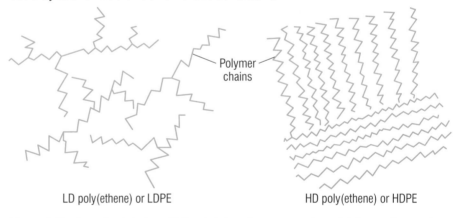

LD poly(ethene) or LDPE

HD poly(ethene) or HDPE

Polymer chains

Figure 3 The branched chains of LD poly(ethene) cannot pack as tightly together as the straighter chains in HD poly(ethene), giving them different properties

Using very high pressures and a trace of oxygen, ethene forms LD poly(ethene). The polymer chains are branched and they can't pack closely together.

Using a catalyst at 50°C and a slightly raised pressure, ethene makes HD poly(ethene). This is made up of straighter poly(ethene) molecules. They can pack more closely together than branched chains. The HD poly(ethene) has a higher softening temperature and is stronger than LD poly(ethene).

  b What do 'LD' and 'HD' stand for in the names of the two types of poly(ethene)?

Thermosoftening and thermosetting polymers

We can classify polymers by looking at what happens to them when they are heated. Some will soften quite easily. They will reset when they cool down. These are called **thermosoftening polymers**. They are made up of individual polymer chains that are tangled together.

Other polymers do not melt when we heat them. These are called **thermosetting polymers**. These have strong covalent bonds forming 'cross links' between their polymer chains. (See Figure 4.)

The tangled web of polymer chains are relatively easy to separate

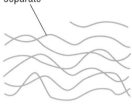

Thermosoftening polymer

Chains fixed together by strong covalent bonds – this is called **cross linking**

Thermosetting polymer

Figure 4 Extensive cross linking by covalent bonds between polymer chains makes a thermosetting plastic that is heat-resistant and rigid

Higher

Bonding in polymers

The atoms in polymer chains are held together by very strong covalent bonds. This is true for all plastics. But the size of the forces *between* polymer molecules in different plastics can be very different.

In thermosoftening polymers the forces between the polymer chains are weak. When we heat the polymer, these weak intermolecular forces are broken. The polymer becomes soft. When the polymer cools down, the intermolecular forces bring the polymer molecules back together. Then the polymer hardens again. This type of polymer can be remoulded.

However, thermosetting polymers are different. Their monomers make covalent bonds between the polymer chains when they are first heated in order to shape them. These covalent bonds are strong, and they stop the polymer from softening. The covalent 'cross links' between chains do not allow them to separate. Even if heated strongly, the polymer will still not soften. Eventually, the polymer will char at high enough temperatures.

Summary questions

1 Copy and complete using the words below:

covalent   thermosetting   tangled   cross links

The polymer chains in a thermosoftening polymer form a .... web. The polymer softens at relatively low temperatures. Other polymers have strong .... bonds between their chains which form .... We call these .... polymers.

2 Why do we use thermosetting polymers to make plastic kettles?

3 Polymer A starts to soften at 100 °C while polymer B softens at 50 °C. Polymer C resists heat but eventually starts to char if heated to very high temperatures.

Explain this using ideas about intermolecular forces. **[H]**

Practical

Modifying a polymer (k)

Take some PVA glue . . .

. . . add a few drops of borax solution

Warm solution of PVA glue

Stir well for about 2 minutes

Slime

The glue becomes slimy because the borax makes the long polymer chains in the glue link together to form a jelly-like substance.

● How could you investigate if the properties of slime depend on how much borax you add?

Figure 5 Electrical sockets are made out of thermosetting plastics. If the plug or wires get hot, the socket will not soften.

Key points

● Monomers affect the properties of the polymers that they produce.

● Changing reaction conditions can also change the properties of the polymer that is produced.

● Thermosoftening polymers will soften or melt easily when heated. Thermosetting polymers will not soften but will eventually char if heated very strongly.

C2 2.6

Nanoscience

?? Did you know ...?

You can get about a million nanometres across a pin-head, and a human hair is about 80000nm wide.

Figure 1 Nanoparticles will save many people from damaged skin and cancers caused by too much UV light

Figure 2 Nanoparticles in cosmetic products can work deeper in the skin

Nanoscience is a new and exciting area of science. 'Nano' is a prefix like 'milli' or 'mega'. While 'milli' means 'one-thousandth', 'nano' means 'one thousand-millionth'.

1 nanometre (1 nm) = 1×10^{-9} metres (= 0.000 000 001 m or a billionth of a metre)

So nanoscience is the science of really tiny things. We are dealing with structures that are just a few hundred atoms in size or even smaller (between 1 and 100 nm in size).

We now know that materials behave very differently at a very tiny scale. Nanoparticles are so tiny that they have a huge surface area for a small volume of material. When we arrange atoms and molecules on a nanoscale, their properties can be truly remarkable.

a How many nanometres make up 1 millimetre?

Nanoscience at work

Here are some uses of nanoscience.

● Glass can be coated with titanium oxide nanoparticles. Sunshine triggers a chemical reaction which breaks down dirt which lands on the window. When it rains the water spreads evenly over the surface of the glass, washing off the broken down dirt.

● Titanium oxide and zinc oxide nanoparticles are also used in modern sun-screens. Scientists can coat nanoparticles of the metal oxide with a coating of silica. The thickness of the silica coating can be adjusted at an atomic level. These coated nanoparticles seem more effective at blocking the Sun's rays than conventional UV absorbers.

● The cosmetics industry is one of the biggest users of this new technology. The nanoparticles in face creams are absorbed deeper into the skin. They are also used in sun tan creams and deodorants.

The delivery of active ingredients in cosmetics can also be applied to medicines. The latest techniques being developed use nanocages of gold to deliver drugs where they need to go in the body. Researchers have found that the tiny gold particles can be injected and absorbed by tumours. Tumours have thin, leaky blood vessels with holes large enough for the gold nanoparticles to pass into. However, they can't get into healthy blood vessels.

When a laser is directed at the tumour the gold nanoparticles absorb energy and warm up. The temperature of the tumour increases enough to change the properties of its proteins but barely warms the surrounding tissue. This destroys the tumour cells without damaging healthy cells.

There is potential to use the gold nanocages to carry cancer-fighting drugs to the tumour at the same time. The carbon nanocages we met in C2 2.3 can also be used to deliver drugs in the body. Incredibly strong, yet light, nanotubes are already being used to reinforce materials (see Figure 3). The new materials are finding uses in sport, such as making very strong but light tennis racquets.

Silver nanoparticles are antibacterial. They also act against viruses and fungi. They are used in sprays to clean operating theatres in hospitals.

Future developments?

Nanotubes are now being developed that can be used as nanowires. This will make it possible to construct incredibly small electronic circuits. Nanotubes can be used to make highly sensitive selective sensors. For example, nanotube sensors have been made that can detect tiny traces of a gas present in the breath of asthmatics before an attack. This will let patients monitor and treat their own condition without having to visit hospital to use expensive machines.

Nanowires would also help to make computers with vastly improved memory capacities and speeds.

Scientists in the US Army are developing nanotech suits – thin, or even spray-on, uniforms which are flexible and tough enough to withstand bullets and blasts. The uniforms would receive aerial views of the battlefield from satellites, transmitted directly to the soldier's brain. There would also be a built-in air conditioning system to keep the body temperature normal. Inside the suit there would be a full range of nanobiosensors that could send medical data back to a medical team.

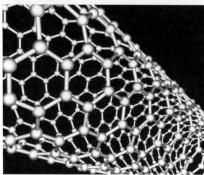

Figure 3 Nanocages can carry drugs inside them and nanotubes can reinforce materials

Possible risks

The large surface area of nanoparticles would make them very effective as catalysts. However, their large surface area also makes them dangerous. If a spark is made by accident, they may cause a violent explosion.

If nanoparticles are used more and more there is also going to be more risk of them finding their way into the air around us. Breathing in tiny particles could damage the lungs. Nanoparticles could enter the bloodstream this way, or from their use in cosmetics, with unpredictable effects. More research needs to be done to find out their effects on health and the environment.

b Why would nanoparticles make very efficient catalysts?

Activity

Whenever we are faced with a possible development in science there are two possible questions – what *can* we do? And what *should* we do? Look at the ideas about the uses of nanoscience and its future development here. Choose one idea and ask yourself 'what *can* we do and what *should* we do?' Present your answers to the rest of your group

Summary questions

1 What do we mean by 'nanoscience'?

2 In his book *Engines of Creation* K. Eric Drexler speculates that one day we may invent a nanomachine that can reproduce itself. Then the world could be overrun by so-called 'grey goo'. Some people are so worried they have called for a halt in nanoscience research. What are your views?

Key points

● Nanoscience is the study of small particles that are between 1 and 100 nanometres in size.

● Nanoparticles behave differently from the materials they are made from on a large scale.

● New developments in nanoscience are very exciting but will need more research into possible issues that might arise from their increased use.

Summary questions

1 Match the sentence halves together:

a	Ionic compounds have	A	.... conduct electricity when molten or in solution.
b	Ionic compounds	B	.... held together by strong electrostatic forces.
c	The oppositely charged ions in an ionic compound are	C	.... a giant lattice of ions.
d	Ionic compounds are made of	D	.... high melting points.

2 The table contains data about some different substances:

Substance	Melting point (°C)	Boiling point (°C)	Electrical conductor
cobalt	1495	2870	Good
ammonia	−78	−33	Poor
magnesium oxide	2852	3600	solid – poor liquid – good
manganese	1244	1962	Good
lithium chloride	605	1340	solid – poor liquid – good
silicon dioxide	1610	2230	Poor
hydrogen bromide	−88	−67	Poor
graphite	3652	4827	Good

a Make a table with the following headings:

Giant covalent, Giant ionic, Simple molecules, Giant metallic.

Now write the name of each substance above in the correct column.

b Which substances are gases at 20 °C?

c One of these substances behaves in a slightly different way than its structure suggests. Why?

3 One use of shape memory alloys is to make spectacle frames. Write down **one** advantage and **one** disadvantage of using a shape memory alloy like this.

4 A certain ionic compound melts at exactly 800°C. A chemical company wants to design a device to activate a warning light and buzzer when the temperature in a chemical reactor rises above 800°C. Suggest how this ionic compound could be used in an alarm.

5 'Both graphite and metals can conduct electricity – but graphite is soft while metals are not.' Use your knowledge of the different structures of graphite and metals to explain this statement. [H]

6 Read the article about the use of nanoparticles in sun creams.

Sun creams

Many sun creams use nanoparticles. These sun creams are very good at absorbing radiation, especially ultraviolet radiation. Owing to the particle size, the sun creams spread more easily, cover better and save money because you use less. The new sun creams are also transparent, unlike traditional sun creams which are white. The use of nanoparticles is so successful that they are now used in more than 300 sun cream products.

Some sun creams contain nanoparticles of titanium oxide. Normal-sized particles of titanium oxide are safe to put on the skin.

It is thought that nanoparticles can pass through the skin and travel around the body more easily than normal-sized particles. It is also thought that nanoparticles might be toxic to some types of cell, such as skin, bone, brain and liver cells.

---

a i How is the size of nanoparticles different from normal-sized particles of titanium oxide?

ii Suggest how the size of nanoparticles might help them to enter the body more easily.

b Give **two** advantages of using nanoparticles in sun creams.

c Why might nanoparticles be dangerous inside the body?

AQA, 2008

AQA Examination-style questions

1 Match each of the substances in the table with a description from the list.

giant covalent   ionic   metal   simple molecule

Substance	Formula	Melting point (°C)	Boiling point (°C)	Does it conduct electricity when liquid?
a	C	3550	4830	No
b	Co	1768	3142	Yes
c	CH_4	−182	−164	No
d	$CaCl_2$	1055	1873	Yes

(4)

2 Copper can be hammered into shape.

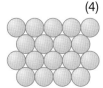

The structure of copper metal can be represented as shown:

a Explain why copper can be hammered into shape. (1)

b Copper can be mixed with zinc to make the alloy called brass. Brass is much harder than copper. Explain why. (2)

c Copper can be mixed with zinc and aluminium to make a shape memory alloy. What is a shape memory alloy? (2)

3 Choose a word from the list to complete each sentence.

different   identical   smart   thermosoftening thermosetting

The polymers low-density poly(ethene) (LDPE) and high-density poly(ethene) (HDPE) are made from monomers that are .... The polymers are produced using catalysts and reaction conditions that are .... LDPE melts at 120°C and HDPE melts at 130°C and they have no cross links between the polymer chains so they are both .... polymers. (3)

4 Chloroethene, C_2H_3Cl, can be polymerised to poly(chloroethene).

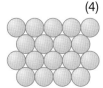

a Explain in terms of its structure why chloroethene is a gas at room temperature. (2)

b Explain in terms of its structure why poly(chloroethene) is a thermosoftening polymer. (2)

[11]

5 The picture shows a copper kettle being heated on a camping stove.

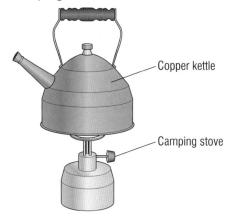

Copper kettle

Camping stove

a *In this question you will be assessed on using good English, organising information clearly and using specialist terms where appropriate.*

Copper is a good material for making a kettle because it has a high melting point.

Explain why copper, like many other metals, has a high melting point.

You should describe the structure and bonding of a metal in your answer. (6)

b An aeroplane contains many miles of electrical wiring made from copper. This adds to the mass of the aeroplane.

It has been suggested that the electrical wiring made from copper could be replaced by lighter carbon nanotubes.

The diagram shows the structure of a carbon nanotube.

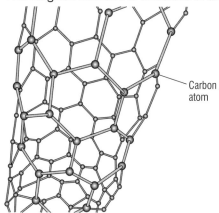

Carbon atom

i What does the term 'nano' tell you about the carbon nanotubes? (1)

ii Like graphite, each carbon atom is joined to three other carbon atoms. Explain why the carbon nanotube can conduct electricity. (2)

AQA, 2010

C2 3.1

The mass of atoms

Learning objectives

- What is an atom's atomic number and mass number?
- What are the relative masses of protons, neutrons and electrons?
- What are isotopes?

Did you know ...?

It would take 1836 electrons to have the same mass as a single proton.

As you know, an atom consists of a nucleus containing positively charged protons, together with neutrons which have no charge. The negatively charged electrons are arranged in energy levels (shells) around the nucleus.

Every atom has the same number of electrons orbiting its nucleus as it has protons in its nucleus. The number of protons in an atom is called its **atomic number**.

The mass of a proton and a **neutron** is the same. This means that the relative mass of a neutron compared with a proton is 1. Electrons are much, much lighter than protons and neutrons. Because of this, the mass of an atom is concentrated in its nucleus. We can ignore the tiny mass of the electrons when we work out the relative mass of an atom.

Type of subatomic particle	Relative mass
Proton	1
Neutron	1
Electron	very small

a What is the atomic number of an atom?
b How does the mass of a proton compare with the mass of a neutron?
c How does the mass of an electron compare with the mass of a neutron or proton?

Mass number

Almost all of the mass of an atom is in its nucleus. This is because the mass of the electrons is so tiny. We call the total number of protons and neutrons in an atom its **mass number**.

We can show the atomic number and mass number of an atom like this:

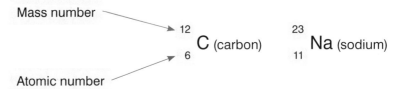

We can work out the number of neutrons in the nucleus of an atom by subtracting its atomic number from its mass number:

number of neutrons = mass number – atomic number

For the two examples above, carbon has 6 protons and a mass number of 12.

So the number of neutrons in a carbon atom is (12 − 6) = 6.

Sodium has an atomic number of 11 and the mass number is 23.

So a sodium atom has (23 − 11) = 12 neutrons. In its nucleus there are 11 protons and 12 neutrons.

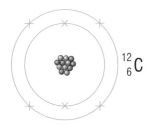

- Proton — Number of protons gives atomic number
- Neutron — Number of protons plus number of neutrons gives mass number

Figure 1 An atom of carbon

d How do we calculate the number of neutrons in an atom?

Isotopes

Atoms of the same element always have the same number of protons. However, they can have different numbers of neutrons.

We give the name **isotopes** to atoms of the same element with different numbers of neutrons.

Isotopes always have the same atomic number but different mass numbers. For example, carbon has two common isotopes, $^{12}_{6}C$ (carbon-12) and $^{14}_{6}C$ (carbon-14). The carbon-12 isotope has 6 protons and 6 neutrons in the nucleus. The carbon-14 isotope has 6 protons and 8 neutrons.

Sometimes the extra neutrons make the nucleus unstable, so it is radioactive. However, not all isotopes are radioactive – they are simply atoms of the same element that have different masses.

e What are isotopes?

Samples of different isotopes of an element have different *physical* properties. For example, they have a different density and they may or may not be radioactive. However, they always have the same *chemical* properties. That's because their reactions depend on their electronic structure. As their atoms will have the same number of electrons, the electronic structure will be same for all isotopes of an element.

For example, hydrogen has three isotopes: hydrogen, deuterium and tritium (see Figure 2). Each has a different mass and tritium is radioactive. However, they can all react with oxygen to make water.

f Which isotope of hydrogen is heaviest?

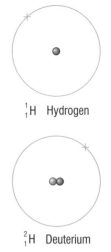

$^{1}_{1}H$ Hydrogen

$^{2}_{1}H$ Deuterium

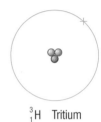

$^{3}_{1}H$ Tritium

Figure 2 The isotopes of hydrogen – they have identical chemical properties but different physical properties

Summary questions

1 Copy and complete using the words below:

electrons isotopes protons mass atomic one

The number of protons in an atom is called its .... number. The relative mass of a neutron compared with a proton is .... Compared with protons and neutrons .... have almost no mass. The total number of .... and neutrons in an atom is called its .... number. Atoms of an element which have different numbers of neutrons are called ....

2 State how many protons there would be in the nucleus of each of the following elements:

a i $^{9}_{4}Be$ ii $^{16}_{8}O$ iii $^{22}_{10}Ne$ iv $^{31}_{15}P$ v $^{79}_{35}Br$.

b State how many neutrons each atom in part **a** has.

3 a How do the physical properties of isotopes of the same element vary?

b Why do isotopes of the same element have identical chemical properties?

Key points

- The relative mass of protons and neutrons is 1.
- The atomic number of an atom is its number of protons (which equals its number of electrons).
- The mass number of an atom is the total number of protons and neutrons in its nucleus.
- Isotopes are atoms of the same element with different numbers of neutrons.

How much?

C2 3.2 Masses of atoms and moles

Learning objectives

- How can we compare the masses of atoms?
- What is the relative atomic mass of an element? [H]
- How can we calculate the relative formula mass of a compound from the elements it is made of?

Balanced symbol equations show us how many atoms of reactants we need to make the products. But when we actually carry out a reaction we really need to know how much to use in grams or cm³.

For example, look at the equation:

$$Mg + 2HCl \rightarrow MgCl_2 + H_2$$

The symbol equation tells us that we need twice as many hydrogen and chlorine atoms as magnesium atoms. However, this doesn't mean that the mass of HCl will be twice the mass of Mg. This is because atoms of different elements have different masses.

To make symbol equations useful in the lab or factory we need to know more about the mass of atoms.

a Why don't symbol equations tell us directly what mass of each reactant to use in a chemical reaction?

Relative atomic masses

The mass of a single atom is so tiny that it would not be practical to use it in experiments or calculations. So instead of working with the real masses of atoms we just focus on the relative masses of different elements. We call these **relative atomic masses (A_r)**.

Relative atomic mass

We use an atom of carbon-12 ($^{12}_6C$) as a standard atom. We give this a 'mass' of exactly 12 units, because it has 6 protons and 6 neutrons. We then compare the masses of atoms of all the other elements with this standard carbon atom. For example, hydrogen has a relative atomic mass of 1 as most of its atoms have a mass that is one-twelfth of a $^{12}_6C$ atom.

The relative atomic mass of an element is usually the same as, or similar to, the mass number of its most common isotope. The A_r takes into account the proportions of any isotopes of the element found naturally. So it is an *average* mass compared with the standard carbon atom. (This is why chlorine has a relative atomic mass of 35.5, although we could never have half a proton or neutron in an atom.)

b Which atom do we use as a standard to compare relative masses of elements?

Figure 1 The relative mass of $^{12}_6C$ atom is 12. Compared with this, the A_r of helium is 4 and the A_r of magnesium is 24.

Higher

Relative formula masses

We can use the A_r of the various elements to work out the **relative formula mass (M_r)** of compounds. This is true whether the compounds are made up of molecules or collections of ions. A simple example is a substance like sodium chloride. We know that the A_r of sodium is 23 and the A_r of chlorine is **35.5**. So the relative formula mass of sodium chloride (NaCl) is:

$$23 \quad + \quad 35.5 \quad = \quad \textbf{58.5}$$
$$A_r\!:\!Na \quad A_r\!:\!Cl \quad M_r\!:\!NaCl$$

Another example is water. Water is made up of hydrogen and oxygen. The A_r of hydrogen is 1, and the A_r of oxygen is 16. Water has the formula H_2O. It contains two hydrogen atoms for every one oxygen, so the M_r is:

$$(1 \times 2) \quad + \quad 16 \quad = \quad \textbf{18}$$
$$A_r\!:\!H \times 2 \quad A_r\!:\!O \quad M_r\!:\!H_2O$$

c What is the relative formula mass of hydrogen sulfide, H_2S? (A_r values: H = 1, S = 32)

We can use the same approach with relatively complicated molecules like sulfuric acid, H_2SO_4. Hydrogen has a A_r of 1, the A_r of sulfur is 32 and the A_r of oxygen 16. This means that the M_r of sulfuric acid is:

$$(1 \times 2) + 32 + (16 \times 4) = 2 + 32 + 64 = \textbf{98}$$

Moles

Saying or writing 'relative atomic mass in grams' or 'relative formula mass in grams' is rather clumsy. So chemists have a shorthand word for it: a **mole**.

They say that the relative atomic mass in grams of carbon (i.e. 12 g of carbon) is a mole of carbon atoms. One mole is simply the relative atomic mass or relative formula mass of any substance expressed in grams. A mole of any substance always contains the same number of atoms, molecules or ions. This is a huge number (6.02×10^{23}).

Did you know ... ?

If you had as many soft drink cans as there are atoms in a mole they would cover the surface of the Earth to a depth of 200 miles!

AQA Examiner's tip

You don't have to remember the number 6.02×10^{23} or the relative atomic masses of elements. But practise calculating the mass of one mole of different substances from their formula and the relative atomic masses that you are given.

Summary questions

1 Copy and complete using the words below:

   atom   elements   formula   relative

   The mass of an individual .... is so small that we use ....
   values when comparing them. We calculate the relative ....
   mass of a compound by adding up the relative atomic masses of its
   .... in the ratio given by its formula.

2 The equation for the reaction of calcium and fluorine is:

   $$Ca + F_2 \rightarrow CaF_2.$$

   a How many moles of fluorine molecules react with one mole of calcium atoms?

   b What is the relative formula mass of CaF_2? (A_r values: Ca = 40, F = 19)

3 The relative atomic mass of helium is 4, and that of sulfur is 32. How many times heavier is a sulfur atom than a helium atom?

4 Define the term 'relative atomic mass' of an element. [H]

Key points

- We compare the masses of atoms by measuring them relative to atoms of carbon-12. [H]

- We work out the relative formula mass of a compound by adding up the relative atomic masses of the elements in it, in the ratio shown by its formula.

- One mole of any substance is its relative formula mass, in grams.

Percentages and formulae

Learning objectives

- How can we calculate the percentage of an element in a compound from its formula?

- How can we calculate the empirical formula of a compound from its percentage composition? [H]

Figure 1 A small difference in the amount of metal in an ore might not seem very much. However, when millions of tonnes of ore are extracted and processed each year, it all adds up!

Maths skills

To calculate the percentage of an element in a compound:

- Write down the formula of the compound.

- Using the A_r values from your data sheet, work out the M_r of the compound. Write down the mass of each element making up the compound as you work it out.

- Write the mass of the element you are investigating as a fraction of the M_r.

- Find the percentage by multiplying your fraction by 100.

We can use the formula mass of a compound to calculate the percentage mass of each element in it. It's not just in GCSE Chemistry books that calculations like this are done! Mining companies decide whether to exploit mineral finds using calculations like these.

Working out the percentage of an element in a compound

Worked example 1

What percentage of the mass of magnesium oxide is actually magnesium?

Solution

We need to know the formula of magnesium oxide: MgO.

The A_r of magnesium is 24 and the A_r of oxygen is 16.

Adding these together gives us the relative formula mass is (M_r), of MgO
24 + 16 = 40

So in 40 g of magnesium oxide, 24 g is actually magnesium.

The fraction of magnesium in the MgO is:

$$\frac{\text{mass of magnesium}}{\text{total mass of compound}} = \frac{24}{40}$$

so the percentage of magnesium in the compound is:

$$\frac{24}{40} \times 100\% = \textbf{60\%}$$

Worked example 2

A pure white powder is found at the scene of a crime. It could be strychnine, a deadly poison with the formula $C_{21}H_{22}N_2O_2$: but is it?

When a chemist analyses the powder, she finds that 83% of its mass is carbon. What is the percentage mass of carbon in strychnine? Is this the same as the white powder?

Solution

Given the A_r values: C = 12, H =1, N = 14, O = 16, the formula mass (M_r) of strychnine is:

$$(12 \times 21) + (1 \times 22) + (14 \times 2) + (16 \times 2) = 252 + 22 + 28 + 32 = 334$$

The percentage mass of carbon in strychnine is therefore:

$$\frac{252}{334} \times 100 = \textbf{75.4\%}$$

This is **not** the same as the percentage mass of carbon in the white powder – so the white powder is not strychnine.

a What is the percentage mass of hydrogen in ammonia, NH_3? (A_r values: N = 14, H = 1)

Higher

Working out the empirical formula of a compound from its percentage composition

We can find the percentage of each element in a compound by experiments. Then we can work out the simplest ratio of each type of atom in the compound. We call this simplest (whole-number) ratio its **empirical formula**.

This is sometimes the same as the actual number of atoms in one molecule (which we call the **molecular formula**) – but not always. For example, the empirical formula of water is H_2O, which is also its molecular formula. However, hydrogen peroxide has the empirical formula HO, but its molecular formula is H_2O_2.

Worked example

A hydrocarbon contains 75% carbon and 25% hydrogen by mass. What is its empirical formula? (A_r values: C = 12, H = 1)

Solution

Imagine we have 100 g of the compound. Then 75 g is carbon and 25 g hydrogen.

Work out the number of moles by dividing the mass of each element by its relative atomic mass:

$$\text{For carbon: } \frac{75}{12} = 6.25 \text{ moles of carbon atoms}$$

For hydrogen: $\frac{25}{1} = 25$ moles of hydrogen atoms

So this tells us that 6.25 moles of carbon atoms are combined with 25 moles of hydrogen atoms.

This means that the ratio is 6.25 (C) : 25 (H).

So the simplest whole number ratio is 1 : 4 (by dividing both numbers by the smallest number in the ratio)

In other words each carbon atom is combined with 4 times as many hydrogen atoms.

So the empirical formula is **CH_4**.

  b A compound contains 40% sulfur and 60% oxygen. What is its empirical formula? (A_r values: S = 32, O = 16)

  c 5.4 g of aluminium react exactly with 4.8 g of oxygen. What is the empirical formula of the compound formed? (A_r values: Al = 27, O = 16)

Maths skills

To work out the formula from percentage masses:

● Change the percentages given to the masses of each element in 100 g of compound.

● Change the masses to moles of atoms by dividing the masses by the A_r values. This tells you how many moles of each different element are present.

● This tells you the ratio of atoms of the different elements in the compound.

● Then the *simplest* whole-number ratio gives you the empirical formula of the compound.   [H]

Summary questions

1 Copy and complete using the words below:

compound   dividing   hundred   formula

The percentage of an element in a .... is calculated by .... the mass of the element in the compound by the relative .... mass of the compound and then multiplying the result by one ....

2 Ammonium nitrate (NH_4NO_3) is used as a fertiliser. What is the percentage mass of nitrogen in it? (A_r values: H = 1, N = 14, O = 16)

3 22.55% of the mass of a sample of phosphorus chloride is phosphorus. What is the empirical formula of this phosphorus chloride?
(A_r values: P = 31, Cl = 35.5)   [H]

Key points

● The relative atomic masses of the elements in a compound and its formula can be used to work out its percentage composition.

● We can calculate empirical formulae given the masses or percentage composition of elements present.   [H]

C2 3.4

Equations and calculations ⓚ

Learning objectives

- What do balanced symbol equations tell us about chemical reactions?

- How do we use balanced symbol equations to calculate masses of reactants and products? [H]

Chemical equations can be very useful. When we want to know how much of each substance is involved in a chemical reaction, we can use the balanced symbol equation.

Think about what happens when hydrogen molecules (H_2) react with chlorine molecules (Cl_2). The reaction makes hydrogen chloride molecules (HCl):

$$H_2 + Cl_2 \rightarrow HCl \text{ (not balanced)}$$

This equation shows the reactants and the product – but it is not balanced.

Here is the balanced equation:

$$H_2 + Cl_2 \rightarrow 2HCl$$

This balanced equation tells us that '1 hydrogen molecule reacts with 1 chlorine molecule to make 2 hydrogen chloride molecules'. But the balanced equation also tells us the number of moles of each substance involved. So our balanced equation also tells us that '1 mole of hydrogen molecules reacts with 1 mole of chlorine molecules to make 2 moles of hydrogen chloride molecules'.

a '2HCl' has two meanings. What are they?

1 hydrogen molecule	1 chlorine molecule	2 hydrogen chloride molecules
H_2 $+$	Cl_2 $\longrightarrow$	$2\,HCl$
1 mole of hydrogen molecules	1 mole of chlorine molecules	2 moles of hydrogen chloride molecules

Using balanced equations to work out reacting masses

This balanced equation above is really useful, because we can use it to work out what mass of hydrogen and chlorine react together. We can also calculate how much hydrogen chloride is made.

To do this, we need to know that the A_r for hydrogen is 1 and the A_r for chlorine is 35.5:

A_r of hydrogen = 1 .... so mass of 1 mole of H_2 = $2 \times 1 = 2\,g$

A_r of chlorine = 35.5 .... so mass of 1 mole of Cl_2 = $2 \times 35.5 = 71\,g$

M_r of HCl = $(1 + 35.5) = 36.5$ .... so mass of 1 mole of HCl = $36.5\,g$

Our balanced equation tells us that 1 mole of hydrogen reacts with 1 mole of chlorine to give 2 moles of HCl. So turning this into masses we get:

1 mole of hydrogen = $1 \times 2\,g$ = $2\,g$

1 mole of chlorine = $1 \times 71\,g$ = $71\,g$

2 moles of HCl = $2 \times 36.5\,g = 73\,g$

Higher

Calculations

These calculations are important when we want to know the mass of chemicals that react together. For example, sodium hydroxide reacts with chlorine gas to make bleach.

Here is the balanced symbol equation for the reaction:

$$2NaOH + Cl_2 \rightarrow NaOCl + NaCl + H_2O$$
sodium hydroxide   chlorine   bleach   salt   water

This reaction happens when chlorine gas is bubbled through a solution of sodium hydroxide.

If we have a solution containing 100 g of sodium hydroxide, how much chlorine gas do we need to convert it to **bleach**? Too much, and some chlorine will be wasted. Too little, and not all of the sodium hydroxide will react.

	Mass of 1 mole of	
	NaOH	**Cl₂**
A_r of hydrogen = 1		
A_r of oxygen = 16	= 23 + 16 + 1 = 40	= 35.5 × 2 = 71
A_r of sodium = 23		
A_r of chlorine = 35.5		

The table shows that 1 mole of sodium hydroxide has a mass of 40 g.

So 100 g of sodium hydroxide is $\frac{100}{40}$ = 2.5 moles.

The balanced symbol equation tells us that for every 2 moles of sodium hydroxide we need 1 mole of chlorine.

So we need $\frac{2.5}{2}$ = 1.25 moles of chlorine.

The table shows that 1 mole of chlorine has a mass of 71 g.

So we will need 1.25 × 71 = **88.75 g** of chlorine to react with 100 g of sodium hydroxide.

Figure 1 Bleach is used in some swimming pools to kill harmful bacteria. Getting the quantities right involves some careful calculation!

Summary questions

1 Copy and complete using the words below:

balanced   equations   mole   mass   product

Symbol .... can tell us about the amounts of substances in a reaction if they are .... To work out the mass of each substance in a reaction we need to know the mass of 1 .... of it. We can then work out the .... of each reactant needed, and the mass of .... that will be formed. [H]

2 a Hydrogen peroxide, H_2O_2, decomposes to form water and oxygen gas. Write a balanced symbol equation for this reaction.

b When hydrogen peroxide decomposes, what mass of hydrogen peroxide is needed to produce 8 g of oxygen gas? (A_r values: H = 1, O = 16) [H]

3 Calcium reacts with oxygen like this:

$$2Ca + O_2 \rightarrow 2CaO$$

What mass of oxygen will react exactly with 60 g of calcium? (A_r values: O = 16, Ca = 40) [H]

Key points

- Balanced symbol equations tell us the number of moles of substances involved in a chemical reaction.

- We can use balanced symbol equations to calculate the masses of reactants and products in a chemical reaction. [H]

C2 3.5 The yield of a chemical reaction

Learning objectives

- What do we mean by the yield of a chemical reaction and what factors affect it?

- How do we calculate the percentage yield of a chemical reaction? [H]

- Why is it important to achieve a high yield in industry and to waste as little energy as possible?

⚮ links

For information about using balanced symbol equations to predict reacting masses, look back to C2 3.4 Equations and calculations.

Many of the substances that we use every day have to be made from other chemicals. This may involve using complex chemical reactions. Examples include food colourings, flavourings and preservatives, the ink in your pen or printer, and the artificial fibres in your clothes. All of these are made using chemical reactions.

Imagine a reaction: A + 2B → C

If we need 1000 kg of C, we can work out how much A and B we need. All we need to know is the relative formula masses of A, B and C and the balanced symbol equation.

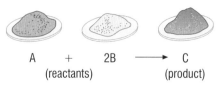

A + 2B ⟶ C
(reactants) (product)

a How many moles of B are needed to react with each mole of A in this reaction?

b How many moles of C will this make?

If we carry out the reaction, it is unlikely that we will get as much of C as we worked out. This is because our calculations assumed that all of A and B would be turned into C. We call the amount of product that a chemical reaction produces its **yield**.

It is useful to think about reactions in terms of their **percentage yield**. This compares the amount of product that the reaction *really* produces with the maximum amount that it could *possibly* produce:

$$\text{Percentage yield} = \frac{\text{amount of product produced}}{\text{maxmimum amount of product possible}} \times 100\%$$

Calculating percentage yield

An industrial example

Limestone is made mainly of calcium carbonate. Crushed lumps of limestone are heated in a rotating lime kiln. The calcium carbonate decomposes to make calcium oxide, and carbon dioxide gas is given off. A company processes 200 tonnes of limestone a day. It collects 98 tonnes of calcium oxide, the useful product. What is the percentage yield of the kiln, assuming limestone contains only calcium carbonate?

(A_r values: Ca = 40, C = 12, O = 16)

calcium carbonate → calcium oxide + carbon dioxide
$$CaCO_3 \rightarrow CaO + CO_2$$

Work out the relative formula masses of $CaCO_3$ and CaO.

M_r of $CaCO_3$ = 40 + 12 + (16 × 3) = 100

M_r of CaO = 40 + 16 = 56

So the balanced symbol equation tells us that:

100 tonnes of $CaCO_3$ could make 56 tonnes of CaO, assuming a 100% yield.

Higher

Therefore 200 tonnes of $CaCO_3$ could make a maximum of (56×2) tonnes of $CaO = 112$ tonnes.

So **percentage yield** $= \dfrac{\text{amount of product produced}}{\text{maximum amount of product possible}} \times 100\%$

$= \dfrac{98}{112} \times 100 = \mathbf{87.5\%}$

We can explain this yield as some of the limestone is lost as dust in the crushing process and in the rotating kiln. There will also be some other mineral compounds in the limestone. It is not 100% calcium carbonate as we assumed in our calculation.

c What is the percentage yield of a reaction?

Very few chemical reactions have a yield of 100% because:

- The reaction may be reversible (so as products form they react to re-form the reactants again).
- Some reactants may react to give unexpected products.
- Some of the product may be lost in handling or left behind in the apparatus.
- The reactants may not be completely pure.
- Some chemical reactions produce more than one product, and it may be difficult to separate the product that we want from the reaction mixture.

Sustainable production

Chemical companies use reactions to make products which they sell. Ideally, they want to use reactions with high yields (that also happen at a reasonable rate). Making a product more efficiently means making less waste. As much product as possible should be made from the reactants.

Chemical factories (or **plants**) are designed by chemical engineers. They design a plant to work as safely and economically as possible. It should waste as little energy and raw materials as possible. This helps the company to make money. It is better for the environment too as it conserves our limited resources. It also reduces the pollution we get when we use fossil fuels as sources of energy.

Summary questions

1. Copy and complete using the words below:

   high   maximum   percentage   product   waste   yield

   The amount of .... made in a chemical reaction is called its ....
   The .... yield tells us the amount of product that is made compared
   to the .... amount that could be made. Reactions with .... yields
   are important because they result in less ....

2. Explain why it is good for the environment if industry finds ways to make products using high yield reactions and processes that waste as little energy as possible.

3. If the percentage yield for a reaction is 100%, 60 g of reactant A would make 80 g of product C. How much of reactant A is needed to make 80 g of product C if the percentage yield of the reaction is only 75%? **[H]**

Key points

- The yield of a chemical reaction describes how much product is made.

- The percentage yield of a chemical reaction tells us how much product is made compared with the maximum amount that could be made (100%).

- Factors affecting the yield of a chemical reaction include product being left behind in the apparatus and difficulty separating the products from the reaction mixture.

- It is important to maximise yield and minimise energy wasted to conserve the Earth's limited resources and reduce pollution.

C2 3.6

Reversible reactions

Learning objectives

- What is a reversible reaction?
- How can we represent reversible reactions?

Figure 1 Indicators undergo reversible reactions, changing colour to show us whether solutions are acidic or alkaline

In all the reactions we have looked at so far the reactants react and form products. We show this by using an arrow pointing *from* the reactants *to* the products:

$$A + B \rightarrow C + D$$
$$\text{reactants} \quad \text{products}$$

But in some reactions the products can react together to make the original reactants again. We call this a **reversible reaction**.

A reversible reaction can go in both directions so we use two arrows in the equation. One arrow points in the forwards direction and one backwards:

$$A + B \rightleftharpoons C + D$$

a What does a single arrow in a chemical equation mean?

b What does a double arrow in a chemical equation mean?

Examples of reversible reactions

Have you ever tried to neutralise an alkaline solution with an acid? It is very difficult to get a solution which is exactly neutral. You can use an indicator to tell when just the right amount of acid has been added. Indicators react in acids to form a coloured compound. They also react in alkalis to form a differently coloured compound.

Litmus is a complex molecule. We will represent it as HLit (where H is hydrogen). HLit is red. If you add alkali, HLit turns into the Lit⁻ ion by losing an H⁺ ion. Lit⁻ is blue. If you then add more acid, blue Lit⁻ changes back to red HLit and so on.

$$\text{HLit} \rightleftharpoons H^+ + Lit^-$$
$$\text{Red litmus} \qquad \text{Blue litmus}$$

c Why does a neutral solution look purple with litmus solution?

Practical

Changing colours

Use litmus solution, dilute hydrochloric acid and sodium hydroxide solution to show the reversible reaction described above.

- Explain the changes you see when adding acid and alkali to litmus.

When we heat ammonium chloride another reversible reaction takes place.

Practical

Heating ammonium chloride

Gently heat a small amount of ammonium chloride in a test tube with a mineral wool plug. Use test tube holders or clamp the test tube at an angle. Make sure you warm the bottom of the tube.

- What do you see happen inside the test tube?

Safety: Wear eye protection for both practicals.

Ammonium chloride breaks down on heating. It forms ammonia gas and hydrogen chloride gas. This is an example of thermal decomposition:

$$\text{ammonium chloride} \xrightarrow{\text{heat}} \text{ammonia} + \text{hydrogen chloride}$$
$$NH_4Cl \longrightarrow NH_3 + HCl$$

The two gases rise up the test tube. When they cool down near the mouth of the tube they react with each other. The gases re-form ammonium chloride again. The white solid forms on the inside of the glass:

$$\text{ammonia} + \text{hydrogen chloride} \rightarrow \text{ammonium chloride}$$
$$NH_3 + HCl \rightarrow NH_4Cl$$

We can show the reversible reactions as:

$$\text{ammonium chloride} \rightleftharpoons \text{ammonia} + \text{hydrogen chloride}$$
$$NH_4Cl \rightleftharpoons NH_3 + HCl$$

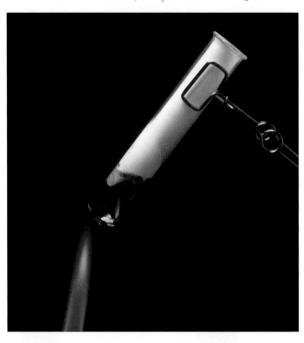

Figure 2 An example of a reversible reaction:

$$\text{ammonium chloride} \rightleftharpoons \text{ammonia} + \text{hydrogen chloride}$$
$$NH_4Cl \rightleftharpoons NH_3 + HCl$$

Summary questions

1 What do we mean by 'a *reversible* chemical reaction'?

2 Phenolphthalein is an indicator. It is colourless in acid and pure water but is pink-purple in alkali. In a demonstration a teacher started with a beaker containing a mixture of water and phenolphthalein. In two other beakers she had different volumes of acid and alkali. The acid and alkali had the same concentration.

   She then poured the mixture into the beaker containing $2\,cm^3$ of sodium hydroxide solution. Finally she poured the mixture into a third beaker with $5\,cm^3$ of hydrochloric acid in it.

   Describe what you would observe happen in the demonstration.

3 We can represent the phenolphthalein indicator as HPhe. Assuming it behaves like litmus, write a symbol equation to show its reversible reaction in acid and alkali. Show the colour of HPhe and Phe⁻ under their formulae in your equation.

Key points

● In a reversible reaction the products of the reaction can react to make the original reactants.

● We can show a reversible reaction using the $\rightleftharpoons$ sign.

C2 3.7

Analysing substances

For hundreds of years we have added salt to food to preserve it. Nowadays, food technologists develop ways to improve the quality of foods. They also analyse foods to ensure they meet legal safety standards.

We call a substance that is added to food to extend its shelf life or to improve its taste or appearance a food additive. Additives that have been approved for use in Europe are given E numbers. The E numbers are like a code to identify the additives. For example, E102 is a yellow food colouring called tartrazine.

a What is a food additive?

Detecting additives

Scientists have many instruments that they can use to identify unknown compounds, including food additives. Many of these are more sensitive, automated versions of techniques we use in school labs.

One technique that is used to identify food additives is paper **chromatography**. It works because some compounds in a mixture dissolve better than others in particular solvents. Their solubility determines how far they travel across the paper.

Figure 1 Modern foods contain a variety of additives to improve their taste or appearance, and to make them keep longer

---

Practical

Detecting dyes in food colourings

Make a chromatogram to analyse various food colourings.

- What can you deduce from your chromatogram?

Figure 2 The technique of paper chromatography that we use in schools. Techniques used to identify food additives are often based on the same principles as the simple tests we do in the school science lab.

Figure 3 A few years ago a batch of red food colouring was found to be contaminated with a chemical suspected of causing cancer. This dye had found its way into hundreds of processed foods. All of these had to be removed from the shelves of our supermarkets and destroyed.

b What happens to the food colourings when you make a paper chromatogram?

Once the compounds in a food have been separated using chromatography, they can be identified. We can compare the chromatogram with others obtained from known substances. For this we must use the same solvent at the same temperature.

Instrumental methods

Many industries need rapid and accurate methods for analysing their products. They use modern instrumental analysis for this task.

Instrumental techniques are also important in fighting pollution. Careful monitoring of the environment using sensitive instruments is now common. This type of analysis is also used all the time in health care.

Modern instrumental methods have a number of benefits over older methods:

● they are highly accurate and sensitive

● they are quicker

● they enable very small samples to be analysed.

Against this, the main disadvantages of using instrumental methods are that the equipment:

● is usually very expensive

● takes special training to use

● gives results that can often be interpreted only by comparison with data from known substances.

c What do you think has aided the development of instrumental methods of chemical analysis?

d Why are these methods important?

∞ links

For more information on the instruments used by chemists to analyse substances, see C2 3.8 Instrumental analysis.

AQA **Examiner's tip**

Although simpler to use than bench chemistry methods, instrumental methods still need trained technicians to operate them.

Figure 4 Compared with the methods of 50 years ago, modern instrumental methods of analysis are quick, accurate and sensitive – three big advantages. They also need far fewer people to carry out the analysis than traditional laboratory analysis.

Summary questions

1 Copy and complete using the words below:

additives   paper   analyse   identify

Food scientists can .... different foods to see what .... have been used. For example, food colourings can be detected by .... chromatography. They can use results from known compounds to positively .... them.

2 a Carry out a survey of some processed foods. Identify some examples of food additives and explain why they have been used.

b Describe how we can separate the dyes in a food colouring and identify them.

3 What are the main advantages and disadvantages of using instrumental analysis compared with traditional practical methods?

Key points

● Additives may be added to food in order to improve its appearance, taste and how long it will keep (its shelf life).

● Food scientists can analyse foods to identify additives, e.g. by using paper chromatography.

● Modern instrumental techniques provide fast, accurate and sensitive ways of analysing chemical substances.

C2 3.8

Instrumental analysis

Learning objectives

- How can we use gas chromatography to separate compounds in a sample mixture?

- How can we use a mass spectrometer to identify the compounds in the sample?

Analysing mixtures

Samples to be analysed are often mixtures of different compounds. So the first step is to separate the compounds. Then they can be identified using one of the many instrumental techniques available. Chemists have developed a technique called gas chromatography–mass spectrometry (GC–MS) to do this task.

- Firstly, they use **gas chromatography** to separate compounds that are easily vaporised.

- Then the separated compounds pass into another instrument – the **mass spectrometer**, which can identify each of them. The mass spectrometer is useful for identifying both elements and compounds. The pattern of peaks it produces identifies the sample.

Gas chromatography

This separation technique is similar to paper chromatography. However, instead of a solvent moving over paper, it has a gas moving through a column packed with a solid.

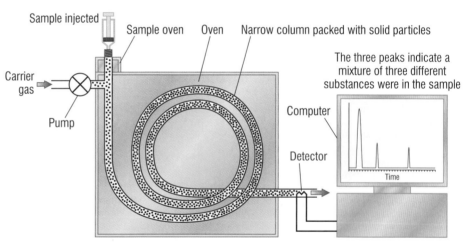

Figure 1 This is the apparatus used in gas chromatography. The solid in the column can be coated in a liquid and is sometimes then known as gas–liquid chromatography.

- First of all, the sample mixture is vaporised.
- A 'carrier' gas moves the vapour through the coiled column.
- The compounds in the sample have different attractions to the material in the column. The compounds with stronger attractions will take longer to get through the column. We say that they have a longer **retention time**.
- The compounds with weak attractions to the material in the column leave it first. They have shorter retention times.

The separated compounds can be recorded on a chart as they leave the column. Look at Figure 2 to see a gas chromatograph.

We can identify the unknown substances in the sample by comparing the chromatograph with the results for known substances. The analysis must have taken place in exactly the same conditions to compare retention times.

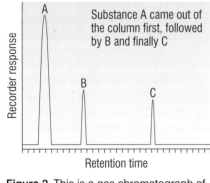

Figure 2 This is a gas chromatograph of a mixture of three different substances. There was more of substance A than B or C in the sample mixture.

Mass spectrometry

To ensure that we identify the unknown substances the gas chromatography apparatus can be attached directly to a **mass spectrometer.** This identifies substances very quickly and accurately and can detect very small quantities in the sample.

Measuring relative molecular masses

A mass spectrometer also provides an accurate way of measuring the relative molecular (formula) mass of a compound. The peak with the largest mass corresponds to an ion with just one electron removed. As you know, the mass of an electron is so small that it can be ignored when we look at the mass of atoms. This peak is called the **molecular ion peak**. It is always found as the last peak on the right as you look at a mass spectrum. The molecular ion peak of the substance analysed in Figure 3 is at 45. So the substance has a relative molecular mass of 45.

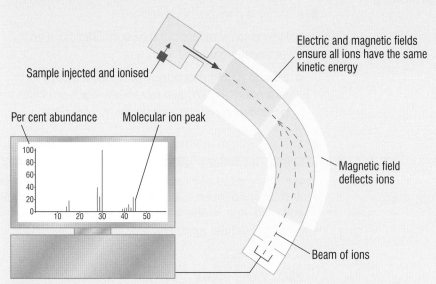

Figure 3 The pattern of peaks (called the mass spectrum) acts like a 'fingerprint' for unknown compounds. The pattern is quickly matched against a database of known compounds stored on computer.
NB You don't need to remember the details of how a mass spectrometer works.

Summary questions

1 Copy and complete using the words below:

chromatography   database   mass   mixture   fingerprint

Separating a .... of compounds can be carried out by gas .... Identifying compounds once they have been separated then uses techniques like .... spectrometry. The pattern of peaks is like a .... for each unknown compound. It is matched against known compounds on a computer ....

2 Describe how a mass spectrometer can be used to find the relative molecular mass of a compound [H]

Key points

- Compounds in a mixture can be separated using gas chromatography.

- Once separated, compounds can be identified using a mass spectrometer.

- The mass spectrometer can be used to find the relative molecular mass of a compound from its molecular ion peak. [H]

Summary questions

1 Match up the parts of the sentences:

a	Neutrons have a relative mass of …	A	… negligible mass compared to protons and neutrons.
b	Electrons have …	B	… 1 compared to protons.
c	Protons have a relative mass of …	C	… found in its nucleus.
d	Nearly all of an atom's mass is …	D	… 1 compared to neutrons.

2 Calculate the mass of 1 mole of each of the following compounds:

a H_2O

b CH_4

c MnO_2

d Al_2O_3

e K_2CO_3

f $KMnO_4$

g $Mn(OH)_2$

(A_r values: C = 12, O = 16, Al = 27, H = 1, Ca = 40, K = 39, Mn = 55)

3 How many moles of:

a Ag atoms are there in 108 g of silver,

b P atoms are there in 93 g of phosphorus,

c Ag atoms are there in 27 g of silver,

d P atoms are there in 6.2 g of phosphorus,

e Fe atoms are there in 0.56 g of iron,

f P_4 molecules are there in 6.2 g of phosphorus?

(A_r values: Ag = 108, P = 31, Fe = 56)

4 a The chemical formula of methane is CH_4. Use the relative atomic masses in question 2 to work out the percentage by mass of carbon in methane.

b In 32 g of methane, work out the mass of hydrogen present in the compound.

5 When aluminium reacts with bromine, 4.05 g of aluminium reacts with 36.0 g of bromine. What is the empirical formula of aluminium bromide?

(A_r values: Al = 27, Br = 80) **[H]**

6 In a lime kiln, calcium carbonate is decomposed to calcium oxide:

$$CaCO_3 \rightarrow CaO + CO_2$$

50.0 tonnes of calcium carbonate gave 26.6 tonnes of calcium oxide. Calculate the percentage yield for the process.

(A_r values: Ca = 40, O = 16, C = 12) **[H]**

7 a What is a reversible reaction?

b How does a reversible reaction differ from an 'ordinary' reaction?

c Ethene (C_2H_4) reacting with steam (H_2O) to form ethanol (C_2H_5OH) is a reversible reaction. Write the balanced symbol equation for this reaction.

8 Sulfur is mined in Poland and is brought to Britain in ships. The sulfur is used to make sulfuric acid. Sulfur is burned in air to produce sulfur dioxide. Sulfur dioxide and air are passed over a heated catalyst to produce sulfur trioxide. Water is added to sulfur trioxide to produce sulfuric acid. The reactions are:

$$S + O_2 \rightleftharpoons SO_2$$
$$2SO_2 + O_2 \rightleftharpoons 2SO_3$$
$$SO_3 + H_2O \rightarrow H_2SO_4$$

Relative atomic masses: H = 1; O = 16; S = 32

a How many moles of sulfuric acid are produced from one mole of sulfur?

b Calculate the maximum mass of sulfuric acid that can be produced from 32 kg of sulfur.

c In an industrial process the mass of sulfuric acid that was produced from 32 kg of sulfur was 94.08 kg. Use your answer to part b to calculate the percentage yield of this process.

d Suggest two reasons why the yield of the industrial process was less than the maximum yield.

e Give two reasons why the industrial process should produce a yield that is as close to the maximum yield as possible. **[H]**

AQA Examination-style questions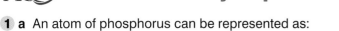

1 a An atom of phosphorus can be represented as:

$$^{31}_{15}P$$

  i What is the number of protons in this atom of phosphorus? (1)
  ii What is the number of neutrons in this atom of phosphorus? (1)
  iii What are the number of electrons in this atom of phosphorus? (1)

b A different atom of phosphorus can be represented as:

$$^{32}_{15}P$$

  i What are these two atoms of phosphorus known as? (1)
  ii Give one way in which these two atoms of phosphorus are different. (1)

2 Toothpastes often contain fluoride ions to help protect teeth from attack by bacteria.

Some toothpastes contain tin(II) fluoride.

This compound has the formula SnF_2.

a Calculate the relative formula mass (M_r) of SnF_2.

(Relative atomic masses: F = 19; Sn = 119) (2)

b Calculate the percentage by mass of fluorine in SnF_2. (2)

c A tube of toothpaste contains 1.2 g of SnF_2. Calculate the mass of fluorine in this tube of toothpaste. (1)

AQA, 2008

3 The diagram shows what happens when ammonium chloride is heated.

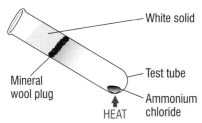

The reaction that takes place is:

$NH_4Cl(s) \rightleftharpoons NH_3(g) + HCl(g)$

a What does $\rightleftharpoons$ in the equation mean? (1)

b Explain why the white solid appears near the top of the test tube. (2)

4 The diagram shows the main parts of an instrumental method called gas chromatography linked to mass spectroscopy (GC–MS).

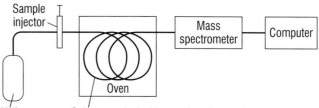

This method separates a mixture of compounds and then helps to identify each of the compounds in the mixture.

a In which part of the apparatus:
  i is the mixture separated? (1)
  ii is the relative molecular mass of each of the compounds in the mixture measured? (1)
  iii are the results of the experiment recorded? (1)

b i Athletes sometimes take drugs because the drugs improve their performance. One of these drugs is ephedrine.
    Ephedrine has the formula:
    $C_{10}H_{15}NO$
    What relative molecular mass (M_r) would be recorded by GC–MS if ephedrine was present in a blood sample taken from an athlete?
    Show clearly how you work out your answer.
    (Relative atomic masses: H = 1; C = 12; N = 14; O = 16.) (2)

  ii Another drug is amphetamine, which has the formula: $C_9H_{13}N$
    The relative molecular mass (M_r) of amphetamine is 135.
    Calculate the percentage by mass of nitrogen in amphetamine. (Relative atomic mass: N = 14.) (2)

c Athletes are regularly tested for drugs at international athletics events. An instrumental method such as GC–MS is better than methods such as titration. Suggest why. (2)

AQA, 2010

5 A chemist thought a liquid hydrocarbon was hexane, C_6H_{14}.

Relative atomic masses: H = 1; C = 12

a Calculate the percentage of carbon in hexane. (2)

b The chemist analysed the liquid hydrocarbon and found that it contained 85.7% carbon. Calculate the empirical formula of the hydrocarbon based on this result. You must show your working to gain full marks. (4)

c Was the liquid hydrocarbon hexane? Explain your answer. [H] (1)

C2 4.1

How fast?

Learning objectives

● What do we mean by the rate of a chemical reaction?

● How can we find out the rate of a chemical reaction?

Figure 1 All living things depend on very precise control of the many chemical reactions happening inside their cells

The rate of a chemical reaction tells us how fast reactants turn into products. In your body, there are lots of reactions taking place all the time. They happen at rates which supply your cells with what they need, whenever required.

Reaction rate is also very important in the chemical industry. Any industrial process has to make money by producing useful products. This means we must make the amount of product needed as cheaply as possible. If it takes too long to produce, it will be hard to make a profit when it is sold. The rate of the reaction must be fast enough to make it quickly and safely.

a What do we mean by the *rate* of a chemical reaction?

b Why is understanding the rate of reactions so important in industry?

How can we find out the rate of reactions?

Reactions happen at all sorts of different rates. Some are really fast, such as a firework exploding. Others are very slow, such as a piece of iron rusting.

There are two ways we can work out the rate of a chemical reaction. We can find out how quickly the reactants are used up as they make products. Or we can find out how quickly the products of the reaction are made.

Here are three ways we can make these kinds of measurement.

Practical

Measuring the decreasing mass of a reaction mixture

We can measure the rate at which the *mass* of a reaction mixture changes if the reaction gives off a gas. As the reaction takes place, the mass of the reaction mixture decreases. We can measure and record the mass at time intervals which we decide.

Some balances can be attached to a computer to monitor the loss in mass continuously.

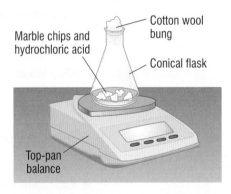

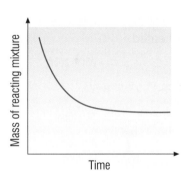

● Why is the cotton wool placed in the neck of the conical flask?

● How would the line on the graph differ if you plot 'Loss in mass' on the vertical axis?

Safety: Wear eye protection.

Practical

Measuring the increasing volume of gas given off

If a reaction produces a gas, we can use the gas to find out the rate of reaction. We do this by collecting the gas and measuring its volume at time intervals.

● What are the sources of error when measuring the volume of gas?

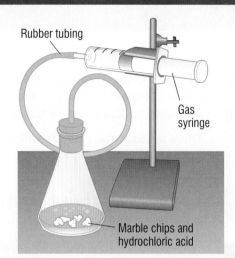

Rubber tubing

Gas syringe

Marble chips and hydrochloric acid

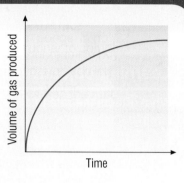

Practical

Measuring the decreasing light passing through a solution

Some reactions in solution make an insoluble solid (precipitate). This makes the solution go cloudy. We can use this to measure the rate at which the solid appears.

The reaction is set up in a flask. Under the flask, we put on a piece of paper marked with a cross. Then we can record the time taken for the cross to disappear. The shorter the time, the faster the reaction rate.

Or we can use a light sensor and data logger. Then we measure the amount of light that passes through the solution, as the graph shows.

● What are the advantages of using a light sensor rather than the 'disappearing cross' method?

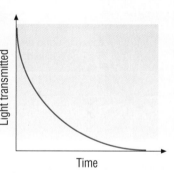

We can summarise these methods of working out the rate of a reaction using this equation:

$$\text{Rate of reaction} = \frac{\text{amount of reactant used or amount of product formed}}{\text{time}}$$

Summary questions

1 Copy and complete using the words below:

products   rate   time   reactants   slope

Measuring the amount of .... which are used up over time or the amount of .... made over time are two ways of finding out the .... of a reaction. The .... of the lines on graphs drawn from these experiments tells us about the rate at any given ....

2 Sketch graphs to show the results of:
   a i   measuring the mass of products formed in a reaction over time.
     ii   measuring the mass of reactants used up in a reaction over time.
   b What does the slope of the graphs at any particular time in part **a** tell us about the reaction?

Key points

● We can find out the rate of a chemical reaction by following the amount of reactants used up over time.

● Alternatively, we can find out the rate of reaction by following the amount of products made over time.

● The slope of the line at any given time on the graphs drawn from such experiments tells us the rate of reaction at that time. The steeper the slope, the faster the reaction.

C2 4.2

Collision theory and surface area

Learning objectives

- What affects the rate of a chemical reaction?
- What is collision theory?
- How does collision theory explain the effect of surface area on reaction rate?

Figure 1 There is no doubt that the chemicals in these fireworks have reacted. But how can we explain what happens in a chemical reaction?

In everyday life we control the rates of chemical reactions. People often do it without knowing! For example, cooking cakes in an oven or revving up a car engine. In chemistry we need to know what affects the rate of reactions. We also need to explain why each factor affects the rate of a reaction.

There are four main factors which affect the rate of chemical reactions:

- temperature
- surface area
- concentration of solutions or pressure of gases
- presence of a catalyst.

Reactions can only take place when the particles (atoms, ions or molecules) of reactants come together. But the reacting particles don't just have to bump into each other. They also need enough energy to react when they collide. This is known as **collision theory**.

The smallest amount of energy that particles must have before they can react is called the **activation energy**.

So reactions are more likely to happen between reactant particles if we:

- increase the chance of reacting particles colliding with each other
- increase the energy that they have when they collide.

If we increase the chance of particles reacting, we will also increase the rate of reaction.

> **a** What must happen before two particles have a chance of reacting?
> **b** Particles must have a minimum amount of energy to be able to react. What is this energy called?

Surface area and reaction rate

Imagine lighting a campfire. You don't pile large logs together and try to set them alight. You use small pieces of wood to begin with. Doing this increases the surface area of the wood. This means there is more wood exposed to react with oxygen in the air.

When a solid reacts in a solution, the size of the pieces of solid affects the rate of the reaction. The particles inside a large lump of solid are not in contact with the solution, so they can't react. The particles inside the solid have to wait for the particles on the surface to react first.

In smaller lumps, or in a powder, each tiny piece of solid is surrounded by solution. More particles are exposed to attack. This means that reactions can take place much more quickly.

> **c** Which has the larger surface area – a log or the same mass of small pieces of wood?
> **d** How does the surface area of a solid affect its rate of reaction?

Figure 2 Cooking – an excellent example of controlling reaction rates!

Practical

Which burns faster?

Make sure you have a heatproof mat under the Bunsen burner and you must wear eye protection.

Try igniting a 2cm length of magnesium ribbon and time how long it takes to burn.

Take a small spatula tip of magnesium powder and sprinkle it into the Bunsen flame.

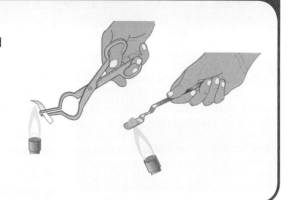

- What safety precautions should you take in this experiment?
- Explain your observations.

Practical

Investigating the effect of surface area

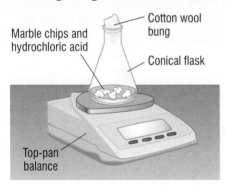

Marble chips and hydrochloric acid — Cotton wool bung — Conical flask — Top-pan balance

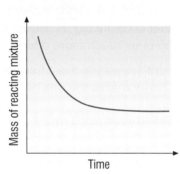

Mass of reacting mixture vs Time

In this investigation you will be measuring the mass lost against time for different sizes of marble (calcium carbonate) chips. You need at least two different sizes of marble chips in order to vary the surface area.

- What variables should you control to make this a fair test?
- Why does this method of finding out the rate of reaction work?
- Use the data collected to draw a graph. Explain what the graph shows. (A data logger would help to plot a graph of the results.)

Safety: Wear eye protection.

Key points

- Particles must collide, with a certain amount of energy, before they can react.

- The minimum amount of energy that particles must have in order to react is called the activation energy.

- The rate of a chemical reaction increases if the surface area of any solid reactants is increased. This increases the frequency of collisions between reacting particles.

Summary questions

1 Copy and complete using the words below:

   energy   activation   collide   frequently   minimum

   Particles can react with each other only when they .... with sufficient .... Reaction rates increase when collisions are more energetic and/or happen more .... The .... amount of energy needed for particles to react is known as the .... energy.

2 Draw a diagram to explain why it is easier to light a fire using small pieces of wood rather than large logs.

3 Why do you digest your food more quickly if you chew it well before you swallow it?

C2 4.3

The effect of temperature

Learning objectives

- How does increasing the temperature affect the rate of reactions?

- How does collision theory explain this effect?

When we increase the temperature, it always increases the rate of reaction. We can use fridges and freezers to reduce the temperature and slow down the rate of reactions. When food goes off it is because of chemical reactions. Reducing the temperature slows down these reactions.

Collision theory tells us why raising the temperature increases the rate of a reaction. There are two reasons:

- particles collide more often
- particles collide with more energy.

Particles collide more often

When we heat up a substance, energy is transferred to its particles. In solutions and in gases, this means that the particles move around faster. And when particles move faster they collide more often. Imagine a lot of people walking around in the school playground blindfolded. They may bump into each other occasionally. However, if they start running around, they will bump into each other much more often.

When particles collide more frequently, there are more chances for them to react. This increases the rate of reaction.

Particles collide with more energy

Particles that are moving around more quickly have more energy. This means that any collisions they have are much more energetic. It's like two people colliding when they're running rather than when they are walking.

When we increase the temperature of a reacting mixture, a higher proportion of the collisions will result in a reaction taking place. This is because a higher proportion of particles have energy greater than the activation energy. This second factor has a greater effect on rate than the increased frequency of collisions.

Around room temperature, if we increase the temperature of a reaction by 10 °C the rate of the reaction will roughly double.

Figure 1 Lowering the temperature will slow down the reactions that make foods go off

Figure 2 Moving faster means it's more likely that you'll bump into someone else – and the collision will be harder too!

a Why does increasing the temperature increase the rate of a reaction?

b How much does a 10 °C rise in temperature increase reaction rate at room temperature?

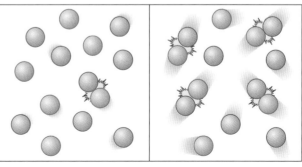

Cold – slow movement, few collisions, little energy

Hot – fast movement, more collisions, more energy

Figure 3 More frequent collisions, with more energy – both of these factors increase the rate of a chemical reaction caused by increasing the temperature

Practical

The effect of temperature on rate of reaction

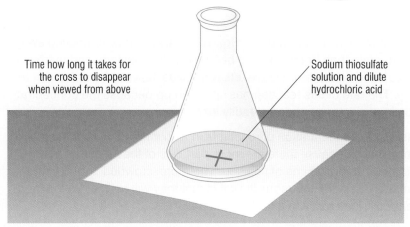

Time how long it takes for the cross to disappear when viewed from above

Sodium thiosulfate solution and dilute hydrochloric acid

When we react sodium thiosulfate solution and hydrochloric acid it makes sulfur. The sulfur is insoluble in water. This makes the solution go cloudy. We can record the length of time it takes for the solution to go cloudy at different temperatures.

- Which variables do you have to control to make this a fair test?
- Why is it difficult to get accurate timings by eye in this investigation?
- How can you improve the **precision** of the data you collect?

Safety: Wear eye protection. Take care if you are an asthmatic.

The results of an investigation like this can be plotted on a graph (see opposite).

The graph shows how the time for the solution to go cloudy changes with temperature.

c What happens to the time it takes the solution to go cloudy as the temperature increases?

Maths skills

As one goes up, the other comes down

In the experiment opposite we can measure the time for an X to disappear as a precipitate forms. This means that the longer the time, the slower the rate of reaction. There is an inverse relationship between time and rate. So as time increases, rate decreases. We say the rate is proportional to 1/time (also written as $time^{-1}$). Therefore, we can plot a graph of temperature against 1/time to investigate the effect of temperature on rate of reaction. [H]

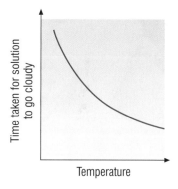

Summary questions

1 Copy and complete using the words below:

   chemical collide decreases doubles energy off quickly rate reducing rise

   When we increase the temperature of a reacting mixture, we increase its .... of reaction. The higher temperature makes the particles move more .... so they .... more often and the collisions have more .... At room temperature, a temperature .... of about 10°C roughly .... the reaction rate. This explains why we use fridges and freezers. .... the temperature .... the rate of the .... reactions which make food go ....

2 Water in a pressure cooker boils at a much higher temperature than water in a saucepan because it is under pressure. Why does food take longer to cook in a pan than it does in a pressure cooker?

Key points

- Reactions happen more quickly as the temperature increases.

- Increasing the temperature increases the rate of reaction because particles collide more frequently and more energetically. More of the collisions result in a reaction because a higher proportion of particles have energy greater than the activation energy.

C2 4.4

The effect of concentration or pressure (k)

Learning objectives

- How does increasing the concentration of reactants in solutions affect the rate of reaction?

- How does increasing the pressure of reacting gases affect the rate of reaction?

Some of our most beautiful buildings are made of limestone or marble. These buildings have stood for centuries. However, they are now crumbling away at a greater rate than before. This is because both limestone and marble are mainly calcium carbonate. This reacts with acids, leaving the stone soft and crumbly. The rate of this reaction has speeded up because the concentration of acids in rainwater has been steadily increasing.

Increasing the concentration of reactants in a solution increases the rate of reaction. That's because there are more particles of the reactants moving around in the same volume of solution. The more 'crowded' together the reactant particles are, the more likely it is that they will collide. So the more frequent collisions result in a faster reaction.

Increasing the pressure of reacting gases has the same effect. It squashes the gas particles more closely together. We have more particles of gas in a given space. This increases the chance that they will collide and react. So increasing the pressure speeds up the rate of the reaction.

a Why does increasing concentration or pressure increase reaction rate?

Figure 1 Limestone statues are damaged by acid rain. This damage happens more quickly as the concentration of the acids in rainwater increases.

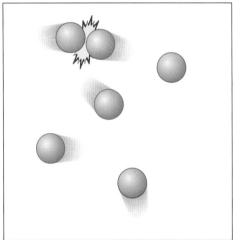

Low concentration/ low pressure

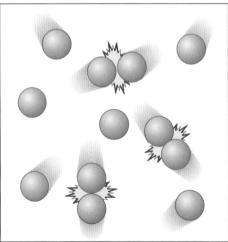

High concentration/ high pressure

Figure 2 Increasing concentration and pressure both mean that particles are closer together. This increases the frequency of collisions between particles, so the reaction rate increases.

Practical

Investigating the effect of concentration on rate of reaction

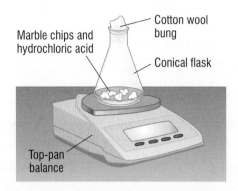

Cotton wool bung

Marble chips and hydrochloric acid

Conical flask

Top-pan balance

We can investigate the effect of changing concentration by reacting marble chips with different concentrations of hydrochloric acid:

$$CaCO_3 + 2HCl \rightarrow CaCl_2 + CO_2 + H_2O$$

We can find the rate of reaction by plotting the mass of the reaction mixture over time. The mass will decrease as carbon dioxide gas is given off in the reaction.

● How do you make this a fair test?

● What conclusion can you draw from your results?

Safety: Wear eye protection.

If we plot the results of an investigation like the one above on a graph they look like the graph opposite:

The graph shows how the mass of the reaction mixture decreases over time at three different concentrations.

b Which line on the graph shows the fastest reaction? How can you tell?

AQA **Examiner's tip**

Increasing concentration or pressure does not increase the energy with which the particles collide. However, it does increase the frequency of collisions.

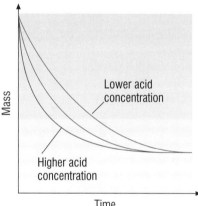

Mass

Lower acid concentration

Higher acid concentration

Time

Summary questions

1 Copy and complete using the words below:

collisions   concentration   faster   frequency   number   pressure
rate   volume

The .... of a reaction is affected by the .... of reactants in solutions and by the .... if the reactants are gases. Both of these tell us the .... of particles that there are in a certain .... of the reaction mixture. Increasing these will increase the .... of .... between reacting particles, making .... reactions.

2 Acidic cleaners are designed to remove limescale when they are used neat. They do not work as well when they are diluted. Using your knowledge of collision theory, explain why this is.

3 You could also follow the reaction in the Practical box above by measuring the volume of gas given off over time. Sketch a graph of volume of gas against time for three different concentrations. Label the three lines as high, medium and low concentration.

Key points

● Increasing the concentration of reactants in solutions increases the frequency of collisions between particles, and so increases the rate of reaction.

● Increasing the pressure of reacting gases also increases the frequency of collisions and so increases the rate of reaction.

C2 4.5 The effect of catalysts ⓚ

Learning objectives

- What is a catalyst?
- How do catalysts affect the rate of reactions?

Figure 1 Catalysts are all around us, in the natural world and in industry. The catalysts in living things are called enzymes. Our planet would be very different without catalysts.

Sometimes a reaction might only work if we use very high temperatures or pressures. This can cost industry a lot of money. However, we can speed up some reactions by using **catalysts**.

   a Apart from using a catalyst, how can we speed up a reaction?

A catalyst is a substance which increases the rate of a reaction. However, it is not changed chemically itself at the end of the reaction.

A catalyst is not used up in the reaction. So it can be used over and over again.

We need different catalysts for different reactions. Many of the catalysts we use in industry involve transition metals. For example, iron is used to make ammonia. Platinum is used to make nitric acid.

   b How is a catalyst affected by a chemical reaction?

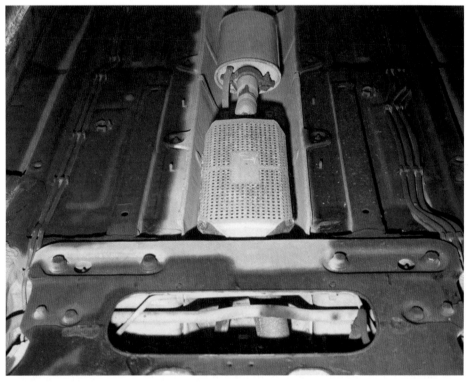

Figure 2 The transition metals platinum and palladium are used in the catalytic converters in cars

We normally use catalysts in the form of powders, pellets or fine gauzes. This gives them the biggest possible surface area.

   c Why is a catalyst in the form of pellets more effective than a whole lump of the catalyst?

Not only does a catalyst speed up a reaction, but it does not get used up in the reaction. We can use a tiny amount of catalyst to speed up a reaction over and over again.

Practical

Investigating catalysis (k)

Rubber tubing

Gas syringe

Hydrogen peroxide solution and catalyst

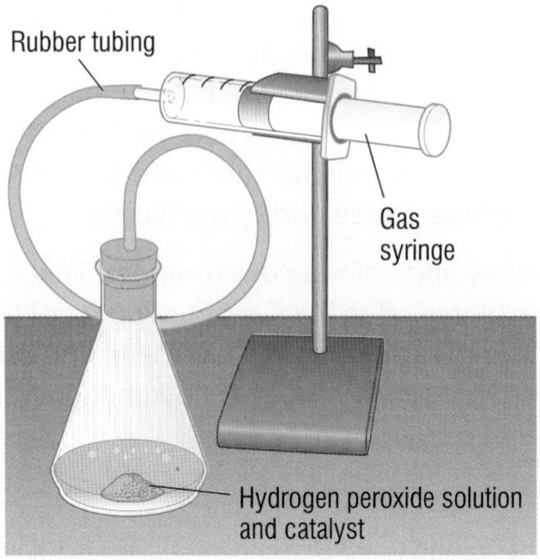

Figure 3 This catalyst is used in the form of pellets to give the largest possible surface area.

We can investigate the effect of different catalysts on the rate of a reaction. We will look at hydrogen peroxide solution decomposing:

$$2H_2O_2 \rightarrow 2H_2O + O_2$$

The reaction produces oxygen gas. We can collect this in a gas syringe using the apparatus shown above.

We can investigate the effect of many different substances on the rate of this reaction. Examples include manganese(IV) oxide and potassium iodide.

- State the independent variable in this investigation.

A table of the time taken to produce a certain volume of oxygen can then tell us which catalyst makes the reaction go fastest.

- What type of graph would you use to show the results of your investigation? Why?

Safety: Wear eye protection.

Summary questions

1 Copy and complete using the words below:

remains   increases   reaction   used

A catalyst .... the rate of a chemical reaction. However, it is not .... up and .... the same chemically after the ....

2 Solid catalysts used in chemical processes are often shaped as tiny beads or cylinders with holes through them. Why are they made in these shapes?

3 Why is the number of moles of catalyst needed to speed up a chemical reaction very small compared with the number of moles of reactants?

Key points

- A catalyst speeds up the rate of a chemical reaction.

- A catalyst is not used up during a chemical reaction.

- Different catalysts are needed for different reactions.

C2 4.6

Catalysts in action

Learning objectives

- Why are catalysts used in so many industrial processes?

- How are new catalysts developed and why are there so many different catalysts?

- What are the disadvantages of using catalysts in industry?

Catalysts are often very expensive precious metals. Gold, platinum and palladium are all costly but are the most effective catalysts for particular reactions. But it is often cheaper to use a catalyst than to pay for the extra energy needed without one. To get the same rate of reaction without a catalyst would require higher temperatures and/or pressures.

So catalysts save money and help the environment. That's because using high temperatures and pressures often involves burning fossil fuels. So operating at lower temperatures and pressures conserves these non-renewable resources. It also stops more carbon dioxide entering the atmosphere.

a Why do catalysts save a chemical company money?

However, many of the catalysts used in industry are transition metals or their compounds. These are often toxic. If they escape into the environment, they build up inside living things. Eventually they poison them. For example, the platinum and palladium used in catalytic converters slowly escape from car exhausts.

So chemists are working to develop new catalysts that are harmless to the environment. The search for the ideal catalyst is often a bit like trial and error. Each reaction is unique. Once a catalyst is found it might be improved by adding small amounts of other chemicals to it. All this takes a lot of time to investigate. However, the research is guided by knowledge of similar catalysed reactions. This knowledge is growing all the time.

Figure 1 Chinese scientists have recently developed a new catalyst for making biodiesel from vegetable oils. It's made from shrimp shells, and is cheaper and more efficient than conventional catalysts. The process that uses the new catalyst also causes less pollution.

Future development

Chemists have developed new techniques to look at reactions. They can now follow the reactions that happen on the surface of the metals in a catalytic converter. These are very fast reactions lasting only a fraction of a second. Knowing how the reactions take place will help them to design new catalysts.

Nanoparticles are also at the cutting edge of work on new catalysts. Scientists can arrange atoms into the best shapes for catalysing a particular reaction they have studied. A small mass of these catalysts has a huge surface area. This has raised hopes that fuel cells will one day take over from petrol and diesel to run cars.

Catalysts in medicine

The catalysts used in making new drugs also contain precious metal compounds. The metal is bonded to an organic molecule. But now chemists can make these catalysts without the metal. The metal was needed to make a stable compound. However, research has resulted in a breakthrough which will mean much cheaper catalysts. There is also no risk of contaminating the drug made with a toxic transition metal.

b Why could it be unsafe to use compounds of transition metals to catalyse reactions to make drugs?

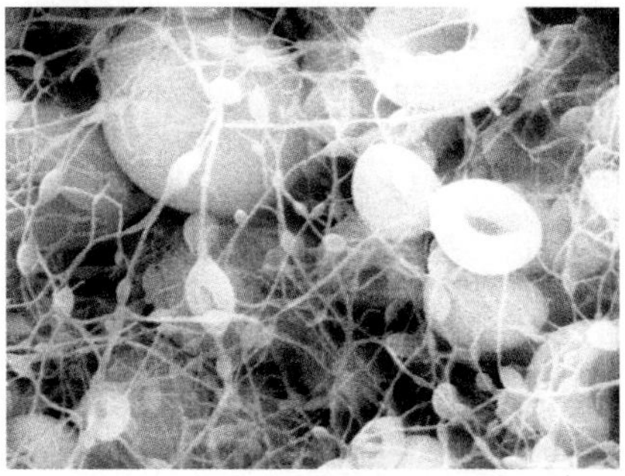

Enzymes

Enzymes are the very efficient catalysts found in living things. For years we've been using enzymes to help clean our clothes. Biological washing powders contain enzymes that help to 'break apart' stain molecules such as proteins at low temperatures. The low temperature washes save energy.

Low-temperature enzyme reactions are the basis of the biotechnology industry. Enzymes are soluble so would have to be separated from the products they make. However, scientists can bind them to a solid. The solution of reactants flows over the solid. No time or money has to be wasted separating out the enzymes to use again. The process can run continuously.

links

For information about nanoparticles, look back to C2 2.6 Nanoscience.

Figure 2 Scientists are developing long nanowires of platinum to use as catalysts in fuel cells. This photo is from an electron microscope. The wires are 1/50 000th of the width of a human hair. The breakthrough has been made in making them over a centimetre in length.

Key points

- Catalysts are used whenever possible in industry to increase rate of reaction and reduce energy costs.

- Traditional catalysts are often transition metals or their compounds, which can be toxic and harm the environment if they escape.

- Modern catalysts are being developed in industry which result in less waste and are safer for the environment.

Summary questions

1 Give two ways in which catalysts are beneficial to the chemical industry.

2 What are the disadvantages of using transition metals or their compounds as catalysts?

3 Do some research to find out four industrial processes that make products using catalysts. Write a word equation for each reaction and name the catalyst used.

Exothermic and endothermic reactions

Learning objectives

- How is energy involved in chemical reactions?
- How can we measure the energy transferred in a chemical reaction?

Whenever chemical reactions take place, energy is involved. That's because energy is always transferred as chemical bonds are broken and new ones are made.

Some reactions transfer energy **from** the reacting chemicals **to** their surroundings. We call these **exothermic** reactions. The energy transferred from the reacting chemicals often heats up the surroundings. This means that we can measure a rise in temperature as the reaction happens.

Some reactions transfer energy **from** the surroundings **to** the reacting chemicals. We call these **endothermic** reactions. As they take in energy from their surroundings, these reactions cause a drop in temperature as they happen.

a What do we call a reaction that releases energy to its surroundings?
b What do we call a reaction that absorbs energy from its surroundings?

Exothermic reactions

Fuels burning are an obvious example of exothermic reactions. For example, when methane (in natural gas) burns it gets oxidised and releases energy.

Respiration is a very special kind of oxidation. It involves reacting sugar with oxygen inside the cells of every living thing. The reaction produces water and carbon dioxide as waste products. Respiration is another exothermic reaction.

Neutralisation reactions between acids and alkalis are also exothermic. We can easily measure the rise in temperature using simple apparatus (see the practical on the next page).

c Give two examples of exothermic reactions.

Figure 1 When a fuel burns in oxygen, energy is transferred to the surroundings. We usually don't need a thermometer to know that there is a temperature change!

Figure 2 All warm-blooded animals rely on exothermic reactions to keep their body temperatures steady

Endothermic reactions

Endothermic reactions are much less common than exothermic ones.

Thermal decomposition reactions are endothermic. An example is the decomposition of calcium carbonate. When heated it forms calcium oxide and carbon dioxide. This reaction only takes place if we keep heating the calcium carbonate strongly. It takes in a great deal of energy from the surroundings.

d Give an example of an endothermic reaction.

Figure 3 When we eat sherbet we can feel an endothermic reaction. Sherbet dissolving in the water in your mouth takes in energy. It provides a slight cooling effect.

Practical

Investigating energy changes **k**

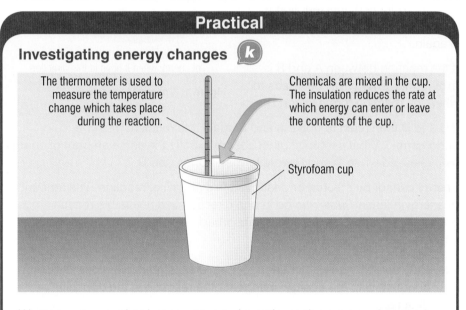

The thermometer is used to measure the temperature change which takes place during the reaction.

Chemicals are mixed in the cup. The insulation reduces the rate at which energy can enter or leave the contents of the cup.

Styrofoam cup

We can use very simple apparatus to investigate the energy changes in reactions. Often we don't need to use anything more complicated than a styrofoam cup and a thermometer.

● State two ways in which you could make the data you collect more accurate.

AQA **Examiner's tip**

Remember that exothermic reactions involve energy EXiting (leaving) the reacting chemicals, so the surroundings get hotter.

In endothermic reactions energy moves INTO (sounds like 'endo'!) the reacting chemicals, so the surroundings get colder.

Key points

● Energy may be transferred to or from the reacting substances in a chemical reaction.

● A reaction in which energy is transferred from the reacting substances to their surroundings is called an exothermic reaction.

● A reaction in which energy is transferred to the reacting substances from their surroundings is called an endothermic reaction.

Summary questions

1 Copy and complete using the words below:

endothermic exothermic changes neutralisation oxidation decomposition

Chemical reactions involve energy .... When a reaction releases energy we say that it is an .... reaction. Two important examples of this type of reaction are .... and .... When a reaction takes in energy we say that it is an .... reaction. An important example of this type of reaction is thermal ....

2 Potassium chloride dissolving in water is an endothermic process. What would you expect to observe when potassium chloride dissolves in a test tube of water?

C2 4.8

Energy and reversible reactions

Energy changes are involved in reversible reactions too. Let's consider an example.

Figure 1 shows a reversible reaction where A and B react to form C and D. The products of this reaction (C and D) can then react to form A and B again.

If the reaction between A and B is exothermic, energy will be released when the reaction forms C and D.

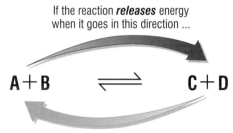

If the reaction **releases** energy when it goes in this direction ...

$$A + B \rightleftharpoons C + D$$

... it will **absorb** exactly the same amount of energy when it goes in this direction

Figure 1 A reversible reaction

If C and D then react to make A and B again, the reaction must be endothermic. What's more, it must absorb exactly the same amount of energy as it released when C and D were formed from A and B.

Energy cannot be created or destroyed in a chemical reaction. The amount of energy released when we go in one direction in a reversible reaction must be exactly the same as the energy absorbed when we go in the opposite direction.

> **a** How does the energy change for a reversible reaction in one direction compare with the energy change for the reaction in the opposite direction?

We can see how this works if we look at what happens when we heat blue copper sulfate crystals. The crystals contain water as part of the lattice formed when the copper sulfate crystallised. We say that the copper sulfate is **hydrated**. Heating the copper sulfate drives off the water from the crystals, producing white **anhydrous** ('without water') copper sulfate. This is an endothermic reaction.

$$CuSO_4 \cdot 5H_2O \rightleftharpoons CuSO_4 + 5H_2O$$

hydrated copper sulfate (blue) $\rightleftharpoons$ anhydrous copper sulfate (white) + water

When we add water to anhydrous copper sulfate we form hydrated copper sulfate. The colour change in the reaction is a useful test for water. The reaction in this direction is exothermic. In fact, so much energy may be produced that we may see steam rising as the water boils.

Figure 2 Hydrated copper sulfate and white anhydrous copper sulfate

Practical

Energy changes in a reversible reaction

Try these reactions yourself. Gently heat a few copper sulfate crystals in a test tube. Observe the changes. When the crystals are completely white allow the tube to cool to room temperature (this takes several minutes). Add two or three drops of water from a dropper and observe the changes. Carefully feel the bottom of the test tube.

● Explain the changes you have observed.

You can repeat this with the same solid, as it is a reversible reaction or try with other hydrated crystals, such as cobalt chloride. Some are not so colourful but the changes are similar.

Safety: Wear eye protection. Avoid skin contact with cobalt chloride.

Figure 3 Blue cobalt chloride paper turns pink when water is added

b What can anhydrous copper sulfate be used to test for?

We can soak filter paper in cobalt chloride solution and allow it to dry in an oven. The blue paper that is produced is called cobalt chloride paper. The paper turns pale pink when water is added to the paper.

c Why does blue cobalt chloride turn pink if left out in the open air?
d When water is added to blue cobalt chloride is energy released or absorbed?

Summary questions

1 A reversible reaction gives out 50 kilojoules (kJ) of energy in the forward reaction. In this reaction W and X react to give Y and Z.
   a Write an equation to show the reversible reaction.
   b What can you say about the energy transfer in the reverse reaction?

2 Blue cobalt chloride crystals turn pink when they become damp. The formula for the two forms can be written as $CoCl_2 \cdot 2H_2O$ and $CoCl_2 \cdot 6H_2O$.
   a How many moles of water will combine with 1 mole of $CoCl_2 \cdot 2H_2O$?
   b Write a balanced chemical equation for the reaction, which is reversible.   [H]
   c How can pink cobalt chloride crystals be changed back to blue cobalt chloride crystals?

Key points

● In reversible reactions, one reaction is exothermic and the other is endothermic.

● In any reversible reaction, the amount of energy released when the reaction goes in one direction is exactly equal to the energy absorbed when the reaction goes in the opposite direction.

C2 4.9

Using energy transfers from reactions

Learning objectives

- How can we use the energy from exothermic reactions?

- How can we use the cooling effect of endothermic reactions?

- What are the advantages and disadvantages of using exothermic and endothermic reactions in the uses described?

Practical

Crystallisation of a supersaturated solution

Dissolve 700 g of sodium ethanoate in 50 cm³ of hot water in a conical flask. Then let the solution cool to room temperature. Now add a small crystal of sodium ethanoate.

- What do you see happen? What does the outside of the flask feel like?

Figure 1 Here is a hand warmer based on the recrystallisation of sodium ethanoate

Warming up

Chemical hand and body warmers can be very useful. These products use exothermic reactions to warm you up. People can take hand warmers to places they know will get very cold. For example, spectators at outdoor sporting events in winter can warm their hands up. People usually use the body warmers to help ease aches and pains.

Some hand warmers can only be used one. An example of this type uses the oxidation of iron to release energy. Iron turns into hydrated iron(III) oxide in an exothermic reaction. The reaction is similar to rusting. Sodium chloride (common salt) is used as a catalyst. This type of hand warmer is disposable. It can be used only once but it lasts for hours.

Other hand warmers can be reused many times. These are based on the formation of crystals from solutions of a salt. The salt used is often sodium ethanoate. A supersaturated solution is prepared. We do this by dissolving as much of the salt as possible in hot water. The solution is then allowed to cool.

A small metal disc in the plastic pack is used to start the exothermic change. When you press this a few times small particles of metal are scraped off. These 'seed' (or start off) the crystallisation. The crystals spread throughout the solution, giving off energy. They work for about 30 minutes.

To reuse the warmer, you simply put the solid pack into boiling water to re-dissolve the crystals. When cool, the pack is ready to activate again.

a Common salt is used as a *catalyst* in some disposable hand warmers. What does this mean?

Exothermic reactions are also used in self-heating cans (see Figure 2). The reaction used to release the energy is usually:

calcium oxide + water → calcium hydroxide

You press a button in the base of the can. This breaks a seal and lets the water and calcium oxide mix. Coffee is available in these self-heating cans.

Development took years and cost millions of pounds. Even then, over a third of the can was taken up with the reactants to release energy. Also, in some early versions, the temperature of the coffee did not rise high enough in cold conditions.

b Which solid is usually used in the base of self-heating coffee cans?

Activity

Hot food

Mountaineers and explorers can take 'self-heating' foods with them on their journeys. One uses the energy released when calcium oxide reacts with water to heat the food.

Design a self-heating, disposable food container for stew.

- Draw a labelled diagram of your container and explain how it works.
- What are the safety issues involved in using your product?

Cooling down

Endothermic processes can be used to cool things down. For example, chemical cold packs usually contain ammonium nitrate and water. When ammonium nitrate dissolves it takes in energy from its surroundings, making them colder. These cold packs are used as emergency treatment for sports injuries. The coldness reduces swelling and numbs pain.

The ammonium nitrate and water (sometimes as a gel) are kept separate in the pack. When squeezed or struck the bag inside the water pack breaks releasing ammonium nitrate. The instant cold packs work for about 20 minutes.

They can only be used once but are ideal where there is no ice available to treat a knock or strain.

The same endothermic change can also be used to chill cans of drinks.

Figure 2 Development of this self-heating can in the USA took about 10 years. The pink circle on the can turns white when the coffee is hot enough. This takes 6–8 minutes.

Figure 3 Instant cold packs can be applied as soon as an injury occurs to minimise damage to the sportsperson

Summary questions

1 a Describe how a disposable hand warmer works.
  b Describe how a re-usable hand warmer works.
  c Give an advantage and a disadvantage of each type of hand warmer.
  d Name one use of an exothermic reaction in the food industry.

2 a Give two uses of endothermic changes.
  b Which endothermic change is often used in cold packs?

Key points

- Exothermic changes can be used in hand warmers and self-heating cans. Crystallisation of a supersaturated solution is used in reusable warmers. However, disposable, one-off warmers can give off heat for longer.

- Endothermic changes can be used in instant cold packs for sports injuries.

Summary questions

1. Select from A, B and C to show how the rate of each reaction, **a** to **d**, could be measured.

a	Gas evolved from reaction mixture	A	Measure mass
b	Mass of reaction mixture changes	B	Measure light transmitted
c	Precipitate produced	C	Measure volume
d	Colour of solution changes		

2. A student carried out a reaction in which she dropped a piece of magnesium ribbon in sulfuric acid with a concentration of 0.5 mol/dm³.

   a Suggest **one** way in which the student could measure the rate of this reaction.

   b i Suggest **three** ways in which the student could increase the rate of this reaction.

   ii Explain how each of these methods changes the rate of the reaction.

3. The following results show what happened when two students investigated the reaction of some marble chips with acid.

Time (minutes)	Investigation 1 Mass of gas produced (g)	Investigation 2 Mass of gas produced (g)
0	0.00	0.00
1	0.54	0.27
2	0.71	0.35
3	0.78	0.38
4	0.80	0.40
5	0.80	0.40

   a The students were investigating the effect of concentration on rate of reaction. How did the students get the data for their table above?

   b Plot a graph of these results with time on the x-axis.

   c After one minute, how does the rate of the reaction in Investigation 2 compare with the rate of reaction in Investigation 1?

   d How does the final mass of gas produced in Investigation 2 compare with that produced in Investigation 1?

   e From the results, what can you say about the concentration of the acids in Investigations 1 and 2?

4. 'When sherbet sweets dissolve in your mouth this is an endothermic process.' Devise an experiment to test your statement. Use words and diagrams to describe clearly what you would do.

5. Two chemicals are mixed and react endothermically. When the reaction has finished, the reaction mixture is allowed to stand until it has returned to its starting temperature.

   a Sketch a graph of temperature (y-axis) against time (x-axis) to show how the temperature of the reaction mixture changes.

   b Label the graph clearly and explain what is happening wherever you have shown the temperature is changing.

6. This student's account of an investigation into the effect of temperature on the rate of a reaction was found on the internet:

   I investigated the effect of temperature on the rate of a reaction. The reaction was between sodium thiosulfate and hydrochloric acid. I set up my apparatus as in this diagram.

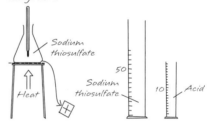

   The cross was put under the flask. I heated the sodium thiosulfate to the temperature I wanted and then added the hydrochloric acid to the flask. I immediately started the watch and timed how long it took for the cross to disappear.

   My results are below.

Temperature of the sodium thiosulfate	Time taken for the cross to disappear
15	110
30	40
45	21

   My conclusion is that the reaction goes faster the higher the temperature.

   a Suggest a suitable prediction for this investigation.

   b Describe one safety feature that is not mentioned in the method.

   c Suggest some ways in which this method could be improved. For each suggestion, say why it is an improvement.

   d Suggest how the table of results could be improved.

   e Despite all of the problems with this investigation, is the conclusion appropriate? Explain your answer.

AQA Examination-style questions

1 A glue is made by mixing together two liquids.

a When the liquids are mixed an exothermic reaction takes place. Complete the sentence below using a word or phrase from the list.

decrease   increase   stay the same

During the reaction the temperature of the mixture will

.... (1)

b The time taken for the glue to set at different temperatures is given in the table below.

Temperature (°C)	Time taken for the glue to set
20	3 days
60	6 hours
90	1 hour

Complete the sentences below using words or phrases from the list.

decreases   increases   stays the same

i When the temperature is increased the time taken for the glue to set .... (1)

ii When the temperature is increased the rate of the setting reaction .... (1)

c Which **two** of the following are reasons why an increase in temperature affects the rate of reaction?

It gives the particles more energy.

It increases the concentration of the particles.

It increases the surface area of the particles.

It makes the particles move faster. (2)

AQA, 2009

2 Instant cold packs are used to treat sports injuries.

One type of cold pack has a plastic bag containing water. Inside this bag is a smaller bag containing ammonium nitrate.

The outer bag is squeezed so that the inner bag bursts. The pack is shaken and quickly gets very cold as the ammonium nitrate dissolves in the water.

a Explain why the pack gets cold. (2)

b Suggest and explain why the pack is shaken after the inner bag has burst. (2)

AQA, 2008

3 A student reacted small pieces of zinc with dilute acid to make hydrogen gas. The graph shows how the volume of hydrogen gas produced changed with time.

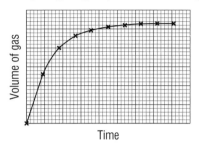

a Describe, as fully as you can, how the rate of this reaction changes with time. (2)

b The student wanted to make the reaction go faster.

Which suggestion would make the reaction go faster?

Use bigger pieces of the same total mass of zinc.

Use more of the dilute acid.

Use zinc powder. (1)

c The student decided to increase the concentration of the acid. Explain, in terms of particles, why increasing the concentration of the acid increases the rate of reaction. (2)

d The student increased the temperature of the reaction by 10 °C. The student found that the reaction went twice as fast. Explain, as fully as you can, why an increase in temperature increases the rate of the reaction. (3)

AQA, 2008

4 Platinum is used as a catalyst in many industrial processes. Platinum is a very expensive metal. The catalysts often contain only about 1% platinum dispersed on an inert support such as aluminium oxide to give a surface area of about 200 m² per gram. Cobalt catalysts with nanosized particles have been developed as an alternative to platinum catalysts for use in some industrial processes.

a Suggest two reasons why platinum is used as a catalyst, even though it is very expensive. (2)

b Explain, in terms of particles, why catalysts like platinum should have a very large surface area. (2)

c Suggest an economic reason and an environmental reason why cobalt catalysts have been developed as alternatives to platinum catalysts. (2)

d Suggest **three** reasons why the use of catalysts is important in industrial processes. (3)

C2 5.1 Acids and alkalis

Learning objectives

- Why are solutions acidic or alkaline?
- What are bases and alkalis?
- How do we measure acidity?

Figure 1 Acids and bases are all around us, in many of the things we buy at the shops, in our schools and factories – and in our bodies too

Acids and bases are an important part of our understanding of chemistry. They play an important part inside us and all other living things.

What are acids and bases?

When we dissolve a substance in water we make an **aqueous solution**. The solution may be acidic, alkaline or neutral. That depends on which substance we have dissolved.

- Soluble hydroxides are called **alkalis**. Their solutions are alkaline. An example is sodium hydroxide solution.
- **Bases**, which include alkalis, are substances that can neutralise **acids**. Metal oxides and metal hydroxides are bases. Examples include iron oxide and copper hydroxide.
- Acids include citric acid, sulfuric acid and ethanoic acid. All acids taste very sour, although many acids are far too dangerous to put in your mouth. Ethanoic acid (in vinegar) and citric acid (in citrus fruit and fizzy drinks) are acids which we regularly eat.
- Pure water is **neutral**.

a Name an alkali.
b What is a base?

One acid that we use in science labs is hydrochloric acid. This is formed when the gas hydrogen chloride (HCl) dissolves in water:

$$HCl(g) \xrightarrow{\text{water}} H^+(aq) + Cl^-(aq)$$

All acids form H$^+$ ions when we add them to water. It is these H$^+$ ions that make a solution acidic. Hydrogen chloride also forms chloride ions (Cl$^-$). The '(aq)' in the equation above is called a **state symbol**. It shows that the ions are in an 'aqueous solution'. In other words, they are dissolved in water.

c What ions do all acids form when we add them to water?

Because alkalis are bases which dissolve in water, they are the bases we often use in experiments. Sodium hydroxide solution is often found in school labs. We get sodium hydroxide solution when we dissolve solid sodium hydroxide in water:

$$NaOH(s) \xrightarrow{\text{water}} Na^+(aq) + OH^-(aq)$$

All alkalis form hydroxide ions (OH$^-$) when we add them to water. It is these hydroxide ions that make a solution alkaline.

d What ions do all alkalis form when we add them to water?
e What does the state symbol '(s)' stand for?

Measuring acidity or alkalinity

Indicators are substances which change colour when we add them to acids and alkalis. Litmus paper is a well-known indicator, but there are many more.

We use the **pH scale** to show how acidic or alkaline a solution is. The scale runs from 0 (most acidic) to 14 (most alkaline). We can use **universal indicator (UI)** to find the pH of a solution. It is a very special indicator made from a number of dyes. It turns a range of colours as the pH changes. Anything in the middle of the pH scale (pH 7) is neutral, neither acid nor alkali.

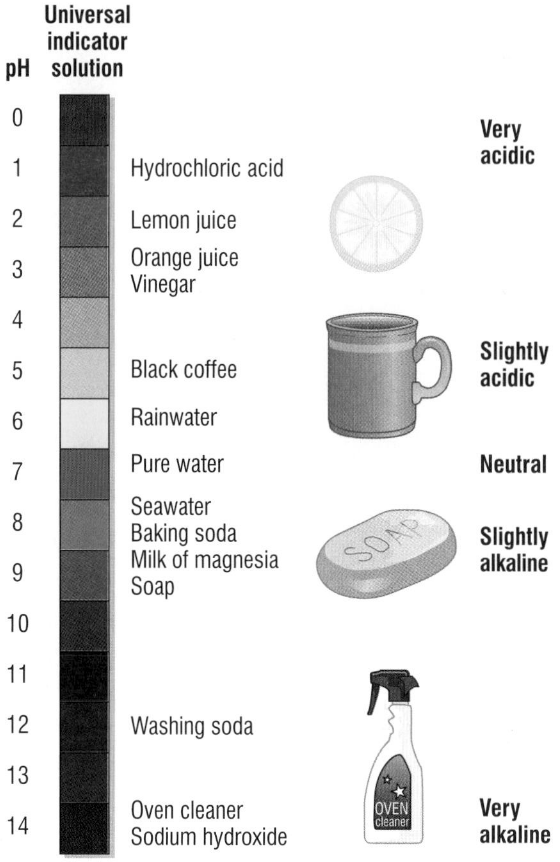

Practical

Which is the most alkaline product?

Compare the alkalinity of various cleaning products.

You can test washing-up liquids, shampoos, soaps, hand-washing liquids, washing powders/liquids and dishwasher powders/tablets.

You could use a pH sensor and data logger to collect your data.

● What are the advantages of using a pH sensor instead of universal indicator solution or paper?

Safety: Wear eye protection.

Maths skills

We can use the mathematical symbols ' > ' (read as 'is greater than') and ' < ' ('is less than') when interpreting pH values.
We can say:
pH < 7 indicates an acidic solution.
i.e. pH values less than 7 are acidic.

pH > 7 indicates an alkaline solution.
i.e. pH values greater than 7 are alkaline.

Figure 2 The pH scale tells us how acidic or alkaline a solution is

pH	Universal indicator solution		
0			Very acidic
1	Hydrochloric acid		
2	Lemon juice		
3	Orange juice / Vinegar		
4			
5	Black coffee		Slightly acidic
6	Rainwater		
7	Pure water		Neutral
8	Seawater / Baking soda		Slightly alkaline
9	Milk of magnesia / Soap		
10			
11			
12	Washing soda		
13			
14	Oven cleaner / Sodium hydroxide		Very alkaline

Summary questions

1 Match the halves of the sentences together:

a	A base that is soluble in water	A	.... a pH of exactly 7.
b	Pure water is neutral with	B	.... form OH⁻ ions when they dissolve in water.
c	Acids are substances that	C	.... is called an alkali.
d	Alkalis are substances that	D	.... is acidic.
e	Indicators are substances that	E	.... form H⁺ ions when they dissolve in water.
f	A solution with a pH less than 7	F	.... change colour when we add them to acids and alkalis.

2 How could you use universal indicator paper as a way of distinguishing between pure water, sodium hydroxide solution and citric acid solution?

Key points

● Acids are substances which produce H^+ ions when we add them to water.

● Bases are substances that will neutralise acids.

● An alkali is a soluble hydroxide. Alkalis produce OH^- ions when we add them to water.

● We can use the pH scale to show how acidic or alkaline a solution is.

C2 5.2 Making salts from metals or bases

Learning objectives

- What is made when acids react with metals?
- What is made when acids react with bases?
- How can we make different salts?

Acids + metals

We can make **salts** by reacting acids with metals. This is only possible if the metal is more reactive than hydrogen. If it is, then the metal will react with an acid to form a salt plus hydrogen gas:

$$\textbf{acid} \quad + \quad \textbf{metal} \quad \rightarrow \quad \textbf{a salt} \quad + \textbf{ hydrogen}$$

$$2HCl(aq) \quad + \quad Mg(s) \quad \rightarrow \quad MgCl_2(aq) \quad + \quad H_2(g)$$

hydrochloric acid + magnesium → magnesium chloride + hydrogen

However, if the metal is very reactive, the reaction with acid is too violent to carry out safely. So metals such as sodium or potassium are never added to acid.

> **a** What does the reaction between an acid and a metal produce?
> **b** What does the state symbol '(g)' stand for?

Acid + insoluble base

When we react an acid with a base, we get a salt and water formed.

The general equation which describes this **neutralisation** reaction is:

$$\textbf{acid + base} \rightarrow \textbf{a salt + water}$$

> **c** What is formed when an acid plus a base react?

The salt that we make depends on the metal or the base that we use, as well as the acid. So bases that contain sodium ions will always make sodium salts. Those that contain potassium ions will always make potassium salts.

In terms of the acid used:

- the salts formed when we neutralise hydrochloric acid are always **chlorides**
- sulfuric acid always makes salts which are **sulfates**
- nitric acid always makes **nitrates**.

The oxide of a transition metal, such as iron(III) oxide, is an example of a base that we can use to make a salt in this way:

$$\text{acid} \quad + \quad \text{base} \quad \rightarrow \quad \text{a salt} \quad + \quad \text{water}$$

$$6HCl(aq) \quad + \quad Fe_2O_3(s) \quad \rightarrow \quad 2FeCl_3(aq) \quad + 3H_2O(l)$$

hydrochloric acid + solid iron(III) oxide → iron(III) chloride solution + water

> **d** Name the salt formed when dilute sulfuric acid reacts with zinc oxide.
> **e** What does the state symbol '(l)' stand for?

Practical

Making a copper salt

We can make copper sulfate crystals from copper oxide (an insoluble base) and sulfuric acid. The equation for the reaction is:

$$acid \quad + \quad base \quad \rightarrow \quad a\ salt \quad + \quad water$$

$$H_2SO_4(aq) \quad + \quad CuO(s) \quad \rightarrow \quad CuSO_4(aq) \quad + \quad H_2O(l)$$

sulfuric acid + copper(ɪɪ) oxide → copper sulfate + water

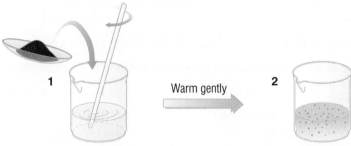

1 Add insoluble copper oxide to sulfuric acid and stir. Warm gently on a tripod and gauze (do not boil).

Warm gently

2 The solution turns blue as the reaction occurs, showing that copper sulfate is being formed. Excess copper oxide can be seen.

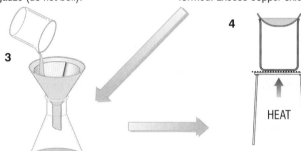

3 When the reaction is complete, filter the solution to remove excess copper oxide

4 HEAT

We can evaporate the water so that crystals of copper sulfate start to form. Stop heating when you see the first crystals appear at the edge of the solution. Then leave for the rest of the water to evaporate off slowly. This will give you larger crystals.

● What does the copper sulfate look like? Draw a diagram if necessary.

Safety: Wear eye protection. Chemicals in this practical are harmful.

Summary questions

1 Copy and complete using the words below:

hydrogen   metals   neutralisation   salt   water

The reaction between an acid and a base is called a .... reaction. When this happens, a .... is formed, together with .... Salts can also be made by reacting acids with some ...., when .... gas is formed along with the salt.

2 a Why wouldn't you add copper metal to dilute sulfuric acid in order to make copper sulfate?

   b Why wouldn't you add potassium metal to dilute nitric acid in order to make potassium nitrate?

   c Describe how you could prepare a sample of copper sulfate crystals from its solution.

Key points

● When we react an acid with a base a neutralisation reaction occurs.

● The reaction between an acid and a base produces a salt and water.

● Salts can also be made by reacting a suitable metal with an acid. This reaction produces hydrogen gas as well as a salt. A sample of the salt made can then be crystallised out of solution by evaporating off water.

C2 5.3

Making salts from solutions ⓚ

Learning objectives

- How can we make salts from an acid and an alkali?
- How can we make insoluble salts?
- How can we remove unwanted ions from solutions?

There are two other important ways of making salts from solutions.

- We can react an acid and an alkali together to form a soluble salt.
- We can make an *insoluble* salt by reacting solutions of two soluble salts together.

Acid + alkali

When an acid reacts with an alkali, a neutralisation reaction takes place.

Hydrochloric acid reacting with sodium hydroxide solution is an example:

$$\text{acid} + \text{alkali} \rightarrow \text{a salt} + \text{water}$$

$$HCl(aq) + NaOH(aq) \rightarrow NaCl(aq) + H_2O(l)$$

hydrochloric acid + sodium hydroxide solution → sodium chloride + water

We can think about neutralisation in terms of $H^+(aq)$ ions reacting with $OH^-(aq)$ ions. They react to form water:

$$H^+(aq) + OH^-(aq) \rightarrow H_2O(l)$$

When we react an acid with an alkali we need to know when the acid and alkali have completely reacted. We can use an indicator for this.

We can make ammonium salts, as well as metal salts, by reacting an acid with an alkali. Ammonia reacts with water to form a weakly alkaline solution:

$$NH_3(aq) + H_2O(l) \rightleftharpoons NH_4^+(aq) + OH^-(aq)$$

Ammonia solution reacts with an acid (for example, nitric acid):

$$\text{acid} + \text{ammonia solution} \rightarrow \text{an ammonium salt} + \text{water}$$

$$HNO_3(aq) + NH_4^+(aq) + OH^-(aq) \rightarrow NH_4NO_3(aq) + H_2O(l)$$

nitric acid + ammonia solution → ammonium nitrate + water

Ammonium nitrate contains a high proportion of nitrogen, and it is very soluble in water. This makes it ideal as a source of nitrogen for plants to take up through their roots. It replaces the nitrogen taken up from the soil by plants as they grow.

Ammonium salts are made by adding ammonia solution to an acid until there is a small excess of ammonia. We can detect the excess ammonia by using universal indicator. We then crystallise the ammonium salt from its solution. The excess ammonia evaporates off.

- **a** Write down a general equation for the reaction between an acid and an alkali.
- **b** Name a salt which is used as a fertiliser to provide crops with nitrogen.

Making insoluble salts

We can sometimes make salts by combining two solutions that contain different soluble salts. When the soluble salts react to make an insoluble salt, we call the reaction a precipitation reaction. That's because the insoluble solid formed is called a **precipitate**.

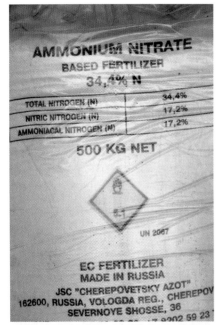

Figure 1 Ammonium nitrate is used as a fertiliser

$$Pb(NO_3)_2(aq) + 2KI(aq) \rightarrow PbI_2(s) + 2KNO_3(aq)$$

lead nitrate   + potassium iodide → lead iodide + potassium nitrate
solution   solution   precipitate   solution

Each of the reactant solutions contains one of the ions of the insoluble salt. In this case, they are lead ions in lead nitrate and iodide ions in potassium iodide. Lead iodide forms a yellow precipitate that we can filter off from the solution.

Practical

Making an insoluble salt

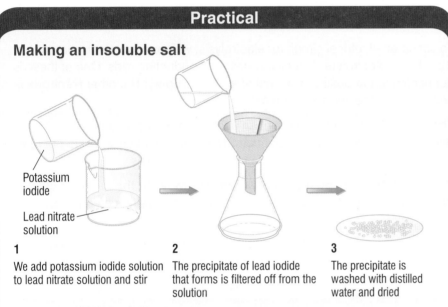

1
We add potassium iodide solution to lead nitrate solution and stir

2
The precipitate of lead iodide that forms is filtered off from the solution

3
The precipitate is washed with distilled water and dried

We can make the salt lead iodide from lead nitrate solution and potassium iodide solution. The equation for the reaction is shown at the top of this page.

● Why is the precipitate of lead iodide washed with distilled water?

Using precipitation

We use precipitation reactions to remove pollutants from the wastewater from factories. The effluent must be treated before it is discharged into rivers and the sea.

Precipitation is used in the removal of metal ions from industrial wastewater. By raising the pH of the water, we can make insoluble metal hydroxides precipitate out. This produces a sludge which we can easily remove from the solution.

The cleaned-up water can then be discharged safely into a river or the sea.

Precipitation can be also used to remove unwanted ions from drinking water.

Figure 2 Water treatment plants use chemical treatments to precipitate out metal compounds which can then be removed by filtering the solution

Summary questions

1 Copy and complete using the words below:

acid alkali insoluble metal polluted precipitation solid neutralisation soluble water indicator

We can make salts by reacting an .... with an .... This makes the salt and .... and is called a .... reaction. We need an .... to tell us when the reaction is complete. We can also make .... salts by reacting two .... salts together. We call this a .... reaction because the salt is formed as a .... This type of reaction is also important when we want to remove .... ions from .... water.

2 Write word equations and a brief method to show how to make the following salts:
   a potassium nitrate (a soluble salt)
   b silver chloride (an insoluble salt). Hint: all nitrates are soluble in water.

Key points

● An indicator is needed when a soluble salt is prepared by reacting an alkali with an acid.

● Insoluble salts can be made by reacting two solutions to produce a precipitate.

● Precipitation is an important way of removing some metal ions from industrial wastewater.

C2 5.4

Electrolysis ⓚ

Learning objectives

- What is electrolysis?
- What types of substance can we electrolyse?
- What is made when we electrolyse substances?

Figure 1 The first person to explain electrolysis was Michael Faraday. He worked on this and many other problems in science nearly 200 years ago.

 Did you know ...?

Electrolysis is also a way of getting rid of unwanted body hair. A small electric current is passed through the base of each individual hair to be removed. The hair is destroyed through chemical changes caused by the electric current, which destroy the cells that make the hair grow.

The word **electrolysis** means 'splitting up using electricity'. In electrolysis we use an electric current to break down an ionic substance. We call the substance that is broken down by electrolysis the **electrolyte**.

a What is electrolysis?
b What do we call the substance broken down by electrolysis?

To set up an electrical circuit for electrolysis, we have two electrodes which dip into the electrolyte. The electrodes are conducting rods. One of these is connected to the positive terminal of a power supply. The other electrode is connected to the negative terminal.

The electrodes are often made of an unreactive (or **inert**) substance. This is often graphite or sometimes platinum. This is so the electrodes do not react with the electrolyte or the products made in electrolysis.

During electrolysis, positively charged ions move to the negative electrode. At the same time, the negative ions move to the positive electrode.

When the ions reach the electrodes they lose their charge and become elements. Gases may be given off or metals deposited at the electrodes. This depends on the compound used and whether it is molten or dissolved in water.

Demonstration

The electrolysis of molten lead bromide

- This demonstration needs a fume cupboard because bromine is toxic and corrosive.
- When does the bulb light up?

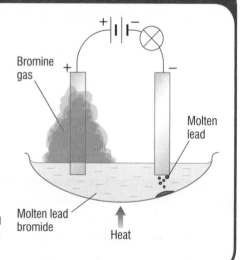

Figure 2 Passing electricity through molten lead bromide. It forms molten lead and brown bromine gas as the electrolyte is broken down by the electricity.

Figure 2 above shows how electricity breaks down lead bromide into lead and bromine:

$$\text{lead bromide} \rightarrow \text{lead} + \text{bromine}$$
$$PbBr_2(l) \rightarrow Pb(l) + Br_2(g)$$

Lead bromide is an ionic substance. Ionic substances do not conduct electricity when they are solid. But once we melt them, the ions are free to move and carry their charge towards the electrodes.

The positive lead ions (Pb^{2+}) move towards the negative electrode. At the same time, the negatively charged bromide ions (Br^-) move towards the positive electrode.

Notice the state symbols in the equation. They tell us that the lead bromide and the lead are molten at the temperature in the dish. The '(l)' stands for 'liquid'. The bromine is given off as a gas, shown as '(g)'.

c Which electrode do positive ions move towards during electrolysis?
d Which electrode do negative ions move towards during electrolysis?

Electrolysis of solutions

Many ionic substances have very high melting points. This can make electrolysis very difficult. But some ionic substances dissolve in water. When this happens, the ions also become free to move around.

However, when electrolysing solutions it is more difficult to predict what will be formed. This is because water also forms ions. So the products at each electrode are not always exactly what we expect.

When we electrolyse a solution of copper bromide, copper ions (Cu^{2+}) move to the negative electrode. The bromide ions (Br^-) move to the positive electrode. Copper bromide is split into its elements at the electrodes (see Figure 3):

$$\text{copper bromide} \rightarrow \text{copper} + \text{bromine}$$
$$CuBr_2(aq) \rightarrow Cu(s) + Br_2(aq)$$

In this case the state symbols in the equation tell us that the copper bromide is dissolved in water. This is shown as '(aq)'. The copper is formed as a solid, shown as '(s)'. The bromine formed remains dissolved in the water – '(aq)'.

Covalent compounds cannot usually be electrolysed unless they react in water to form ions, e.g. acids in water.

⃕ links

For more information about the effect of water in electrolysis, see C2 5.5 Changes at the electrodes and C2 5.7 Electrolysis of brine.

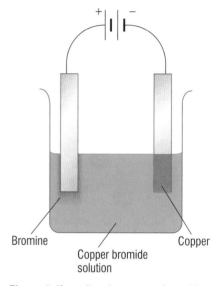

Bromine / Copper bromide solution / Copper

Figure 3 If we dissolve copper bromide in water, we can decompose it by electrolysis. Copper metal is formed at the negative electrode. Brown bromine appears in solution around the positive electrode.

Summary questions

1 Copy and complete using the words below:

ions   molten   move   solution

For the current to flow in electrolysis, the .... must be able to .... between the electrodes. This can only happen if the substance is in .... or if it is ....

2 Predict the products formed at each electrode when the following compounds are melted and then electrolysed:
   a zinc iodide
   b lithium bromide
   c iron(III) fluoride.

3 Solid ionic substances do not conduct electricity. Using words and diagrams explain why they conduct electricity when molten or in solution.

Key points

- Electrolysis breaks down a substance using electricity.

- Ionic compounds can only be electrolysed when they are molten or in solution. That's because their ions are then free to move to the electrodes.

- In electrolysis, positive ions move to the negative electrode while negative ions move to the positive electrode.

Changes at the electrodes

C2 5.5

Learning objectives

- What happens to the ions during electrolysis?

- How can we represent what happens at each electrode? **[H]**

- How does water affect the products of electrolysis?

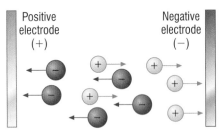

Figure 1 An ion always moves towards the oppositely charged electrode

During electrolysis, ions move towards the electrodes. The direction they move in depends on their charge. As we saw in C2 5.4, positive ions move towards the negative electrode. Negative ions move towards the positive electrode.

When ions reach an electrode, they either lose or gain electrons. What happens depends on their charge.

Negatively charged ions *lose* electrons to become neutral atoms. Positively charged ions *gain* electrons to become neutral atoms.

a How do negatively charged ions become neutral atoms in electrolysis?
b How do positively charged ions become neutral atoms in electrolysis?

The easiest way to think about this is to look at an example:

Think back to the electrolysis of molten lead bromide. The lead ions (Pb^{2+}) move towards the negative electrode. When they get there, each ion gains two electrons to become a neutral lead atom.

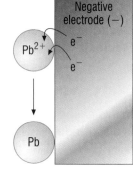

Gaining electrons is called **reduction.** We say that the lead ions are **reduced.** 'Reduction' is simply another way of saying 'gaining electrons'.

The negatively charged bromide ions (Br^-) move towards the positive electrode. Once there, each ion loses one electron to become a neutral bromine atom. Two bromine atoms then form a covalent bond to make a bromine molecule, Br_2.

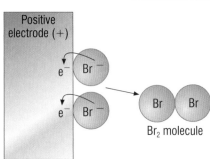

Losing electrons is called **oxidation.** We say that the bromide ions are **oxidised**. 'Oxidation' is another way of saying 'losing electrons'.

Half equations

We represent what is happening at each electrode using **half equations**.

At the negative electrode:

$$Pb^{2+} + 2e^- \rightarrow Pb \quad \text{(notice how an electron is written as 'e}^-\text{')}$$

At the positive electrode:

$$2\,Br^- \rightarrow Br_2 + 2e^-$$

Sometimes half equations can show the electrons being removed from negative ions, like this:

$$2Br^- - 2e^- \rightarrow Br_2$$

You can write the half equation for negative ions either way. They both show the same change.

Higher

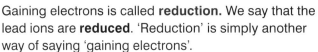
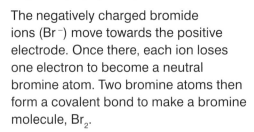

AQA *Examiner's tip*

Oxidation and reduction reactions don't have to involve oxygen. More generally they involve the transfer of electrons.

Remember **OILRIG** – **O**xidation **I**s **L**oss (of electrons), **R**eduction **I**s **G**ain (of electrons).

The effect of water

In aqueous solutions, electrolysis is more complex because of the ions from water. There is a rule for working out what will happen. Remember that if two elements can be produced at an electrode, the less reactive element will usually be formed. In solution we will always have the positively charged metal ions and H^+ ions (from water) attracted to the negative electrode.

Look at Figure 2. It shows what happens in the electrolysis of a solution of a potassium compound. Hydrogen is less reactive than potassium. So hydrogen is produced at the negative electrode rather than potassium.

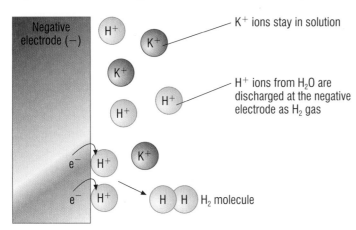

Negative electrode (−)

K^+ ions stay in solution

H^+ ions from H_2O are discharged at the negative electrode as H_2 gas

H_2 molecule

Figure 2 Here is the negative electrode in the electrolysis of a solution of a potassium compound. Hydrogen is less reactive than potassium, so hydrogen gas is given off at the negative electrode.

So what happens at the positive electrode in the electrolysis of aqueous solutions?

Hydroxide ions from water are often discharged. That is unless the solution contains a reasonably high concentration of a halide ion (group VII ions). In this case the halide ion is discharged. So the 'order of discharge' at the positive electrode is:

halide ion > hydroxide > all other negatively charged ions.

When hydroxide ions are discharged, we see oxygen gas given off at the positive electrode.

Summary questions

1 Copy and complete using the words below:

gain   less   lose   oxidised   reduced

During electrolysis, positively charged ions .... electrons and are .... At the same time, negatively charged ions .... electrons and are .... When electrolysis is carried out in water, the .... reactive element is usually produced.

2 Predict what is formed at each electrode in the electrolysis of:
   a molten potassium oxide
   b copper chloride solution
   c magnesium sulfate solution.

3 Copy and balance the following half equations where necessary:
   a $Cl^- \rightarrow Cl_2 + e^-$
   b $O^{2-} \rightarrow O_2 + e^-$
   c $Ca^{2+} + e^- \rightarrow Ca$
   d $Al^{3+} + e^- \rightarrow Al$
   e $Na^+ + e^- \rightarrow Na$
   f $H^+ + e^- \rightarrow H_2$ [H]

Key points

● In electrolysis, the ions move towards the oppositely charged electrodes.

● At the electrodes, negative ions are oxidised while positive ions are reduced.

● When electrolysis happens in water, the less reactive element, between hydrogen and the metal, is usually produced at the negative electrode. At the positive electrode, we often get oxygen gas given off from discharged hydroxide ions.

C2 5.6 The extraction of aluminium

Learning objectives

- How is aluminium obtained from aluminium oxide?
- Why is cryolite used in the process?
- What happens at each electrode in the process?

You already know that aluminium is a very important metal. The uses of the metal or its alloys include:

- pans
- overhead power cables
- aeroplanes
- cooking foil
- drink cans
- window and patio door frames
- bicycle frames and car bodies.

a Why is aluminium used to make overhead power cables?

Aluminium is quite a reactive metal. It is less reactive than magnesium but more reactive than zinc or iron. Carbon is not reactive enough to use in its extraction so we must use electrolysis. The compound electrolysed is aluminium oxide, Al_2O_3.

We get aluminium oxide from bauxite ore. The ore is mined by open cast mining. Bauxite contains mainly aluminium oxide. However, it is mixed with other rocky impurities. So the first step is to separate aluminium oxide from the ore. The impurities contain a lot of iron(III) oxide. This colours the waste solution from the separation process rusty brown. The solution has to be stored in large lagoons.

Figure 1 Aluminum alloys have a low density but are very strong

Electrolysis of aluminium oxide

To electrolyse the aluminium oxide we must first melt it. This enables the ions to move to the electrodes.

Unfortunately aluminium oxide has a very high melting point. It melts at 2050°C. However, chemists have found a way of saving at least some energy. This is done by mixing the aluminium oxide with molten cryolite. Cryolite is another ionic compound. The molten mixture can be electrolysed at about 850°C. The electrical energy transferred to the electrolysis cells keeps the mixture molten.

b Why must aluminium oxide be molten for electrolysis to take place?

The overall reaction in the electrolysis cell is:

$$\text{aluminium oxide} \xrightarrow{\text{electrolysis}} \text{aluminium} + \text{oxygen}$$
$$2Al_2O_3(l) \longrightarrow 4Al(l) + 3O_2(g)$$

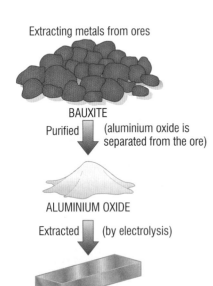

Extracting metals from ores

BAUXITE

Purified (aluminium oxide is separated from the ore)

ALUMINIUM OXIDE

Extracted (by electrolysis)

ALUMINIUM METAL

Figure 2 Extracting aluminium from its ore. This process requires a lot of energy. The purification stage makes aluminium hydroxide. This is separated from the impurities but then must be heated to turn it back to pure aluminium oxide. Then even more energy is needed melting and electrolysing the oxide.

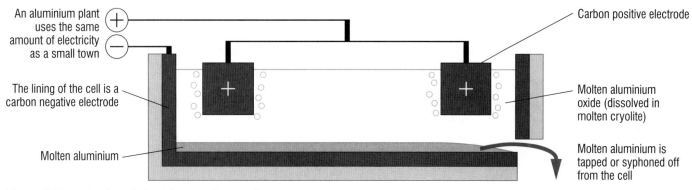

An aluminium plant uses the same amount of electricity as a small town

The lining of the cell is a carbon negative electrode

Molten aluminium

Carbon positive electrode

Molten aluminium oxide (dissolved in molten cryolite)

Molten aluminium is tapped or syphoned off from the cell

Figure 3 The extraction of aluminium by electrolysis

At the negative (–) electrode:

Each aluminium ion (Al^{3+}) gains 3 electrons. The ions turn into aluminium atoms. We say that the Al^{3+} ions are reduced to form Al atoms.

The aluminium metal formed is molten at the temperature of the cell and collects at the bottom. It is siphoned or tapped off.

At the positive (+) electrode:

Each oxide ion (O^{2-}) loses 2 electrons. The ions turn into oxygen atoms. We say that the O^{2-} ions are oxidised to form oxygen atoms. These bond in pairs to form molecules of oxygen gas (O_2).

The oxygen reacts with the hot, positive carbon electrodes, making carbon dioxide gas. So the positive electrodes gradually burn away. They need to be replaced in the cells regularly.

   c Are the oxide ions reduced or oxidised in the electrolysis of molten aluminium oxide?

Summary questions

1 Copy and complete using the words below:

   positive oxygen extraction carbon cryolite negative energy

   In the .... of aluminium, aluminium oxide is dissolved in molten .... in order to use less .... to melt it. The aluminium metal is collected at the .... electrode in the cells, while oxygen is formed at the .... electrode. The electrodes used are made of .... The positive electrodes burn away as they react with .... and form carbon dioxide gas.

2 **a** Explain which ions are oxidised and which ions are reduced in the electrolysis of molten aluminium oxide.
  b Why are the positive electrodes replaced regularly in the industrial electrolysis of aluminium oxide? Include a word equation.

3 Write half equations for the changes at each electrode in the electrolysis of molten aluminium oxide. [H]

Key points

● Aluminium oxide is electrolysed in the manufacture of aluminium metal.

● The aluminium oxide is mixed with molten cryolite to lower its melting point.

● Aluminium forms at the negative electrode and oxygen at the positive electrode.

● The positive carbon electrodes are replaced regularly as they gradually burn away.

C2 5.7 Electrolysis of brine

Learning objectives

- What is produced when we electrolyse brine?
- How do we use these products?

Practical

Electrolysing brine in the lab

Turn off the electricity once the tubes are nearly full of gas to avoid inhaling chlorine gas (toxic).

- How can you positively test for the gases collected?

Test the solution near the negative electrode with universal indicator solution.

- What does the indicator tell us?

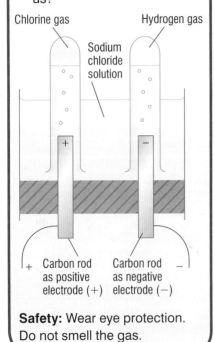

Safety: Wear eye protection. Do not smell the gas.

⚲ links

For information about what happens when two Ions are attracted to an electrode, see C2 5.2 Making salts from metals or bases.

The electrolysis of **brine** (concentrated sodium chloride solution) is a very important industrial process. When we pass an electric current through brine we get three products:

- chlorine gas is produced at the positive electrode
- hydrogen gas is produced at the negative electrode
- sodium hydroxide solution is also formed.

We can summarise the electrolysis of brine as:

$$\text{sodium chloride solution} \xrightarrow{\text{electrolysis}} \text{hydrogen} + \text{chlorine} + \text{sodium hydroxide solution}$$

a What are the three products made when we electrolyse brine?

At the positive electrode (+):

The negative chloride ions (Cl^-) are attracted to the positive electrode. When they get there, they each lose one electron. The chloride ions are oxidised, as they lose electrons. The chlorine atoms bond together in pairs and are given off as chlorine gas (Cl_2).

At the negative electrode (−):

There are H^+ ions in brine, formed when water breaks down:

$$H_2O \rightleftharpoons H^+ + OH^-$$

These positive hydrogen ions are attracted to the negative electrode. The sodium ions (Na^+) are also attracted to the same electrode. But remember in C2 5.5, we saw what happens when two ions are attracted to an electrode. It is the less reactive element that gets discharged. In this case, hydrogen ions are discharged and sodium ions stay in solution.

When the H^+ ions get to the negative electrode, they each gain one electron. The hydrogen ions are reduced, as they each gain an electron. The hydrogen atoms formed bond together in pairs and are given off as hydrogen gas (H_2).

The remaining solution:

You can test the solution around the negative electrode with indicator. It shows that the solution is alkaline. This is because we can think of brine as containing aqueous ions of Na^+ and Cl^- (from salt) and H^+ and OH^- (from water). The Cl^- and H^+ ions are removed during electrolysis. So this leaves a solution containing Na^+ and OH^- ions, i.e. a solution of sodium hydroxide.

Look at the way we can electrolyse brine in industry in Figure 1.

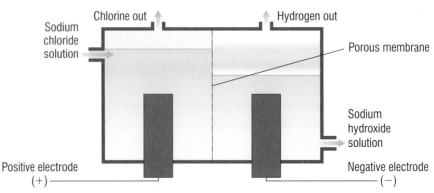

Figure 1 In industry, brine can be electrolysed in a cell in which the two electrodes are separated by a porous membrane. This is called a diaphragm cell.

Half equations for the electrolysis of brine

The half equations for what happens in the electrolysis of brine are:

At the positive electrode (+):

$$2Cl^-(aq) \rightarrow Cl_2(g) + 2e^-$$

[remember that this can also be written as: $2Cl^-(aq) - 2e^- \rightarrow Cl_2(g)$]

At the negative electrode (−):

$$2H^+(aq) + 2e^- \rightarrow H_2(g)$$

Using chlorine

We can react chlorine with the sodium hydroxide produced in the electrolysis of brine. This makes a solution of **bleach**. Bleach is very good at killing bacteria.

Chlorine is also important in making many other disinfectants, as well as plastics such as PVC.

b What is chlorine used for?

Using hydrogen

The hydrogen that we make by electrolysing brine is particularly pure. This makes it very useful in the food industry. We make margarine by reacting hydrogen with vegetable oils.

c What is hydrogen used for?

Using sodium hydroxide

The sodium hydroxide from the electrolysis of brine is used to make soap and paper. It is also used to make bleach (see above).

d What is sodium hydroxide used for?

Figure 2 The chlorine made when we electrolyse brine is used to kill bacteria in drinking water, and also in swimming pools

Summary questions

1 Copy and complete using the words below:

hydrogen bleach hydroxide chlorine

When we pass an electric current through brine we can collect .... gas at the positive electrode, and .... gas at the negative electrode. Sodium .... solution is formed in the cell. Two of these products are also used to make ....

2 We can electrolyse *molten* sodium chloride. Compare the products formed with those from the electrolysis of sodium chloride solution. What are the differences?

3 For the electrolysis of brine, write half equations, including state symbols, for the reactions **a** at the positive electrode and **b** at the negative electrode. [11]

Key points

- When we electrolyse brine we get three products – chlorine gas, hydrogen gas and sodium hydroxide solution (an alkali).
- Chlorine is used to make bleach, which kills bacteria, and to make plastics.
- Hydrogen is used to make margarine.
- Sodium hydroxide is used to make bleach, paper and soap.

C2 5.8

Electroplating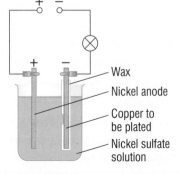

Learning objectives

- Why do we electroplate objects?

- How can we electroplate a metal object?

Most of us will use an electroplated objected at some time each day. You might use a chromium-plated kettle to boil water or ride a bicycle with chromium-plated handlebars. You could open a tin-plated steel can for a meal or put on some gold- or silver-plated jewellery.

An electroplated object is coated with a thin layer of metal by electrolysis.

> a Name four metals that we can use to electroplate another metal.

Why do we electroplate objects?

There can be different reasons why we electroplate objects. These include:

- to protect the metal beneath from corroding
- to make the object look more attractive
- to increase the hardness of a surface and its resistance to scratching
- to save money by using a thin layer of a precious metal instead of the pure expensive metal. This also helps people who are allergic to nickel – a metal often used to make cheap jewellery.

Electroplating saves money in making cheaper jewellery. However, using electroplating to protect large metal surfaces against rusting and damage makes things more expensive. In the long term, though, this can still make economic sense because we don't have to replace objects so often.

Figure 1 Chromium-plated objects look very shiny and attractive. The chromium layer does not corrode away so it protects the steel beneath from rusting.

Electroplating a metal object

You can try to nickel plate some copper foil in the experiment below.

Practical

Nickel plating copper metal

Your teacher will melt some wax in a metal tray. Using tongs you can dip in a piece of copper foil.

Let the wax set. Then scratch a simple design in the wax. You want the design to be plated with nickel so get this area as free from wax as possible.

Set up the apparatus as shown in the diagram. Using a small current for a long time will give best results.

When you have finished, rinse the copper foil in water, dry, then scrape off the rest of the wax.

- What happens at the negative electrode?

Figure 2 So-called 'tin' cans actually contain very little tin. The layer on the steel can be only a few thousandths of a millimetre thick! The tin keeps air and water away from the iron in steel and stops it rusting – at least until the tin gets scratched! Tin is quite a soft metal, unlike chromium.

Wax
Nickel anode
Copper to be plated
Nickel sulfate solution

Explaining electroplating

The metal object to be plated (the copper foil in this case) is used as the negative electrode. The positive electrode is made from the plating metal (nickel). The electrolysis takes place in a solution containing nickel ions. In the previous experiment we use nickel sulfate solution.

At the positive electrode made of the plating metal:

Nickel atoms in the electrode are oxidised. They lose 2 electrons each and form nickel ions (Ni^{2+}) which go into the solution.

At the negative electrode to be plated:

Nickel ions (Ni^{2+}) from the solution are reduced. They gain 2 electrons and form nickel atoms which are deposited on the copper electrode.

> **b** Where are the nickel atoms oxidised?
> **c** What is formed when nickel atoms are oxidised?

Higher

Electroplating half equations

Here are the half equations at each electrode in electroplating by nickel:

At the positive nickel electrode:

$$Ni(s) \rightarrow Ni^{2+}(aq) + 2e^-$$

At the negative electrode to be plated:

$$Ni^{2+}(aq) + 2e^- \rightarrow Ni(s)$$

Summary questions

1 Copy and complete using the words below:

atoms negative nickel plating deposited electrons oxidised reduced

In electroplating, a solution of the .... metal is electrolysed. In the case of nickel plating, the positive electrode is made of .... The nickel atoms are .... and go into the solution. At the .... electrode, the nickel ions gain .... and are .... They form nickel .... and are .... on the object to be plated.

2 What are the economic advantages and disadvantages of electroplating a metal object?

3 In making 'chrome' objects, chromium metal is used to electroplate a steel object. The steel is first electroplated with nickel because chromium does not stick well on steel. Give the half equation at the negative electrode for the nickel, then the chromium, plating processes. Include state symbols in your answer. (Chromium ions are Cr^{3+}) **[H]**

Key points

- We can electroplate objects to improve their appearance, protect their surface and to use smaller amounts of precious metals.

- The object to be electroplated is made the negative electrode in an electrolysis cell. The plating metal is made the positive electrode. The electrolyte contains ions of the plating metal.

Summary questions

1 Zinc sulfate crystals can be made from an insoluble base and sulfuric acid.

   a i Name the insoluble base that can be used to make zinc sulfate.

     ii Write a word equation to show the reaction.

   b Describe how you could make crystals of zinc sulfate from the reaction in **a ii**.

2 Write balanced symbol equations, including state symbols, to describe the reactions below. (Each reaction forms a salt.)

   a Potassium hydroxide (an alkali) and sulfuric acid.

   b Zinc oxide (an insoluble base) and nitric acid.

   c Calcium metal and hydrochloric acid.

   d Barium nitrate and sodium sulfate (this reaction produces an insoluble salt – Hint: all sodium salts are soluble). **[H]**

3 Select A or B to describe correctly what happens at the positive electrode (+) and negative electrode (–) in electrolysis for **a** to **f**.

   A Positive electrode

   B Negative electrode

   a Positive ions move towards this.

   b Negative ions move towards this.

   c Reduction happens here.

   d Oxidation happens here.

   e Connected to the negative terminal of the power supply.

   f Connected to the positive terminal of the power supply.

4 Make a table to show which of the following ions would move towards the positive electrode and which towards the negative electrode during electrolysis. (You may need to use a copy of the periodic table to help you.)

   sodium   iodide   calcium   fluoride
   oxide   zinc   aluminium   bromide

5 The diagram shows an industrial process used for the electrolysis of sodium chloride solution.

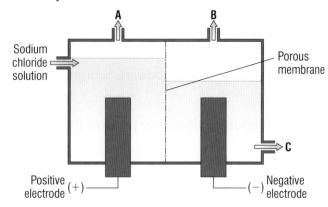

Identify the products **A**, **B** and **C** on the diagram using substances from the list.

chlorine gas   oxygen gas   hydrogen gas
sodium hydroxide solution   sodium metal

6 Water can be split into hydrogen and oxygen using electrolysis. The word equation for this reaction is:

water → hydrogen + oxygen

   a Write a balanced symbol equation for this reaction using the correct chemical symbols.

   b Write half equations to show what happens at the positive and negative electrodes. **[H]**

   c When some water is electrolysed it produces 2 moles of hydrogen. How much oxygen is produced?

   d Where does the energy needed to split water into hydrogen and oxygen come from during electrolysis?

7 Copy and complete the following half equations:

   a $K^+ \rightarrow K$

   b $Ba^{2+} \rightarrow Ba$

   c $I^- \rightarrow I_2$

   d $O^{2-} \rightarrow O_2$ **[H]**

8 Electrolysis can be used to produce a thin layer of metal on the surface of a metal object. Using words and diagrams, describe how you would cover a small piece of steel with copper. Make sure that you write down the half equation that describes what happens at the surface of the steel. **[H]**

AQA Examination-style questions

1 Hydrogen chloride gas reacts with water to make hydrochloric acid. The equation for the reaction is:

$HCl(g) \rightarrow H^+(aq) + Cl^-(aq)$

a Which of the following shows that an acid has been made?

   A An aqueous solution has been made.

   B Hydrogen ions have been made.

   C Chloride ions have been made. (1)

b Choose a number from the list for the pH of hydrochloric acid.

   1 7 12 (1)

c Hydrochloric acid reacts with sodium hydroxide solution to produce a salt and water.

   i Choose a word from the list that describes sodium hydroxide. (1)

      alcohol alkali insoluble

   ii Choose a word from the list to complete the sentence.
The reaction between hydrochloric acid and sodium hydroxide is an example of .... (1)

      combustion neutralisation oxidation

   iii Name the salt made when hydrochloric acid reacts with sodium hydroxide. (1)

2 Lead chloride is a white insoluble salt. It can be made by mixing lead nitrate solution with sodium chloride solution. Both of these solutions are colourless.

a What would you **see** when lead nitrate solution is mixed with sodium chloride solution? (1)

b Write a word equation for the reaction. (2)

c A mining company produces wastewater that contains dissolved lead ions. Suggest how the company could treat the wastewater to reduce the concentration of lead ions. (2)

3 *In this question you will be assessed on using good English, organising information clearly and using specialist terms where appropriate.*

Copper(II) oxide is an insoluble base.

Describe how you could make crystals of copper(II) sulfate from copper(II) oxide. (6)

4 The diagram shows a nickel spoon being coated with silver.

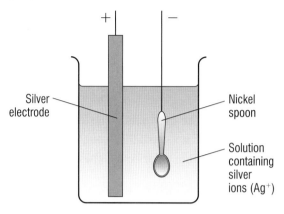

a Explain why silver ions in the solution move towards the spoon. (2)

b Use words from the list to complete the sentence.

gaining losing sharing electron neutron proton

When silver ions reach the spoon they change into silver atoms by .... an .... (2)

c Suggest one reason why spoons made from nickel are coated with silver. (1)

AQA, 2002

5 Magnesium is manufactured by the electrolysis of molten magnesium chloride. The container is made of steel, which is the negative electrode. Carbon (graphite) is used for the positive electrode.

a Steel and carbon (graphite) both conduct electricity.

   i Suggest one other reason why the negative electrode is made of steel. (1)

   ii Suggest one other reason why the positive electrode is made of carbon (graphite). (1)

b Magnesium chloride melts at 950°C. It is mixed with sodium and calcium chloride so that it can be electrolysed at 750°C.

   i Suggest one way this benefits the manufacturer. (1)

   ii Suggest one way this benefits the environment. (1)

c Complete and balance the equations for the reactions at the electrodes.

   i At the negative electrode: $Mg^{2+} + e^- \rightarrow Mg$ (1)

   ii At the positive electrode: $Cl^- \rightarrow Cl_2 + e^-$ **[H]** (1)

1 Calcium chloride is an ionic compound.

Use a table showing the charges on ions to help you answer this question.

a Which of these is the formula of calcium chloride?

CaF Ca_2F CaF_2 Ca_2F_2 (1)

b A sodium ion can be represented in the following way:

Draw diagrams like this to show the ions in calcium chloride.   (4)

c Calcium chloride is a crystalline solid with a high melting point.

Explain why calcium chloride has these properties.   (3)

2 A company extracts copper from an ore that contains the mineral chalcopyrite, $CuFeS_2$.

a Calculate the relative formula mass (M_r) of $CuFeS_2$. (*Relative atomic masses (A_r): Cu = 63.5; Fe = 56; S = 32*)   (2)

b What is the percentage by mass of copper in chalcopyrite?   (2)

c Suggest one reason why the company might prefer to use an ore containing the mineral chalcocite, Cu_2S.   (1)

d The company uses the copper it produces to restore items made of copper. It electroplates the copper items with a new coating of copper. Pure copper is used as the positive electrode and the copper item is the negative electrode. The electrolyte is a solution containing copper(II) sulfate.

  i Draw a diagram showing how you could electroplate a copper spoon in the laboratory.   (3)

  ii Explain how copper is deposited onto the spoon by electrolysis.   (3)

3 A blackcurrant-flavoured drink was analysed for artificial colours and flavours.

A scientist used paper chromatography to identify the artificial colours in the drink. The result of the chromatography is shown in the diagram.

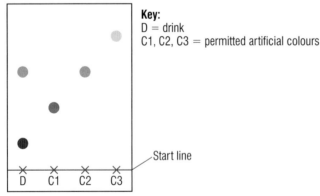

Key:
D = drink
C1, C2, C3 = permitted artificial colours

a *In this question you will be assessed on using good English, organising information clearly and using specialist terms where appropriate.*

Describe how the chromatography was done to produce this result.   (6)

b What conclusions can you make about the colours in the drink?   (3)

c To identify the flavour compounds in the drink the scientist put a sample of the drink into a gas chromatography column linked to a mass spectrometer. The output of the column showed five main peaks.

  i What was the purpose of the gas chromatography column?   (1)

  ii What was the purpose of the mass spectrometer?   (1)

4 A student carried out an experiment to make aspirin. The method is given below.

1. Weigh 2.00 g of salicylic acid.

2. Add 4 cm³ of ethanoic anhydride (an excess).

3. Add 5 drops of concentrated sulfuric acid.

4. Warm the mixture for 15 minutes.

5. Add ice cold water to remove the excess ethanoic anhydride.

6. Cool the mixture until a precipitate of aspirin is formed.

7. Collect the precipitate and wash it with cold water.

8. The precipitate of aspirin is dried and weighed.

a The equation for this reaction is:

$$C_7H_6O_3 + C_4H_6O_3 \rightarrow C_9H_8O_4 + CH_3COOH$$
salicylic acid   aspirin

The relative formula mass (M_r) of salicylic acid, $C_7H_6O_3$, is 138.

The relative formula mass (M_r) of aspirin, $C_9H_8O_4$, is 180.

Calculate the maximum mass of aspirin that could be made from 2.00 g of salicylic acid. (2)

b The student made 1.10 g of aspirin from 2.00 g of salicylic acid.

Calculate the percentage yield of aspirin for this experiment. (2)

c Suggest **one** possible reason why this method does not give the maximum amount of aspirin. (1)

d The student made another compound with properties similar to aspirin. The student sent this compound to a laboratory for analysis. The analysis showed that the compound contained 75.7% C, 8.80% H and 15.5% O.

Calculate the empirical formula of this compound. You must show all of your working to gain full marks. (4)

[H]

5 The element carbon has several forms.

a Diamond is one form of carbon. Explain, in terms of structure and bonding, why diamond is very hard. (3)

b *In this question you will be assessed on using good English, organising information clearly and using specialist terms where appropriate.*

Another form of carbon is graphite. Graphite is used for the contacts in electric motors because it conducts electricity and is soft and slippery. Explain, in terms of structure and bonding, why graphite has these properties. (6)

c Carbon can also form fullerenes. The first fullerene to be discovered has a structure that contains 60 carbon atoms. Other fullerenes contain a few hundred atoms.

i What is the basic unit of the structure of fullerenes? (1)

ii Give two reasons why there has been much research interest in the fullerenes since their discovery in 1985. (2)

[H]

AQA **Examiner's tip**

Always show your working when you do a calculation. If you make a mistake calculating the final answer you may still gain some marks if you show that you know how to do the calculation.

AQA **Examiner's tip**

Q5 b requires you to describe the structure and bonding in graphite and use this to explain the properties given in the question. You need to link the properties clearly to particular points in your description. Before writing your answer, briefly list the key points that you know about the structure and bonding in graphite and then link these to the properties. Then write your answer in a logical order, giving as much detail as you can.

P2 1.1

Distance–time graphs

Figure 1 Capturing the land speed record

??? Did you know ... ?

- Usain Bolt broke the 100 m sprint record in August 2009 in a time of 9.58 seconds – an average speed of 10.44 metres per second (100 ÷ 9.58). By the time you read this, there will probably be a new record.

- A cheetah is faster than any other animal. It can run about 30 metres every second – but only for about 20 seconds! This is nearly as fast as a vehicle travelling at 70 miles per hour (mph).

- The land speed record at present is 763 mph, which is more than Mach 1, the speed of sound. The Bloodhound Project is aiming to set a new record of 1000 mph.

Some motorways have marker posts every kilometre. If you are a passenger in a car on a motorway, you can use these posts to check the speed of the car. You need to time the car as it passes each post. The table below shows some measurements made on a car journey.

Distance (metres, m)	0	1000	2000	3000	4000	5000	6000
Time (seconds, s)	0	40	80	120	160	200	240

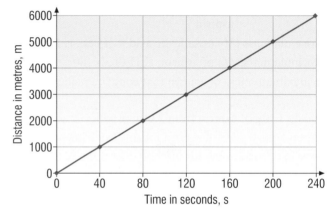

Figure 2 A distance–time graph

Look at the readings plotted on a graph of distance against time in Figure 2.

The graph shows that:

- the car took 40 s to go from each marker post to the next. So its speed was **constant** (or uniform).

- the car went a distance of 25 metres every second (= 1000 metres ÷ 40 seconds). So its speed was 25 metres per second.

If the car had travelled faster, it would have gone further than 1000 metres every 40 seconds. So the line on the graph would have been **steeper**. In other words, the **gradient** of the line would have been greater.

The gradient of a line on a distance–time graph represents speed.

a What can you say about the gradient of the line if the car had travelled slower than 25 metres per second?

Speed

For an object moving at constant **speed**, we can calculate its speed using the formula:

$$\text{speed in metres per second, m/s} = \frac{\text{distance travelled in metres, m}}{\text{time taken in seconds, s}}$$

The scientific unit of speed is the metre per second, usually written as metre/second or m/s.

Speed in action

Long-distance vehicles are fitted with recorders called **tachographs.** These can check that their drivers don't drive for too long. Look at the distance–time graphs in Figure 3 for three lorries, X, Y and Z, on the same motorway.

- X went fastest because it travelled furthest in the same time.
- Y travelled more slowly than X. From the graph, you can see it travelled 30000 metres in 1250 seconds. So its speed was:

$$\text{distance} \div \text{time} = 30000\,\text{m} \div 1250\,\text{s} = 24\,\text{m/s}.$$

b Calculate the speed of X.

- Z stopped for some of the time. Its speed was zero in this time.

c How long did Z stop for?
d Calculate the **average** speed of Z, using the total distance Z travels in its journey.

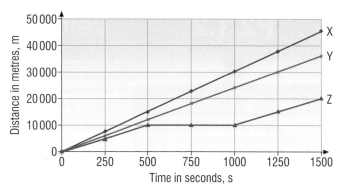

Figure 3 Comparing distance–time graphs

Practical

Be a distance recorder!

Take the measurements needed to plot distance–time graphs for a person:

- walking
- running
- riding a bike.

Remember that you must always label the graph axes, which includes units.

- Work out the average speeds.

Figure 4 Measuring distance

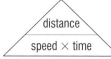 *Maths skills*

Rearranging the speed formula

If two of the three quantities are known, the third can be found. It may help to use the speed formula triangle below:

```
      distance
   ─────────────
   speed × time
```

Cover up the unknown quantity and the triangle tells you how to use the other two known quantities.

Summary questions

1 Copy and complete sentences **a** to **c** using the words below:

   distance   gradient   speed

   a The unit of .... is the metre/second.
   b An object moving at a constant speed travels the same .... every second.
   c The steeper the .... of the line on a distance–time graph of a moving object, the greater its speed is.

2 A vehicle on a motorway travels 1800 m in 60 seconds. Calculate:
   a the average speed of the vehicle in m/s.
   b how far it would travel in 300 seconds if it continued travelling at this speed.

3 A car on a motorway travels 10 kilometres in six minutes. A coach takes seven minutes to travel the same distance. Which vehicle was travelling faster, the car or the coach? Give a reason for your answer.

Key points

- The distance–time graph for any object that is
  - stationary is a horizontal line
  - moving at constant speed is a straight line that slopes upwards.

- The gradient of a distance–time graph for an object represents the object's speed.

- Speed in metres per second, m/s =

  $$\frac{\text{distance travelled in metres, m}}{\text{time taken in seconds, s}}$$

P2 1.2 Velocity and acceleration

Learning objectives

- What is the difference between speed and velocity?
- What is acceleration and what is its unit?
- How can we calculate the acceleration of an object?
- What is deceleration?

Figure 2 You experience plenty of changes in velocity on a corkscrew ride!

Figure 3 On a test circuit

When you visit a fairground, do you like the rides that throw you round? Your speed and your direction of motion keep changing. We use the word **velocity** for speed in a given direction. An exciting ride would be one that changes your velocity often and unexpectedly!

Velocity is speed in a given direction.

- An object moving steadily round in a circle has a constant speed. Its direction of motion changes continuously as it goes round so its velocity is not constant.

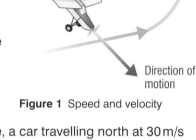

Direction of motion

Figure 1 Speed and velocity

- Two moving objects can have the same speed but different velocities. For example, a car travelling north at 30 m/s on a motorway has the same speed as a car travelling south at 30 m/s. But their velocities are not the same because they are moving in opposite directions.

a How far apart are the two cars 10 seconds after they pass each other?

Acceleration

A car maker claims their new car 'accelerates more quickly than any other new car'. A rival car maker is not pleased by this claim and issues a challenge. Each car in turn is tested on a straight track with a velocity recorder fitted.

The results are shown in the table:

Time from a standing start (seconds, s)	0	2	4	6	8	10
Velocity of car X (metre per second, m/s)	0	5	10	15	20	25
Velocity of car Y (metre per second, m/s)	0	6	12	18	18	18

Which car has a greater **acceleration**? The results are plotted on the velocity–time graph in Figure 4. You can see the velocity of Y goes up from zero faster than the velocity of X does. So Y accelerates more in the first 6 seconds.

The acceleration of an object is its change of velocity per second. The unit of acceleration is the metre per second squared, abbreviated to m/s^2.

Any object with a changing velocity is accelerating. We can work out its acceleration using the equation:

Acceleration

$$\text{(metres per second squared, m/s}^2) = \frac{\text{change in velocity in metres per second, m/s}}{\text{time taken for the change in seconds, s}}$$

For an object that accelerates steadily from an initial velocity u to a final velocity v, its change of velocity = final velocity − initial velocity = $v - u$.

Therefore, we can write the equation for acceleration as:

$$\text{acceleration, } a = \frac{v - u}{t}$$

Where:
v = the final velocity in metres per second,
u = the initial velocity in metres per second,
t = time taken in seconds.

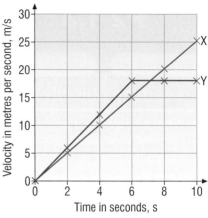

Figure 4 Velocity–time graph

 Maths skills

Worked example

In Figure 4, the velocity of Y increases from 0 to 18 m/s in 6 seconds. Calculate its acceleration.

Solution

Change of velocity = $v - u$ = 18 m/s − 0 m/s = 18 m/s

Time taken, t = 6 s

Acceleration, $a = \dfrac{\text{change in velocity in metres per second, m/s}}{\text{time taken for the change in seconds, s}} = \dfrac{v - u}{t}$

$$= \frac{18\,\text{m/s}}{6\,\text{s}} = 3\,\text{m/s}^2$$

b Calculate the acceleration of X in Figure 4.

Deceleration

A car decelerates when the driver brakes. We use the term **deceleration** or **negative acceleration** for any situation where an object slows down.

Summary questions

1 Copy and complete **a** to **c** using the words below:

acceleration   speed   velocity

   a An object moving steadily round in a circle has a constant ....
   b If the velocity of an object increases by the same amount every second, its .... is constant.
   c Deceleration is when the .... of an object decreases.

2 The velocity of a car increased from 8 m/s to 28 m/s in 8 s without change of direction. Calculate:
   a its change of velocity
   b its acceleration.

3 The driver of a car increased the speed of the car as it joined the motorway. It then travelled at constant velocity before slowing down as it left the motorway at the next junction.
   a i When did the car decelerate?
   ii When was the acceleration of the car zero?
   b When the car joined the motorway, its velocity increased from 5.0 metres per second to 25 metres per second in 10 seconds. What was its acceleration during this time?

Key points

- Velocity is speed in a given direction.

- Acceleration is change of velocity per second. The unit of acceleration is the metre per second squared (m/s^2).

- Acceleration = change of velocity ÷ time taken.

- Deceleration is the change of velocity per second when an object slows down.

P2 1.3

More about velocity–time graphs

Learning objectives

- What can we say if a velocity–time graph is a horizontal line?
- How can we tell from a velocity–time graph if an object is accelerating or decelerating?
- What does the area under a velocity–time graph represent? **[H]**

Figure 2 Measuring motion using a computer

⬭ links

For more information on variables and relationships between them, see H3 Using data.

Investigating acceleration

We can use a motion sensor linked to a computer to record how the velocity of an object changes. Figure 1 shows how we can do this, using a trolley as the moving object. The computer can also be used to display the measurements as a velocity–time graph.

Test A: If we let the trolley accelerate down the runway, its velocity increases with time. Look at the velocity–time graph from a test run in Figure 2.

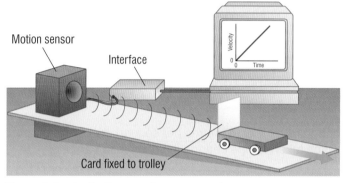

Figure 1 A velocity–time graph on a computer

- The line goes up because the velocity increases with time. So it shows the trolley was accelerating as it ran down the runway.
- The line is straight, which tells us that the increase in velocity was the same every second. In other words, the acceleration of the trolley was constant.

Test B: If we make the runway steeper, the trolley accelerates faster. This would make the line on the graph in Figure 2 steeper than for test A. So the acceleration in test B is greater.

The gradient of a line is a measure of its steepness. The tests show that **the gradient of the line on a velocity–time graph represents acceleration.**

a If you made the runway less steep than in test A, would the line on the graph be steeper or less steep than in A?

Practical

Investigating acceleration

Use a motion sensor and a computer to find out how the gradient of a runway affects a trolley's acceleration.

- Name **i** the independent variable, and **ii** the dependent variable in this investigation.
- What relationship do you find between the variables?

Braking

Braking reduces the velocity of a vehicle. Look at the graph in Figure 3. It is the velocity–time graph for a vehicle that brakes and stops at a set of traffic lights. The velocity is constant until the driver applies the brakes.

Using the gradient of the line:

- The section of the graph for constant velocity is horizontal. The gradient of the line is zero so the acceleration in this section is zero.

- When the brakes are applied, the velocity decreases to zero and the vehicle decelerates. The gradient of the line is negative in this section. So the acceleration is negative.

b How would the gradient of the line differ if the deceleration had taken longer?

Look at the graph in Figure 3 again.

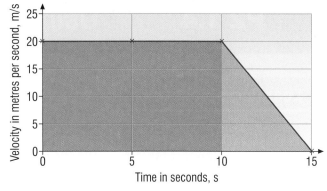

Figure 3 Braking

Using the area under the line

- Before the brakes are applied, the vehicle moves at a velocity of 20 m/s for 10 s. It therefore travels 200 m in this time (= 20 m/s × 10 s). This distance is represented on the graph by the area under the line from 0 s to 10 s. This is the shaded rectangle on the graph.

- When the vehicle decelerates in Figure 3, its velocity drops from 20 m/s to 0 m/s in 5 s. We can work out the distance travelled in this time from the area of the purple triangle in Figure 3. This area is ½ × the height × the base of the triangle. So the vehicle must have travelled a distance of 50 m when it was decelerating.

The area under the line on a velocity–time graph represents distance travelled.

c Would the total distance travelled be greater or smaller if the deceleration had taken longer? **[H]**

??? Did you know ... ?

A speed camera flashes when a vehicle travelling over the speed limit has gone past. Some speed cameras flash twice and measure the distance the car travels between flashes.

Summary questions

1 Match each of the following descriptions to one of the lines, labelled A, B, C and D, on the velocity–time graph.
 1 Accelerated motion throughout
 2 Zero acceleration
 3 Accelerated motion, then decelerated motion
 4 Deceleration

———— A   ———— C
———— B   ········ D

2 Look at the graph in Question 1. Which line represents the object that travelled:
 a the furthest distance? **[H]**
 b the least distance? **[H]**

3 Look again at the graph in Question 1.
 a Show that the object that produced the data for line A (the horizontal line) travelled a distance of 160 m. **[H]**
 b Which one of the other three lines represents the motion of an object that decelerated throughout its journey? **[H]**
 c Calculate the distance travelled by this object. **[H]**

Key points

- If a velocity–time graph is a horizontal line, the acceleration is zero.

- The gradient of the line on a velocity–time graph represents acceleration.

- The area under the line on a velocity–time graph represents distance travelled. **[H]**

P2 1.4 Using graphs (k)

Learning objectives

- How can we calculate speed from a distance–time graph? [H]

- How can we calculate acceleration from a velocity–time graph? [H]

- How can we calculate distance from a velocity–time graph? [H]

Using distance–time graphs

For an object moving at constant speed, we saw at the start of this chapter that the distance–time graph is a straight line sloping upwards.

The speed of the object is represented by the gradient of the line. To find the gradient, we need to draw a triangle under the line, as shown in Figure 1. The height of the triangle represents the distance travelled and the base represents the time taken. So

$$\text{the gradient of the line} = \frac{\text{the height of the triangle}}{\text{the base of the triangle}}$$

and this represents the object's speed.

a Find the speed of the object in the graph in Figure 1.

For a moving object with a changing speed, the distance–time graph is not a straight line. The graphs in Figure 2 show two examples.

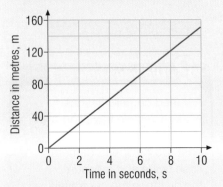

Figure 1 A distance–time graph for constant speed

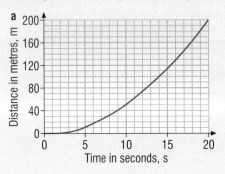
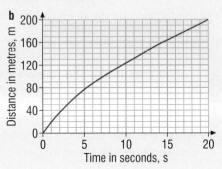

Figure 2 Distance–time graphs for changing speed

In Figure 2a, the gradient of the graph increases gradually, so the object's speed must have increased gradually.

b What can you say about the speed in Figure 2b?

Using velocity–time graphs

Look at the graph in Figure 3. It shows the velocity–time graph of an object X moving with a constant acceleration. Its velocity increases at a steady rate. So the graph shows a straight line that has a constant gradient.

To find the acceleration from the graph, remember the gradient of the line on a velocity–time graph represents the acceleration.

In Figure 3, the gradient is given by the height divided by the base of the triangle under the line.

The height of the triangle represents the change of velocity and the base of the triangle represents the time taken.

Therefore, the gradient represents the acceleration, because:

$$\text{acceleration} = \frac{\text{change of velocity}}{\text{time taken}}$$

Figure 3 A velocity–time graph for constant acceleration

Maths skills

Worked example

Use the graph in Figure 3 to find the acceleration of object X.

Solution

The height of the triangle represents an increase of velocity of 8 m/s (= 12 m/s – 4 m/s).

The base of the triangle represents a time of 10 s.

Therefore, the acceleration = $\dfrac{\text{change of velocity}}{\text{time taken}} = \dfrac{8\,\text{m/s}}{10\,\text{s}} = 0.8\,\text{m/s}^2$

To find the distance travelled from the graph, remember the area under a line on a velocity–time graph represents the distance travelled. The shape under the line in Figure 3 is a triangle on top of a rectangle. So the distance travelled is represented by the area of the triangle plus the area of the rectangle under it.

Look at the worked example opposite.

Maths skills

Worked example

Use the graph in Figure 3 to calculate the distance moved by object X.

Solution

The area of the triangle = ½ × height × base.

Therefore, the distance represented by the area of triangle = ½ × 8 m/s × 10 s
= 40 m

The area of the rectangle under the triangle = height × base

Therefore, the distance represented by the area of the rectangle = 4 m/s × 10 s
= 40 m

So the distance travelled by X = 40 m + 40 m = 80 m

Summary questions

1 Copy and complete **a** to **c** using the words below:

acceleration   distance   speed

a The area under the line of a velocity–time graph represents ....

b The gradient of a line on a distance–time graph represents ....

c The gradient of a line on a velocity–time graph represents .... [H]

2 The graph shows how the velocity of a cyclist on a straight road changes with time.

a Describe the motion of the cyclist.

b Use the graph to work out
   i the initial acceleration of the cyclist
   ii the distance travelled by the cyclist in the first 40 s. [H]

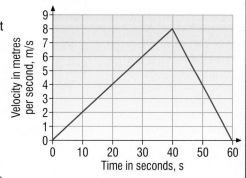

3 In a motorcycle test, the speed from rest was recorded at intervals.

Time (seconds, s)	0	5	10	15	20	25	30
Velocity (metre per second, m/s)	0	10	20	30	40	40	40

a Plot a velocity–time graph of these results.

b What was the initial acceleration?

c How far did it move in:
   i the first 20 s?
   ii the next 10 s? [H]

Key points

- The speed of an object is given by the gradient of the line on its distance–time graph. [H]

- The acceleration of an object is given by the gradient of the line on its velocity–time graph. [H]

- The distance travelled by an object is given by the area under the line of its velocity–time graph. [H]

Summary questions

1 A model car travels round a circular track at constant speed.

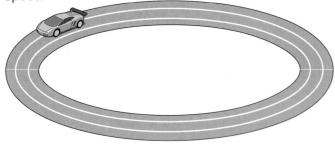

a If you were given a stopwatch, a marker, and a tape measure, how would you measure:

  i the time taken by the car to travel 10 laps

  ii the distance the car travels in 10 laps.

b If the car travels 36 metres in 30 seconds, calculate its speed.

2 A train travels at a constant speed of 35 m/s. Calculate:

a how far it travels in 20 s

b how long it takes to travel a distance of 1400 m.

3 The figure shows the distance–time graph for a car on a motorway.

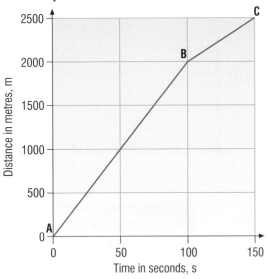

a Which part of the journey was faster, A to B or B to C?

b i How far did the car travel from A to B and how long did it take?

  ii Calculate the speed of the car between A and B.

4 a A car took 8 s to increase its velocity from 8 m/s to 28 m/s. Calculate:

  i its change of velocity

  ii its acceleration.

b A vehicle travelling at a velocity of 24 m/s slowed down and stopped in 20 s. Calculate its deceleration.

5 The figure shows the velocity–time graph of a passenger jet before it took off.

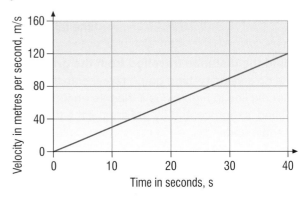

a Calculate the acceleration of the jet.

b Calculate the distance it travelled before it took off. [H

6 The table below shows how the velocity of a train changes as it travelled from one station to the next.

Time (seconds)	0	20	40	60	80	100	120	140	160
Velocity (m/s)	0	5	10	15	20	20	20	10	0

a Plot a velocity–time graph using this data.

b Calculate the acceleration in each of the three parts of the journey.

c Calculate the total distance travelled by the train.

d Show that the average speed for the train's journey was 12.5 m/s. [H

7 A motorcyclist started from rest and accelerated steadily to 25 m/s in 5 seconds then slowed down steadily to a halt 30 seconds after she started.

a Draw a velocity–time graph for this journey.

b Show that the acceleration of the motorcyclist in the first 5 seconds was 5.0 m/s².

c Calculate the deceleration of the motorcyclist in the last 25 seconds.

d Use your graph to show that the total distance travelled by the motorcyclist was 375 metres. [H

AQA Examination-style questions

1 The table gives values of distance and time for a child travelling along a straight track competing in an egg and spoon race.

Time (seconds)	0	5	10	15	20	25
Distance (metres)	0	8	20	20	24	40

a Copy the graph axes below on to graph paper. Plot a graph of distance against time for the child. (3)

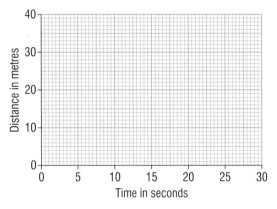

b Name the dependent variable shown on the graph. (1)

c What type of variable is this? (1)

d Use your graph to estimate the distance travelled in 22 seconds. (1)

e Use your graph to estimate the time taken for the child to travel 15 metres. (1)

f Describe the motion of the child between 10 seconds and 15 seconds.
Give a reason for your answer. (2)

2 The graph shows how far a runner travels during a charity running race.

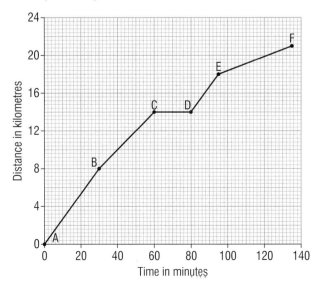

a What was the distance of the race? (1)

b How long did it take the runner to complete the race? (1)

c For how long did the runner rest during the race? (1)

d Between which two points was the runner moving the fastest?
Give a reason for your answer. (2)

e Between which two points did the runner travel at the same speed as they did between A and B? (1)

f Calculate the speed of the runner between B and C in metres per second.
Write down the equation you use. Show clearly how you work out your answer. (3)

3 A cyclist is travelling along a straight road. The graph shows how the velocity changes with time for part of the journey.

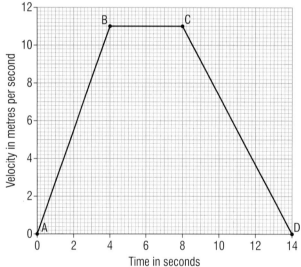

a Explain how the acceleration can be found from a velocity–time graph. (1)

b Copy and complete the following sentences using the list of words and phrases below. Each one can be used once, more than once or not at all.

is stationary   travels at a constant speed
accelerates   decelerates

   i Between A and B the cyclist .... (1)
   ii Between B and C the cyclist .... (1)
   iii Between C and D the cyclist .... (1)

c i Use the graph to find the maximum speed of the cyclist. (2)

   ii Use the graph to calculate the distance travelled in metres between 4 and 8 seconds. Show clearly how you work out your answer. (2)

   iii Use the graph to calculate the total distance travelled in metres.
Show clearly how you work out your answer. [H] (6)

P2 2.1

Forces between objects

Learning objectives

- What can forces do?

- What is the unit of force?

- When two objects interact, what can we say about the forces acting?

?? Did you know ...?

Quicksand victims sink because they can't get enough support from the sand. The force of gravity on the victim (acting downwards) is greater than the upwards force of the sand on the victim. People caught in quicksand should not struggle but flatten themselves on the surface and crawl to a safe place.

When you apply a **force** to a tube of toothpaste, be careful not to apply too much force. The force you apply to squeeze the tube changes its shape and pushes toothpaste out of the tube. If you apply too much force, the toothpaste might come out too fast.

A force can change the shape of an object or change its state of rest or its motion.

Equal and opposite forces

Whenever two objects push or pull on each other, they exert equal and opposite forces on one another. The unit of force is the newton (abbreviated as N).

- A boxer who punches an opponent with a force of 100 N experiences a reverse force of 100 N from his opponent.

- Two roller skaters pull on opposite ends of a rope. The skaters move towards each other. This is because they pull on each other with equal and opposite forces. Two newtonmeters could be used to show this.

Figure 1 Equal and opposite forces

 Practical

Action and reaction

Test this with a friend if you can, using roller skates and two newtonmeters. Don't forget to wear protective head gear!

- What did you find out?

- Comment on the precision of your readings.

a A hammer hits a nail with a downward force of 50 N. What is the size and direction of the force of the nail on the hammer?

In the mud

A car stuck in mud can be difficult to shift. A tractor can be very useful here. Figure 2 shows the idea. At any stage, the force of the rope on the car is equal and opposite to the force of the car on the rope.

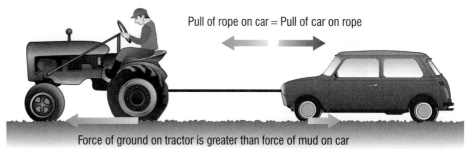

Pull of rope on car = Pull of car on rope

Force of ground on tractor is greater than force of mud on car

Figure 2 In the mud

To pull the car out of the mud, the force of the ground on the tractor needs to be greater than the force of the mud on the car. These two forces aren't necessarily equal to one another because the objects are not the same.

b A lorry tows a broken-down car. When the force of the lorry on the tow rope is 200 N, what is the force of the tow rope on the lorry?

Friction in action

The driving force on a car is the force that makes it move. This is sometimes called the engine force or the **motive force**. This force is due to **friction** between the ground and the tyre of each drive wheel. Friction acts where the tyre is in contact with the ground.

When the car moves forwards:

- the force of friction of the ground on the tyre is in the forward direction
- the force of friction of the tyre on the ground is in the reverse direction.

The two forces are equal and opposite to one another.

c What happens if there isn't enough friction between the tyre and the ground?

Direction of car

Force of tyre on road   Force of road on tyre

Figure 3 Driving force

Summary questions

1 a When the brakes of a moving car are applied, what is the effect of the braking force on the car?

b When you sit on a cushion, what is the effect of your weight on the cushion?

c When you kick a football, what is the effect of the force of your foot on the ball?

2 Copy and complete **a** and **b** using the words below:

downwards   equal   opposite   upwards

a The force on a ladder resting against a wall is .... and .... to the force of the wall on the ladder.

b A book is at rest on a table. The force of the book on the table is .... The force of the table on the book is ....

3 When a student is standing at rest on bathroom scales, the scales read 500 N.

a What is the size and direction of the force of the student on the scales?

b What is the size and direction of the force of the scales on the student?

Key points

- A force can change the shape of an object or change its motion or its state of rest.

- The unit of force is the newton (N).

- When two objects interact, they always exert equal and opposite forces on each other.

P2 2.2

Resultant force

Learning objectives

● What is a resultant force?

● What happens if the resultant force on an object is:
  – zero?
  – not zero?

● How do we calculate the resultant force when an object is acted on by two forces acting along the same line?

Wherever you are at this moment, at least two forces are acting on you. These are the force of gravity on you and a force supporting you. Most objects around you are acted on by more than one force. We can work out the effect of the forces on an object by replacing them with a single force, the **resultant force**. This is a single force that has the same effect as all the forces acting on the object.

Zero resultant force

When the resultant force on an object is zero, the object:

● remains stationary if it was at rest, or

● continues to move at the same speed and in the same direction if it was already moving.

If two forces only act on the object, they must be equal to each other and act in opposite directions.

⬯ links

For more information on using data to draw conclusions, see H3 Using data.

⚙ Practical

Investigating forces

Make and test a model hovercraft floating on a cushion of air from a balloon.

And/or:

Use a glider on an air track to investigate the relationship between force and acceleration.

● What relationship do you find between force and acceleration?

---

1 **A glider on a linear air track** floats on a cushion of air. Provided the track is level, the glider moves at constant velocity (i.e. with no change of speed or direction) along the track. That's because friction is absent. The resultant force on the glider is zero.

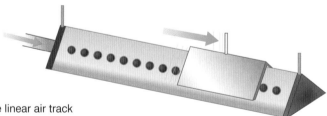

Figure 1 The linear air track

a What happens to the glider if the air track blower is switched off, and why?

2 **When a heavy crate is pushed across a rough floor at a constant velocity,** the resultant force on the crate is zero. The push force on the crate is equal in size but acts in the opposite direction to the force of friction of the floor on the crate.

b What difference would it make if the floor were smooth?

Push force

Friction

Figure 2 Overcoming friction

Non-zero resultant force

When the resultant force on an object is not zero, the movement of the object depends on the size and direction of the resultant force.

1 **When a jet plane is taking off**, the thrust force of its engines is greater than the force of air resistance on it. The resultant force on it is the difference between the thrust force and the force of air resistance on it. The resultant force is therefore non-zero. The greater the resultant force, the quicker the take-off is.

   c What can you say about the thrust force and the force of air resistance when the plane is moving at constant velocity at constant height?

2 **When a car driver applies the brakes**, the braking force is greater than the force from the engine. The resultant force is the difference between the braking force and the engine force. It acts in the opposite direction to the car's direction. So it slows the car down.

   d What can you say about the resultant force if the brakes had been applied harder?

The examples above show that if an object is acted on by two unequal forces acting in opposite directions, the resultant force is:

● equal to the difference between the two forces
● in the direction of the larger force.

Note what happens if the two forces act in the same direction. The resultant force is equal to the sum of the two forces and acts in the same direction as the two forces.

Figure 3 A passenger jet on take-off

Figure 4 Braking

Summary questions

1 Copy and complete **a** to **c** using the words below:

greater than   less than   equal to

A car starts from rest and accelerates along a straight flat road.
  a The force of air resistance on it is .... the driving force of its engine.
  b The resultant force is .... zero.
  c The downward force of the car on the road is .... the support force of the road on the car.

2 A jet plane lands on a runway and stops.
  a What can you say about the direction of the resultant force on the plane as it lands?
  b What can you say about the resultant force on the plane when it has stopped?

3 A car is stuck in the mud. A tractor tries to pull it out.
  a The tractor pulls the car with a force of 250 N but the car doesn't move. Explain why the car doesn't move.
  b Increasing the tractor force to 300 N pulls the car steadily out of the mud. What is the force of the mud on the car now?

Key points

● The resultant force is a single force that has the same effect as all the forces acting on an object.

● If the resultant force on an object is zero, the object stays at rest or at constant velocity. If the resultant force on an object is not zero, the velocity of the object will change.

● If two forces act on an object along the same line, the resultant force is:
  1 their sum if the forces act in the same direction
  2 their difference if the forces act in opposite directions.

P2 2.3 Force and acceleration

Learning objectives

- How does the acceleration of an object depend on the size of the resultant force?

- What effect does the mass of the object have on its acceleration?

- How do we calculate the resultant force on an object from its acceleration and its mass?

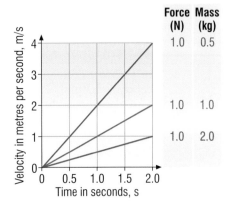

Figure 2 Velocity–time graph for different combinations of force and mass

Force (N)	Mass (kg)
1.0	0.5
1.0	1.0
1.0	2.0

∞ links

For more information on how to work out the acceleration from the gradient of the line, look back at P2 1.4 Using graphs.

 Maths skills

Worked example

Calculate the resultant force on an object of mass 6.0 kg when it has an acceleration of 3.0 m/s².

Solution

Resultant force
= mass × acceleration
= 6.0 kg × 3.0 m/s² = 18.0 N

Practical

Investigating force and acceleration

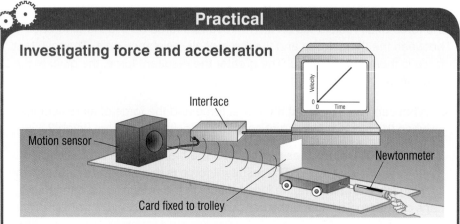

Figure 1 Investigating the link between force and motion

We can use the apparatus above to accelerate a trolley with a constant force.

Use the newtonmeter to pull the trolley along with a constant force.

You can double or treble the total moving mass by using double-deck and triple-deck trolleys.

A motion sensor and a computer record the velocity of the trolley as it accelerates.

- What are the advantages of using a data logger and computer in this investigation?

You can display the results as a velocity–time graph on the computer screen.

Figure 2 shows velocity–time graphs for different masses. You can work out the acceleration from the gradient of the line, as explained in the previous chapter.

Look at some typical results in the table below:

Resultant force (newtons)	0.5	1.0	1.5	2.0	4.0	6.0
Mass (kilograms)	1.0	1.0	1.0	2.0	2.0	2.0
Acceleration (m/s²)	0.5	1.0	1.5	1.0	2.0	3.0
Mass × acceleration (kg m/s²)	0.5	1.0	1.5	2.0	4.0	6.0

The results show that the resultant force, the mass and the acceleration are linked by the equation

resultant force = **mass** × **acceleration**
(newtons, N) (kilograms) (metres/second²)

We can write the word equation above using symbols as follows:

resultant force, $F = ma$,

Where F = resultant force in newtons
m = mass in kilograms
a = acceleration in metres/second².

a Calculate the resultant force on a sprinter of mass 80 kg who accelerates at 8 m/s².

Higher

Maths skills

Worked example

Calculate the acceleration of an object of mass 5.0 kg acted on by a resultant force of 40 N.

Solution

Rearranging $F = ma$ gives $a = \dfrac{F}{m} = \dfrac{40\,N}{5.0\,kg} = 8.0\,m/s^2$

b Calculate the acceleration of a car of mass 800 kg acted on by a resultant force of 3200 N.

Speeding up or slowing down

If the velocity of an object changes, it must be acted on by a resultant force. Its acceleration is always in the same direction as the resultant force.

- The velocity of the object increases if the resultant force is in the **same** direction as the velocity. We say its acceleration is positive because it is in the same direction as its velocity.
- The velocity of the object decreases (i.e. it decelerates) if the resultant force is **opposite** in direction to its velocity. We say its acceleration is negative because it is opposite in direction to its velocity.

Summary questions

1 Copy and complete **a** to **c** using the words below. Each word can be used more than once.

acceleration   resultant force   mass   velocity

a A moving object decelerates when a .... acts on it in the opposite direction to its ....

b The greater the .... of an object is, the less its acceleration is when a .... acts on it.

c The .... of a moving object increases when a .... acts on it in the same direction as it is moving in.

2 Copy and complete the following table:

	a	b	c	d	e
Force (newtons, N)		200	840		5000
Mass (kilograms, kg)	20		70	0.40	
Acceleration (metres/second squared, m/s²)	0.80	5.0		6.0	0.20

3 A car and a trailer have a total mass of 1500 kg.

Tow bar

a Find the force needed to accelerate the car and the trailer at 2.0 m/s².

b The mass of the trailer is 300 kg. Find the force of the tow bar on the trailer.

Maths skills

We can rearrange the equation $F = ma$ to give

$$a = \frac{F}{m} \quad or \quad m = \frac{F}{a}$$

Did you know … ?

If you're in a car that suddenly brakes, your neck pulls on your head and slows it down. The equal and opposite force of your head on your neck can injure your neck.

Figure 3 A 'whiplash' injury

AQA Examiner's tip

- If an object is accelerating, it can be speeding up or changing direction. If it is decelerating, it is slowing down.
- If an object is accelerating or decelerating, there must be a resultant force acting on it.

Key points

- The bigger the resultant force on an object is, the greater its acceleration is.
- The greater the mass of an object is, the smaller its acceleration is for a given force.
- Resultant force (newtons, N) = mass (kilograms) × acceleration (metres/second²)

On the road

Learning objectives

- What forces oppose the driving force of a car?
- What does the stopping distance of a vehicle depend on?
- What factors can increase the stopping distance of a vehicle?

Did you know ...?

The mass of a BMW Mini Cooper car is just over 1000 kg.

Did you know ...?

When the brakes of a car are applied, friction between the brake pads and the car wheels causes kinetic energy to be transferred by heating to the brakes and the brake pads. If the brake pads wear away too much, they need to be replaced.

Practical

Reaction times

Use an electronic stopwatch to test your own reaction time. Ask a friend to start the stopwatch when you are looking at it with your finger on the stop button. The read-out from the watch will give your reaction time.

- How can you make your data as precise as possible?
- What conclusions can you draw?

Forces on the road

For any car travelling at constant velocity, the resultant force on it is zero. This is because the driving force of its engine is balanced by the resistive forces (i.e. friction and air resistance). The resistive forces are mostly due to air resistance. Friction between parts of the car that move against each other also contributes.

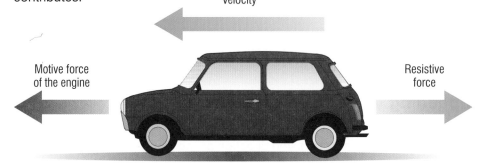

Figure 1 Constant velocity

A car driver uses the accelerator pedal (also called the gas pedal) to vary the driving force of the engine.

a What do you think happens if the driver presses harder on the accelerator?

The **braking force needed to stop a vehicle** in a certain distance depends on:

- the speed of the vehicle when the brakes are first applied
- the mass of the vehicle.

We can see this using the equation 'resultant force = mass × acceleration', in which the braking force is the resultant force.

1 The greater the speed, the greater the deceleration needed to stop the vehicle in a certain distance. So the braking force must be greater than at low speed.

2 The greater the mass, the greater the braking force needed for a given deceleration.

Stopping distances

Driving tests always ask about **stopping distances**. This is the shortest distance a vehicle can safely stop in, and is in two parts:

The thinking distance: the distance travelled by the vehicle in the time it takes the driver to react (i.e. during the driver's reaction time).

The braking distance: the distance travelled by the vehicle during the time the braking force acts.

stopping distance = thinking distance + braking distance

Figure 2 shows the stopping distance for a vehicle on a dry flat road travelling at different speeds. Check for yourself that the stopping distance at 31 m/s (70 miles per hour) is 96 m.

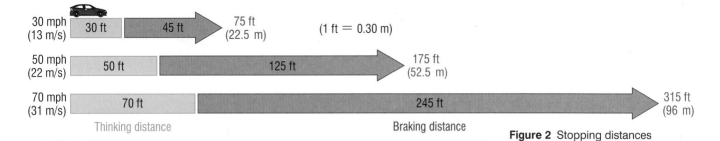

(1 ft = 0.30 m)

Thinking distance   Braking distance

Figure 2 Stopping distances

b What are the thinking distance, the braking distance in metres and the stopping distance at 13 m/s (30 mph)? (1 foot = 0.3 metres).

Maths skills

- The thinking distance is equal to the car's speed multiplied by the driver's reaction time. So it is directly proportional to the car's speed.
- The braking distance is equal to the average speed of the car during braking multiplied by the braking time. Since both of these quantities are directly proportional to the car's speed (before the brakes are applied), the braking distance is directly proportional to the square of the car's speed.

Factors affecting stopping distances

1 **Tiredness, alcohol and drugs** all increase reaction times. Distractions such as using a mobile phone can also affect reaction time. All these factors increase the thinking distance (because thinking distance = speed × reaction time). Therefore, the stopping distance is greater.
2 **The faster a vehicle is travelling**, the further it travels before it stops. This is because the thinking distance and the braking distance both increase with increased speed.
3 **In adverse road conditions**, for example on wet or icy roads, drivers have to brake with less force to avoid skidding. Stopping distances are therefore greater in poor road conditions.
4 **Poorly maintained vehicles**, for example with worn brakes or tyres, take longer to stop because the brakes and tyres are less effective.

c Why are stopping distances greater in poor visibility?

Figure 3 Stopping distances are further than you might think!

Summary questions

1 Each of the following factors affects the thinking distance or the braking distance of a vehicle. Which of these two distances is affected in these?
   a The road surface condition affects the .... distance.
   b The tiredness of a driver increases his or her .... distance.
   c Poorly maintained brakes affects the .... distance.

2 **a** Use the chart in Figure 2 to work out, in metres, the increase in
   i the thinking distance   **ii** the braking distance
   iii the stopping distance from 13 m/s (30 mph) to 22 m/s (50 mph).
   b A driver has a reaction time of 0.8 s. Calculate her thinking distance at a speed of   **i** 15 m/s   **ii** 30 m/s.

3 When the speed of a car is doubled:
   a Explain why the thinking distance of the driver is doubled, assuming the driver's reaction time is unchanged.
   b Explain why the braking distance is more than doubled.

Key points

- Friction and air resistance oppose the driving force of a car.

- The stopping distance of a car depends on the thinking distance and the braking distance.

- High speed, poor weather conditions and poor maintenance all increase the braking distance. Poor reaction time and high speed both increase the thinking distance.

P2 2.5

Falling objects

Learning objectives

- What is the difference between mass and weight?
- What can we say about the motion of a falling object acted on only by gravity?
- What is terminal velocity?

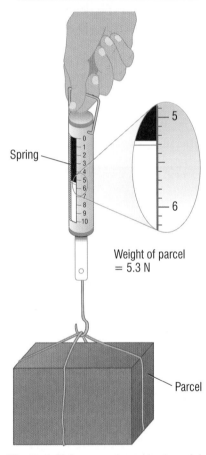

Spring

Weight of parcel = 5.3 N

Parcel

Figure 1 Using a newtonmeter to weigh an object

Maths skills

Worked example

Calculate the weight in newtons of a person of mass 55 kg.

Solution

Weight = mass × gravitational field strength = 55 kg × 10 N/kg = 550 N

How to reduce your weight

Your weight is due to the gravitational force of attraction between you and the Earth. This force is very slightly weaker at the equator than at the poles. So if you want to reduce your weight, go to the equator. However, your mass will be the same no matter where you are.

- The **weight** of an object is the force of gravity on it. Weight is measured in newtons.
- The **mass** of an object is the quantity of matter in it. Mass is measured in kilograms.

We can measure the weight of an object using a newtonmeter.

The weight of an object:

- of mass 1 kg is 10 N
- of mass 5 kg is 50 N.

The force of gravity on a 1 kg object is the **gravitational field strength** at the place where the object is. The unit of gravitational field strength is the newton per kilogram (N/kg).

The value of the Earth's gravitational field strength at its surface is about 10 N/kg.

If we know the mass of an object, we can calculate the force of gravity on it (i.e. its weight) using the equation:

$$\text{weight} = \text{mass} \times \text{gravitational field strength}$$
$$\text{(newtons, N)} \quad \text{(kilograms, kg)} \quad \text{(newtons/kilogram, N/kg)}$$

We can write the word equation above using symbols as follows:

$$\text{weight, } W = mg,$$

Where:
W = weight in newtons, N
m = mass in kilograms, kg
g = gravitational field strength in newtons per kilogram, N/kg

a Calculate the weight of a steel bar of mass 20 kg.

The forces on falling objects

If we release an object above the ground, it falls because of its weight (i.e. the force of gravity on it).

If the object falls with no other forces acting on it, the resultant force on it is its weight. It accelerates downwards at a constant acceleration of 10 m/s². This is called the acceleration due to gravity. For example, if we release a 1 kg object above the ground:

- the force of gravity on it is 10 N, and
- its acceleration (= force/mass = 10 N/1 kg) = 10 m/s².

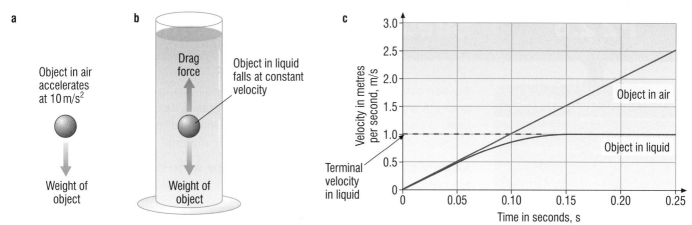

Figure 2 Falling objects. **a** Falling in air, **b** falling in a liquid, **c** velocity–time graph for **a** and **b**.

If the object falls in a fluid, the fluid drags on the object. The **drag force** increases with speed. At any instant, the resultant force on the object is its weight minus the drag force on it.

● The acceleration of the object decreases as it falls. This is because the drag force increases as it speeds up. So the resultant force on it decreases and therefore its acceleration decreases.

● The object reaches a constant velocity when the drag force on it is equal and opposite to its weight. We call this velocity its **terminal velocity**. The resultant force is then zero, so its acceleration is zero.

When an object moves through the air (i.e. the fluid is air) the drag force is called **air resistance**. This is not shown in Figure 2a because air resistance is very small in a short descent.

b Why does an object released in water eventually reach a constant velocity?

Summary questions

1 Copy and complete **a** to **c** using the words below:

   equal to   greater than   less than

   When an object is released in a fluid:

   a The drag force on it is .... its weight before it reaches its terminal velocity.

   b Its acceleration is .... zero after it reaches its terminal velocity.

   c The resultant force on it is initially .... its weight.

2 The gravitational field strength at the surface of the Earth is 10 N/kg. For the Moon, it is 1.6 N/kg.

   a Calculate the weight of a person of mass 50 kg at the surface of the Earth.

   b Calculate the weight of the same person if she was on the surface of the Moon.

3 A parachutist of mass 70 kg supported by a parachute of mass 20 kg reaches a constant speed.

   a Explain why the parachutist reaches a constant speed.

   b Calculate:

   i the total weight of the parachutist and the parachute

   ii the size and direction of the force of air resistance on the parachute when the parachutist falls at constant speed.

Practical

Investigating falling

Release an object with and without a parachute.

Make suitable measurements to compare the two situations.

● Why does the object fall at constant speed when the parachute is open?

● Evaluate the quality of the data you collected. How could you improve your data?

Figure 3 Using a parachute

Key points

● The weight of an object is the force of gravity on it. Its mass is the quantity of matter in it.

● An object acted on only by gravity accelerates at about 10 m/s².

● The terminal velocity of a falling object is the velocity it reaches when it is falling in a fluid. The weight is then equal to the drag force on the object.

P2 2.6 Stretching and squashing

Learning objectives

- How do we measure the extension of an object when it is stretched?
- How does the extension of a spring vary with the force applied to it?
- What is the spring constant of a spring?

Did you know ... ?

Rubber and other soft materials such as flowers dipped in liquid nitrogen become as brittle as glass. Such frozen materials shatter when struck with a hammer or explode when hit with a projectile.

Figure 2 A flower dipped in nitrogen and then smashed

Table 1 Weight versus length measurements for a rubber strip

Weight (N)	Length (mm)	Extension (mm)
0	120	0
1.0	152	32
2.0	190	70
3.0	250	
4.0		

Squash players know that hitting a squash ball changes the ball's shape briefly. A squash ball is **elastic** because it regains its original shape. A rubber band is also elastic as it regains its original length after it is stretched and then released. Rubber is an example of an elastic material.

An elastic object regains its original shape when the forces deforming it are removed.

Practical

Stretch tests

We can investigate how easily a material stretches by hanging weights from it, as shown in Figure 1.

- The strip of material to be tested is clamped at its upper end. A weight hanger is attached to the material to keep it straight.
- The length of the strip is measured using a metre ruler. This is its original length.
- The weight hung from the material is increased by adding weights one at a time. The strip stretches each time more weight is hung from it.
- The length of the strip is measured each time a weight is added. The total weight added and the total length of the strip are recorded in a table.

Figure 1 Investigating stretching

The increase of length from the original is called the **extension**. This is calculated each time a weight is added and recorded, as shown in Table 1.

The extension of the strip of material at any stage = its length at the stage – its original length

The measurements may be plotted on a graph of extension on the vertical axis against weight on the horizontal axis. Figure 3 shows the results for strips of different materials and a steel spring plotted on the same axes.

- The steel spring gives a straight line through the origin. This shows that the extension of the steel spring is **directly proportional** to the weight hung on it. For example, doubling the weight from 2.0 N to 4.0 N doubles the extension of the spring.
- The rubber band does not give a straight line. When the weight on the rubber band is doubled from 2.0 N to 4.0 N, the extension more than doubles.
- The polythene strip does not give a straight line either. As the weight is increased from zero, the polythene strip stretches very little at first then it 'gives' and stretches easily.

a Which part of a plastic shopping bag 'gives' if you overload the bag?

Elastic energy

When an elastic object is stretched, elastic potential energy is stored in the object. This is because work is done on the object by the stretching force.

When the stretching force is removed, the elastic energy stored in the object is released. Some of this energy may be transferred into kinetic energy of the object or may make its atoms vibrate more so it becomes warmer.

Hooke's law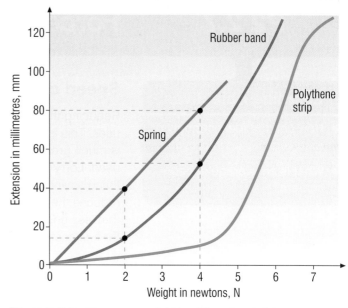

In the tests above, the extension of a steel spring is directly proportional to the force applied to it. We can use the graph to predict what the extension would be for any given force. But if the force is too large, the spring stretches more than predicted. This is because the spring has been stretched beyond its **limit of proportionality**.

Figure 3 Extension versus weight for different materials

The extension of a spring is directly proportional to the force applied, provided its limit of proportionality is not exceeded.

The above statement is known as **Hooke's law**. If the extension of any stretched object or material is directly proportional to the stretching force, we say it obeys Hooke's law.

1 The lines on the graph in Figure 3 show that rubber and polythene have a low limit of proportionality. Beyond this limit, they do not obey Hooke's law. A steel spring has a much higher limit of proportionality.

2 Hooke's law may be written as an equation:

Force applied =	**spring constant**	×	**extension**
(in newtons, N)	(in newtons per metre, N/m)		(in metres, m)

The **spring constant** is equal to the force per unit extension needed to extend the spring, assuming its limit of proportionality is not reached. The stiffer a spring is, the greater its spring constant is.

b A spring has a spring constant of 25 N/m. How much force is needed to make the spring extend by 0.10 m?

Maths skills

We can write the word equation for Hooke's law using symbols as follows:

$$F = k \times e,$$

Where:
F = force in newtons, N
k = the spring constant in newtons per metre, N/m
e = extension in metres, m.

Summary questions

1 Copy and complete **a** to **c** using the words below.

   elastic limit   extension   length

   a When a steel spring is stretched, its .... is increased.
   b When a strip of polythene is stretched beyond its .... , its length is permanently increased.
   c When rubber is stretched and unstretched, its .... afterwards is zero.

2 What is meant by:
   a the limit of proportionality of a spring?
   b the spring constant of a spring?

3 **a** In Figure 3, when the weight is 4.0 N, what is the extension of:
   i the spring   **ii** the rubber band   **iii** the polythene strip?
   b i What is the extension of the spring when the weight is 3.0 N?
   ii Calculate the spring constant of the spring

Key points

- The extension is the difference between the length of the spring and its original length.

- The extension of a spring is directly proportional to the force applied to it, provided the limit of proportionality is not exceeded.

- The spring constant of a spring is the force per unit extension needed to stretch it.

P2 2.7

Force and speed issues

Learning objectives

- How can the fuel economy of road vehicles be improved?
- What is an average speed camera?

Speed costs

Reducing the speed of a vehicle reduces the fuel it uses. This is because air resistance at high speed is much greater than at low speed. So more fuel is used. Lorry drivers can reduce their fuel usage by fitting a wind deflector over the cab. The deflector reduces the air resistance on the lorry. This means that less engine force and less power are needed to maintain a certain speed. So fuel costs are reduced because less fuel is needed.

Figure 1 A wind deflector on a lorry

a When a vehicle is accelerating, what can you say about the engine force and the air resistance?

Activity

The shape of a wind deflector on a lorry affects air resistance. Investigate the effect of the deflector shape by testing a trolley with a box on (or a toy lorry) without a deflector then fitted with deflectors of different shapes. You could use a hairdryer to blow air at the 'lorry' and use a newtonmeter to measure the force needed to stop it being blown backwards. (See P2 3.1 Figure 2.)

Speed kills!

- At 20 mph, the stopping distance of a car is 12 metres.
- At 40 mph, the stopping distance is 36 metres.
- At 60 mph, the stopping distance is 72 metres.

If someone walks across a road in front of a car, a driver travelling slowly is much more likely to stop safely than a speeding driver. The force on a person struck by a car increases with speed. Even at 20 mph, it can be many times the person's weight. A speed limit of 20 mph is in place outside many schools now.

Speed cameras

Speed cameras are very effective in discouraging motorists from speeding. A speeding motorist caught by a speed camera is fined and can lose his or her driving licence. On some motorways,

- Speed limits can vary according to the amount of traffic on the motorway.
- Speed cameras may be linked. These can catch out motorists who slow down for a speed camera then speed up.

In some areas, residents are supplied with 'mobile' speed cameras to catch speeding motorists. Some motorists think this is going too far and that speed cameras should not be used in this way. Lots of motorists say speed cameras are being used by local councils to increase their income.

Are speed cameras effective?

A report from one police force said that where speed cameras had been introduced:

- average speeds fell by 17%
- deaths and serious injuries fell by 55%.

Another police force reported that, in their area, as a result of installing more speed cameras in 2003:

- There were no child deaths in road accidents for the first time since 1927.
- 420 fewer children were involved in road accidents compared with the previous year.

b Discuss whether or not the statements above prove the argument that speed cameras save lives.

Anti-skid surfaces

Have you noticed that road surfaces near road junctions and traffic lights are often different from normal road surfaces?

- The surface is rougher than normal. This gives increased friction between the surface and a vehicle tyre, so it reduces the chance of skidding when a driver in a car applies the brakes.
- The surface is lighter in colour so it is marked out clearly from a normal road surface.

Skidding happens when the brakes are applied too harshly. The wheels lock and the tyres slide on the road as a result. Increased friction between the tyres and the road allows more force to be applied without skidding happening, so the stopping distance is reduced.

Figure 3 A speed camera

Figure 4 An anti-skid surface

Summary questions

1 The legal limit for a driver with alcohol in the blood is 80 milligrams per litre. Above this level, reaction times become significantly longer. The thinking distance of a normal car driver (i.e. one with no alcohol in the blood) travelling at 30 mph is 9.0 m (30 feet).

  a i What would this distance be for a driver whose reaction time is 20% longer than that of a normal driver?

    ii Drivers at the legal limit are 80% more likely to be in a road accident than normal drivers. Researchers think that a reduction of the legal limit to 40 milligrams per litre would cut the risk from 80% to 20%. Discuss whether or not the present legal limit should be reduced.

  b The braking distance for a car at 30 mph is 13.5 m and 6.0 m at 20 mph.

    i Thinking distance is directly proportional to speed. Show that the thinking distance at 20 mph is 6.0 m.

    ii Calculate the reduction in the stopping distance.

  c Many parents want the speed limit outside schools to be reduced to 20 mph. Explain why this would reduce road accidents outside schools significantly.

2 Campaigners in the village of Greystoke want the council to resurface the main road at the traffic lights in the village. A child was killed crossing the road at the traffic lights earlier in the year. The council estimates it would cost £45 000. They say they can't afford it. Campaigners have found some more data to support their case.

- There are about 50 000 road accidents each year in the UK.
- The cost of road accidents is over £8 billion per year.
- Anti-skid surfaces have cut accidents by about 5%.

  a Estimate how much each road accident costs.

  b Imagine you are one of the campaigners. Write a letter to your local newspaper to challenge the council's response that they can't afford to resurface the road.

Key points

- Fuel economy of road vehicles can be improved by reducing the speed or fitting a wind deflector.

- Average speed cameras are linked in pairs and they measure the average speed of a vehicle.

- Anti-skid surfaces increase the friction between a car tyre and the road surface. This reduces skids, or even prevents skids altogether.

Summary questions

1 A student is pushing a box across a rough floor. Friction acts between the box and the floor.

a Copy and complete sentences **i** and **ii** using the words below:

in the same direction as   in the opposite direction to

  i The force of friction of the box on the floor is .... the force of friction of the floor on the box.

  ii The force of the student on the box is .... the force of friction of the box on the floor.

b The student is pushing the box towards a door. Which direction, towards the door or away from the door, is:

  i the force of the box on the student?

  ii the force of friction of the student on the floor?

2 a The weight of an object of mass 100 kg on the Moon is 160 N.

  i Calculate the gravitational field strength on the Moon.

  ii Calculate the weight of the object on the Earth's surface.

  The gravitational field strength near the Earth's surface is 10 N/kg.

b Calculate the acceleration and the resultant force in each of the following situations.

  i A sprinter of mass 80 kg accelerates from rest to a speed of 9.6 m/s in 1.2 s.

  ii A train of mass 70 000 kg decelerates from a velocity of 16 m/s to a standstill in 40 s without change of direction.

3 The figure shows the velocity–time graphs for a metal object X dropped in air and a similar object Y dropped in a tank of water.

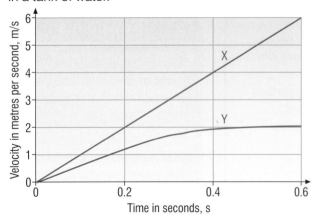

a What does the graph for X tell you about its acceleration?

b In terms of the forces acting on Y, explain why it reached a constant velocity.

4 Copy and complete **a** to **c** using the words below:
decreasing   increasing   terminal

a When the resultant force on an object is not zero and acts in the opposite direction to the object's velocity, its velocity is ....

b When an object falls in a fluid and the drag force on it is less than its weight, its velocity is ....

c When the drag force on an object falling in a fluid is equal to its weight, the object moves at its .... velocity.

5 a Explain why the stopping distance of a car is increased if:

  i the road is wet instead of dry

  ii the driver is tired instead of alert.

b A driver travelling at 18 m/s takes 0.7 s to react when a dog walks into the road 40 m ahead. The braking distance for the car at this speed is 24 m.

  i Calculate the distance travelled by the car in the time it takes the driver to react.

  ii How far in front of the dog does the car stop?

6 In a Hooke's law test on a spring, the following results were obtained.

Weight (N)	Length (mm)	Extension (mm)
0	245	0
1.0	285	40
2.0	324	
3.0	366	
4.0	405	
5.0	446	
6.0	484	

a Copy and complete the third column of the table.

b Plot a graph of the extension on the vertical axis against the weight on the horizontal axis.

c If a weight of 7.0 N is suspended on the spring, what would be the extension of the spring?

d i Calculate the spring constant of the spring.

  ii An object suspended on the spring gives an extension of 140 mm. Calculate the weight of the object.

7 a A racing cyclist accelerates at 5 m/s² when she starts from rest. The total mass of the cyclist and her bicycle is 45 kg. Calculate:

  i the resultant force that produces this acceleration

  ii the total weight of the cyclist and the bicycle.

b Explain why she can reach a higher speed by crouching than by staying upright.

AQA Examination-style questions

1 a The tractor is pulling a trailer. The force acting on the trailer is labelled A, and the force acting on the tractor is labelled B.

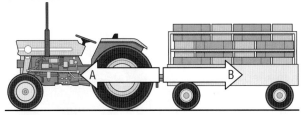

Copy and complete the following sentences using the list of words and phrases below. Each one can be used once, more than once or not at all.

A and B are the same   A is greater than B
B is greater than A

i If the tractor and trailer are accelerating .... (1)
ii If the tractor and trailer are moving at a constant speed .... (1)

b The driving force from the tractor is 12000 N and the total resistive forces are 10000 N.
i Calculate the resultant force. (2)
ii Calculate the acceleration of the tractor and trailer. Mass of the tractor and trailer = 2300 kg Write down the equation you use. Show clearly how you work out your answer and give the unit. (2)

2 A car is travelling at 30 m/s when the vehicle in front suddenly stops. The car travels 19 m before the driver applies the brake.

a What is the name given to this distance? (1)

b Calculate the reaction time of the driver. Write down the equation you use. Show clearly how you work out your answer. (2)

c The driver applies the brakes and stops 6 seconds later. Calculate the deceleration of the car. Write down the equation you use. Show clearly how you work out your answer. (2)

d The braking distance is 81 m. What is the total stopping distance in metres? (1)

e Give two factors that would increase reaction time. (2)

3 The diagram shows the forces acting on a dragster just before it reaches its top speed. The resistive forces are represented by arrow **X**. The driving force is shown by arrow **Y**.

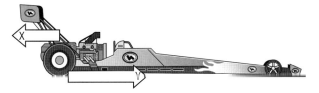

a What is the main type of resistive force acting on the dragster? (1)

b If the driving force remains the same, what will happen to force X?
Give a reason for your answer. (2)

c The dragster slows down by applying its brakes and using a parachute. The velocity–time graph shows the motion of the dragster from a stationary start until it stops.

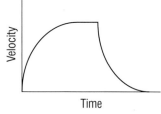

Explain, in terms of energy changes, the shape of the graph when the brakes are applied. (3)

4 A student carries out an experiment to find if extension is proportional to the force applied for an elastic hair bobble. She measures the extension with one and then two 0.1 kg masses. She holds the bobble with one hand and the ruler in the other.

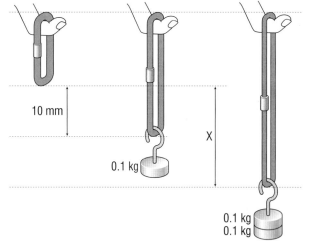

a If the extension is proportional to the force applied, what value should the student expect to obtain for distance X? (1)

b Give the name of the form of energy stored in the stretched hair bobble. (1)

c Calculate the weight of one of the 0.1 kg masses. (g = 10 N/kg) (2)

d *In this question you will be assessed on using good English, organising information clearly and using specialist terms where appropriate.*
The student is unable to draw a valid conclusion because she has not carried out the investigation with sufficient precision. Describe the improvements she could make in order to carry out the investigation more precisely and gain sufficient data to draw a valid conclusion. (6)

P2 3.1 Energy and work ⓚ

Learning objectives

- What do we mean by 'work' in science?
- What is the relationship between work and energy?
- How do we calculate the work done by a force?
- What happens to the work done to overcome friction?

Working out

In a fitness centre or a gym, you have to work hard to keep fit. Raising weights and pedalling on an exercise bike are just two ways to keep fit. Whichever way you choose to keep fit, you have to apply a force to move something. So the work you do causes **transfer** of energy.

a When you pedal on an exercise bike, where does the energy transferred go to?

Figure 1 Working out

When an object is moved by a force, we say **work** is done on the object by the force. The force therefore transfers energy to the object. The amount of energy transferred to the object is equal to the work done on it. For example, to raise an object, you need to apply a force to it to 'overcome' the force of gravity on it. If the work you do on the object is 20 J, the energy transferred to it must be 20 J. So its gravitational potential energy increases by 20 J.

Energy transferred = work done

The work done by a force depends on the size of the force and the distance moved. We use the following equation to calculate the work done by a force when it moves an object:

work done = force applied × distance moved in the direction of the force
(joules, J)   (newtons, N)   (metres, m)

We can write the word equation above using symbols:

$$W = F \times d$$

Where:
W = work done in joules, J
F = force in newtons, N
d = distance moved in metres in the direction of the force, m.

🖩 Maths skills

Worked example

A builder pushed a wheelbarrow a distance of 5.0 m across flat ground with a force of 50 N. How much work was done by the builder?

Solution

Work done = force applied × distance moved = 50 N × 5.0 m = 250 J

b How much work is done when a force of 2000 N pulls a truck through a distance of 40 m in the direction of the force?

??? Did you know ... ?

Imagine pulling a 40 tonne truck over 40 metres. On level ground, a pull force of about 2000 N is needed. Very few people can manage to pull with such force. Don't even try it though. The people who have done it are very, very strong and have trained specially for it.

Practical

Doing work

Carry out a series of experiments to calculate the work done in performing the tasks below. Use a newtonmeter to measure the force applied and a metre ruler to measure the distance moved.

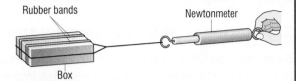

Figure 2 At work

1 Drag a small box a measured distance across a rough surface.

2 Repeat the test above with two rubber bands wrapped around the box as shown in Figure 2.

● What is the resolution of your measuring instruments? Repeat your tests and comment on the precision of your repeat measurements. Can you be confident about the accuracy of your results?

c Why is more work done than the calculated value in the practical with rubber bands?

Friction at work

Work done to overcome friction is mainly transferred into energy by heating.

1 If you rub your hands together vigorously, they become warm. Your muscles do work to overcome the friction between your hands. The work you do is transferred into energy that warms your hands.

2 Brake pads become hot if the brakes are applied for too long a time. Friction between the brake pads and the wheel discs opposes the motion of the wheel. The kinetic energy of the vehicle is transferred into energy that heats the brake pads and the wheel discs, as well as the surrounding air. A small proportion of the energy will be transferred to the surroundings by sound waves if the brakes 'squeal'.

Summary questions

1 Copy and complete **a** and **b** using the words below:

gravitational potential   kinetic   sound   wasted

a When a rower pulls on an oar, the work done by the rower is transferred into .... energy of the boat and .... energy by heating the water.

b When an electric motor is used to raise a car park barrier, the work done by the motor is transferred into .... energy of the barrier and .... energy.

2 A car is brought to a standstill when the driver applies the brakes.

a Explain why the brake pads become warm.

b The car travelled a distance of 20 metres after the brakes were applied. The braking force on the car during this time was 7000 N. Calculate the work done by the braking force.

3 Calculate the work done when:

a a force of 20 N makes an object move 4.8 m in the direction of the force

b an object of weight 80 N is raised through a height of 1.2 m.

Key points

● Work is done on an object when a force makes the object move.

● Energy transferred = work done

● Work done (joules) = force (newtons) × distance moved in the direction of the force (metres).

● Work done to overcome friction is transferred as energy that heats the objects that rub together and the surroundings.

P2 3.2 Gravitational potential energy

Maths skills

Worked example

A student of weight 300 N climbs on a platform which is 1.2 m higher than the floor. Calculate the increase of her gravitational potential energy.

Solution

Increase of GPE = 300 N × 1.2 m
= 360 J

Note: We often use the abbreviation 'GPE' or E_p for gravitational potential energy.

Did you know ... ?

You use energy when you hold an object stationary in your outstretched hand. The biceps muscle of your arm is in a state of contraction. Energy must be supplied to keep the muscles contracted. No work is done on the object because it doesn't move. The energy supplied heats the muscles and is transferred by heating to the surroundings.

Gravitational potential energy transfers

Every time you lift an object up, you do some work. Some of your muscles transfer chemical energy from your muscles into **gravitational potential energy** of the object.

Gravitational potential energy is energy stored in an object because of its position in the Earth's gravitational field.

The force you need to lift an object steadily is equal and opposite to the force of gravity on the object. Therefore, the upward force you need to apply to it is equal to its weight. For example, a force of 80 N is needed to lift a box of weight 80 N.

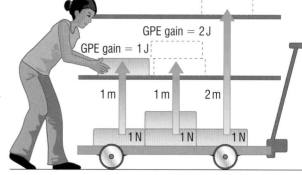

Figure 1 Using joules

- **When an object is moved up**, its gravitational potential energy increases. The increase of its gravitational potential energy is equal to the work done on it by the lifting force.

- **When an object moves down**, its gravitational potential energy decreases. The decrease of its gravitational potential energy is equal to the work done by the force of gravity acting on it.

The work done when an object moves up or down depends on:

1 how far it is moved vertically (its change of height)

2 its weight.

Using the formula $W = F \times d$ (work done = force applied × distance moved in the direction of the force), we can therefore say:

> the change of its gravitational = its weight × its change of height
> potential energy (in joules)   (in newtons)   (in metres)

a Read the 'Did you know?' box. What happens to the energy supplied to the muscles to keep them contracted?

Gravitational potential energy and mass

Astronauts on the Moon can lift objects much more easily than they can on the Earth. This is because, at their surfaces, the gravitational field strength of the Moon is only about a sixth of the Earth's gravitational field strength.

In P2 2.5, 'Falling objects', we saw that the weight of an object in newtons is equal to its mass × the gravitational field strength.

Therefore, when an object is lifted or lowered, because its change of gravitational potential energy is equal to its weight × its change of height:

> change of gravitational = mass × gravitational field × change of height
> potential energy (in J)   (in kg)   strength (in N/kg)   (in metres)

We can write the word equation on the previous page using symbols:

$$E_p = m \times g \times h$$

Where:

E_p = change of GPE in joules, J
m = mass in kilograms, kg
g = gravitational field strength in newtons per kilogram, N/kg
h = change in height in metres, m.

 Maths skills

Worked example

A 2.0 kg object is raised through a height of 0.4 m. Calculate the gain of gravitational potential energy of the object. The gravitational field strength of the Earth at its surface is 10 N/kg.

Solution

Gain of GPE = mass × gravitational field strength × height gain

$$= 2.0 \, kg \times 10 \, N/kg \times 0.4 \, m$$
$$= 8.0 \, J$$

Power and energy

Power is the rate of transfer of energy. If energy E (in joules) is transferred in time t (in seconds):

$$\text{power, } P \text{ (in watts)} = \frac{E}{t}$$

b A weightlifter raises a 20 kg metal bar through a height of 1.5 m.
  i Calculate the gain of gravitational potential energy. The gravitational field strength of the Earth at its surface is 10 N/kg.
  ii The bar is raised by the weightlifter in 0.5 seconds. Calculate the power of the weightlifter.

Summary questions

1 Copy and complete **a** to **c** using the words below. Each word can be used more than once.

decreases   increases   stays the same

  a When a ball falls, its gravitational potential energy ....
  b When a car travels along a level road, the gravitational potential energy of the car ....
  c When a child on a swing moves from one extreme to the opposite extreme, her gravitational potential energy .... then ....

2 A student of weight 450 N steps on a box of height 0.20 m.
  a Calculate the gain of gravitational potential energy of the student.
  b Calculate the work done by the student if she steps on and off the box 50 times.

3 **a** A weightlifter raises a steel bar of mass 25 kg through a height of 1.2 m. Calculate the change of gravitational potential energy of the bar. The gravitational field strength at the surface of the Earth is 10 N/kg.
  b The weightlifter then drops the bar and it falls vertically to the ground. Assume air resistance is negligible. What is the change of its gravitational potential energy in this fall?

Key points

● The gravitational potential energy of an object depends on its weight and how far it moves vertically.

● The gravitational potential energy of an object increases when the object goes up and decreases when the object goes down.

● The change of gravitational potential energy of an object is equal to its mass × the gravitational field strength × its change of height.

P2 3.3 Kinetic energy

Learning objectives

- What does the kinetic energy of an object depend on?
- How can we calculate kinetic energy?
- What is elastic potential energy?

?? Did you know ... ?

Sports scientists design running shoes:

- to reduce the force of each impact when the runner's foot hits the ground
- to return as much kinetic energy as possible to each foot in each impact.

Figure 2 A sports shoe

a Some of the kinetic energy of the runner's foot is wasted in each impact. What is this energy transferred into?

Practical

Investigating a catapult

Use rubber bands to 'catapult' a trolley along a horizontal runway. Find out how the speed of the trolley depends on how much the catapult is pulled back before the trolley is released. For example, see if the distance needs to be doubled to double the speed. Figure 1 shows how the speed of the trolley can be measured.

Practical

Investigating kinetic energy

- The kinetic energy of an object is the energy it has due to its motion. It depends on its mass and its speed.

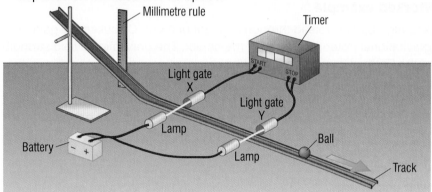

Figure 1 Investigating kinetic energy

Figure 1 shows how we can investigate how the **kinetic energy** of a ball depends on its speed.

1 The ball is released on a slope from a measured height above the foot of the slope. We can calculate the gravitational potential energy it loses from its mass × gravitational field strength × its drop of height. This is equal to its gain of kinetic energy.

2 The ball is timed, using light gates, over a measured distance between X and Y after the slope.

- Why do light gates improve the quality of the data you can collect in this investigation?

Some sample measurements for a ball of mass 0.5 kg are shown in the table:

Height drop to foot of slope (metres, m)	0.05	0.10	0.16	0.20
Initial kinetic energy of ball (joules, J)	0.25	0.50	0.80	1.00
Time to travel 1.0 m from X to Y (seconds, s)	0.98	0.72	0.57	0.50
Speed (metres/second, m/s)	1.02			2.00

Work out the speed in each case. The first and last values have been worked out for you. Can you see a link between speed and the height drop? The results show that the greater the height drop, the faster the speed is. So we can say that the kinetic energy of the ball increases if the speed increases.

The kinetic energy formula

The table shows that when the height drop is increased by four times from 0.05 m to 0.20 m, the speed doubles. The height drop is directly proportional to the (speed)^2. Since the height drop is a measure of the ball's kinetic energy, we can say that the ball's kinetic energy is directly proportional to the square of its speed.

b Check the other measurements in the table to see if they fit this rule.

The exact link between the kinetic energy of an object and its speed is given by the equation:

kinetic energy = ½ × **mass** × **speed²**
(joules, J)   (kilograms, kg)   (metres/second)², (m/s)²

 Maths skills

We can write this word equation using symbols:

$$E_K = ½ × m × v^2$$

Where:
E_K = kinetic energy in joules, J
m = mass in kilograms, kg
v = speed in metres/second, m/s².

 Maths skills

Worked example

Calculate the kinetic energy of a vehicle of mass 500 kg moving at a speed of 12 m/s.

Solution

kinetic energy = ½ × mass × speed² = 0.5 × 500 kg × (12 m/s)² = 36 000 J.

 *Examiner's tip*

Don't forget to square the speed when calculating kinetic energy. This is a common mistake.

Kinetic energy recovery systems (KERS) in vehicles store energy when the vehicle brakes and use it later. In 2009, some Formula 1 racing cars were fitted with a flywheel. The kinetic energy of the vehicle could be transferred to the flywheel in braking and used later to boost the vehicle's speed when overtaking. Other vehicles, including hybrid cars, use an electric generator to transfer kinetic energy into electrical energy, which is then stored in a battery.

Using elastic potential energy

When you stretch a rubber band or a bowstring, the work you do is stored in it as **elastic potential energy**. Figure 3 shows one way you can **transfer** elastic potential energy into kinetic energy.

An object is **elastic** if it regains its shape after being stretched or squashed. A rubber band is an example of an elastic object.

Elastic potential energy is the energy stored in an elastic object when work is done on it to change its shape.

Figure 3 Using elastic potential energy

Summary questions

1 Copy and complete **a** and **b** using the words below.

elastic potential   kinetic   gravitational potential

A student on a trampoline falls on to the trampoline and rebounds.
   a Before she rebounds, the impact decreases her .... energy to zero.
   b During the rebound, ... energy changes into .... energy and .... energy.

2 **a** A catapult is used to fire an object into the air. Describe the energy transfers when the catapult is:
   i stretched
   ii released.
   b An object of weight 2.0 N fired vertically upwards from a catapult reaches a maximum height of 5.0 m. Calculate:
   i the gain of gravitational potential energy of the object
   ii the kinetic energy of the object when it left the catapult.

3 A car moving at a constant speed has 360 000 J of kinetic energy. When the driver applies the brakes, the car stops in a distance of 100 m.
   a Calculate the force that stops the vehicle.
   b The speed of the car was 30 m/s when its kinetic energy was 360 000 J. Calculate its mass.

Key points

- The **kinetic energy** of a moving object depends on its mass and its speed.

- Kinetic energy (J) = ½ × mass (kg) × speed² (m/s)²

- **Elastic potential energy** is the energy stored in an elastic object when work is done on the object.

P2 3.4

Momentum (k)

Learning objectives

- How can we calculate momentum?
- What is the unit of momentum?
- What happens to the total momentum of two objects when they collide?

Figure 1 A contact sport

Momentum is important to anyone who plays a contact sport. In a game of rugby, a player with a lot of momentum is very difficult to stop.

The momentum of a moving object = mass × velocity.

So momentum has a size and a direction.

The unit of momentum is the kilogram metre/second (kg m/s).

We can write the word equation above using symbols: $p = m \times v$

Where:
p = momentum in kilograms metres/second, kg m/s
m = mass in kilograms, kg
v = speed in metres/second, m/s.

Maths skills

Worked example

Calculate the momentum of a sprinter of mass 50 kg running at a velocity of 10 m/s.

Solution

Momentum = mass × velocity = 50 kg × 10 m/s = 500 kg m/s

a Calculate the momentum of a 40 kg person running at 6 m/s.

Practical

Investigating collisions

When two objects collide, the momentum of each object changes. Figure 2 shows how to use a computer and a motion sensor to investigate a collision between two trolleys.

Trolley A is given a push so it collides with a stationary trolley B. The two trolleys stick together after the collision. The computer gives the velocity of A before the collision and the velocity of both trolleys afterwards.

- What does each section of the velocity–time graph show?

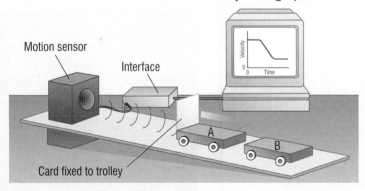

Figure 2 Investigating collisions

1 **For two trolleys of the same mass**, the velocity of trolley A is halved by the impact. The combined mass after the collision is twice the moving mass before the collision. So the momentum (= mass × velocity) after the collision is the same as before the collision.

2 **For a single trolley pushed into a double trolley**, the velocity of A is reduced to one-third. The combined mass after the collision is three times the initial mass. So once again, the momentum after the collision is the same as the momentum before the collision.

In both tests, the total momentum is unchanged (i.e. is conserved) by the collision. This is an example of the **conservation of momentum**. It applies to any system of objects provided the system is a closed system, which means no resultant force acts on it.

Figure 3 A 'shunt' collision

In general, the **law of conservation of momentum** states that

in a closed system, the total momentum before an event is equal to the total momentum after the event.

We can use this law to predict what happens whenever objects collide or push each other apart in an 'explosion'. Momentum is conserved in any collision or explosion provided no external forces act on the objects.

Maths skills

Worked example

A 0.5 kg trolley A is pushed at a velocity of 1.2 m/s into a stationary trolley B of mass 1.5 kg as shown in Figure 4. The two trolleys stick to each other after the impact.

Calculate:

a the momentum of the 0.5 kg trolley before the collision

b the velocity of the two trolleys straight after the impact.

Solution

a Momentum = mass × velocity = 0.5 kg × 1.2 m/s = 0.6 kg m/s.

b The momentum after the impact = the momentum before the impact = 0.6 kg m/s

(1.5 kg + 0.5 kg) × velocity after the impact = 0.6 kg m/s

the velocity after the impact = $\dfrac{0.6\,\text{kg m/s}}{2\,\text{kg}}$ = 0.3 m/s

b Calculate the speed after the collision if trolley A had a mass of 1.0 kg.

Summary questions

1 Complete **a** and **b** using the words below:

force   mass   momentum   velocity

  a The momentum of a moving object is its .... × its ....

  b .... is conserved when objects collide, provided no external .... acts.

2 **a** Calculate the momentum of an 80 kg rugby player running at a velocity of 5 m/s.

  b An 800 kg car moves with the same momentum as the rugby player in part **a**. Calculate the velocity of the car.

3 A 1000 kg rail wagon moving at a velocity of 5.0 m/s on a level track collides with a stationary 1500 kg wagon. The two wagons move together after the collision.

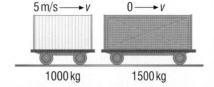

1000 kg   1500 kg

Figure 5

  a Calculate the momentum of the 1000 kg wagon before the collision.

  b Show that the wagons move at a velocity of 2.0 m/s after the collision.

Did you know ...?

If a vehicle crashes into the back of a line of cars, each car in turn is 'shunted' into the one in front. Momentum is transferred along the line of cars to the one at the front.

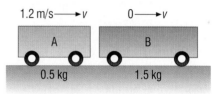

1.2 m/s→v   0→v

A   B

0.5 kg   1.5 kg

Figure 4 Worked example

Maths skills

Worked example

A 3000 kg truck moving at a velocity of 16 m/s crashes into the back of a stationary 1000 kg car. The two vehicles move together immediately after the impact. Calculate their velocity.

Solution

Let *v* represent the velocity of the vehicles after the impact.

momentum of the truck before the impact = 48 000 kg m/s

momentum of car before impact = 0 m/s

momentum of truck after impact = 3000 kg × *v*

momentum of car after impact = 1000 kg × *v*

3000 *v* + 1000 *v* = 48 000 + 0

4000 *v* = 48 000; *v* = 12 m/s

Key points

● Momentum = mass × velocity

● The unit of momentum is kg m/s.

● Momentum is conserved whenever objects interact, provided the objects are in a closed system so that no external forces act on them.

Work, energy and momentum

P2 3.5 Explosions

Learning objectives

- Why does momentum have a direction as well as size?

- When two objects push each other apart
  - do they move away at different speeds?
  - why is their total momentum zero?

If you are a skateboarder, you will know that the skateboard can shoot away from you when you jump off it. Its momentum is in the opposite direction to your own momentum. What can we say about the total momentum of objects when they fly apart from each other?

Practical

Investigating a controlled explosion

Figure 1 shows controlled explosion using trolleys. When the trigger rod is tapped, a bolt springs out and the trolleys recoil (spring back) from each other.

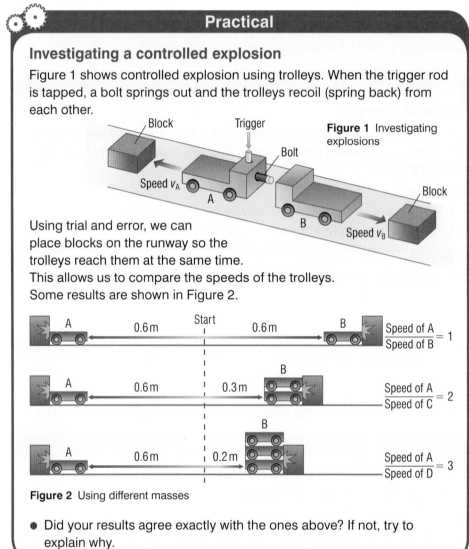

Figure 1 Investigating explosions

Using trial and error, we can place blocks on the runway so the trolleys reach them at the same time.
This allows us to compare the speeds of the trolleys.
Some results are shown in Figure 2.

Figure 2 Using different masses

- Did your results agree exactly with the ones above? If not, try to explain why.

- Two single trolleys travel equal distances in the same time. This shows that they recoil at equal speeds.

- A double trolley only travels half the distance that a single trolley does. Its speed is half that of the single trolley.

In each test:
1 the mass of the trolley × the speed of the trolley is the same, and
2 they recoil in opposite directions.

So momentum has size and direction. The results show that the trolleys recoil with equal and opposite momentum.

a Why does a stationary rowing boat recoil when someone jumps off it?

Conservation of momentum

In the trolley examples:

- momentum of A after the explosion = (mass of A × velocity of A)
- momentum of B after the explosion = (mass of B × velocity of B)
- total momentum before the explosion = 0 (because both trolleys were at rest).

Using conservation of momentum gives:

(mass of A × velocity of A) + (mass of B × velocity of B) = 0

Therefore

(mass of A × velocity of A) = – (mass of B × velocity of B)

The minus sign after the equal sign tells us that the momentum of B is in the opposite direction to the momentum of A. The equation tells us that A and B move apart with equal and opposite amounts of momentum. So the total momentum after the explosion is the same as before it.

Momentum in action

When a shell is fired from an artillery gun, the gun barrel recoils backwards. The recoil of the gun barrel is slowed down by a spring. This lessens the backwards motion of the gun.

b In the worked example, if the mass of the gun had been much greater than 2000 kg, why would the speed of the shell have been greater?

Maths skills

Worked example

An artillery gun of mass 2000 kg fires a shell of mass 20 kg at a velocity of 120 m/s. Calculate the recoil velocity of the gun.

Solution

Applying the conservation of momentum gives:

mass of gun × recoil velocity of gun = – (mass of shell × velocity of shell)

If we let V represent the recoil velocity of the gun,

$2000\,kg \times V = -(20\,kg \times 120\,m/s)$

$V = \dfrac{2400\,kg\,m/s}{2000\,kg} = -1.2\,m/s$

Figure 3 An artillery gun in action

Summary questions

1 A 60 kg skater and a 80 kg skater standing in the middle of an ice rink push each other away. Copy and complete **a** to **c** using the words below:

force   momentum   velocity

80 kg   60 kg

Figure 4

   a They move apart with equal and opposite ....
   b The 60 kg skater moves away with a bigger .... than the other skater.
   c They push each other with equal and opposite ....

2 In Question 1, the 60 kg skater moves away at 2.0 m/s. Calculate:
   a her momentum
   b the velocity of the other skater.

3 A 600 kg cannon recoils at a speed of 0.5 m/s when a 12 kg cannon ball is fired from it.
   a Calculate the velocity of the cannon ball when it leaves the cannon.
   b Calculate the kinetic energy of:
      i the cannon
      ii the ball.

Key points

- Momentum is mass × velocity and velocity is speed in a certain direction.

- When two objects push each other apart, they move apart:
  – with different speeds if they have unequal masses
  – with equal and opposite momentum so their total momentum is zero.

P2 3.6 Impact forces

Crumple zones at the front end and rear end of a car are designed to lessen the force of an impact. The force changes the momentum of the car.

- In a front-end impact, the momentum of the car is reduced.

- In a rear-end impact (where a vehicle is struck from behind by another vehicle), the momentum of the car is increased.

In both cases the effect of a crumple zone is to increase the impact time and so lessen the impact force.

Practical

Investigating impacts

We can test an impact using a trolley and a brick, as shown in Figure 1. When the trolley hits the brick, the plasticine flattens on impact, making the impact time longer. This is the key factor that reduces the impact force.

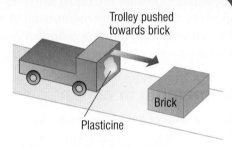

Figure 1 Investigating impacts

Figure 2 A crash test. Car makers test the design of a crumple zone by driving a remote control car into a brick wall.

a Why is rubber matting under a child's swing a good idea?

Impact time

Let's see why making the impact time longer reduces the impact force.

Suppose a moving trolley hits another object and stops. The impact force on the trolley acts for a certain time (the impact time) and causes it to stop. A soft pad on the front of the trolley would increase the impact time and would allow the trolley to travel further before it stops. The momentum of the trolley would be lost over a longer time and its kinetic energy would be transferred over a greater distance.

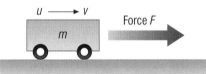

Figure 3 Impact force

1 The kinetic energy of the trolley is transferred to the pad as work done by the impact force in squashing the pad.

2 Since work done = force × distance, the impact force is therefore reduced because the distance is increased.

   The longer the impact time is, the more the impact force is reduced.

If we know the impact time, we can calculate the impact force as follows:

- From P2 1.2, since acceleration = change of velocity ÷ time taken, we can work out the deceleration by dividing the change of velocity by the impact time.

- From P2 2.3, since force = mass × acceleration, we can now calculate the impact force by multiplying the mass of the trolley by the deceleration.

The above method shows how much the impact force can be reduced by increasing the impact time. Car safety features such as crumple zones and side bars increase the impact time and so reduce the impact force.

b In a car crash, why does wearing a car seat belt reduce the impact force on the wearer?

??? Did you know ...?

Scientists at Oxford University have developed new lightweight material for bullet-proof vests. The material is so strong and elastic that bullets bounce off it.

Maths skills

Worked example

A bullet of mass 0.004 kg moving at a velocity of 90 m/s is stopped by a bulletproof vest in 0.0003 s.

Calculate **a** the deceleration and **b** the impact force.

Solution

a Initial velocity of bullet = 90 m/s

Final velocity of bullet = 0

Change of velocity = final velocity − initial velocity

$$= 0 - 90\,\text{m/s} = -90\,\text{m/s}$$

(where the minus sign tells us the change of velocity is a decrease)

$$\text{Deceleration} = \frac{\text{change of velocity}}{\text{impact time}} = \frac{-90\,\text{m/s}}{0.0003\,\text{s}} = -300\,000\,\text{m/s}^2$$

b Using 'force = mass × acceleration', impact force = 0.004 kg × −300 000 m/s² = −1200 N

c Calculate the impact force if the impact time had been 0.0002 s.

Two-vehicle collisions

When two vehicles collide, they exert equal and opposite impact forces on each other at the same time. The change of momentum of one vehicle is therefore equal and opposite to the change of momentum of the other vehicle. The total momentum of the two vehicles is the same after the impact as it was before the impact, so momentum is conserved – assuming no external forces act.

For example, suppose a fast-moving truck runs into the back of a stationary car. The impact decelerates the truck and accelerates the car. Assuming the truck's mass is greater than the mass of the car, the truck loses momentum and the car gains momentum.

Did you know ...?

We sometimes express the effect of an impact on an object or person as a force to weight ratio. We call this the **g-force**. For example, a g-force of 2 g means the force on an object is twice its weight. You would experience a g-force of:

- about 3–4 g on a fairground ride that whirls you round
- about 10 g in a low-speed car crash
- more than 50 g in a high-speed car crash. You would be lucky to survive!

Summary questions

1 Copy and complete **a** to **c** using the words below:

equal   greater   smaller

a The greater the mass of a moving object is the .... the force needed to stop it in a certain time.

b When two objects collide, they exert .... forces on each other.

c When two vehicles collide, the vehicle with the .... mass has a greater change of velocity.

2 **a** An 800 kg car travelling at 30 m/s is stopped safely when the brakes are applied. What deceleration and braking force is required to stop it in **i** 6.0 s? **ii** 30 s?

b If the vehicle in part **a** had been stopped in a collision lasting less than a second, explain why the force on it would have been much greater.

3 A 2000 kg van moving at a velocity of 12 m/s crashes into the back of a stationary truck of mass 10 000 kg. Immediately after the impact, the two vehicles move together.

a Show that the velocity of the van and the truck immediately after the impact was 2 m/s.

b The impact lasted for 0.3 seconds. Calculate the **i** deceleration of the van **ii** force of the impact on the van

Key points

- When vehicles collide, the force of the impact depends on mass, change of velocity, and the duration of the impact.

- The longer the impact time is, the more the impact force is reduced.

- When two vehicles collide,
  - they exert equal and opposite forces on each other
  - their total momentum is unchanged.

P2 3.7

Car safety

Learning objectives

- Why do seat belts and air bags reduce the force on people in car accidents?

- How do side impact bars and crumple zones work?

- How can we work out if a car in a crash was 'speeding'?

When you travel in a car, you want to feel safe if the car is in a crash. In this topic, we look at different car safety features that are designed to keep us safe.

Clunk click!

When seat belts were first introduced, some car users claimed they should not be forced by law to wear them. A very successful campaign was launched to convince car users to 'belt up'. It included the catchy phrase '*Clunk click every trip*'. As a result, deaths and injuries in road accidents fell significantly.

A **seat belt** stops its wearer from continuing forwards when the car suddenly stops. Someone without a seat belt would hit the windscreen in a 'short sharp' impact and suffer major injury.

- The time taken to stop someone in a car is longer if they are wearing a seat belt than if they are not. So the decelerating force is reduced by wearing a seat belt.

- The seat belt acts across the chest so it spreads the force out. Without the seat belt, the force would act on the head when it hits the windscreen.

  a A seat belt 'locks' when in an impact. What would happen to the wearer if it didn't lock?

Figure 1 An air bag in action

Air bags

Most new cars are fitted with front air bags that protect the driver and the front passenger. Some new cars also have side air bags. These bags protect people in the car from an impact on the side of the car. In a car crash, an inflated air bag spreads the force of an impact across the upper part of the body. It also increases the duration of the impact time. So the effect of the force is lessened compared with a seat belt.

Child car seats

Any baby or child in a car must be strapped in a child car seat. This law applies to children up to 12 years old or up to 1.35 metres in height. Different types of child car seat must be used for babies up to 9 months old, infants up to about 4 years old and children over 4.

- Baby seats must face backwards.

- Children under 4 years old should usually be in a child car seat fitted to a back seat.

The law was brought in to reduce deaths and serious injuries of children in cars. Before the law was passed, dozens of children were killed and hundreds were seriously injured each year in car accidents. Many such accidents happened during the school run. The driver is responsible for making sure every child in their car is seated safely in a correct type of seat.

  b Why are ordinary car seat belts unsafe for children?

Figure 2 A child car seat

Safety costs

Car makers need to sell cars. If their cars are too expensive, people won't buy them. Safety features add to the cost of a new car. Some safety features (e.g. seat belts) are required by law and some (e.g. side impact bars) are optional.

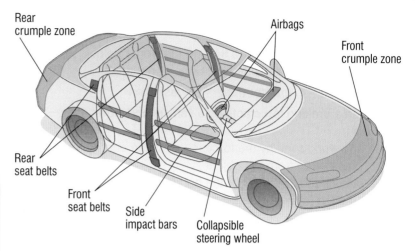

Figure 3 Car safety features

Activity

a With the help of your friends, find out what safety features are in new cars. Find out if they are compulsory or optional. List the price (including tax) of each car.

b Use your information to say if cheaper cars have fewer safety features than more expensive cars.

Activity

Brakes are very important vehicle safety features! Flywheel brakes can transfer large amounts of energy very quickly and very efficiently, unlike ordinary friction brakes which can overheat and wear away. Electric brakes (see P2 3.3) waste energy due to the heating effect of the electric current.

a State and explain the advantages of fitting flywheel brakes in addition to friction brakes in a racing car.

b Explain why flywheel brakes would be better than electric brakes for additional braking on a racing car.

Summary questions

1 Why are rear-facing car seats for babies safer than front-facing seats?

2 Explain why an inflated air bag in front of a car user reduces the force on a user in a 'head-on' crash.

3 A car crashed into a lorry that was crossing a busy road. The speed limit on the road was 60 miles per hour (27 m/s).

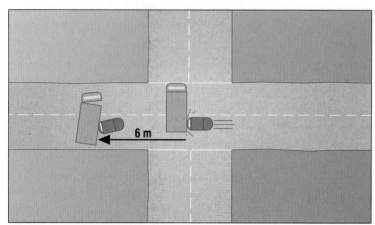

Figure 4 A road accident

The following measurements were made by police officers at the scene of a road crash:

● The car and lorry ended up 6 m from the point of impact.

● The car's mass was 750 kg and the lorry's mass was 2150 kg.

The speed of a vehicle for a braking distance of 6 m is 9 m/s.

a Use this speed to calculate the momentum of the car and the lorry immediately after the impact.

b Use conservation of momentum to calculate the velocity of the car immediately before the collision.

c Was the car travelling over the speed limit before the crash?

Key points

● Seat belts and air bags spread the force across the chest and they also increase the impact time.

● Side impact bars and crumple zones 'give way' in an impact so increasing the impact time.

● We can use the conservation of momentum to find the speed of a car before an impact.

Summary questions 🄺

1 a Copy and complete **i** and **ii** using the words below.
Each term can be used once, twice or not at all.

equal to   greater than   less than

When a braking force acts on a vehicle and slows it down,

  i the work done by the force is .... the energy transferred from the object

  ii the kinetic energy after the brakes have been applied is .... the kinetic energy before they were applied.

b A student pushes a trolley of weight 150 N up a slope of length 20 m. The slope is 1.2 m high.

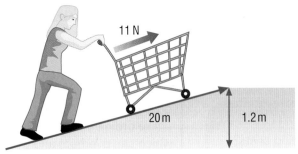

11 N

20 m   1.2 m

  i Calculate the gravitational potential energy gained by the trolley.

  ii The student pushed the trolley up the slope with a force of 11 N. Show that the work done by the student was 220 J.

  iii Give one reason why all the work done by the student was not transferred to the trolley as gravitational potential energy.

2 A 700 kg car moving at 20 m/s is stopped in a distance of 80 m when the brakes are applied.

  a Show that the kinetic energy of the car at 20 m/s is 140 000 J.

  b Calculate the braking force on the car.

3 A student of mass 40 kg standing at rest on a skateboard of mass 2.0 kg jumps off the skateboard at a speed of 0.30 m/s. Calculate:

  a the momentum of the student

  b the recoil velocity of the skateboard.

4 A car bumper is designed not to bend in impacts at less than 4 m/s. It was fitted to a car of mass 900 kg and tested by driving the car into a wall at 4 m/s. The time of impact was measured and found to be 1.8 s.

Show that the deceleration of the car was 2.2 m/s².

5 a Copy and complete **i** and **ii** using the words below.
Each term can be used once, twice or not at all.

elastic potential energy   kinetic energy
gravitational potential energy

An object is catapulted from a catapult.

  i .... is stored in the catapult when it is stretched.

  ii The object has .... when it leaves the catapult.

b A stone of mass 0.015 kg is catapulted into the air and it reaches a height of 20 m before it descends and hits the ground some distance away.

  i Calculate the increase of gravitational potential energy of the stone when it reached its maximum height (*g* = 10 N/kg).

  ii State two reasons why the catapult stored more energy than that calculated in part **b i**?

6 A 1200 kg rail wagon moving at a velocity of 3.0 m/s on a level track collides with a stationary wagon of mass 800 kg. The 1200 kg truck is slowed down to a velocity of 1.0 m/s as a result of the collision.

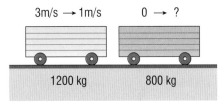

3m/s → 1m/s   0 → ?

1200 kg   800 kg

a Calculate the momentum of the 1200 kg wagon

  i before the collision

  ii after the collision.

b Calculate

  i the momentum, and

  ii the velocity of the 800 kg wagon after the collision.

c Calculate the kinetic energy of:

  i the 1200 kg wagon before the collision

  ii the 1200 kg wagon after the collision

  iii the 800 kg wagon after the collision.

d Give a reason why the total kinetic energy after the collision is not equal to the total kinetic energy before the collision.

AQA Examination-style questions

1 a Copy and complete the following sentences using the list of words and phrases below. Each one can be used once.

kinetic energy   work   power
gravitational potential energy

  i Energy is transferred when .... is done. (1)
  ii .... is the energy that an object has by virtue of its position in a gravitational field. (1)
  iii The .... of an object depends on its mass and speed. (1)
  iv .... is the energy transferred in a given time. (1)

b Explain why a meteorite 'burns up' as it enters the Earth's atmosphere. Use ideas about work and energy. (3)

2 The diagram shows three cars, **A**, **B** and **C**, travelling along a straight, level road.

A
Speed
40 m/s
650 kg

B
18 m/s
1250 kg

C
15 m/s
1500 kg

a Calculate the momentum of each of the vehicles and explain which one has the greatest momentum. Write down the equation you use. Show clearly how you work out your answer and give the unit. (3)

b Car **C,** travelling at 15 m/s, crashes into the back of car **A** when car **A** is stationary. The cars move together after the collision.
  i Calculate the total momentum of the cars just after the collision. (1)
  ii Calculate the speed of the two cars just after the collision. (2)

c Explain, using ideas about momentum changes, how the crumple zone at the front of car **C** may reduce the chance of injury to the occupants during the collision. (3)

3 When ploughing a field a horse and plough move 170 m and the horse pulls with a force of 800 N.

a Calculate the work done by the horse.

  Write down the equation you use. Show clearly how you work out your answer and give the unit. (3)

b i The horse takes 3 minutes to plough 170 m. Calculate the power of the horse. Write down the equation you use. Show clearly how you work out your answer and give the unit. (3)
  ii Calculate the kinetic energy of the horse. Write down the equation you use. Show clearly how you work out your answer and give the unit. Mass of horse = 950 kg (3)

c Explain why the horse has to do more work if the field slopes uphill than it would do on level ground. (2)

4 The picture shows a catapult.

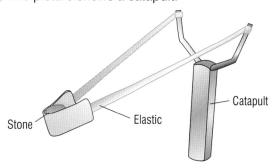

Catapult
Stone   Elastic

When a force is applied to the stone, work is done in stretching the elastic and the stone moves backwards.

a Calculate the work done if the average force applied to the stone is 20 N. The force moves it backwards 0.15 m. Write down the equation you use. Show clearly how you work out your answer and give the unit. (3)

b Calculate the maximum speed of the stone after the catapult is released. The mass of the stone is 0.049 kg. Assume all the work done is transferred to the stone as kinetic energy when the catapult is released. Write down the equation you use. Show clearly how you work out your answer and give the unit. (3)

P2 4.1 Electrical charges

Current electricity

Learning objectives

- What happens when insulating materials are rubbed together?
- What is transferred when objects become charged?
- What happens when charges are brought together?

??? Did you know ...?

Take off a woolly jumper and listen out! You can hear it crackle as tiny sparks from static electricity are created. If the room is dark, you can even see the sparks.

You can get charged up just by sitting in a plastic chair. If this happens, you may feel a slight shock from static electricity when you stand up.

Have you ever stuck a balloon on a ceiling? All you need to do is to rub the balloon on your clothing before you touch it on the ceiling. The rubbing action charges the balloon with **static electricity**. In other words, the balloon becomes electrically charged. The charge on the balloon attracts it to the ceiling.

a Why does a TV screen crackle when you switch it on?

Demonstration

The Van de Graaff generator

A Van de Graaff generator can make your hair stand on end. The dome charges up when the generator is switched on. Massive sparks are produced if the charge on the dome builds up too much.

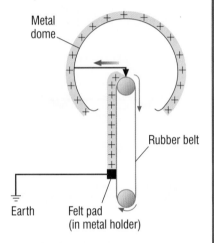

Figure 1 The Van de Graaff generator

The Van de Graaff generator charges up because:
- the belt rubs against a felt pad and becomes charged
- the belt carries the charge onto an insulated metal dome
- sparks are produced when the dome can no longer hold any more charge.
- Why should you keep away from a Van de Graaff generator?

Inside the atom

The **protons** and **neutrons** make up the nucleus of the atom. Electrons move about in the space round the nucleus.
- A proton has a positive charge.
- An electron has an equal negative charge.
- A neutron is uncharged.

An uncharged atom has equal numbers of electrons and protons. Only electrons can be transferred to or from an atom. A charged atom is referred to as an **ion**.

1 Adding electrons to an uncharged atom makes it negative (because the atom then has more electrons than protons).

2 Removing electrons from an uncharged atom makes it positive (because the atom has fewer electrons than protons).

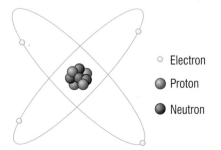

Electron
Proton
Neutron

Figure 2 Inside an atom

Charging by friction

Some insulators become charged by rubbing them with a dry cloth.

● Rubbing a polythene rod with a dry cloth transfers electrons to the surface atoms of the rod from the cloth. So the polythene rod becomes negatively charged.

● Rubbing a perspex rod with a dry cloth transfers electrons from the surface atoms of the rod on to the cloth. So the perspex rod becomes positively charged.

b Glass is charged positively when it is rubbed with a cloth. Does glass gain or lose electrons when it is charged?

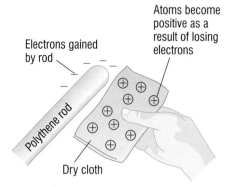

Atoms become positive as a result of losing electrons
Electrons gained by rod
Polythene rod
Dry cloth

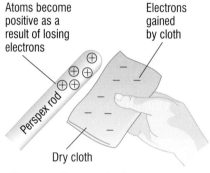

Atoms become positive as a result of losing electrons
Electrons gained by cloth
Perspex rod
Dry cloth

Figure 3 Charging by friction

Practical

The force between two charged objects

Two charged objects exert a force on each other. Figure 4 shows how you can investigate this force.

● What happens?

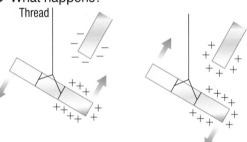

Thread

Figure 4 The law of force for charges

Your results in the experiment above should show that:

● two objects with the same type of charge (i.e. like charges) repel each other

● two objects with different types of charge (i.e. unlike charges) attract each other.

Like charges repel. Unlike charges attract.

c What force keeps the electrons inside an atom?

Summary questions

1 Copy and complete **a** and **b** using the words below. Each word can be used more than once.

to   from   loses   gains

a When a polythene rod is charged using a dry cloth, it becomes negative because it .... electrons that transfer .... it .... the cloth.

b When a perspex rod is charged using a dry cloth, it becomes positive because it .... electrons that transfer .... it .... the cloth.

2 When rubbed with a dry cloth, perspex becomes positively charged. Polythene and ebonite become negatively charged. State whether or not attraction or repulsion takes place when:

a a perspex rod is held near a polythene rod

b a perspex rod is held near an ebonite rod

c a polythene rod is held near an ebonite rod.

Key points

● Certain insulating materials become charged when rubbed together.

● Electrons are transferred when objects become charged:

  – Insulating materials that become positively charged when rubbed lose electrons.

  – Insulating materials that become negatively charged when rubbed gain electrons.

● Like charges repel; unlike charges attract.

Current electricity

Electric circuits

Learning objectives

- Why are electric circuits represented by circuit diagrams?

- What is the difference between a battery and a cell?

- What determines the size of an electric current?

- How can we calculate the size of an electric current from the charge flow and the time taken?

An electric torch can be very useful in a power cut at night. But it needs to be checked to make sure it works. Figure 1 shows what is inside a torch. The circuit shows how the torch bulb is connected to the switch and the two cells.

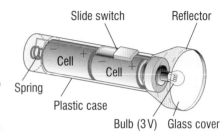

Figure 1 An electric torch

a Why does the switch have to be closed to turn the torch bulb on?

A circuit diagram shows us how the components in a circuit are connected together. Each component has its own symbol. Figure 2 shows the symbols for some of the components you will meet in this course. The function of each component is also described. You need to recognise these symbols and remember what each component is used for – otherwise you'll get mixed up in your exams. More importantly, you could get a big shock if you mix them up!

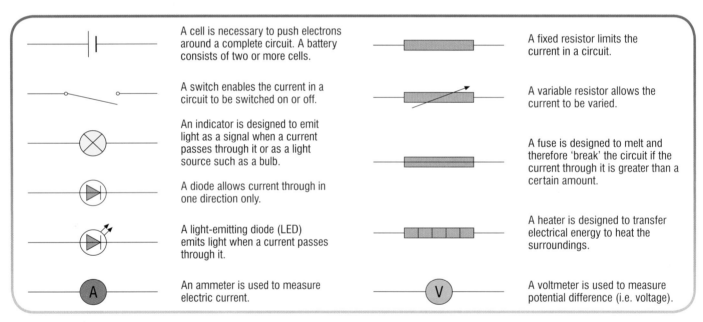

A cell is necessary to push electrons around a complete circuit. A battery consists of two or more cells.

A switch enables the current in a circuit to be switched on or off.

An indicator is designed to emit light as a signal when a current passes through it or as a light source such as a bulb.

A diode allows current through in one direction only.

A light-emitting diode (LED) emits light when a current passes through it.

An ammeter is used to measure electric current.

A fixed resistor limits the current in a circuit.

A variable resistor allows the current to be varied.

A fuse is designed to melt and therefore 'break' the circuit if the current through it is greater than a certain amount.

A heater is designed to transfer electrical energy to heat the surroundings.

A voltmeter is used to measure potential difference (i.e. voltage).

Figure 2 Components and symbols

b What components are in the circuit diagram in Figure 3?

⊂⊃ links

See P2 4.4 for two other symbols you need to know.

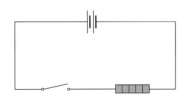

Figure 3

Electric current

An electric current is a flow of charge. When an electric torch is on, millions of **electrons** pass through the torch bulb and through the cell every second. Each electron carries a negative charge. Metals contain lots of electrons that move about freely between the positively charged metal ions. These electrons stop the ions moving away from each other. The electrons pass through the bulb because its filament is made of a metal. The electrons transfer energy from the cell to the torch bulb.

The size of an electric current is the rate of flow of electric charge. This is the flow of charge per second. The greater the number of electrons that pass through a component, the bigger the current passing through it.

Electric charge is measured in **coulombs (C)**. Electric current is measured in **amperes (A)** sometimes abbreviated as 'amps'.

An electric current of 1 ampere is a rate of flow of charge of 1 coulomb per second. If a certain amount of charge flows steadily through a wire or a component in a certain time,

the current in amperes = $\dfrac{\textbf{charge flow in coulombs}}{\textbf{time taken in seconds}}$

We can write the equation above using symbols as follows:

$$I = \frac{Q}{t}$$

Where:
I = current in amperes, A
Q = charge in coulombs, C
t = time taken in seconds, s.

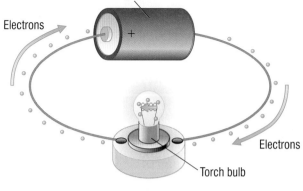

Cell

Electrons

Electrons

Torch bulb

Figure 4 Electrons on the move

Maths skills

Worked example

A charge of 8.0 C passes through a bulb in 4.0 seconds. Calculate the current through the bulb.

Solution

$$I = \frac{Q}{t} = \frac{8.0\,\text{C}}{4.0\,\text{s}} = 2.0\,\text{A}$$

Practical

Circuit tests

Connect a variable resistor in series with the torch bulb and a cell, as shown in Figure 6.

Adjust the slider of the variable resistor. This alters the amount of current flowing through the bulb and therefore affects its brightness.

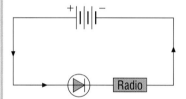

Figure 6 Using a variable resistor

- In Figure 6, the torch bulb goes dim when the slider is moved one way. What happens if the slider is moved back again?
- What happens if you include a diode in the circuit?

Summary questions

1 Name the numbered components in the circuit diagram in Figure 7.

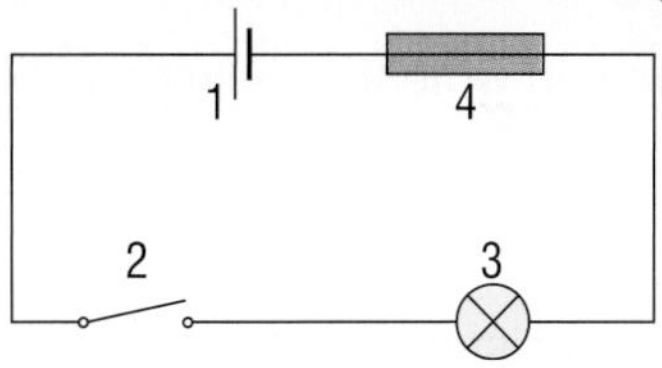

2 **a** Redraw the circuit diagram in Question 1 with a diode in place of the switch so it allows current through.

 b What further component would you need in this circuit to alter the current in it?

3 **a** What is a light-emitting diode?

 b What is a variable resistor used for?

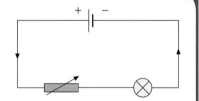

Figure 7

?? Did you know ... ?

You would damage a portable radio if you put the batteries in the wrong way round, unless a diode is in series with the battery. The diode only allows current through when it is connected as shown in Figure 5.

Radio

Figure 5 Using a diode

c Would the radio in Figure 5 work if the diode was turned round in the circuit?

Key points

- Every component has its own agreed symbol. A circuit diagram shows how components are connected together.

- A battery consists of two or more cells connected together.

- The size of an electric current is the rate of flow of charge.

- Electric current = charge flow/time taken

P2 4.3 Resistance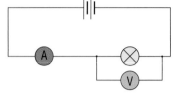

Learning objectives

- What do we mean by potential difference?
- What is resistance and what is its unit?
- What is Ohm's law?
- What happens if you reverse the current in a resistor?

 Maths skills

Worked example

The energy transferred to a bulb is 24 J when 8.0 C of charge passes through it. Calculate the potential difference across the bulb.

Solution

$V = \dfrac{W}{Q} = \dfrac{24\,J}{8.0\,C} = 3.0\,V$

AQA Examiner's tip

Ammeters are always connected in series and voltmeters are always connected in parallel.

Maths skills

Rearranging the equation

$R = \dfrac{V}{I}$ gives $V = IR$ or $I = \dfrac{V}{R}$

Ammeters and voltmeters

Look at the circuit in Figure 1. The battery forces electrons to pass through the ammeter and the bulb.

- The ammeter measures the current through the torch bulb. It is connected in **series** with the bulb so the current through them is the same. The ammeter reading gives the current in amperes (or milliamperes (mA) for small currents, where 1 mA = 0.001 A).

Figure 1 Using an ammeter and a voltmeter

- The voltmeter measures the **potential difference** (pd) across the torch bulb. This is the amount of work done or energy transferred to the bulb by each coulomb of charge that passes through it. The unit of potential difference is the **volt (V)**. We sometimes use the word 'voltage' for potential difference.

- The voltmeter is connected in **parallel** with the torch bulb so it measures the pd across it. The voltmeter reading gives the pd in volts (V).

When charge flows steadily through a component,

$$\frac{\text{the potential difference}}{\text{across the component in volts}} = \frac{\text{work done in joules}}{\text{charge in coulombs}}$$

We can write the equation above using symbols as:

$$V = \frac{W}{Q}$$

Where:
V = the potential difference in volts, V
W = work done or energy transferred in joules, J
Q = charge in coulombs, C.

Electrons passing through a torch bulb have to push their way through lots of vibrating ions in the metal filament. The ions resist the passage of electrons through the torch bulb.

We define the **resistance** of an electrical component as:

$$\text{Resistance (ohms)} = \frac{\text{potential difference (volts)}}{\text{current (amperes)}}$$

The unit of resistance is the **ohm**. The symbol for the ohm is the Greek letter Ω (omega). Note that a resistor in a circuit limits the current. For a given pd, the larger the resistance of a resistor, the smaller the current is.

We can write the definition above as:

$$R = \frac{V}{I}$$

Where:
R = resistance (ohms)
V = potential difference (volts)
I = current (amperes).

    a The current through a wire is 0.5 A when the potential difference across it is 4.0 V. Calculate the resistance of the wire.

Higher

Practical

Investigating the resistance of a wire

Does the resistance of a wire change when the current through it is changed? Figure 2 shows how we can use a variable resistor to change the current through a wire. Make your own measurements and use them to plot a current–potential difference graph like the one in Figure 2.

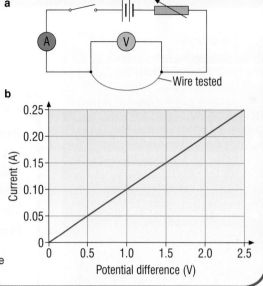
a

- Discuss how your measurements compare with the ones from the table used to plot the graph in Figure 2.
- Calculate the resistance of the wire you tested.

Current (A)	0	0.05	0.10	0.15	0.20	0.25
Potential difference (V)	0	0.50	1.00	1.50	2.00	2.50

Figure 2 Investigating the resistance of a wire.
a Circuit diagram **b** A current–potential difference graph for a wire

b Calculate the resistance of the wire that gave the results in the practical table.

Current–potential difference graphs

The graph in Figure 2 is a straight line through the origin. This means that the current is directly proportional to the potential difference. In other words, the resistance (= pd ÷ current) is constant. This was first discovered for a wire at constant temperature by Georg Ohm and is known as **Ohm's law**:

The current through a resistor at constant temperature is directly proportional to the potential difference across the resistor.

We say a wire is an **ohmic conductor** because its resistance is constant. As shown in Figure 3, reversing the pd makes no difference to the shape of the line. The resistance is the same whichever direction the current is in.

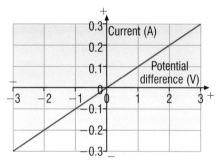

Figure 3 A current–potential difference graph for a resistor

Summary questions

1 Copy and complete **a** and **b** using the words below. Each word can be used once, twice or not at all.

decreases   increases   reverses   stays the same

a If the current through a resistor is decreased, the pd across the resistor ....

b If the current through a resistor is reversed, the pd across the resistor .... and the resistance of the resistor ....

2 Calculate the missing value in each line of the table, using the equation $V = IR$ or a rearrangement of it.

Resistor	Current (A)	Potential difference (V)	Resistance (Ω)
W	2.0	12.0	
X	4.0		20
Y		6.0	3.0

Key points

- The potential difference across a component (in volts) =

$$\frac{\text{work done or energy transferred (in joules)}}{\text{charge (in coulombs)}}$$

- Resistance (in ohms) =

$$\frac{\text{potential difference (volts)}}{\text{current (amperes)}}$$

- Ohm's law states that the current through a resistor at constant temperature is directly proportional to the potential difference across the resistor.

- Reversing the current through a component reverses the pd across it.

P2 4.4

More current–potential difference graphs

Learning objectives

- What happens to the resistance of a filament bulb as its temperature increases?

- How does the current through a diode depend on the potential difference across it?

- What happens to the resistance of a thermistor as its temperature increases and of an LDR as the light level increases?

Have you ever switched a light bulb on only to hear it 'pop' and fail? Electrical appliances can fail at very inconvenient times. Most electrical failures are because too much current passes through a component in the appliance.

Practical

Investigating different components

We can use the circuit in Figure 2 on the previous page to find out if the resistance of a component depends on the current. We can also see if reversing the component in the circuit has any effect.

Make your own measurements using a resistor, a filament bulb and a diode.

Plot your measurements on a current–potential difference graph. Plot the 'reverse' measurements on the negative section of each axis.

- Why can you use a line graph to display your data? (See H3 Using data.)

Using current–potential difference graphs

A filament bulb

Figure 1 shows the graph for a torch bulb (i.e. a low-voltage filament bulb).

- The line **curves** away from the current axis. So the current is *not* directly proportional to the potential difference. The filament bulb is a non-ohmic conductor.

- The resistance (= potential difference/current) increases as the current increases. So the resistance of a filament bulb increases as the filament temperature increases.

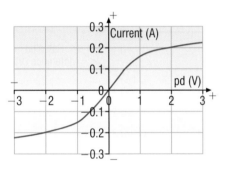

Figure 1 A current–potential difference graph for a filament bulb

The resistance of the metal filament increases as its temperature increases. This is because the ions in the metal filament vibrate more as the temperature increases. So they resist the passage of the electrons through the filament more.

- Reversing the potential difference makes no difference to the shape of the curve. The resistance is the same for the same current, regardless of its direction.

    a Calculate the resistance of the filament bulb at   **i** 0.1 A   **ii** 0.2 A.

The diode

Look at Figure 2, a graph for a diode.

- In the 'forward' direction, the line curves towards the current axis. So the current is not directly proportional to the potential difference. A diode is not an ohmic conductor.

- In the reverse direction, the current is negligible. So its resistance in the reverse direction is much higher than in the forward direction.

Note that a light-emitting diode (LED) emits light when a current passes through it in the forward direction.

    b What can we say about the forward resistance of a diode as the current increases?

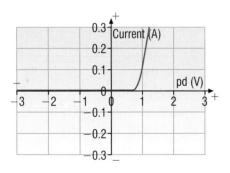

Figure 2 A current–potential difference graph for a diode

Thermistors and light-dependent resistors (LDRs)

We use thermistors and LDRs in sensor circuits. A thermistor is a temperature-dependent resistor. The resistance of an LDR depends on how much light is on it.

Test a thermistor and then an LDR in series with a battery and an ammeter.

● What did you find out about each component tested?

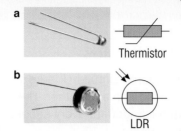

Figure 3 a A thermistor and its circuit symbol **b** An LDR and its circuit symbol

Current–potential difference graphs for a thermistor and an LDR

For a thermistor, Figure 4 shows the current–potential difference graph at two different temperatures.

● At constant temperature, the line is straight so its resistance is constant.
● If the temperature is increased, its resistance decreases.

For a light-dependent resistor, Figure 5 shows the current–potential difference graph in bright light and in dim light.

c What does the graph tell us about an LDR's resistance if the light intensity is constant?
d If the light intensity is increased, what happens to the resistance of the LDR?

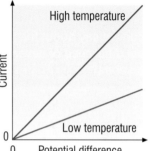

Figure 4 Thermistor graph

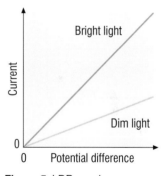

Figure 5 LDR graph

Summary questions

1 Copy and complete sentences **a** to **d** using the words below:

   diode   filament bulb   resistor   thermistor

   a The resistance of a .... decreases as its temperature increases.
   b The resistance of a .... depends on which way round it is connected in a circuit.
   c The resistance of a .... increases as the current through it increases.
   d The resistance of a .... does not depend on the current through it.

2 A thermistor is connected in series with an ammeter and a 3.0 V battery, as shown.

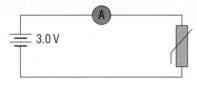

Figure 6

   a At 15 °C, the current through the thermistor is 0.2 A and the potential difference across it is 3.0 V. Calculate its resistance at this temperature.
   b State and explain what happens to the ammeter reading if the thermistor's temperature is increased.

3 The thermistor in Figure 6 is replaced by a light-dependent resistor (LDR). State and explain what happens to the ammeter reading when the LDR is covered.

Key points

● *Filament bulb:* resistance increases with increase of the filament temperature.

● *Diode:* 'forward' resistance low; 'reverse' resistance high.

● *Thermistor:* resistance decreases if its temperature increases.

● *LDR:* resistance decreases if the light intensity on it increases.

Series circuits

P2 4.5

Learning objectives

- What can we say about the current and potential difference for components in a series circuit?
- How can we find the total resistance of resistors in series?
- What can we say about the potential difference of several cells in series?

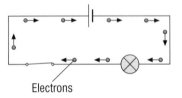

Electrons

Figure 1 A torch bulb circuit

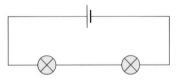

Figure 2 Bulbs in series

Table 1

Filament bulb	Voltmeter V_1 (volts)	Voltmeter V_2 (volts)
normal	1.5	0.0
dim	0.9	0.6
very dim	0.5	1.0

Circuit rules

In the torch circuit in Figure 1, the bulb, the cell and the switch are connected in series with each other. The same number of electrons passes through each component every second. So the same current passes through each component.

The same current passes through components in series with each other.

a If the current through the bulb is 0.12 A, what is the current through the cell?

In Figure 2, each electron from the cell passes through two bulbs. The electrons are pushed through each bulb by the cell. The potential difference (or **voltage**) of the cell is a measure of the energy transferred from the cell by each electron that passes through it. Since each electron in the circuit in Figure 2 goes through both bulbs, the potential difference of the cell is shared between the bulbs. This rule applies to any series circuit.

The total potential difference of the voltage supply in a series circuit is shared between the components.

b In Figure 2, if the potential difference of the cell is 1.2V and the potential difference across one bulb is 0.8V, what is the potential difference across the other bulb?

Cells in series

What happens if we use two or more cells in series in a circuit? Provided we connect the cells so they act in the same direction, each electron gets a push from each cell. So an electron would get the same push from a battery of three 1.5V cells in series as it would from a single 4.5 V cell.

In other words, provided the cells act in the same direction:

The total potential difference of cells in series is the sum of the potential difference of each cell.

Practical

Investigating potential differences in a series circuit

Figure 3 shows how to test the potential difference rule for a series circuit. The circuit consists of a filament bulb in series with a variable resistor and a cell. We can use the variable resistor to see how the voltmeter readings change when we alter the current. Make your own measurements.

- How do they compare with the data in Table 1?

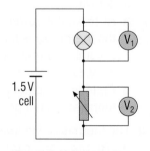

Figure 3 Voltage tests

The measurements in the table show that the voltmeter readings for each setting add up to 1.5 V. This is the potential difference of the cell. The share of the cell's potential difference across each component depends on the setting of the variable resistor.

c What would voltmeter V_2 read if voltmeter V_1 showed 0.4 V?

The resistance rule for components in series

In Figure 3, suppose the current through the bulb is 0.1 A when the bulb is dim.

Using data from Table 1:

- the resistance of the bulb would then be 9 Ω (= 0.9 V ÷ 0.1 A),
- the resistance of the variable resistor at this setting would be 6 Ω (= 0.6 V ÷ 0.1 A).

If we replaced these two components by a single resistor, what should its resistance be for the same current of 0.1 A? We can calculate this because we know the potential difference across it would be 1.5 V (from the cell). So the resistance would need to be 15 Ω (= 1.5 V ÷ 0.1 A). This is the sum of the resistance of the two components. The rule applies to any series circuit.

The total resistance of components in series is equal to the sum of the resistance of each component.

d What is the total resistance of a 2 Ω resistor in series with a 3 Ω resistor?

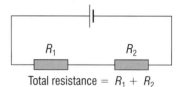

Total resistance = $R_1 + R_2$

Figure 4 Resistors in series

AQA *Examiner's tip*

Remember that in a series circuit the same current passes through all the components.

Summary questions

1 Copy and complete **a** and **b** using the words below. Each word can be used once, twice or not at all.

greater than   less than   the same as

For the circuit in Figure 5:
a The current through the battery is .... the current through resistor P.
b The potential difference across resistor Q is .... the potential difference across the battery.

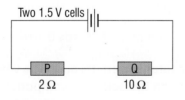

Two 1.5 V cells

P
2 Ω

Q
10 Ω

Figure 5

2 A 1.5 V cell is connected to a 3.0 Ω resistor and 2.0 Ω resistor in series with each other.
a Draw the circuit diagram for this arrangement.
b Calculate:
  i the total resistance of the two resistors
  ii the current through the resistors.

3 For the circuit in Question 1, each cell has a potential difference of 1.5 V.
a Calculate:
  i the total resistance of the two resistors
  ii the total potential difference of the two cells.
b Show that the current through the battery is 0.25 A.
c Calculate the potential difference across each resistor.

Key points

- For components in series:
  - the current is the same in each component
  - adding the potential differences gives the total potential difference

- Adding the resistances gives the total resistance of resistors in series.

- For cells in series, acting in the same direction, the total potential difference is the sum of their individual potential differences.

P2 4.6 Parallel circuits

Learning objectives

- What can we say about the currents in the components in a parallel circuit?
- What can we say about the potential differences across the components in a parallel circuit?
- How can we calculate current through a resistor in a parallel circuit?

Did you know ...?

A bypass is a parallel route. A heart bypass is another route for the flow of blood. A road bypass is a road that passes a town centre instead of going through it. For components in parallel, charge flows separately through each component. The total flow of charge is the sum of the flow through each component.

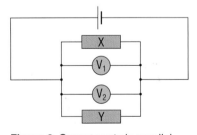

Figure 2 Components in parallel

Practical

Investigating parallel circuits

Figure 1 shows how you can investigate the current through two bulbs in parallel with each other. You can use ammeters in series with the bulbs and the cell to measure the current through each component.

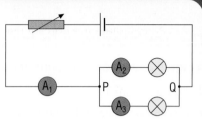

Figure 1 At a junction

Set up your own circuit and collect your data.

- How do your measurements compare with the ones for different settings of the variable resistor shown in Table 1 below?
- Discuss if your own measurements show the same pattern.

Look at the sample data below.

Table 1

Ammeter A_1 (A)	Ammeter A_2 (A)	Ammeter A_3 (A)
0.50	0.30	0.20
0.30	0.20	0.10
0.18	0.12	0.06

In each case, the reading of ammeter A_1 is equal to the sum of the readings of ammeters A_2 and A_3.

This shows that the current through the cell is equal to sum of the currents through the two bulbs. This rule applies wherever components are in parallel.

a If ammeter A_1 reads 0.40 A and A_2 reads 0.1 A, what would A_3 read?

The total current through the whole circuit is the sum of the currents through the separate components.

Potential difference in a parallel circuit

Figure 2 shows two resistors X and Y in parallel with each other. A voltmeter is connected across each resistor. The voltmeter across resistor X shows the same reading as the voltmeter across resistor Y. This is because each electron from the cell either passes through X or through Y. So it delivers the same amount of energy from the cell, whichever resistor it goes through. In other words:

For components in parallel, the potential difference across each component is the same.

Calculations on parallel circuits

Components in parallel have the same potential difference across them.
The current through each component depends on the resistance of the
component.

- The bigger the resistance of the component, the smaller the current through
  it. The resistor which has the largest resistance passes the smallest current.
- We can calculate the current using the equation:

$$\text{current (amperes)} = \frac{\text{potential difference (volts)}}{\text{resistance (ohms)}}$$

b A $3\,\Omega$ resistor and a $6\,\Omega$ resistor are connected in parallel in a circuit.
Which resistor passes the most current?

Maths skills

Worked example

The circuit diagram shows three resistors $R_1 = 1\,\Omega$, $R_2 = 2\,\Omega$ and $R_3 = 6\,\Omega$
connected in parallel to a 6 V battery.

Calculate:

a the current through each resistor

b the current through the battery.

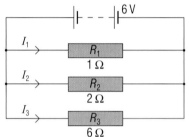

Figure 3

Solution

a $I_1 = \dfrac{V_1}{R_1} = \dfrac{6}{1} = 6\,\text{A}$

$I_2 = \dfrac{V_2}{R_2} = \dfrac{6}{2} = 3\,\text{A}$

$I_3 = \dfrac{V_3}{R_3} = \dfrac{6}{6} = 1\,\text{A}$

b The total current from the battery $= I_1 + I_2 + I_3 = 6\,\text{A} + 3\,\text{A} + 1\,\text{A} = 10\,\text{A}$

Summary questions

1 Copy and complete **a** and **b** using the words below:

current   potential difference

a Components in parallel with each other have the same ....
b For components in parallel, each component has a different ....

2 A 1.5 V cell is connected across a $3\,\Omega$ resistor in parallel with a $6\,\Omega$ resistor.
a Draw the circuit diagram for this circuit.
b Show that the current through:
  i the $3\,\Omega$ resistor is 0.50 A   **ii** the $6\,\Omega$ resistor is 0.25 A.
c Calculate the current passing through the cell.

3 The circuit diagram shows three
resistors $R_1 = 2\,\Omega$, $R_2 = 3\,\Omega$ and
$R_3 = 6\,\Omega$ connected to each other
in parallel and to a 6 V battery.
Calculate:
a the current through each resistor
b the current through the battery.

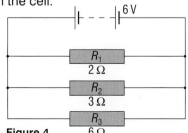

Figure 4

Key points

- For components in parallel:
  - the total current is the sum of the currents through the separate components
  - the bigger the resistance of a component, the smaller its current is.
- In a parallel circuit the potential difference is the same across each component.
- To calculate the current through a resistor in a parallel circuit, use this equation:

  current (amperes)
  $= \dfrac{\text{potential difference (volts)}}{\text{resistance (ohms)}}$

Summary questions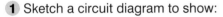

1 Sketch a circuit diagram to show:

a a torch bulb, a cell and a diode connected in series so that the torch bulb is on

b a variable resistor, two cells in series and a torch bulb whose brightness can be varied by adjusting the variable resistor.

2 Match each component in the list to each statement **a** to **d** that describes it.

diode   filament bulb   resistor   thermistor

a Its resistance increases if the current through it increases.

b The current through it is proportional to the potential difference across it.

c Its resistance decreases if its temperature is increased.

d Its resistance depends on which way round it is connected in a circuit.

3 a Sketch a circuit diagram to show two resistors P and Q connected in series to a battery of two cells in series with each other.

b In the circuit in part **a**, resistor P has a resistance of 4 Ω, resistor Q has a resistance of 2 Ω and each cell has a potential difference of 1.5 V. Calculate:
  i the total potential difference of the two cells
  ii the total resistance of the two resistors
  iii the current in the circuit
  iv the potential difference across each resistor.

4 a Sketch a circuit diagram to show two resistors R and S in parallel with each other connected to a single cell.

b In the circuit in part **a**, resistor R has a resistance of 2 Ω, resistor S has a resistance of 4 Ω and the cell has a potential difference of 2 V. Calculate:
  i the current through resistor R
  ii the current through resistor S
  iii the current through the cell in the circuit.

5 Copy and complete **a** and **b** using the phrases below. Each option can be used once, twice or not at all.

different from   equal to

a For two components X and Y in series, the potential difference across X is usually .... the potential difference across Y.

b For two components X and Y in parallel, the potential difference across X is .... the potential difference across Y.

6 Figure 1 shows a light-dependent resistor is series with a 200 Ω resistor, a 3.0 V battery and an ammeter.

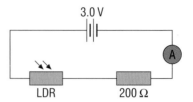

3.0 V

LDR   200 Ω

Figure 1

a With the LDR in daylight, the ammeter reads 0.010 A.
  i Calculate the potential difference across the 200 Ω resistor when the current through it is 0.010 A.
  ii Show that the potential difference across the LDR is 1.0 V when the ammeter reads 0.010 A.

b If the LDR is then covered, explain whether the ammeter reading increases or decreases or stays the same.

7 In Figure 1 in Question 6, the LDR is replaced by a 100 Ω resistor and a voltmeter connected in parallel with this resistor.

a Draw the circuit diagram for this circuit.

b Calculate:
  i the total resistance of the two resistors in the circuit
  ii the current through the ammeter
  iii the voltmeter reading
  iv the potential difference across the 200 Ω resistor.

8 Figure 2 shows a light-emitting diode (LED) in series with a resistor and a 3.0 V battery.

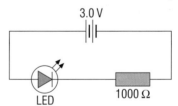

3.0 V

LED   1000 Ω

Figure 2

a The LED in the circuit emits light. The potential difference across it when it emits light is 0.6 V.
  i Explain why the potential difference across the 1000 Ω resistor is 2.4 V.
  ii Calculate the current in the circuit.

b If the LED in the circuit is reversed, what would be the current in the circuit? Give a reason for your answer.

9 State and explain how the resistance of a filament bulb changes when the current through the filament is increased.

[H]

AQA Examination-style questions Ⓚ

1 A plastic rod is rubbed with a dry cloth.

a Explain how the rod becomes negatively charged. (3)

b What charge is left on the cloth? (1)

c What happens if the negatively charged rod is brought close to another negatively charged rod? (1)

2 a Copy and complete the table of circuit symbols and their names. (5)

Circuit symbol	Name
—(V)—	i
ii	ammeter
—[⟋]—	iii
iv	LDR
—⊣⊢··⊣⊢—	v

b Copy and complete the following sentences using the list of words and phrases below. Each word can be used once, more than once or not at all.

energy transferred charge resistance voltage

Electric current is a flow of ....

The potential difference between two points in a circuit is the .... per unit of .... that passes between the points.

The greater the .... the lower the current for a given potential difference. (4)

3 Complete the following calculations. Write down the equation you use. Show clearly how you work out your answer and give the unit.

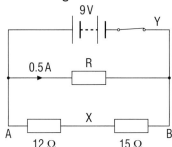

a i Calculate the potential difference between A and B. (1)

ii The potential difference across the 15 Ω resistor is 5 V.
Calculate the potential difference across the 12 Ω resistor. (1)

b i Calculate the combined resistance of the 12 Ω and the 15 Ω resistors in series. (1)

ii Calculate the current that flows through the circuit at X. (2)

iii Calculate the current flowing through the circuit at Y. (1)

c Calculate the resistance of the resistor labelled R. (2)

d Calculate the charge that flows through resistor R in 2 minutes. (3)

e Calculate the work done (energy transferred) by the cell if the total charge that has flowed through it is 3000 C. (2)

4 a Sketch and label a graph of current against potential difference for a diode. (3)

b The graph of current against potential difference for a filament bulb is shown.

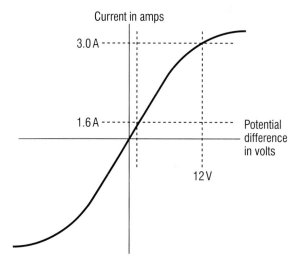

i Calculate the potential difference when the resistance of the filament bulb is 2 Ω when the current is 1.6 A. Write down the equation you use. Show clearly how you work out your answer and give the unit. (2)

ii Calculate the resistance at a potential difference of 12 V. Write down the equation you use. Show clearly how you work out your answer and give the unit. (3)

c *In this question you will be assessed on using good English, organising information clearly and using specialist terms where appropriate.*

Explain the change in resistance of the filament bulb in terms of ions and electrons. **[H]** (6)

P2 5.1   Alternating current ⓚ

Learning objectives

- What is meant by direct current and alternating current?
- What do we mean by the peak voltage of an alternating potential difference?
- What do we mean by the live wire and the neutral wire of a mains circuit?
- How do we use an oscilloscope to measure the frequency of an alternating current?   [H]

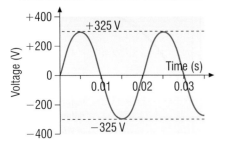

Figure 1 Mains voltage *v*. time

The battery in a torch makes the current to go round the circuit in one direction only. We say the current in the circuit is a **direct current** (dc) because it is in one direction only.

When you switch a light on at home, you use **alternating current** (ac) because mains electricity is an ac supply. An alternating current repeatedly reverses its direction. It flows one way then the opposite way in successive cycles. Its **frequency** is the number of cycles it passes through each second.

In the UK, the mains frequency is 50 cycles per second (or 50 Hz). A light bulb works just as well at this frequency as it would with a direct current.

a Why would a much lower frequency than 50 Hz be unsuitable for a light bulb?

Mains circuits

Every mains circuit has a **live wire** and a **neutral wire**. The current through a mains appliance alternates. That's because the mains supply provides an alternating potential difference between the two wires.

The neutral wire is **earthed** at the local substation. The potential difference between the live wire and 'earth' is usually referred to as the 'potential' or voltage of the live wire. The live wire is dangerous because its voltage repeatedly changes from + to − and back every cycle. It reaches over 300 V in each direction, as shown in Figure 1.

Practical

The oscilloscope

We use an oscilloscope to show how an alternating potential difference (pd) changes with time.

1 Connect a signal generator to an oscilloscope, as shown in Figure 2.

  – The trace on the oscilloscope screen shows electrical waves. They are caused by the potential difference increasing and decreasing continuously.

  – The highest potential difference is reached at each peak. The peak potential difference or

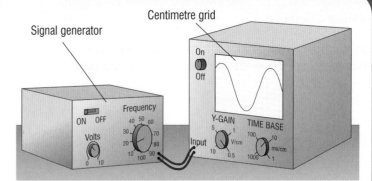

Figure 2 Using an oscilloscope

the **peak voltage** is the difference in volts between the peak and the middle level of the waves. Increasing the pd of the ac supply makes the waves on the screen taller.

  – Increasing the frequency of the ac supply increases the number of cycles you see on the screen. So the waves on the screen get squashed together.

- How would the trace change if the pd of the ac supply were reduced?

2 Connect a battery to the oscilloscope. You should see a flat line at a constant potential difference.

- What difference is made by reversing the battery?

Measuring an alternating potential difference

We can use an **oscilloscope** to measure the peak potential difference and the frequency of a low voltage ac supply. For example, in Figure 2:

- the peak voltage is 2.1 V if the peaks are 8.4 cm above the troughs. Each peak is 4.2 cm above the middle which is at zero pd. The **Y-gain control** at 0.5 V/cm tells us each centimetre of height is due to a potential difference of 0.5 V. So the peak potential difference is 2.1 V (= 0.5 V/cm × 4.2 cm).

- the frequency is 12.5 Hz if each cycle on the screen is 8 cm across. The **time base control** at 10 milliseconds per centimetre (ms/cm) tells us each centimetre across the screen is a time interval of 10 ms. So the time taken for one cycle is 80 ms (= 10 ms/cm × 8 cm). The frequency is therefore 12.5 Hz (= 1/80 ms or 1/0.08 s).

Note: the frequency of ac supply = $\dfrac{1}{\text{the time for one cycle}}$

More about mains circuits

Look at Figure 1 again. It shows how the potential of the live wire varies with time.

- The live wire alternates between +325 V and −325 V. In terms of electrical power, this is equivalent to a direct voltage of 230 V. So we say the voltage of the mains is 230 V.

Each cycle in Figure 1 takes 0.02 second. The frequency of the mains supply (the number of cycles per second) is therefore 50 Hz (= $\dfrac{1}{0.02 \text{ seconds}}$)

b What is the maximum potential difference between the live wire and the neutral wire in Figure 1?

Summary questions

1 Choose the correct potential difference from the list for each appliance **a** to **d**.

1.5 V   12 V   230 V   325 V

- **a** a car battery
- **b** the mains voltage
- **c** a torch cell
- **d** the maximum potential of the live wire.

2 In Figure 2, how would the trace on the screen change if the frequency of the ac supply was:
- **a** increased
- **b** reduced?

3 In Figure 2, what is the frequency if one cycle measures 4 cm across the screen for the same time base setting? [H]

4 **a** How does an alternating current differ from a direct current?
b Figure 4 shows a diode and a resistor in series with each other connected to an ac supply. Explain why the current in the circuit is a direct current not an alternating current.

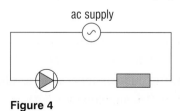

Figure 4

Key points

- Direct current is in one direction only. Alternating current repeatedly reverses its direction.

- The peak voltage of an alternating potential difference is the maximum voltage measured from zero volts.

- A mains circuit has a live wire that is alternately positive and negative every cycle and a neutral wire at zero volts.

- To measure the frequency of an a.c. supply, we measure the time period of the waves then use the formula:
  frequency = $\dfrac{1}{\text{time taken for 1 cycle}}$. [H]

P2 5.2

Cables and plugs

Learning objectives

- What is the casing of a mains plug or socket made from and why?

- What is in a mains cable?

- What colour are the live, neutral and earth wires?

- Why does a 3-pin plug include an earth pin?

Did you know ...?

Mains electricity is dangerous. By law, mains wiring must be done by properly qualified electricians.

When you plug in a heater with a metal case into a wall **socket**, you 'earth' the metal case automatically. This stops the metal case becoming 'live' if the live wire breaks and touches the case. If the case did become live and you touched it, you would be electrocuted.

Plastic materials are very good insulators. An appliance with a plastic case is doubly-insulated and carries the double insulation ▣ symbol.

Plugs, sockets and cables

The outer casings of **plugs**, sockets and **cables** of all mains circuits and appliances are made of hard-wearing electrical insulators. That's because plugs, sockets and cables contain live wires. Most mains appliances are connected via a wall socket to the mains using a cable and a **three-pin plug**.

Sockets are made of stiff plastic materials with the wires inside. Figure 1 shows part of a wall socket circuit. It has an earth wire as well as a live wire and a neutral wire.

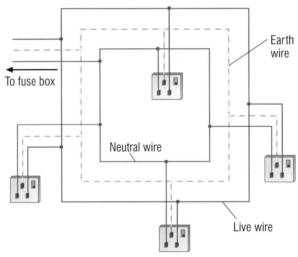

Figure 1 A wall socket circuit

- The earth wire of this circuit is connected to the ground at your home.

- The longest pin of a three-pin plug is designed to make contact with the earth wire of a wall socket circuit. So when you plug an appliance with a metal case to a wall socket, the case is automatically earthed.

a Why are sockets wired in parallel with each other?

Plugs have cases made of stiff plastic materials. The live pin, the neutral pin and the earth pin, stick out through the plug case. Figure 2 shows inside a three-pin plug.

- The pins are made of brass because brass is a good conductor and does not rust or oxidise. Copper isn't as hard as brass even though it conducts better.

- The case material is an electrical insulator. The inside of the case is shaped so the wires and the pins cannot touch each other when the plug is sealed.

- The plug contains a fuse between the live pin and the live wire. If too much current passes through the wire in the fuse, it melts and cuts the live wire off.

b Why is brass, an alloy of copper and zinc, better than copper for the pins of a three-pin plug?

- The brown wire is connected to the live pin.
- The blue wire is connected to the neutral pin.
- The green and yellow wire (of a three-core cable) is connected to the earth pin. A two-core cable does not have an earth wire.

Cables used for mains appliances (and for mains circuits) consist of two or three insulated copper wires surrounded by an outer layer of rubber or flexible plastic material.

- Copper is used for the wires because it is a good electrical conductor and it bends easily.
- Plastic is a good electrical insulator and therefore prevents anyone touching the cable from receiving an electric shock.
- Two-core cables are used for appliances which have plastic cases (e.g. hairdryers, radios).
- Cables of different thicknesses are used for different purposes. For example, the cables joining the wall sockets in a house must be much thicker than the cables joining the light fittings. This is because more current passes along wall socket cables than along lighting circuits. So the wires in them must be much thicker. This stops the heating effect of the current making the wires too hot.

c Why are cables that are worn away or damaged dangerous?
d In Figure 3, which wire in each cable is the earth wire?

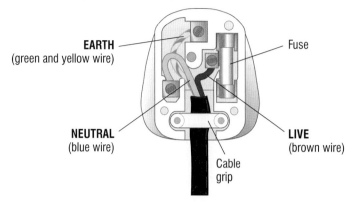

Figure 2 Inside a three-pin plug

EARTH (green and yellow wire)
Fuse
NEUTRAL (blue wire)
Cable grip
LIVE (brown wire)

Figure 3 Mains cables

Summary questions

1 Copy and complete **a** to **e** using the words below:

   earth   live   neutral   series   parallel

   a The .... wire in a mains plug is blue.
   b If too much current passes through the fuse, it blows and cuts the .... wire off.
   c Appliances plugged into the same mains circuit are in .... with each other.
   d The metal frame of an appliance is connected to the .... wire of a mains circuit when it is plugged in.
   e The fuse in a plug is in .... with the live wire.

2 **a** Match the list of parts 1–4 in a three-pin plug with the list of materials A–D.

1 cable insulation	**A** brass	
2 case	**B** copper	
3 pin	**C** rubber	
4 wire	**D** stiff plastic	

   b Explain your choice of material for each part in **a**.

3 **a** Why is each of the three wires in a three-core mains cable insulated?
   b How is the metal case of an electrical appliance connected to earth?

Key points

- **Sockets** and **plug cases** are made of stiff plastic materials that enclose the electrical connections. Plastic is used because it is a good electrical insulator.

- **Mains cable** consists of two or three insulated copper wires surrounded by an outer layer of flexible plastic material.

- In a **three-pin plug** or a three-core cable, the live wire is brown, the neutral wire is blue, and the earth wire is green and yellow.

- The earth wire is connected to the longest pin and is used to earth the metal case of a mains appliance.

P2 5.3

Fuses

Mains electricity

Learning objectives

● What do we use a fuse for?

● Why is a fuse always on the 'live' side of an appliance?

● What is a circuit breaker?

● Why are appliances with plastic cases not earthed?

??? Did you know ...?

If a live wire inside the appliance touches a neutral wire, a very large current passes between the two wires at the point of contact. We call this a short circuit. If the fuse blows, it cuts the current off.

If you need to buy a **fuse** for a mains appliance, make sure you know the fuse rating. Otherwise, the new fuse might 'blow' as soon as it is used. Worse still, it might let too much current through and cause a fire.

● A fuse contains a thin wire that heats up and melts if too much current passes through it. If this happens, we say the fuse 'blows'.

● The rating of a fuse is the maximum current that can pass through it without melting the fuse wire.

● The fuse should always be in series with the live wire between the live wire and the appliance. If the fuse blows, the appliance is then cut off from the live wire.

A fuse in a mains plug must always have the correct current rating for the appliance. If the current rating is too large, the fuse will not blow when it should. The heating effect of the current could set the appliance or its connecting cable on fire. Provided the correct fuse is fitted, the connecting cable must be thick enough (so its resistance is small enough) to make the heating effect of the current in the cable insignificant.

a What would happen if the current rating of the fuse was too small?

a   b

Figure 1 a A cartridge fuse **b** A rewireable fuse

The importance of earthing

Figure 2 shows why an electric heater is made safer by earthing its metal frame.

In Figure 2a, the heater works normally and its frame is earthed. The frame is safe to touch.

In Figure 2b, the earth wire is broken. The frame would become live if the live wire touched it.

AQA Examiner's tip

The earth wire protects the user and the fuse protects the appliance and the wiring of the circuit.

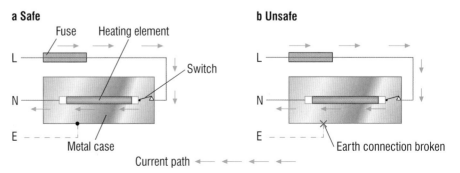

Figure 2 a and b Earthing an electric heater

In Figure 2c, the heater element has touched the unearthed frame so the frame is live. Anyone touching it would be electrocuted. The fuse provides no protection to the user as a current of no more than 20 mA can be lethal.

In Figure 2d, the earth wire has been repaired but the heater element still touches the frame. The current is greater than in **a** or **b** because it only passes through part of the heater element. Because the frame is earthed, anyone touching it would not be electrocuted. But Figure 2d is still dangerous. This is because although the current might not be enough to blow the fuse, it might cause the wires of the appliance to overheat.

b Why is the current in Figure 2d greater than normal?

Circuit breakers

A **circuit breaker** is an electromagnet switch that opens (switches off or 'trips') when there is a fault. This stops the current in the live wire flowing. The electromagnet is in series with the live wire. If the current in the live wire is too large, the magnetic field of the electromagnet is strong enough to pull the switch contacts apart. Once the switch is open, it stays open. It can then be reset once the fault that made it trip has been put right.

Circuit breakers are used instead of fuses. They work faster than fuses and can be reset more quickly.

The **Residual Current Circuit Breaker (RCCB)** works even faster than the ordinary circuit breaker described above. An RCCB cuts off the current in the live wire when it is different from the current in the neutral wire. The RCCB can be used where there is no earth connection. The RCCB is also more sensitive than either a fuse or an ordinary circuit breaker.

c What should you do if a circuit breaker trips again after being reset?

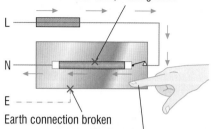

c Deadly Heating element touches the metal case, making it live

Earth connection broken

Victim touches the metal case, and because the earth wire is broken, conducts current to earth

d Still dangerous as it may overheat

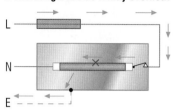

Figure 2 c and d

Figure 3 A circuit breaker

Key points

- A fuse contains a thin wire that heats up, melts, and cuts off the current if the current is too large.

- A fuse is always fitted in series with the live wire. This cuts the appliance off from the live wire if the fuse blows.

- A circuit breaker is an electromagnetic switch that opens (i.e. 'trips') and cuts off the current if too much current passes through the circuit breaker.

- A mains appliance with a plastic case does not need to be earthed because plastic is an insulator and cannot booomo livo.

Summary questions

1 a What is the purpose of a fuse in a mains circuit?
  b Why is the fuse of an appliance always on the live side?
  c What advantages does a circuit breaker have compared with a fuse?

2 Figure 4 shows the circuit of an electric heater that has been wired incorrectly.
  a Does the heater work when the switch is closed?
  b When the switch is open, why is it dangerous to touch the element?
  c Redraw the circuit correctly wired.

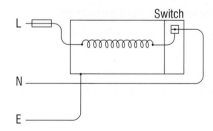

Figure 4

3 a What is the difference between an ordinary circuit breaker and a Residual Current Circuit Breaker (RCCB)?
  b What are the advantages of an RCCB mains socket compared with an ordinary mains socket with a fuse in it?

P2 5.4

Electrical power and potential difference

Learning objectives

- What is the relationship between power and energy?
- How can we calculate electrical power and what is its unit?
- How can we calculate the correct current for a fuse?

Did you know ... ?

A surgeon fitting an artificial heart in a patient needs to make sure the battery will last a long time. Even so, the battery may have to be replaced every few years.

Figure 1 An artificial heart

When you use an electrical appliance, it transfers electrical energy into other forms of energy. The **power** of the appliance, in watts, is the energy it transfers, in joules per second. We can show this as the following equation:

$$\textbf{Power (watts, W)} = \frac{\textbf{energy transferred (joules, J)}}{\textbf{time (seconds, s)}}$$

We can write the equation for the power of an appliance as:

$$P = \frac{E}{t}$$

Where:
P = power in watts, W
E = energy transferred in joules, J
t = time taken in seconds, s.

Maths skills

Worked example

A light bulb transfers 30 000 J of electrical energy when it is on for 300 s. Calculate its power.

Solution

$$\text{Power} = \frac{\text{energy transferred}}{\text{time}} = \frac{30\,000\,J}{300\,s} = 100\,W$$

a The human heart transfers about 30 000 J of energy in about 8 hours. Calculate an estimate of the power of the human heart.

Calculating power

Millions of electrons pass through the circuit of an artificial heart every second. Each electron transfers a small amount of energy to it from the battery. So the total energy transferred to it each second is large enough to enable the appliance to work.

For any electrical appliance:

- the current through it is the charge that flows through it each second
- the potential difference across it is the energy transferred to the appliance by each coulomb of charge that passes through it
- the power supplied to it is the energy transferred to it each second. This is the electrical energy it transfers every second.

Therefore:

the energy transfer to the appliance each second = the charge flow per second × the energy transfer per unit charge.

In other words:

$$\begin{array}{ccc} \textbf{power supplied} & = & \textbf{current} \times \textbf{potential difference} \\ \text{(watts, W)} & & \text{(amperes, A)} \qquad \text{(volts, V)} \end{array}$$

The equation can be written as:

$$P = I \times V$$

Where:
P = electrical power in watts, W
I = current in amperes, A
V = potential difference in volts, V.

For example, the power supplied to:

- a 4A, 12V electric motor is 48W (= 4A × 12V)
- a 0.1A, 3V torch lamp is 0.3W (= 0.1A × 3.0V).

b Calculate the power supplied to a 5A, 230V electric heater.

Rearranging the equation $P = I \times V$ gives:

potential difference, $V = \dfrac{P}{I}$ or

current, $I = \dfrac{P}{V}$

Choosing a fuse

Domestic appliances are often fitted with a 3A, 5A or 13A fuse. If you don't know which one to use for an appliance, you can work it out. You use the power rating of the appliance and its potential difference (voltage). The next time you change a fuse, do a quick calculation to make sure its rating is correct for the appliance (see the worked example opposite).

c Why would a 13A fuse be unsuitable for a 230V, 100W table lamp?

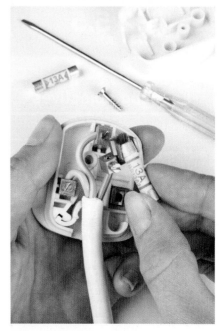

Figure 2 Changing a fuse

 Maths skills

Worked example

a Calculate the normal current through a 500W, 230V heater.

b Which fuse, 3A, 5A or 13A, would you use for the appliance?

Solution

a Current = $\dfrac{500\,W}{230\,V}$ = 2.2A

b You would use a 3A fuse.

Summary questions

1 Copy and complete **a** and **b** using the words below. Each word can be used more than once.

current   potential difference   power

a When an electrical appliance is on, ... is supplied to it as a result of .... passing through it.

b When an electrical appliance is on, a .... is applied to it which causes .... to pass through it.

2 a Calculate the power supplied to each of the following devices in normal use:

i a 12V, 3A light bulb
ii a 230V, 2A heater.

b Which type of fuse, 3A, 5A or 13A, would you select for:

i a 24W, 12V heater?
ii a 230V, 800W microwave oven?

3 a Why would a 3A fuse be unsuitable for a 230V, 800W microwave oven?

b The heating element of a 12V heater has a resistance of 4.0Ω. When the heating element is connected to a 12V power supply, calculate:

i the current through it
ii the electrical power supplied to it.

Key points

- The power supplied to a device is the energy transferred to it each second.

- Electrical power supplied (watts)

  = current (amperes) × potential difference (volts)

- Correct rating (in amperes) for a fuse:

  = $\dfrac{\text{electrical power (watts)}}{\text{potential difference (volts)}}$

Electrical energy and charge

Learning objectives

- What is an electric current?

- How do we calculate the flow of electric charge from the current?

- What energy transfers take place when charge flows through a resistor?

- How is the energy transferred by a flow of charge related to potential difference? [H]

- What can we say about the electrical energy supplied by the battery in a circuit and the electrical energy transferred to the components? [H]

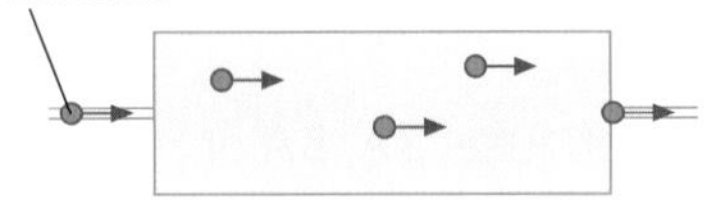

Calculating charge

When an electrical appliance is on, electrons are forced through the appliance by the potential difference of the power supply unit. The potential difference causes a flow of charge through the appliance carried by electrons.

As explained in P2 4.2, the electric current is the rate of flow of charge through the appliance. The unit of charge, the **coulomb (C)**, is the amount of charge flowing through a wire or a component in 1 s when the current is 1 A.

The charge passing along a wire or through a component in a certain time depends on the current and the time.

We can calculate the charge using the equation:

$$\underset{\text{(coulombs)}}{\text{charge}} = \underset{\text{(amperes)}}{\text{current}} \times \underset{\text{(seconds)}}{\text{time}}$$

The equation can be written as: $Q = I \times t$

Where:

Q = charge in coulombs, C
I = current in amperes, A
t = time in seconds, s.

a Calculate the charge flowing in 50 s when the current is 3 A.

Electrons

Charge flow = current × time

Figure 1 Charge and current

Maths skills

Worked example

Calculate the charge flow when the current is 8 A for 80 s.

Solution

Charge flow = current × time
= 8 A × 80 s
= 640 C

Energy and potential difference

When a resistor is connected to a battery, electrons are made to pass through the resistor by the battery. Each electron repeatedly collides with the vibrating metal ions of the resistor, transferring energy to them. The ions of the resistor therefore gain kinetic energy and vibrate even more. The resistor becomes hotter.

When charge flows through a resistor, energy is transferred to the resistor so the resistor becomes hotter.

The energy transferred in a certain time in a resistor depends on:

- the amount of charge that passes through it
- the potential difference across the resistor.

Because energy = power × time = potential difference × current × time, we can calculate the energy transferred using the equation:

$$\underset{\text{(joules, J)}}{\text{energy transferred}} = \underset{\text{(volts, V)}}{\text{potential difference}} \times \underset{\text{(coulombs, C)}}{\text{charge}}$$

The equation can be written as:

$$E = V \times Q$$

Where: E = energy transferred in joules, J
V = potential difference in volts, V
Q = charge in coulombs, C.

b Calculate the energy transferred when the charge flow is 30 C and the pd is 4 V.

Higher

Energy transfer in a circuit

The circuit in Figure 2 shows a 12 V battery in series with a torch bulb and a variable resistor. When the voltmeter reads 10 V, the potential difference across the variable resistor is 2 V.

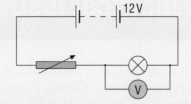

Figure 2 Energy transfer in a circuit

Each coulomb of charge:

● leaves the battery with 12 J of energy (because energy from the battery = charge × battery potential difference)

● transfers 10 J of energy to the torch bulb (because energy transfer to bulb = charge × potential difference across bulb)

● transfers 2 J of energy to the variable resistor.

The energy transferred to the bulb makes the bulb hot and emit light. The energy transferred to the variable resistor makes the resistor warm, so energy is therefore transferred to the surroundings by both bulb and resistor.

So the energy from the battery is equal to the sum of the energy transferred to the bulb and to the variable resistor.

Maths skills

Worked example

Calculate the energy transferred in a component when the charge passing through it is 30 C and the potential difference is 20 V.

Solution

Energy transferred = 20 V × 30 C
= 600 J

AQA Examiner's tip

Make sure you know and understand the relationship between charge, current and time.

Summary questions

1 Copy and complete **a** to **d** using the words below:

charge   current   energy   potential difference

  a The coulomb is the unit of ....

  b Charge flowing through a resistor transfers .... to the resistor.

  c A .... is the rate of flow of charge.

  d Energy transferred = ... × charge.   **[H]**

2 a Calculate the charge flow for:

    i a current of 4 A for 20 s

    ii a current of 0.2 A for 60 minutes.

  b Calculate the energy transfer:

    i for a charge flow of 20 C when the potential difference is 6.0 V

    ii for a current of 3 A that passes through a resistor for 20 s, when the potential difference is 5 V.   **[H]**

3 In Figure 3, a 4.0 Ω resistor and an 8.0 Ω resistor in series with each other are connected to a 6.0 V battery.

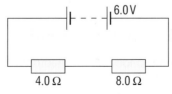

Figure 3

  Calculate:

  a the resistance of the two resistors in series

  b the current through the resistors

  c the charge flow through each resistor in 60 seconds

  d the potential difference across each resistor

  e the energy transferred to each resistor in 60 seconds

  f the energy supplied by the battery in 60 seconds.   **[H]**

Key points

● An electric current is the rate of flow of charge.

● Charge (coulombs) = current (amperes) × time (seconds). **[H]**

● When an electrical charge flows through a resistor, energy transferred to the resistor makes it hot.

● Energy transferred (joules) = potential difference (volts) × charge flow (coulombs). **[H]**

● When charge flows round a circuit for a certain time, the electrical energy supplied by the battery is equal to the electrical energy transferred to all the components in the circuit. **[H]**

P2 5.6

Electrical issues

Learning objectives

- Why are electrical faults dangerous?
- How can we prevent electrical faults?
- When choosing an electrical appliance, what factors in addition to cost should we consider?
- How do different forms of lighting compare in terms of cost and energy efficiency?

Activity

Spot the hazards!

How many electrical faults and hazards can you find in Shockem Hall? See how many you can spot in the main hall.

Figure 1 Shockem Hall

??? Did you know ... ?

What kills you – current or voltage? Mains electricity is dangerous. A current of no more than about 0.03 A through your body would give you a severe shock and might even kill you. Your body has a resistance of about 1000 Ω including contact resistance at the skin. If your hands get wet, your resistance is even lower.

An electrical fault is dangerous. It could give someone a nasty shock or even electrocute them, resulting in death. Also, a fault can cause a fire. This happens when too much current passes through a wire or an appliance and heats it up.

Fault prevention

Electrical faults can happen if sockets, plugs, cables or appliances are damaged. Users need to check for loose fittings, cracked plugs and sockets and worn cables. Any such damaged items need to be repaired or replaced by a qualified electrician.

- If a fuse blows or a circuit breaker trips when a mains appliance is in use, switch the appliance off. Then don't use it until it has been checked by a qualified electrician.
- If an appliance (or its cable or plug or socket) overheats and/or you get a distinctive burning smell from it, switch it off. Again, don't use it until it has been checked.

Too many appliances connected to a socket may cause the socket to overheat. If this happens, switch the appliances and the socket off and disconnect the appliances from the socket.

Smoke alarms and infrared sensors connected to an alarm system are activated if a fire breaks out. An electrical fault could cause an appliance or a cable to become hot and could set fire to curtains or other material in a room. Smoke alarms and sensors should be checked regularly to make sure they work properly.

An electrician selecting a cable for an appliance needs to use:

- a two-core cable if the appliance is 'double-insulated' and no earth wire is needed
- a three-core cable if an earth wire is needed because the appliance has a metal case
- a cable with conductors of suitable thickness so the heating effect of the current in the cable is insignificant.

  a i If a mains appliance suddenly stops working, why is it a mistake to replace the fuse straightaway?

    ii Should the cable of an electric iron be a two-core or a three-core cable?

New bulbs for old

When choosing an electrical appliance, most people compare several different appliances. The cost of the appliance is just one factor that may need to be considered. Other factors might include the power of the appliance and its efficiency.

If you want to replace a bulb, a visit to an electrical shop can present you with a bewildering range of bulbs.

A filament bulb is very inefficient. The energy from the hot bulb gradually makes the plastic parts of the bulb socket brittle and they crack.

Low energy bulbs are much more efficient so they don't become hot like filament bulbs do. Different types of low energy bulb are now available:

- **Low-energy compact fluorescent bulbs (CFLs)** are now used for room lighting instead of filament bulbs.
- **Low-energy light-emitting diodes (LEDs)** used for spotlights are usually referred to as high-power LEDs. They operate at low voltage and low power. They are much more efficient than filament bulbs or halogen bulbs and they last much longer.

This table gives more information about these different bulbs.

Type	Power	Efficiency	Lifetime in hours	Cost of bulb	Typical use
Filament bulb	100 W	20%	1000	50p	room lighting
Halogen bulb	100 W	25%	2500	£2.00	spotlight
Low-energy compact fluorescent bulb (CFL)	25 W	80%	15 000	£2.50	room lighting
Low-energy light-emitting diode (LED)	2 W	90%	30 000	£7.00	spotlight

b A householder wants to replace a 100 W room light with a row of low-energy LEDs with the same light output. Use the information in the table above to answer the following questions.
   i How many times would the filament bulb need to be replaced in the lifetime of an LED?
   ii How many LEDs would be needed to give the same light output as a 100 W filament bulb?
   iii The householder reckons the cost of the electricity for each LED at 10p per kWh over its lifetime of 30 000 hours would be £6. Show that the cost of the electricity for a 100 W bulb over this time would be £300.
   iv Use your answers above to calculate how much the householder would save by replacing the filament bulb with LEDs.

Did you know ...?

All new appliances like washing machines and freezers sold in the EU are labelled clearly with an efficiency rating. The rating is from A (very efficient) to G (lowest efficiency). Light bulbs are also labelled in this way on the packaging.

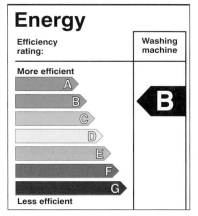

Figure 2 Efficiency measures

Key points

- Electrical faults are dangerous because they can cause electric shocks and fires.
- Never touch a mains appliance (or plug or socket) with wet hands. Never touch a bare wire or a terminal at a potential of more than 30 V.
- Check cables, plugs and sockets for damage regularly. Check smoke alarms and infrared sensors regularly.
- When choosing an electrical appliance, the power and efficiency rating of the appliance need to be considered.
- Filament bulbs and halogen bulbs are much less efficient than low energy bulbs.

Summary questions

1 An 'RCCB' socket should be used for mains appliances such as lawnmowers where there is a possible hazard when the appliance is used. Such a socket contains a residual current circuit breaker instead of a fuse. This type of circuit breaker switches the current off if the live current and the neutral current differ by more than 30 mA. This can happen, for example, if the blades of a lawnmower cut into the cable.

Create a table to show a possible 'electrical' hazard for each of these appliances: lawnmower, electric drill, electric saw, hairdryer, vacuum cleaner. The first entry has been done for you.

Appliance	Hazard
Lawnmower	The blades might cut the cable.

Summary questions

1 a In a mains circuit, which wire:
  i is earthed at the local sub-station
  ii alternates in potential?

b An oscilloscope is used to display the potential difference of an alternating voltage supply unit. How would the trace change if:
  i the pd is increased
  ii the frequency is increased?

2 Copy and complete **a** and **b** using the words below. Each word can be used more than once.

earth   live   neutral

a When a mains appliance is switched on, current passes through it via the .... wire and the .... wire.

b In a mains circuit:
  i the .... wire is blue
  ii the .... wire is brown
  iii the .... wire is green and yellow.

3 a Copy and complete the following sentences:
  i Wall sockets are connected in .... with each other.
  ii A fuse in a mains plug is in .... with the appliance and cuts off the .... wire if too much current passes through the appliance.

b i What is the main difference between a fuse and a circuit breaker?
  ii Give two reasons why a circuit breaker is safer than a fuse.

4 a i Calculate the current in a 230 V, 2.5 kW electric kettle.
  ii Which fuse, 3 A, 5 A or 13 A, would you fit in the kettle plug?

b Calculate the power supplied to a 230 V electric toaster when the current through it is 4.0 A.

5 A 5 Ω resistor is in series with a bulb, a switch and a 12 V battery.

a Draw the circuit diagram.

b When the switch is closed for 60 seconds, a direct current of 0.6 A passes through the resistor. Calculate:
  i the energy supplied by the battery
  ii the energy transferred to the resistor
  iii the energy transferred to the bulb.   [H]

c The bulb is replaced by a 25 Ω resistor.
  i Calculate the total resistance of the two resistors.
  ii Show that a current of 0.4 A passes through the battery.

  iii Calculate the power supplied by the battery and the power delivered to each resistor.

6 When a 6 V bulb operates normally, the electrical power supplied to it is 15 W.
  a Calculate:
  i the current through the bulb when it operates normally
  ii the resistance of the bulb when it operates normally.

b If the bulb is connected to a 3 V battery, state and explain why its resistance is less than at 6 V.

7 A 12 V 36 W bulb is connected to a 12 V supply.

  a Calculate:
  i the current through the bulb.
  ii the charge flow through the bulb in 200 s.   [H]

  b i Show that 7200 J of electrical energy is delivered to the bulb in 200 s.

  ii Calculate the energy delivered to the bulb by each coulomb of charge that passes through it.   [H]

8 An electrician has the job of connecting a 6.6 kW electric oven to the 230 V mains supply in a house.

  a Calculate the current needed to supply 6.6 kW of electrical power at 230 V.

  b The table below shows the maximum current that can pass safely through five different mains cables. For each cable the cross-sectional area (csa) of each conductor is given in square millimetres (mm²).

	Cross-sectional area of conductor (mm²)	Maximum safe current (A)
A	1.0	14
B	1.5	18
C	2.5	28
D	4.0	36
E	6.0	46

  i To connect the oven to the mains supply, which cable should the electrician choose? Give a reason for your answer.

  ii State and explain what would happen if she chose a cable with thinner conductors?

AQA Examination-style questions

1 The pictures show situations in which electricity is not being used safely.

For each picture **a**, **b** and **c**, explain how electricity is not being used safely.

a
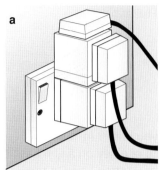
(2)

b
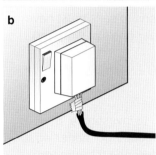
(2)

c
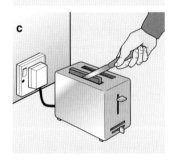
(2)

d The colour of the earth wire in a plug is .... (1)

e The pins of the plug are made of brass because it is a good .... (1)

f The voltage on the neutral wire is about .... V. (1)

g RCCB stands for .... (1)

2 Most domestic appliances are connected to the 230 V mains supply with a 3-pin plug containing a fuse. 3 A, 5 A and 13 A fuses are available.

a A bulb for a desk lamp has a normal current of 0.26 A.
   i Which of the three fuses should be used? (1)
   ii Calculate the power of the lamp. (2)
   iii Calculate how many coulombs of charge pass through the lamp if it is left on for 1 hour. [H] (3)

b i Calculate the current passing through a 1.15 kW electric fan heater. (2)
   ii Which fuse should be used in the plug for this heater? (1)

c Calculate how much electrical energy is transferred when the fan heater is left on for 30 minutes. Write down the equation you use. Show clearly how you work out your answer and give the unit. (3)

d *In this question you will be assessed on using good English, organising information clearly and using specialist terms where appropriate.*

The heater is made of metal and has an earth wire connected to it. Explain how the fuse and earth wire together protect the wiring of the circuit. (6)

3 A kettle is connected to the UK mains supply and boiled. An energy monitoring device measures that 420 000 J has been transferred to the kettle in the time it takes to boil.

a Calculate how much charge has flowed through the kettle. Write down the equation you use. Show clearly how you work out your answer and give the unit. [H] (3)

b The power of the kettle is 2.2 kW. How long did the kettle take to boil? (3)

4 An oscilloscope is connected to a power supply. The trace is shown on a centimetre grid.

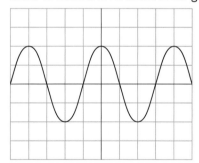

a Explain how you know that it is an ac supply being measured. (1)

b Give the peak voltage if each division on the y-axis is 2 V/cm. (1)

c Each x-axis division is 0.01 s/cm.
   i Calculate the time period of the supply. (1)
   ii Calculate the frequency of the supply. [H] (2)

d Describe the position and appearance of the trace on the screen if the supply was switched to 6 V dc. (2)

P2 6.1

Observing nuclear radiation

Learning objectives

- What is a radioactive substance?
- What types of radiation are given out from a radioactive substance?
- When does a radioactive source give out radiation (radioactive decay)?
- Where does background radiation come from?

A key discovery

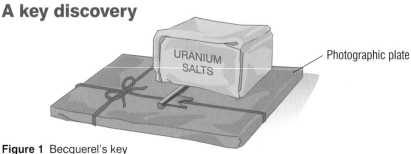

Figure 1 Becquerel's key

If your photos showed a mysterious image, what would you think? In 1896, the French physicist, **Henri Becquerel**, discovered the image of a key on a film he developed. He remembered the film had been in a drawer under a key. On top of that there had been a packet of uranium salts. The uranium salts must have sent out some form of radiation that passed through paper (the film wrapper) but not through metal (the key).

Marie Curie

Becquerel asked a young research worker, **Marie Curie**, to investigate. She found that the salts gave out radiation all the time. It happened no matter what was done to them. She used the word **radioactivity** to describe this strange new property of uranium.

She and her husband, Pierre, did more research into this new branch of science. They discovered new radioactive elements. They named one of the elements **polonium**, after Marie's native country, Poland.

a You can stop a lamp giving out light by switching it off. Is it possible to stop uranium giving out radiation?

Becquerel and the Curies were awarded the Nobel Prize for the discovery of radioactivity. When Pierre died in a road accident, Marie went on with their work. She was awarded a second Nobel Prize in 1911 for the discovery of polonium and radium. She died in 1934 from leukaemia, a disease of the blood cells. It was probably caused by the radiation from the radioactive materials she worked with.

Figure 2 Marie Curie 1867–1934

Practical

Investigating radioactivity

We can use a **Geiger counter** to detect radioactivity. Look at Figure 3. The counter clicks each time a particle of radiation from a radioactive substance enters the Geiger tube.

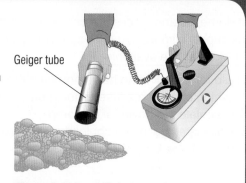

Figure 3 Using a Geiger counter

What stops the radiation? Ernest Rutherford carried out tests to answer this question about a century ago. He put different materials between the radioactive substance and a detector.

He discovered two types of radiation:

● One type (**alpha radiation**, symbol α) was stopped by paper.

● The other type (**beta radiation**, symbol β) went through the paper.

Scientists later discovered a third type, **gamma radiation** (symbol γ), even more penetrating than beta radiation.

> **b** Can gamma radiation go through paper?

A radioactive puzzle

Why are some substances radioactive? Every atom has a nucleus made up of protons and neutrons. Electrons move about in energy levels (or shells) surrounding the nucleus.

Most atoms each have a stable nucleus that doesn't change. But the atoms of a radioactive substance each have a nucleus that is unstable. An unstable nucleus becomes stable by emitting alpha, beta or gamma radiation. We say an unstable nucleus **decays** when it emits radiation.

We can't tell when an unstable nucleus will decay. It is a **random** event that happens without anything being done to the nucleus.

> **c** Why is the radiation from a radioactive substance sometimes called 'nuclear radiation'?

The origins of background radiation

A Geiger counter clicks even when it is not near a radioactive source. This effect is due to **background radiation**. This is radiation from radioactive substances:

● in the environment (e.g. in the air or the ground or in building materials), or

● from space (cosmic rays), or

● from devices such as X-ray tubes.

Some of these radioactive substances are present because of nuclear weapons testing and nuclear power stations. But most of it is from naturally occurring substances in the Earth. For example, radon gas is radioactive and is a product of the decay of uranium found in the rocks in certain areas.

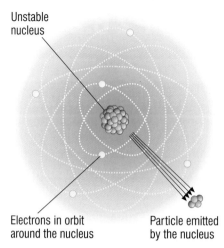

Unstable nucleus

Electrons in orbit around the nucleus

Particle emitted by the nucleus

Figure 4 Radioactive decay

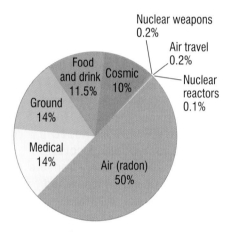

Nuclear weapons 0.2%
Air travel 0.2%
Nuclear reactors 0.1%
Food and drink 11.5%
Cosmic 10%
Ground 14%
Medical 14%
Air (radon) 50%

Figure 5 The origins of background radiation

Key points

● A radioactive substance contains unstable nuclei that become stable by emitting radiation.

● There are three main types of radiation from radioactive substances – alpha, beta and gamma radiation.

● Radioactive decay is a random event – we cannot predict or influence when it will happen.

● Background radiation is from radioactive substances in the environment or from space or from devices such as X-ray machines.

Summary questions

1 Copy and complete **a** and **b** using the words below. Each word can be used more than once.

protons   neutrons   nucleus   radiation

  a The .... of an atom is made up of .... and ....

  b When an unstable .... decays, it emits ....

2 **a** The radiation from a radioactive source is stopped by paper. What type of radiation does the source emit?

  b The radiation from a different source goes through paper. What can you say about this radiation?

3 **a** Explain why some substances are radioactive.

  b State two sources of background radioactivity.

P2 6.2

The discovery of the nucleus

Learning objectives

- How was the nuclear model of the atom established?

- Why was the plum pudding model of the atom rejected?

- Why was the nuclear model accepted?

Did you know ...?

Ernest Rutherford was awarded the Nobel Prize in 1908 for his discoveries on radioactivity. His famous discovery of the nucleus was made in 1913. He was knighted in 1914 and made a member of the House of Lords in 1931. He hoped that no one would discover how to release energy from the nucleus until people learned to live at peace with their neighbours. He died in 1937 before the discovery of nuclear fission.

Figure 2 Ernest Rutherford

Practical

Lucky strike!

Fix a small metal disc about 2 cm thick at the centre of a table. Hide the disc under a cardboard disc about 20 cm in diameter. See if you can hit the metal disc with a rolling marble.

Ernest Rutherford made many important discoveries about radioactivity. He discovered that alpha and beta radiation consists of different types of particles. He realised alpha (α) particles could be used to probe the atom. He asked two of his research workers, Hans Geiger and Ernest Marsden, to investigate. They used a thin metal foil to scatter a beam of alpha particles. Figure 1 shows the arrangement they used.

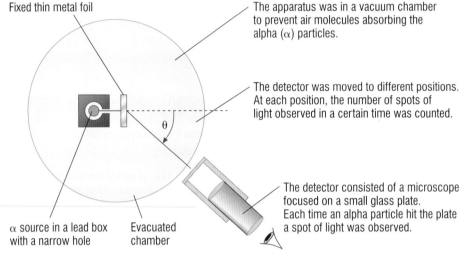

Fixed thin metal foil

The apparatus was in a vacuum chamber to prevent air molecules absorbing the alpha (α) particles.

The detector was moved to different positions. At each position, the number of spots of light observed in a certain time was counted.

The detector consisted of a microscope focused on a small glass plate. Each time an alpha particle hit the plate a spot of light was observed.

α source in a lead box with a narrow hole

Evacuated chamber

Figure 1 Alpha particle scattering

They measured the number of alpha particles deflected per second through different angles. The results showed that:

- most of the alpha particles passed straight through the metal foil
- the number of alpha particles deflected per minute decreased as the angle of deflection increased
- about 1 in 10 000 alpha particles were deflected by more than 90°.

    a If you kicked a football at an empty goal and the ball bounced back at you, what would you conclude?

Rutherford was astonished by the results. He said it was like firing 'naval shells' at tissue paper and discovering the occasional shell rebounds. He knew that α particles are positively charged. He deduced from the results that there is a nucleus at the centre of every atom that is:

- positively charged because it repels α particles (remember that like charges repel and unlike charges attract)
- much smaller than the atom because most α particles pass through without deflection
- where most of the mass of the atom is located.

Using this model, Rutherford worked out the proportion of α particles that would be deflected for a given angle. He found an exact agreement with Geiger and Marsden's measurements. He used his theory to estimate the diameter of the nucleus. He found it was about 100 000 times smaller than the atom.

Rutherford's nuclear model of the atom was quickly accepted because:

- It agreed exactly with the measurements Geiger and Marsden made in their experiments.
- It explains radioactivity in terms of changes that happen to an unstable nucleus when it emits radiation.
- It predicted the existence of the neutron, which was later discovered.

b What difference would it have made if Geiger and Marsden's measurements had not fitted Rutherford's nuclear model?

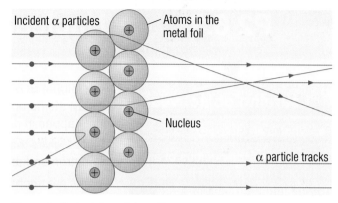

Figure 3 Alpha (α) particle paths

Goodbye to the plum pudding model!

Before the nucleus was discovered in 1914, scientists didn't know what the structure of the atom was. They did know atoms contained electrons and they knew these are tiny negatively charged particles. But they didn't know how the positive charge was arranged in an atom, although there were different models in circulation. Some scientists thought the atom was like a 'plum pudding' with:

- the positively charged matter in the atom evenly spread about (as in a pudding), and
- electrons buried inside (like plums in the pudding).

Rutherford's discovery meant farewell to the 'plum pudding' atom.

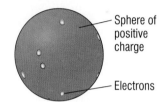

Figure 4 The plum pudding atom

Did you know ...?

Almost all the mass of an atom is in its nucleus. The density of the nucleus is about a thousand million million times the density of water. A matchbox of nuclear matter would weigh about a million million tonnes!

Summary questions

1 Copy and complete **a** to **c** using the words below:

charge   diameter   mass

a A nucleus has the same type of .... as an alpha particle.
b A nucleus has a much smaller .... than the atom.
c Most of the .... of the atom is in the nucleus.

2 **a** Figure 5 shows four possible paths, labelled A, B, C and D, of an alpha particle deflected by a nucleus. Which path would the alpha particle travel along?
b Explain why each of the other paths in part **a** is not possible.

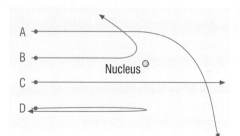

Figure 5

3 **a** Describe two differences between the nuclear model of the atom and the plum pudding model.
b Explain why the alpha-scattering experiment led to the acceptance of the nuclear model of the atom and the rejection of the plum pudding model.

Key points

- Rutherford used the measurements from alpha-scattering experiments to prove that an atom has a small positively charged central nucleus where most of the mass of the atom is located.
- The plum pudding model could not explain why some alpha particles were scattered through large angles.
- The nuclear model of the atom correctly explained why the alpha particles are scattered and why some are scattered through large angles.

P2 6.3 Nuclear reactions

Learning objectives

- What is an isotope?

- How does the nucleus of an atom change when it emits an alpha particle or a beta particle?

- How can we represent the emission of an alpha or a beta particle from a nucleus? [H]

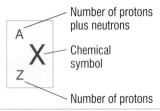

- Number of protons plus neutrons
- Chemical symbol
- Number of protons

Example: the symbol for the uranium isotope with 92 protons and 146 neutrons is

$$^{238}_{92}U \text{ (or sometimes U-238)}$$

Figure 1 Representing an isotope

Table 1

	Relative mass	Relative charge
proton	1	+1
neutron	1	0
electron	0.0005	-1

The nucleus emits an α particle and forms a new nucleus

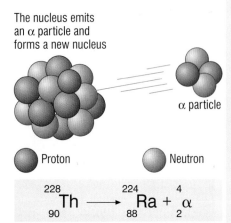

α particle

Proton   Neutron

$$^{228}_{90}Th \longrightarrow ^{224}_{88}Ra + ^{4}_{2}\alpha$$

Figure 2 α emission

In α (alpha) or β (beta) decay, the number of protons in a nucleus changes. In α decay, the number of neutrons also changes. We will now look at the changes that happen in α and β decay and how we can represent these changes.

Table 1 gives the relative masses and the relative electric charges of a proton, a neutron and an electron.

Atoms are uncharged. They have equal numbers of protons (+) and electrons (−). A charged particle, called an ion, is formed when an atom gains or loses one or more electrons. Then there are unequal numbers of protons and electrons in the ion.

The atoms of the same element each have the same number of protons. The number of protons in a nucleus is given the symbol Z. It is called the **atomic number** (or **proton number**).

Isotopes are atoms of the same element with different numbers of neutrons. The isotopes of an element have nuclei with the same number of protons but a different number of neutrons.

The number of protons and neutrons in a nucleus is called its **mass number**. We give it the symbol A.

An isotope of an element X, which has Z protons and A protons plus neutrons, is represented by the symbol $^{A}_{Z}X$. For example, the uranium isotope $^{238}_{92}U$ contains 92 protons and 146 neutrons (= 238 − 92) in each nucleus. So its relative mass is 238 and the relative charge of the nucleus is +92.

> **a** How many protons and how many neutrons are in the nucleus of the uranium isotope $^{235}_{92}U$?

Radioactive decay

An unstable nucleus becomes more stable by emitting an α (alpha) or a β (beta) particle or by emitting γ (gamma) radiation.

α emission

An α particle consists of two protons and two neutrons. Its relative mass is 4 and its relative charge is +2. So we can represent it by the symbol $^{4}_{2}\alpha$.

When an unstable nucleus emits an α particle, its atomic number goes down by 2 and its mass number goes down by 4.

For example, the thorium isotope $^{228}_{90}Th$ decays by emitting an α particle. So it forms the radium isotope $^{224}_{88}Ra$.

Figure 2 shows an equation to represent this decay.
- The numbers along the top represent the mass number which is the number of protons and neutrons in each nucleus and in the α particle.
- The equation shows that the total number of protons and neutrons after the change (= 224 + 4) is equal to the total number of neutrons and protons before the change (= 228).
- The numbers along the bottom represent the atomic number which is the number of protons in each nucleus and in the α particle.
- The equation shows that the total number of protons after the change (= 88 + 2) is equal to the total number of protons before the change (= 90).

Higher

b How many protons and how many neutrons are in $^{228}_{90}$Th and $^{224}_{88}$Ra?

β emission

- A β particle is an electron created and emitted by a nucleus which has too many neutrons compared with its protons. A neutron in the nucleus changes into a proton and a β particle. This is instantly emitted at high speed by the nucleus.
- The relative mass of a β particle is effectively zero and its relative charge is −1. So we can represent a β particle by the symbol $^{0}_{-1}$β.

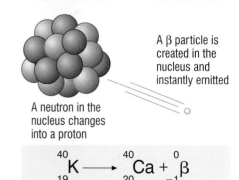

A β particle is created in the nucleus and instantly emitted

A neutron in the nucleus changes into a proton

$$^{40}_{19}K \longrightarrow\ ^{40}_{20}Ca +\ ^{0}_{-1}\beta$$

Figure 3 β emission

- When an unstable nucleus emits a β particle, the atomic number of the nucleus goes up by 1 but its mass number stays the same (because a neutron changes into a proton).

For example, the potassium isotope $^{40}_{19}$K decays by emitting a β particle. So it forms a nucleus of the calcium isotope $^{40}_{20}$Ca.

- The numbers along the top represent the mass number which is the number of protons and neutrons for each nucleus and −1 for the β particle, as explained below.
- The equation shows that the total number of protons and neutrons after the change (= 40 + 0) is equal to the total number of neutrons and protons before the change (= 40).
- The numbers along the bottom represent the atomic number. This is the number of protons for each nucleus and −1 for the β particle, as explained below.
- The equation shows that the total number of protons after the change (= 20 −1) is equal to the total number of protons before the change (= 19).

(Note the relative charge of the β particle is −1 so we represent its atomic number as −1 in these nuclear equations, even though it has no protons at all.)

c How many protons and how many neutrons are in $^{40}_{19}$K and $^{40}_{20}$Ca?

γ emission

γ radiation is emitted by some unstable nuclei after an α particle or a β particle has been emitted. γ radiation is uncharged and has no mass. So it does not change the number of protons or the number of neutrons in a nucleus.

Key points

- Isotopes of an element are atoms with the same number of protons but different numbers of neutrons. Therefore they have the same atomic number but different mass numbers.

α decay	β decay
Change in the nucleus	
Nucleus loses 2 protons and 2 neutrons	A neutron in the nucleus changes into a proton
Particle emitted	
2 protons and 2 neutrons emitted as an α particle	An electron is created in the nucleus and instantly emitted
Equation	[H]
$^{A}_{Z}X \rightarrow\ ^{A-4}_{Z-2}Y +\ ^{4}_{2}\alpha$	$^{A}_{Z}X \rightarrow\ ^{A}_{z+1}Y +\ ^{0}_{-1}\beta$

Summary questions

1 How many protons and how many neutrons are there in the nucleus of each of the following isotopes?

   a $^{12}_{6}$C   **b** $^{60}_{27}$Co   **c** $^{235}_{92}$U

2 A substance contains the radioactive isotope $^{238}_{92}$U, which emits alpha radiation. The product nucleus X emits beta radiation and forms a nucleus Y. How many protons and how many neutrons are present in:

   a a nucleus of $^{238}_{92}$U   **b** a nucleus of X   **c** a nucleus of Y?

3 Copy and complete the following equations for α and β decay.

   a $^{235}_{92}$U → $^{?}_{?}$Th + $^{4}_{?}$α   **b** $^{64}_{29}$Cu → $^{?}_{?}$Zn + $^{?}_{-1}$β   [H]

Higher

More about alpha, beta and gamma radiation

Learning objectives

- How far can each type of radiation travel in air and what stops it?

- What is alpha, beta and gamma radiation?

- How can we separate a beam of alpha, beta and gamma radiation?

- Why is alpha, beta and gamma radiation dangerous?

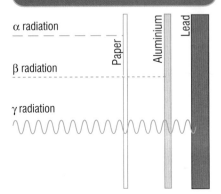

Figure 2 The penetrating powers of α, β and γ radiation

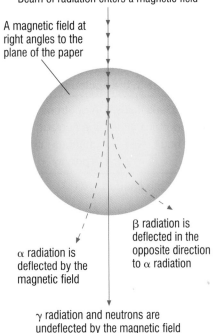

Figure 3 Radiation in a magnetic field

Penetrating power

Alpha radiation can't penetrate paper. But what stops beta and gamma radiation? And how far can each type of radiation travel through air? We can use a Geiger counter to find out, but we must take account of background radiation. To do this we should:

1 Measure the count rate (which is the number of counts per second) without the radioactive source present. This is the background count rate, the count rate due to background radiation.

2 Measure the count rate with the source in place. Subtracting the background count rate from this gives the count rate due to the source alone.

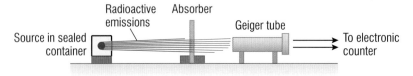

Figure 1 Absorption tests

We can then test absorber materials and the range in air.

- To test different materials, we need to place each material between the tube and the radioactive source. Then we measure the count rate. We can add more layers of material until the count rate due to the source is zero. The radiation from the source has then been stopped by the absorber material.

- To test the range in air, we need to move the tube away from the source. When the tube is beyond the range of the radiation, the count rate due to the source is zero.

The table below shows the results of the two tests.

Type of radiation	Absorber materials	Range in air
alpha (α)	Thin sheet of paper	about 5 cm
beta (β)	Aluminium sheet (about 5 mm thick) Lead sheet (2–3 mm thick)	about 1 m
gamma (γ)	Thick lead sheet (several cm thick) Concrete (more than 1 m thick)	unlimited

Gamma radiation spreads out in air without being absorbed. It does get weaker as it spreads out.

  a Why is a radioactive source stored in a lead-lined box?

The nature of alpha, beta and gamma radiation

We can separate these radiations using a magnetic field or an electric field.

Deflection by a magnetic field

- β radiation is easily deflected, in the same way as electrons. So the radiation consists of negatively charged particles. In fact, a β particle is a fast-moving electron. It is emitted by an unstable nucleus that contains too many neutrons.

- α radiation is deflected in the opposite direction to β radiation. So α radiation consists of positively charged particles. α particles are harder to deflect than β radiation. This is because an α particle has a much greater mass than a β particle has. An alpha particle is two protons and two neutrons stuck together, the same as a helium nucleus.
- γ radiation is not deflected by a magnetic field or an electric field. This is because gamma radiation is electromagnetic radiation so is uncharged.

Figure 4 Radiation passing through an electric field

Deflection by an electric field

α and β particles passing through an electric field are deflected in opposite directions, as shown in Figure 4.

- The α particles are attracted towards the negative plate because they are positively charged.
- The β particles are attracted towards the positive plate because they are negatively charged,

In Figures 3 and 4, an alpha particle is deflected much less than the beta particle. The charge of an alpha particle is twice that of a beta particle, so the force is twice as great. But the mass of an alpha particle is about 8000 times that of a beta particle, so the deflection of the alpha particle is much less.

b How do we know that gamma radiation is not made up of charged particles?

Figure 5 Radioactive warnings

Radioactivity dangers

The radiation from a radioactive substance can knock electrons out of atoms. The atoms become charged because they lose electrons. The process is called **ionisation**. (Remember that a charged particle is called an ion.)

X-rays also cause ionisation. Ionisation in a living cell can damage or kill the cell. Damage to the genes in a cell can be passed on if the cell generates more cells. Strict safety rules must always be followed when radioactive substances are used.

Alpha radiation is more dangerous in the body than beta or gamma radiation. This is because it has a greater ionising effect than beta or gamma radiation.

c Why should long-handled tongs be used to move a radioactive source?

Summary questions

1 Copy and complete **a** and **b** using the words below. Each word can be used more than once.

alpha beta gamma

a Electromagnetic radiation from a radioactive substance is called .... radiation.

b A thick metal plate will stop .... and .... radiation but not .... radiation.

2 Which type of radiation is:

a uncharged **b** positively charged **c** negatively charged?

3 **a** Explain why ionising radiation is dangerous.

b Explain how you would use a Geiger counter to find the range of the radiation from a source of α radiation.

Key points

- **α radiation** is stopped by paper, has a range of a few centimetres in air and consists of particles, each composed of two protons and two neutrons.

- **β radiation** is stopped by thin metal, has a range of about a metre in air and consists of fast-moving electrons emitted from the nucleus.

- **γ radiation** is stopped by thick lead, has an unlimited range in air and consists of electromagnetic radiation.

- A magnetic or an electric field can be used to separate a beam of alpha, beta and gamma radiation.

- Alpha, beta and gamma radiation ionise substances they pass through. Ionisation in a living cell can damage or kill the cell.

P2 6.5

Half-life

Learning objectives

- What do we mean by the 'half-life' of a radioactive source?
- What do we mean by the activity of a radioactive source?
- What happens to the activity of a radioactive isotope as it decays?

Every atom of an element always has the same number of protons in its nucleus. However, the number of neutrons in the nucleus can differ. Each type of atom is called an isotope. (So isotopes of an element contain the same number of protons but different numbers of neutrons.)

The **activity** of a radioactive isotope is the number of atoms that decay per second. As the nucleus of each unstable atom (the 'parent' atom) decays, the number of parent atoms goes down. Therefore the activity of the sample decreases.

We can use a Geiger counter to monitor the activity of a radioactive sample. We need to measure the **count rate** due to the sample. This is the number of counts per second (or per minute). The graph below shows how the count rate of a sample decreases.

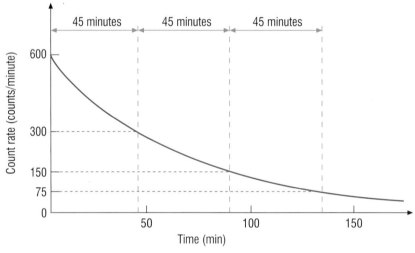

Figure 1 Radioactive decay: a graph of count rate against time

The graph shows that the count rate decreases with time. The count rate falls from:

- 600 counts per minute (c.p.m.) to 300 c.p.m. in the first 45 minutes
- 300 counts per minute (c.p.m.) to 150 c.p.m. in the next 45 minutes.

The average time taken for the count rate (and therefore the number of parent atoms) to fall by half is always the same. This time is called the **half-life**. The half-life shown on the graph is 45 minutes.

a What will the count rate be after 135 minutes from the start?

The half-life of a radioactive isotope is the average time it takes:

- **for the number of nuclei of the isotope in a sample (and therefore the mass of parent atoms) to halve**
- **for the count rate the isotope in a sample to fall to half its initial value.**

Did you know ...?

Some radioactive isotopes have half-lives of a fraction of a second, whereas others have half-lives of more than a billion years. The nitrogen isotope N-12 has a half-life of 0.0125 seconds. The uranium isotope U-238 has a half-life of 4.5 billion years.

The random nature of radioactive decay

Radioactive decay is a random process. We can't predict *when* an individual atom will suddenly decay. But we *can* predict how many atoms will decay in a certain time – because there are so many of them. This is a bit like throwing dice. You can't predict what number you will get with a single throw. But if you threw 1000 dice, you would expect one-sixth to come up with a particular number.

Suppose we start with 1000 unstable atoms. Look at the graph on the right:

If 10% decay every hour:

- 100 atoms will decay in the first hour, leaving 900
- 90 atoms (= 10% of 900) will decay in the second hour, leaving 810.

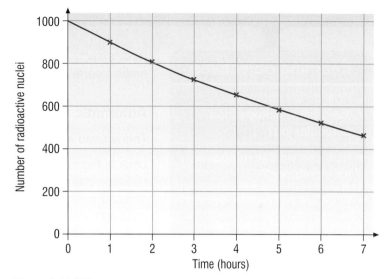

Figure 2 Half-life

The table below shows what you get if you continue the calculations. The results are plotted as a graph in Figure 2.

Time from start (hours)	0	1	2	3	4	5	6	7
No. of unstable atoms present	1000	900	810	729	656	590	530	477
No. of unstable atoms that decay in the next hour	100	90	81	73	66	59	53	48

b Use the graph in Figure 2 to work out the half-life of this radioactive isotope.

Summary questions

1 Copy and complete **a** and **b** using the words below. Each word can be used more than once.

half-life   stable   unstable

a In a radioactive substance, ... atoms decay and become ....

b The .... of a radioactive isotope is the time taken for the number of .... atoms to decrease to half.

2 A radioactive isotope has a half-life of 15 hours. A sealed tube contains 8 milligrams of this isotope.
What mass of the isotope is in the tube:
a 15 hours later?
b 45 hours later?

3 A sample of a radioactive isotope contains 320 million atoms of the isotope. How many atoms of the isotope are present after:
a one half-life
b five half-lives?

Key points

- The **half-life** of a radioactive isotope is the average time it takes for the number of nuclei of the isotope in a sample to halve.

- The activity of a radioactive source is the number of nuclei that decay per second.

- The number of atoms of a radioactive isotope and the activity both decrease by half every half-life.

P2 6.6   Radioactivity at work

Learning objectives

- How do we choose a radioactive isotope for a particular job?
- How can we use radioactivity for monitoring?
- What are radioactive tracers?
- What is radioactive dating?

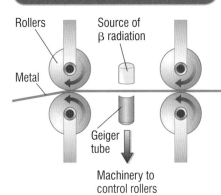

Figure 1 Thickness monitoring using a radioactive source

Radioactivity has many uses. For each use, we need a radioactive isotope that emits a certain type of radiation and has a suitable half-life.

Automatic thickness monitoring

This is used when making metal foil.

Look at Figure 1. The radioactive source emits β radiation. The amount of radiation passing through the foil depends on the thickness of the foil. A detector on the other side of the metal foil measures the amount of radiation passing through it.

- If the thickness of the foil increases too much, the detector reading drops.
- The detector sends a signal to the rollers to increase the pressure on the metal sheet.

This makes the foil thinner again.

a What happens if the thickness of the foil decreases too much?

b Why is alpha radiation not used here?

Radioactive tracers

These are used to trace the flow of a substance through a system. For example, doctors use radioactive iodine to find out if a patient's kidney is blocked.

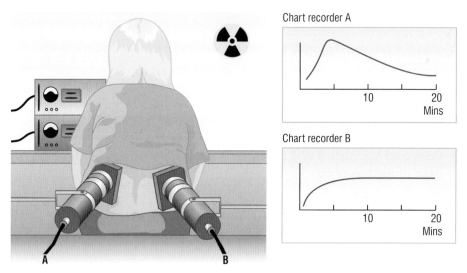

Figure 2 Using a tracer to monitor a patient's kidneys

Before the test, the patient drinks water containing a tiny amount of the radioactive substance. A detector is then placed against each kidney. Each detector is connected to a chart recorder.

- The radioactive substance flows in and out of a normal kidney. So the detector reading goes up then down.
- For a blocked kidney, the reading goes up and stays up. This is because the radioactive substance goes into the kidney but doesn't flow out again.

Radioactive iodine is used for this test because:

- Its half-life is 8 days, so it lasts long enough for the test to be done but decays almost completely after a few weeks.
- It emits gamma radiation, so it can be detected outside the body.
- It decays into a stable product.

c In Figure 2, which kidney is blocked, A or B?

Radioactive dating

This is used to find the age of ancient material. We can use:

- **Carbon dating** – this is used to find the age of ancient wood and other organic material. Living wood contains a tiny proportion of radioactive carbon. This has a half-life of 5600 years. When a tree dies, it no longer absorbs any carbon. So the amount of radioactive carbon in it decreases. To find the age of a sample, we need to measure the count rate from the wood. This is compared with the count rate from the same mass of living wood. For example, suppose the count rate in a sample of wood is half the count rate of an equal mass of living wood. Then the sample must be 5600 years old.

- **Uranium dating** – this is used to find the age of igneous rocks. These rocks contain radioactive uranium, which has a half-life of 4500 million years. Each uranium atom decays into an atom of lead. We can work out the age of a sample by measuring the number of atoms of uranium and lead. For example, if a sample contains 1 atom of lead for every atom of the uranium, the age of the sample must be 4500 million years. This is because there must have **originally** been 2 atoms of uranium for each atom of uranium now present.

d What could you say about an igneous rock with uranium but no lead in it?

Summary questions

1 Copy and complete **a** to **c** using the words below. Each word can be used more than once.

   alpha   beta   gamma

   a In the continuous production of thin metal sheets, a source of .... radiation should be used to monitor the thickness of the sheets.

   b A radioactive tracer given to a hospital patient needs to emit .... or .... radiation.

   c The radioactive source used to trace a leak in an underground pipeline should be a source of .... radiation.

2 **a** Explain why γ radiation is not suitable for monitoring the thickness of metal foil.

   b When a radioactive tracer is used, why is it best to use a radioactive isotope that decays into a stable isotope?

3 **a** What are the ideal properties of a radioactive isotope used as a medical tracer?

   b A sample of old wood was carbon dated and found to have 25% of the count rate measured in an equal mass of living wood. The half-life of the radioactive carbon is 5600 years. How old is the sample of wood?

Key points

- The use we can make of a radioactive isotope depends on:
  a its half-life
  b the type of radiation it gives out.

- For monitoring, the isotope should have a long half-life.

- Radioactive tracers should be β or γ emitters that last long enough to monitor but not too long.

- For radioactive dating of a sample, we need a radioactive isotope that is present in the sample which has a half-life about the same as the age of the sample.

Summary questions

1 a How many protons and how many neutrons are in a nucleus of each of the following isotopes?

    i $^{14}_{6}C$

    ii $^{228}_{90}Th$

  b $^{14}_{6}C$ emits a β particle and becomes an isotope of nitrogen (N).

    i How many protons and how many neutrons are in this nitrogen isotope?

    ii Write down the symbol for this isotope.

  c $^{228}_{90}Th$ emits an α particle and becomes an isotope of radium (Ra).

    i How many protons and how many neutrons are in this isotope of radium?

    ii Write down the symbol for this isotope.

2 Which type of radiation, alpha, beta or gamma:

  a can pass through lead?

  b travels no further than about 10 cm in air?

  c is stopped by an aluminium metal plate but not by paper?

  d consists of electrons?

  e consists of helium nuclei?

  f is uncharged?

3 The table below gives information about four radioactive isotopes **A**, **B**, **C** and **D**.

Isotope	Type of radiation emitted	Half-life
A californium-241	alpha	4 minutes
B cobalt-60	gamma	5 years
C hydrogen-3	beta	12 years
D strontium-90	beta	28 years

  Match each statement 1 to 4 with **A**, **B**, **C** or **D**.

  1 the isotope that gives off radiation with an unlimited range

  2 the isotope that has the longest half-life

  3 the isotope that decays the fastest

  4 the isotope with the smallest mass of each atom.

4 The following measurements were made of the count rate due to a radioactive source.

Time (hours)	0	0.5	1.0	1.5	2.0	2.5
Count rate due to the source (counts per minute)	510	414	337	276	227	188

  a Plot a graph of the count rate (on the vertical axis) against time.

  b Use your graph to find the half-life of the source.

5 In a carbon dating experiment of ancient wood, a sample of the wood gave a count rate of 0.4 counts per minute. The same mass of living wood gave a count rate of 1.6 counts per minute.

  a How many half-lives did the count rate take to decrease from 1.6 to 0.4 counts per minute?

  b The half-life of the radioactive carbon in the wood is 5600 years. What is the age of the sample?

6 In an investigation to find out what type of radiation was emitted from a given source, the following measurements were made with a Geiger counter.

Source	Average count rate (in counts per minute)
No source present	29
Source at 20 mm from tube with no absorber between	385
Source at 20 mm from tube with a sheet of metal foil between	384
Source at 20 mm from tube with a 10 mm thick aluminium plate between	32

  a What caused the count rate when no source was present?

  b What was the count rate due to the source with no absorbers present?

  c What type of radiation was emitted by the source? Explain how you arrive at your answer.

7 Figure 1 shows the path of two α particles labelled A and B that are deflected by the nucleus of an atom.

  a Why are they deflected by the nucleus?

  b Why is B deflected less than A?

  c Why do most α particles directed at a thin metal foil pass straight through it?

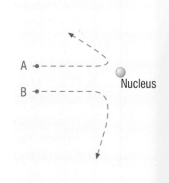

Figure 1

AQA Examination-style questions

1 Diagrams **A** and **B** show two atoms of carbon.

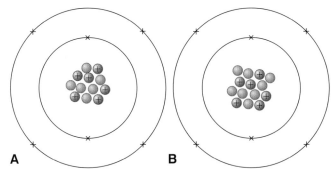

A   **B**

a Copy and complete the following sentences using the list of words and phrases below. Each one can be used once, more than once or not at all.

electrons   positive   isotopes   nuclear
plum pudding   negative   nucleus   ions   neutrons

Particles shown by the symbol **x** in the diagram are called .... They orbit the .... of an atom. This is made up of protons and .... Protons have a .... charge. This diagram shows the .... model of the atom which replaced the .... model. (6)

b Explain how a carbon **ion** would be different from atom **A**. (1)

c Give the mass number of atom **A**. (1)

d Give the atomic number of atom **A**. (1)

e Compare atom **B** with atom **A**. (3)

2 a A geologist wishes to know what types of radiation are emitted by three radioactive rock samples. Different absorbers are placed between each sample and a detector. The counts per second are shown in the table.

Absorber	Counts per second		
	Sample 1	Sample 2	Sample 3
1 cm of air	140	80	120
paper	90	50	70
3 mm of aluminium	30	49	0
1 cm of lead	0	1	0

For each sample state which of the three types of radiation (alpha, beta, gamma) are emitted. A rock may emit more than one type. (3)

b Describe the nature of an alpha particle. (2)

c List the three types of nuclear radiation in order of their relative ionising power from the least ionising to the most ionising. (3)

d The source of radiation shown below emits alpha, beta and gamma. When the radiation travels through air in an electric field between two plates, the three types of radiation behave differently.

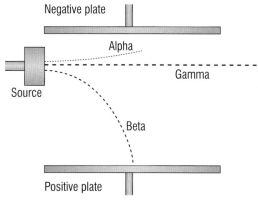

i An alpha particle has more charge than a beta particle. Explain why the beta particle is deflected more by the electric field and in the opposite direction. **[H]** (3)

ii Explain why the gamma radiation is not affected by the electric field. (1)

iii Explain why the alpha particle does not reach the plate. (2)

3 Technetium-99 is a gamma-emitting radioisotope used as a tracer inside the body in order to diagnose problems with various organs. Cobalt-60 is a gamma emitter used for radiotherapy where the source is used outside the body to kill cancer cells on the inside.

	Half-life	Radiation	Relative ionising power
technetium-99	6.0 hours	gamma	1
cobalt-60	5.3 years	gamma	10

a Technetium–99 emits a gamma ray and then decays to an isotope of ruthenium (Ru) by beta decay. Balance the nuclear equation by giving the appropriate atomic numbers and mass numbers.

$$^{99}_{43}Tc \rightarrow \, ^{(i)}_{(ii)}Ru + \, ^{(iii)}_{(iv)}\beta$$ **[H]** (4)

b *In this question you will be assessed on using good English, organising information clearly and using specialist terms where appropriate.*

Explain why cobalt-60 is not used as a medical tracer in humans and why technetium-99 is used for this purpose. (6)

P2 7.1

Nuclear fission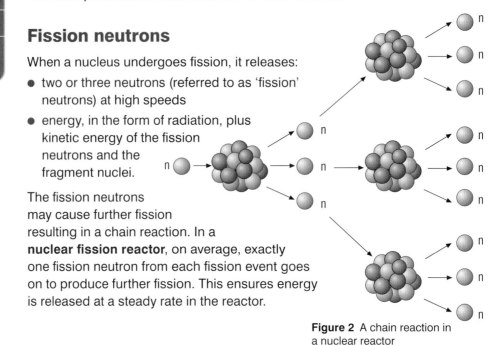

Learning objectives

- What is nuclear fission?
- Which radioactive isotopes undergo fission?
- What is a chain reaction?
- How is a chain reaction in a nuclear reactor controlled?

Chain reactions

Energy is released in a nuclear reactor as a result of **nuclear fission**. In this process, the nucleus of an atom of a fissionable substance splits into two smaller 'fragment' nuclei. This event can cause other fissionable nuclei to split. This then produces a **chain reaction** of fission events.

Fission neutrons

When a nucleus undergoes fission, it releases:

- two or three neutrons (referred to as 'fission' neutrons) at high speeds
- energy, in the form of radiation, plus kinetic energy of the fission neutrons and the fragment nuclei.

The fission neutrons may cause further fission resulting in a chain reaction. In a **nuclear fission reactor**, on average, exactly one fission neutron from each fission event goes on to produce further fission. This ensures energy is released at a steady rate in the reactor.

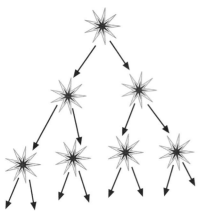

In a chain reaction, each reaction causes more reactions which cause more reactions, etc. etc.

Figure 1 A chain reaction

Figure 2 A chain reaction in a nuclear reactor

a What would happen if, on average, more than one fission neutron per event went on to produce further fission?

Fissionable isotopes

The fuel in a nuclear reactor must contain fissionable isotopes.

- Most reactors at the present time are designed to use 'enriched uranium' as the fuel. This consists mostly of the non-fissionable uranium isotope $^{238}_{92}U$ (U-238) and about 2–3% of the uranium isotope $^{235}_{92}U$ (U-235) which is fissionable. In comparison, natural uranium is more than 99% U-238.
- The U-238 nuclei in a nuclear reactor do not undergo fission but they change into other heavy nuclei, including plutonium-239 (the isotope $^{239}_{94}Pu$). This isotope is fissionable. It can be used in a different type of reactor but not in a uranium reactor.

Inside a nuclear reactor

A nuclear reactor consists of uranium fuel rods spaced evenly in the reactor core. Figure 3 shows a cross-section of a pressurised water reactor (PWR).

- The reactor core contains the fuel rods, control rods and water at high pressure. The fission neutrons are slowed down by collisions with the atoms in the water molecules. This is necessary as fast neutrons do not cause further fission of U-235. We say the water acts as a **moderator** because it slows down the fission neutrons.

- **Control rods** in the core absorb surplus neutrons. This keeps the chain reaction under control. The depth of the rods in the core is adjusted to maintain a steady chain reaction.
- The water acts as a **coolant**. Its molecules gain kinetic energy from the neutrons and the fuel rods. The water is pumped through the core. Then it goes through sealed pipes to and from a heat exchanger outside the core. The water transfers energy for heating to the heat exchanger from the core.
- The reactor core is made of thick steel to withstand the very high temperature and pressure in the core. The core is enclosed by thick concrete walls. These absorb radiation that escapes through the walls of the steel vessel.

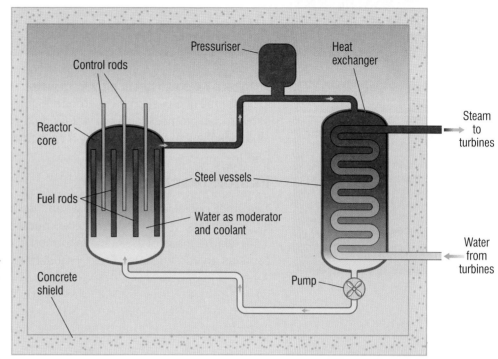

Figure 3 A nuclear reactor

b What would happen if the control rods were removed from the core?

AQA **Examiner's tip**

During nuclear fission a large nucleus breaks up into two smaller nuclei. Make sure you know how to spell 'fission' – with two s's.

Summary questions

1 Copy and complete **a** and **b** using the words below. Each word can be used more than once.

nucleus   uranium-235   uranium-238   plutonium-239

   a Nuclear fission happens when a .... of .... or .... splits.

   b A nucleus of .... in a nuclear reactor changes without fission into a nucleus of ....

2 Put the statements A to D in the list below into the correct sequence to describe a steady chain reaction in a nuclear reactor.

   A a U-235 nucleus splits
   B a neutron hits a U-235 nucleus
   C neutrons are released
   D energy is released

3 Look at the chain reaction shown in Figure 4.

   a i Which of the nuclei A to F have been hit by a neutron?

   ii What has happened to these nuclei?

   Figure 4

   iii Which two of the other nuclei A to F could undergo fission from a fission neutron shown?

   b State one process that could happen to a fission neutron that does not produce further fission.

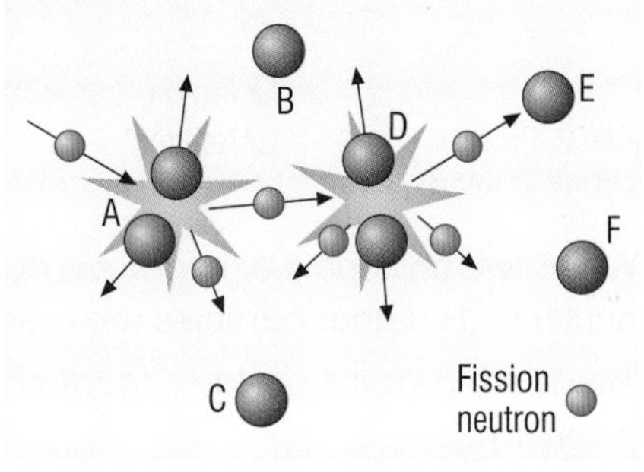

Fission neutron

Key points

- Nuclear fission is the splitting of a nucleus into two approximately equal fragments and the release of two or three neutrons.

- Nuclear fission occurs when a neutron hits a uranium-235 nucleus or a plutonium-239 nucleus and the nucleus splits.

- A chain reaction occurs in a nuclear reactor when each fission event causes further fission events.

- In a nuclear reactor, control rods absorb fission neutrons to ensure that, on average, only one neutron per fission goes on to produce further fission.

P2 7.2

Nuclear fusion

Learning objectives

- What is nuclear fusion?
- How can nuclei be made to fuse together?
- Where does the Sun's energy come from?
- Why is it difficult to make a nuclear fusion reactor?

Imagine if we could get energy from water. Stars release energy as a result of fusing small nuclei such as hydrogen to form larger nuclei. Water contains lots of hydrogen atoms. A glass of water could provide the same amount of energy as a tanker full of petrol. But only if we could make a fusion reactor here on Earth.

Fusion reactions

Two small nuclei release energy when they are fused together to form a single larger nucleus. This process is called **nuclear fusion**. It releases energy only if the relative mass of the nucleus formed is no more than about 55 (about the same as an iron nucleus). Energy must be supplied to create bigger nuclei.

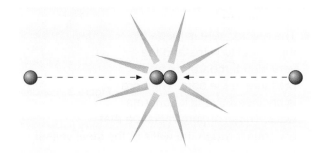

Figure 1 A nuclear fusion reaction

The Sun is about 75 per cent hydrogen and 25 per cent helium. The core is so hot that it consists of a 'plasma' of bare nuclei with no electrons. These nuclei move about and fuse together when they collide. When they fuse, they release energy. Figure 2 shows how protons fuse together to form a $_2^4$He nucleus. Energy is released at each stage.

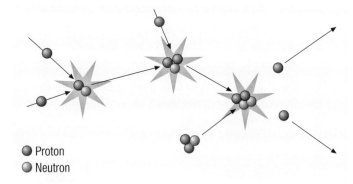

Figure 2 Fusion reactions in the Sun

- Proton
- Neutron

- When two protons (i.e. hydrogen nuclei) fuse, they form a 'heavy hydrogen' nucleus, $_1^2$H. Other particles are created and emitted at the same time.
- Two more protons collide separately with two $_1^2$H nuclei and turn them into heavier nuclei.
- The two heavier nuclei collide to form the helium nucleus $_2^4$He.
- The energy released at each stage is carried away as kinetic energy of the product nucleus and other particles emitted.

a Look at Figure 2 and work out what is formed when a proton collides with a $_1^2$H nucleus.

Fusion reactors

There are enormous technical difficulties with making fusion a useful source of energy. The plasma of light nuclei must be heated to very high temperatures before the nuclei will fuse. This is because two nuclei approaching each other will repel each other due to their positive charges. If the nuclei are moving fast enough, they can overcome the force of repulsion and fuse together.

In a fusion reactor:

● the plasma is heated by passing a very large electric current through it

● the plasma is contained by a magnetic field so it doesn't touch the reactor walls. If it did, it would go cold and fusion would stop.

Scientists have been working on these problems since the 1950s. A successful fusion reactor would release more energy than it uses to heat the plasma. At the present time, scientists working on experimental fusion reactors are able to do this by fusing heavy hydrogen nuclei to form helium nuclei – but only for a few minutes!

b Why is a fusion reactor unlikely to explode?

Figure 3 An experimental fusion reactor

A promising future

Practical fusion reactors could meet all our energy needs.

● The fuel for fusion reactors is readily available as heavy hydrogen and is naturally present in sea water.

● The reaction product, helium, is a non-radioactive inert gas, so is harmless.

● The energy released could be used to generate electricity.

In comparison, fission reactors mostly use uranium, which is only found in certain parts of the world. Also, they produce nuclear waste that has to be stored securely for many years. However, fission reactors have been in operation for over 50 years, unlike fusion reactors, which are still under development.

Summary questions

1 Copy and complete **a** and **b** using the words below:

   large   small   stable

   a When two .... nuclei moving at high speed collide, they form a .... nucleus.

   b Energy is released in nuclear fusion if the product nucleus is not as .... as an iron nucleus.

2 **a** Why does the plasma of light nuclei in a fusion reactor need to be very hot?

   b Why would a fusion reactor that needs more energy than it produces not be much use?

3 **a** How many protons and how many neutrons are present in a $_1^2$H nucleus?

   b Copy and complete the equation below to show the reaction that takes place when two $_1^2$H nuclei fuse together to form a helium nucleus.

   $$_1^2H + _1^2H \rightarrow _?^?He$$

   [H]

Key points

● Nuclear fusion is the process of forcing two nuclei close enough together so they form a single larger nucleus.

● Nuclear fusion can be brought about by making two light nuclei collide at very high speed.

● Energy is released when two light nuclei are fused together. Nuclear fusion in the Sun's core releases energy.

● A fusion reactor needs to be at a very high temperature before nuclear fusion can take place. The nuclei to be fused are difficult to contain

Energy from the nucleus

P2 7.3

Nuclear issues

Learning objectives

- What is radon gas and why is it dangerous?
- How safe are nuclear reactors?
- What happens to nuclear waste?

∞ links

For more information on ionising radiation, look back at P2 6.4 More about alpha, beta and gamma radiation.

??? Did you know ... ?

Nuclear waste

Used fuel rods are very hot and very radioactive.

- After removal from a reactor, they are stored in large tanks of water for up to a year. The water cools the rods down.
- Remote-control machines are then used to open the fuel rods. The unused uranium and plutonium are removed chemically from the used fuel. These are stored in sealed containers so they can be used again.
- The remaining material contains many radioactive isotopes with long half-lives. This radioactive waste must be stored in secure conditions for many years.

Figure 2 Storage of nuclear waste

Radioactivity all around us

When we use a Geiger counter, it clicks even without a radioactive source near it. This is due to background **radiation.** Radioactive substances are found naturally all around us.

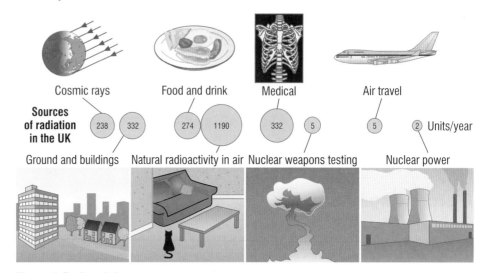

Figure 1 Radioactivity

Figure 1 shows the sources of background radiation. As explained in P2 6.4, the radiation from radioactive substances is hazardous, as it ionises substances it passes through. The numbers in Figure 1 tell you the **radiation dose** or how much radiation on average each person gets in a year from each source.

- Medical sources include X-rays as well as radioactive substances, as X-rays have an ionising effect. People who work in jobs that involve the use of ionising radiation have to wear personal radiation monitors to ensure they are not exposed to too much ionising radiation.
- Background radiation in the air is due mostly to radon gas that seeps through the ground from radioactive substances in rocks deep underground. Radon gas emits alpha particles so it is a health hazard if it is breathed in. It can seep into homes and other buildings in certain locations. In homes and buildings where people are present for long periods, methods need to be taken to reduce exposure to radon gas. For example, pipes under the building can be installed and fitted to a suction pump to draw the gas out of the ground before it seeps into the building.

a What is the biggest source of background radioactivity?
b Which source in the chart contributes least to background radioactivity?

Chernobyl

In 1986, a nuclear reactor in Ukraine exploded. Emergency workers and scientists struggled for days to contain the fire. A cloud of radioactive material from the fire drifted over many parts of Europe, including Britain. More than 100 000 people were evacuated from Chernobyl and the surrounding area. Over 30 people died in the accident. Many more have developed leukaemia or cancer since then. It was and remains (up to now) the world's worst nuclear accident.

Could it happen again?

- Most nuclear reactors are of a different design.
- The Chernobyl accident did not have a high-speed shutdown system like most reactors have.
- The operators at Chernobyl ignored safety instructions.
- There are thousands of nuclear reactors in the world. They have been working safely for many years.

Radioactive risks

The effect on living cells of radiation from radioactive substances depends on:

- the type and the amount of radiation received (the dose)
- whether the source of the radiation is inside or outside the body
- how long the living cells are exposed to the radiation.

Figure 3 Chernobyl

	Alpha radiation	Beta radiation	Gamma radiation
source inside the body	**very dangerous** – affects all the surrounding tissue	**dangerous** – reaches cells throughout the body	
source outside the body	**some danger** – absorbed by skin; damages skin cells		

- The larger the dose of radiation someone gets, the greater the risk of cancer. High doses kill living cells.
- The smaller the dose, the less the risk – but it is never zero. So there is a very low level of risk to each and every one of us because of background radioactivity.

Workers who are at risk from ionising radiations cut down their exposure to the radiation by:

- keeping as far as possible from the source of radiation, using special handling tools with long handles
- spending as little time as possible in 'at-risk' areas
- shielding themselves from the radiation by staying behind thick concrete barriers and/or using thick lead plates.

> **c** Why does radioactive waste need to be stored **i** securely **ii** for many years?
> **d** Why is a source of alpha radiation very dangerous inside the body but not outside it?

Summary questions

1 In some locations, the biggest radiation hazard comes from radon gas which seeps up through the ground and into buildings. The dangers of radon gas can be minimised by building new houses that are slightly raised on brick pillars and modifying existing houses. Radon gas is an α-emitting isotope.
   a Why is radon gas dangerous in a house?
   b Describe one way of making an existing house safe from radon gas.

2 Should the UK government replace our existing nuclear reactors with new reactors, either fission or fusion or both? Answer this question by discussing the benefits and drawbacks of new fission and fusion reactors.

Did you know ... ?

New improved nuclear reactors

Most of the world's nuclear reactors in use now will need to be replaced in the next 20 years. New improved 'third generation' nuclear reactors will replace them. The new types of reactors have:

- a standard design to cut down costs and construction time
- a longer operating life – typically 60 years
- more safety features, such as convection of outside air through cooling panels along the reactor walls
- much less effect on the environment.

Key points

- Radon gas is an α-emitting isotope that seeps into houses in certain areas through the ground.

- There are thousands of fission reactors safely in use in the world. None of them are of the same type as the Chernobyl reactors that exploded.

- Nuclear waste is stored in safe and secure conditions for many years after unused uranium and plutonium (to be used in the future) is removed from it.

P2 7.4

The early universe

Learning objectives

- What is a galaxy?

- What was the universe like in the billions of years before stars and galaxies were formed?

- What is the force responsible for the formation of stars and galaxies?

??? *Did you know …?*

In the Cold War, US satellites detected bursts of gamma radiation from space. At first, the US military thought nuclear weapons were being tested in space by Russia. Then astronomers found the bursts were from violent events long ago in distant galaxies – maybe stars being sucked into black holes!

The Big Bang that created the universe was about 13 thousand million (13 billion) years ago. Space, time and radiation were created in the Big Bang. At first, the universe was a hot glowing ball of radiation and matter. As it expanded, its temperature fell. Now the universe is cold and dark, except for hot spots we call stars.

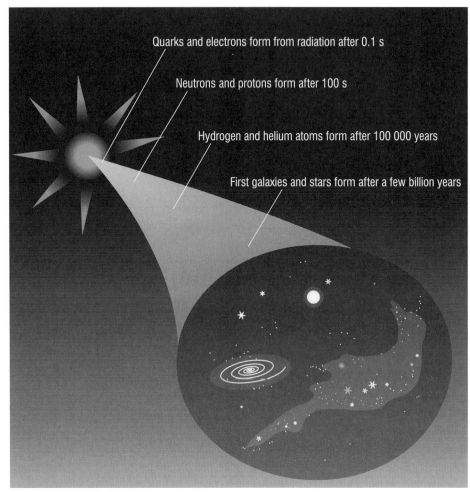

Quarks and electrons form from radiation after 0.1 s

Neutrons and protons form after 100 s

Hydrogen and helium atoms form after 100 000 years

First galaxies and stars form after a few billion years

Figure 1 Timeline for the universe

The stars we see in the night sky are all in the Milky Way galaxy, our home galaxy. The Sun is just one of billions of stars in the Milky Way galaxy. Using powerful telescopes, we can see many more stars in the Milky Way galaxy. We can also see individual stars in other galaxies.

We now know there are billions of galaxies in the universe. There is vast empty space between them. Light from the furthest galaxies that we can see has taken billions of years to reach us.

a Why do powerful telescopes give us a picture of the universe long ago?

Figure 2 Andromeda – the nearest big galaxy to the Milky Way

The Dark Age of the universe

As the universe expanded, it became transparent as radiation passed through the empty space between its atoms. The background microwave radiation that causes the spots on an untuned television was released at this stage. The Dark Age of the universe had begun!

For the next few billion years, the universe was a completely dark, patchy, expanding cloud of hydrogen and helium. Then the stars and galaxies formed and lit up the universe!

b How long, to the nearest billion years, has background microwave radiation been travelling for?

Figure 3 Arno Allan Penzias and Robert Woodrow Wilson standing on the radio antenna that unexpectedly discovered the universe's microwave background radiation

The force of gravity takes over

Uncharged atoms don't repel each other. But they can attract each other. During the Dark Age of the universe, the force of gravitational attraction was at work without any opposition from repulsive forces.

As the universe continued to expand, it became more patchy as the denser parts attracted nearby matter. Gravity pulled more matter into the denser parts and turned them into gigantic clumps.

Eventually, the force of gravity turned the clumps into galaxies and stars. A few billion years after the Big Bang, the Dark Age came to an end, as the stars lit up the universe.

c Why would the force of gravity between two helium nuclei be unable to pull the nuclei together?

Figure 4 The force of gravity takes over

Summary questions

1 Copy and complete **a** to **c** using the words below:

attracted   cooled   expanded   formed

   a As the universe .... , it ....
   b Uncharged atoms .... each other.
   c Galaxies and stars .... from uncharged atoms.

2 **a i** Why can't we take a photo of the Milky Way galaxy from outside?
     ii Why can't we take photos of a distant galaxy at different stages in its formation?
   b i Why do the stars in a galaxy not drift away from each other?
     ii Why are there vast spaces between the galaxies?

3 Put these events in the correct sequence with the earliest event first.
   1 Cosmic background radiation was released.
   2 Hydrogen nuclei were first fused to form helium nuclei.
   3 The Big Bang took place.
   4 Neutrons and protons formed.

Key points

● A galaxy is a collection of billions of stars held together by their own gravity.

● Before galaxies and stars formed, the universe was a dark patchy cloud of hydrogen and helium.

● The force of gravity pulled matter into galaxies and stars.

P2 7.5

The life history of a star

Learning objectives

- What is a protostar?
- What are the stages in the life of a star?
- What will eventually happen to the Sun?
- What is a supernova?

The birth of a star

Stars form out of clouds of dust and gas.

- The particles in the clouds are pulled together by their own gravitational attraction. The clouds merge together. They become more and more concentrated to form a **protostar**, the name for a star to be.
- As a protostar becomes denser, it gets hotter. If it becomes hot enough, the nuclei of hydrogen atoms and other light elements fuse together. Energy is released in this fusion so the core gets hotter and brighter and starts to shine. A star is born!
- Objects may form that are too small to become stars. Such objects may be attracted by a protostar to become **planets**.

a Where does the energy to heat a protostar come from?

Shining stars

Stars like the Sun radiate energy because of hydrogen fusion in the core. They are called **main sequence stars** because this is the main stage in the life of a star. It can maintain its energy output for millions of years until the star runs out of hydrogen nuclei to fuse together.

- Energy released in the core keeps the core hot so the process of fusion continues. Radiation flows out steadily from the core in all directions.
- The star is stable because the forces within it are balanced. The force of gravity that makes a star contract is balanced by the outward force of the radiation from its core. These forces stay in balance until most of the hydrogen nuclei in the core have been fused together.

b Why doesn't the Sun collapse under its own gravity?

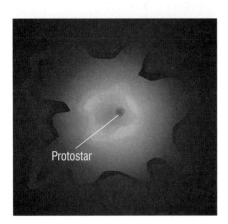

Protostar

Figure 1 Star birth

The end of a star

When a star runs out of hydrogen nuclei to fuse together, it reaches the end of its main sequence stage and it swells out.

Stars about the same size as the Sun (or smaller) swell out, cool down and turn red.

- The star is now a **red giant**. At this stage, helium and other light elements in its core fuse to form heavier elements.
- When there are no more light elements in its core, fusion stops and no more radiation is released. Due to its own gravity, the star collapses in on itself. As it collapses, it heats up and turns from red to yellow to white. It becomes a **white dwarf**. This is a hot, dense white star much smaller in diameter than it was. Stars like the Sun then fade out, go cold and become **black dwarfs**.

Stars much bigger than the Sun end their lives much more dramatically.

- Such a star swells out to become a red **supergiant** which then collapses.
- In the collapse, the matter surrounding the star's core compresses the core more and more. Then the compression suddenly reverses in a cataclysmic explosion known as a **supernova**. Such an event can outshine an entire galaxy for several weeks.

??? Did you know ... ?

- The Sun is about 5000 million years old and will probably continue to shine for another 5000 million years.
- The Sun will turn into a red giant bigger than the orbit of Mercury. By then, the human race will probably have long passed into history. But will intelligent life still exist?

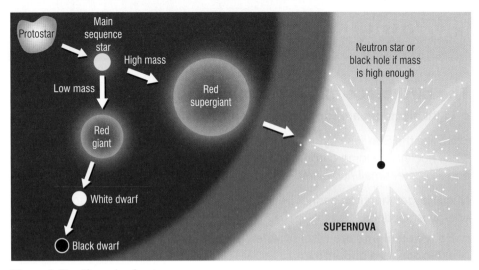

Figure 2 The life cycle of a star

c What force causes a red giant to collapse?

What remains after a supernova occurs?

The explosion compresses the core of the star into a **neutron star**. This is an extremely dense object composed only of neutrons. If the star is massive enough, it becomes a **black hole** instead of a neutron star. The gravitational field of a black hole is so strong that nothing can escape from it. Not even light, or any other form of electromagnetic radiation, can escape.

d What force causes matter to be dragged into a black hole?

Figure 3 M87 is a galaxy that spins so fast at its centre that it is thought to contain a black hole with a billion times more mass than the Sun

Summary questions

1 a The list below shows some of the stages in the life of a star like the Sun. Put the stages in the correct sequence.

  A main sequence
  B protostar
  C red giant
  D white dwarf

b i Which stage in the above list is the Sun at now?

  ii What will happen to the Sun after it has gone through the above stages?

2 a Copy and complete **i** and **ii** using the words below. Each word can be used more than once.

  collapse expand explode

  i The Sun will eventually .... then ....
  ii A red supergiant will .... then ....

b i What is the main condition needed for a supergiant to form a black hole?

  ii Why is it not possible for light to escape from a black hole?

3 a i What force makes a red supergiant collapse?

  ii What force prevents a main sequence star from collapsing?

b Why does a white dwarf eventually become a black dwarf?

Key points

- A protostar is a gas and dust cloud in space that can go on to form a star.

Low mass star:
Protostar → main sequence star → red giant → white dwarf → black dwarf

High mass star:
Protostar → main sequence star → red supergiant → supernova → neutron star → black hole if sufficient mass

- The Sun will eventually become a black dwarf.

- A supernova is the explosion of a supergiant after it collapses.

P2 7.6 How the chemical elements formed

Learning objectives

- What chemical elements are formed inside stars?
- What chemical elements are formed in supernovas?
- Why does the Earth contain heavy elements?

The birthplace of the chemical elements

- **Light elements are formed as a result of fusion in stars.**

Stars like the Sun fuse hydrogen nuclei (i.e. protons) into helium and similar small nuclei, including carbon. When it becomes a red giant, it fuses helium and the other small nuclei into larger nuclei.

Nuclei larger than iron cannot be formed by this process because too much energy is needed.

- **Heavy elements are formed when a massive star collapses then explodes as a supernova.**

The enormous force of the collapse fuses small nuclei into nuclei larger than iron. The explosion scatters the star into space.

The debris from a supernova contains all the known elements from the lightest to the heaviest. Eventually, new stars form as gravity pulls the debris together.

Planets form from debris surrounding a new star. As a result, such planets will be composed of all the known elements too.

a Lead (Pb) is much heavier than iron (Fe). How did the lead we use form?

Did you know ... ?

The Crab Nebula is the remnants of a supernova explosion that was observed in the 11th century. In 1987, a star in the southern hemisphere exploded and became the biggest supernova to be seen for four centuries. Astronomers realised that it was Sandaluk II, a star in the Andromeda galaxy millions of light years from Earth.

If a star near the Sun exploded, the Earth would probably be blasted out of its orbit. We would see the explosion before the shock wave hit us.

Figure 1 The Crab Nebula

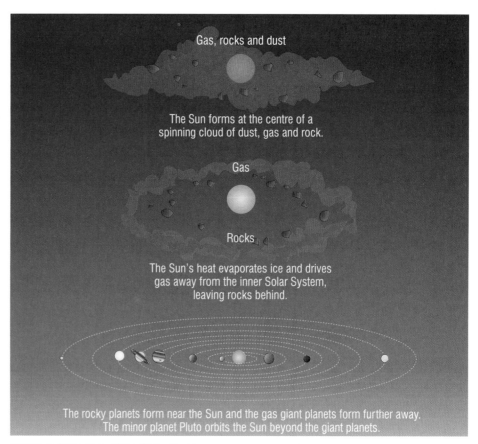

Gas, rocks and dust

The Sun forms at the centre of a spinning cloud of dust, gas and rock.

Gas

Rocks

The Sun's heat evaporates ice and drives gas away from the inner Solar System, leaving rocks behind.

The rocky planets form near the Sun and the gas giant planets form further away. The minor planet Pluto orbits the Sun beyond the giant planets.

Figure 2 Formation of the Solar System

Molecules of carbon-based chemicals are present in space. Life on Earth probably developed from chemicals reacting in lightning storms.

So are we looking for any scientific evidence about life on other planets, either in our own Solar System or around other stars?

- *Space probes sent to Mars* have tested the atmosphere, rocks and soil on Mars looking for microbes or chemicals that might indicate life was once present on Mars. Water is necessary for life. Astronomers now have strong evidence of the presence of 'underground' water breaking through to the surface of Mars.

- *The search for extra-terrestrial intelligence,* known as **SETI**, has gone on for more than 40 years using radio telescopes. Signals from space would indicate the existence of living beings with technologies at least as advanced as our own. No signals have been detected – yet!

Figure 3 The NASA Exploration Rovers looked for signs of life on Mars

Planet Earth

The heaviest known natural element is uranium. It has a half-life of 4500 million years. The presence of uranium in the Earth is evidence that the Solar System must have formed from the remnants of a supernova.

Elements such as plutonium are heavier than uranium. Scientists can make these elements by bombarding heavy elements like uranium with high-speed neutrons. They would have been present in the debris which formed the Solar System. Elements heavier than uranium formed then have long since decayed.

b Plutonium-239 has a half-life of about 24 000 years.
Why is it not found naturally like uranium?

c Why is carbon an important element?

Summary questions

1 Match each statement below with an element in the list.

helium   hydrogen   iron   uranium

a Helium nuclei are formed when nuclei of this element are fused.

b This element is formed in a supernova explosion.

c Stars form nuclei of these two elements (and others not listed) by fusing smaller nuclei.

d The early universe mostly consisted of this element.

2 Copy and complete **a** to **c** using the words below. Each word can be used more than once.

galaxy   planets   stars   supernova

a Fusion inside .... creates light elements. Fusion in a .... creates heavy elements.

b A .... scatters the elements throughout a ....

c .... and planets formed from the debris of a .... contain all the known elements.

3 Uranium-238 is a radioactive isotope found naturally in the Earth. It has a half-life of about 4500 million years. It was formed from lighter elements.

a i What is the name of the physical process in which this isotope is formed?

ii What is the name for the astronomical event in which the above process takes place?

b Why has all the uranium in the Earth not decayed by now?

Key points

- Elements as heavy as iron are formed inside stars as a result of nuclear fusion.

- Elements heavier than iron are formed in supernovas as well as light elements.

- The Sun and the rest of the Solar System were formed from the debris of a supernova.

Summary questions *k*

1 a Copy and complete **i** to **iii** using the words below:

decreases   increases   stays the same

When energy is released at a steady rate in a nuclear reactor,

  i the number of fission events each second in the core ....

  ii the amount of uranium-235 in the core ....

  iii the number of radioactive isotopes in the fuel rods ....

b Explain what would happen in a nuclear reactor if:

  i the coolant fluid leaked out of the core

  ii the control rods were pushed further into the reactor core.

2 a i What do we mean by nuclear fusion?

  ii Why do two nuclei repel each other when they get close?

  iii Why do they need to collide at high speed in order to fuse together?

b Give two reasons why nuclear fusion is difficult to achieve in a reactor.

3 a Copy and complete **i** to **iii** using the words below. Each word can be used more than once.

fission   fusion

  i In a .... reactor, two small nuclei join together and release energy.

  ii In a .... reactor, a large nucleus splits and releases energy.

  iii The fuel in a .... reactor contains uranium-235.

b State two advantages that nuclear fusion reactors would have in comparison with nuclear fission reactors.

4 a i What physical process causes energy to be released in the Sun?

  ii Which element is used in the physical process named in part **i** to release energy in the Sun?

b How will the Sun change in the next stage of its life cycle when it has used up all the element named in part **a ii**?

5 Copy and complete **a** to **d** using the words below. Each word can be used more than once.

galaxy   planet   stars

a A .... isn't big enough to be a star.

b The Sun is inside a ....

c .... became hot after they formed from matter pulled together by the force of gravity.

d The force of gravity keeps .... together inside a ....

6 a What force pulls dust and gas in space?

b Why do large planets like Jupiter not produce their own light?

c What is the name for the type of reaction that releases energy in the core of the Sun?

7 a The stages in the development of the Sun are listed below. Put the stages in the correct sequence.

  A dust and gas

  B present stage

  C protostar

  D red giant

  E white dwarf

b i After the white dwarf stage, what will happen to the Sun?

  ii What will happen to a star that has much more mass than the Sun?

8 a i What is a supernova?

  ii How could we tell the difference between a supernova and a distant star like the Sun at present?

b i What is a black hole?

  ii What would happen to stars and planets near a black hole?

9 a i Which element as well as hydrogen is formed in the early universe?

  ii Which of the two elements is formed from the other one in a star?

b i Which two of the elements listed below is not formed in a star that gives out radiation at a steady rate?

carbon   iron   lead   uranium

  ii How do we know that the Sun formed from the debris of a supernova?

AQA Examination-style questions

1 a Copy and complete the following diagram to show how a chain reaction may occur inside a nuclear fuel rod containing many uranium-235 nuclei. (3)

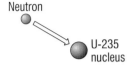

Neutron

U-235 nucleus

b Name the other fissionable substance that is used in some nuclear reactors. (1)

c The passages below reflect some of the conflicting opinions about nuclear power.

> Nuclear power is a low-emission source of energy and is the only readily available, large-scale alternative to fossil fuels for a continuous, reliable supply of electricity. The waste from nuclear power occupies a tiny volume and can be safely returned to the Earth for underground storage.

> A new generation of nuclear power stations will only reduce our emissions by four per cent by 2024: far too little, far too late, to stop global warming. They will create tens of thousands of tonnes of the most hazardous radioactive waste, which remains dangerous for up to a million years.

  i What are the 'emissions' that both sources refer to? (1)

  ii Why can nuclear waste remain dangerous for millions of years? (2)

  iii Give one advantage and one disadvantage of the storage of nuclear waste underground. (2)

  iv Explain why it would not be possible to replace fossil fuels with wind power alone. (1)

d For over 50 years scientists have been experimenting with fusion reactors with the aim of eventually generating electricity. The latest research project, called ITER, is scheduled to start operating in France in 2018 and is a collaboration between many countries.

  i State two of the potential benefits of fusion power. (2)

  ii Why are some people opposed to the research into fusion power? (2)

2 a Copy and complete the following sentences using the list of words and phrases below. Each one can be used once, more than once or not at all.

  split   fusion   join   a larger one   fission two smaller nuclei

  The Sun's energy is produced by nuclear .... This is where atomic nuclei .... to form .... (3)

b Which element was the first to form in the universe? (1)

c The red super giant star Betelgeuse is likely to explode as a supernova and then form a neutron star. The red supergiant VV Cephei is likely to explode as a supernova and become a black hole. What causes the fate of these two stars to be different? (2)

d Which type of star produces all the elements up to iron? (1)

e The diagram shows the forces acting within a star. The grey arrows show the outward force created by radiation. Star A is stable but in star B the outward force has become less.

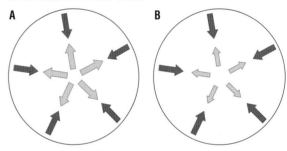

  i What type of force is counteracting the outward force from radiation? (1)

  ii What is about to happen to star B? (1)

  iii Suggest why the force from radiation may suddenly decrease. (2)

3 *In this question you will be assessed on using good English, organising information clearly and using specialist terms where appropriate.*

Explain how the solar system formed and why there were elements heavier than iron present when it formed. (6)

1 A toy cannon uses a spring to fire a metal ball bearing.

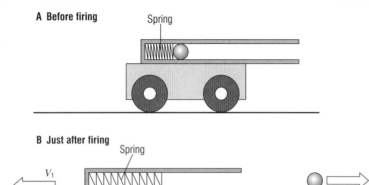

A Before firing   Spring

B Just after firing   Spring

v_1

a Calculate the deceleration of the cannon after it is fired and recoils to the left. The initial velocity of the cannon was −0.3 m/s, then it slows down and stops in 0.6 seconds. (2)

To find out how fast the ball bearing travels when it is fired, the student measures the recoil velocity (v_1) of the cannon using a light gate.

b What is meant by the conservation of momentum? (2)

c Calculate the velocity of the ball bearing if v_1 is −0.3 m/s.

Mass of cannon = 0.15 kg

Mass of ball bearing = 0.0045 kg

Write down the equation you use. Show clearly how you work out the answer and give the unit. **[H]** (3)

d Calculate the kinetic energy of the cannon just after it is fired. (2)

e i Calculate the spring constant if the force required to compress the spring a distance of 2 cm was 23 N. (3)

ii Describe the energy transfers that take place between diagram **A** and diagram **B**. **[H]** (2)

2

12 V

S   18 Ω

18 Ω   **L2**

A   **L1**   **B**   18 Ω **C**

L3

a Explain why the resistance between B and C is less than the resistance between A and B when switch S is closed. (2)

b The potential difference between A and B is 8 V when switch S is closed. What is the potential difference between B and C? (1)

c i Calculate the current through bulb L1. (2)

ii Calculate the current through bulb L3. (1)

d Switch S is opened.

i Explain what effect this will have on the brightness of bulb L1. (3)

ii Calculate the resistance between A and C. (1)

iii Show that the current through L1 is now 0.33 A. (2)

iv Calculate the total power delivered to both bulbs. (2)

e With the switch open the battery will deliver 500 C of charge before the bulbs start to dim. How long can the circuit be left on before this happens? (2)

AQA Examiner's tip

Both acceleration and deceleration are calculated using the same equation. The object is decelerating if the equation gives a negative value for the acceleration.

Learn definitions and laws like the one for the law of conservation of momentum.

AQA Examiner's tip

Good knowledge of the circuit rules is essential to answer this question.

When you are calculating the current through a component, make sure you are using the potential difference across that component only.

3 Plutonium-239 has a half-life of 24 200 years and decays into uranium-235 with a half-life of 703 million years. These substances are both *fissionable*.

a i Explain what is meant by *fissionable*. (2)

ii What is meant by 'a half-life of 24 200 years'? (2)

iii A sample of plutonium-239 of mass 0.8 kg is being stored. How many years will pass before the sample contains 0.7 kg of uranium-235? Show clearly how you work out your answer. (3)

iv If the sample were kept at a higher temperature and pressure, what effect would this have on your answer to part **a iii**? (1)

b Explain how a small amount of uranium-235 is found in the Earth's crust in rocks such as granite, when hardly any plutonium is found occurring naturally and nearly all of it is formed in nuclear reactors. (3)

c Name one other natural source of background radiation that we are constantly exposed to, apart from rocks. (1)

d Plutonium (Pu) has 94 protons. Copy and complete the following decay equation to show how it decays into uranium-235. **[H]** (6)

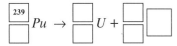

e List the stages below in the correct order to describe the life cycle of a star that is about the same size as the Sun. One of the stages is not part of the life cycle of this type of star. (5)

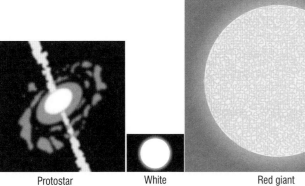

Protostar   White dwarf   Red giant

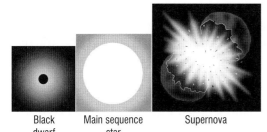

Black dwarf   Main sequence star   Supernova

4 *In this question you will be assessed on using good English, organising information clearly and using specialist terms where appropriate.*

In 1911 Ernest Rutherford published a scientific paper in which he suggested the existence of a very small region at the centre of every atom where most of the charge and mass is concentrated. Rutherford was interpreting the results of an experiment carried out by his research workers Geiger and Marsden in 1909.

Outline the main results of this experiment and explain why these results led Rutherford to suggest the existence of the atomic nucleus. (6)

H1 How science works for us

Learning objectives

- What are 'continuous' and 'categoric variables'?

- What is meant by 'repeatable evidence', 'reproducible evidence' and 'valid evidence'?

- What is the link between the independent and dependent variable?

- What is a 'hypothesis' and a 'prediction'?

- How do we reduce risks in hazardous situations?

Science works for us all day, every day. Working as a scientist you will have knowledge of the world around you and particularly about the subject you are working with. You will observe the world around you. An enquiring mind will then lead you to start asking questions about what you have observed.

Science usually moves forward by slow steady steps. Each small step is important in its own way. It builds on the body of knowledge that we already have.

Thinking scientifically

Deciding on what to measure

Variables can be one of two different types:

- A **categoric variable** is one that is best described by a label (usually a word). The colour of eyes is a categoric variable, e.g. blue or brown eyes.

- A **continuous variable** is one that we measure, so its value could be any number. Temperature (as measured by a thermometer or temperature sensor) is a continuous variable, e.g. 37.6°C, 45.2°C. Continuous variables can have values (called a quantity) that can be given by any measurements made (e.g. light intensity, flow rate etc.).

When designing your investigation you should always try to measure continuous data whenever you can. If this is not always possible, you should then try to use ordered data. If there is no other way to measure your variable then you have to use a label (categoric variable).

Making your investigation repeatable, reproducible and valid

When you are designing an investigation you must make sure that others can repeat any results you get – this makes it **reproducible**. You should also plan to make each result **repeatable**. You can do this by getting consistent sets of repeat measurements.

You must also make sure you are measuring the actual thing you want to measure. If you don't, your data can't be used to answer your original question. This seems very obvious but it is not always quite so easy. You need to make sure that you have controlled as many other variables as you can, so that no-one can say that your investigation is not **valid**.

How might an independent variable be linked to a dependent variable?

The **independent variable** is the one you choose to vary in your investigation.

The **dependent variable** is used to judge the effect of varying the independent variable.

These variables may be linked together. If there is a pattern to be seen (for example as one thing gets bigger the other also gets bigger), it may be that:

- changing one has caused the other to change
- the two are related, but one is not necessarily the cause of the other.

Starting an investigation

Observation

As scientists we use observations to ask questions. We can only ask useful questions if we know something about the observed event. We will not have all of the answers, but we know enough to start asking the correct questions.

When you are designing an investigation you have to observe carefully which variables are likely to have an effect.

What is a hypothesis?

A **hypothesis** is an idea based on observation that has some really good science to try to explain it.

You will need to make your own hypothesis for your controlled assessment. When making hypotheses you can be very imaginative with your ideas. However, you should have some scientific reasoning behind those ideas so that they are not totally bizarre.

Remember, your explanation might not be correct, but you think it is. The only way you can check out your hypothesis is to make it into a prediction and then test it by carrying out an investigation.

observation + knowledge ⟶ hypothesis ⟶ prediction ⟶ investigation

Starting to design an investigation

An investigation starts with a prediction. You, as the scientist, predict that there is a relationship between two variables.

You should think about a preliminary investigation to find the most suitable range and interval for the independent variable.

Making your investigation safe

Remember that when you design your investigation, you must:
- look for any potential hazards
- decide how you will reduce any risk.

You will need to write these down in your plan.

In Section 1 of the ISA you will be asked to:
- write down your plan
- make a risk assessment
- make a prediction
- draw a blank table ready for the results.

AQA *Examiner's tip*

Observations, backed up by really creative thinking and good scientific knowledge can lead into a hypothesis.

Key points

- Continuous data can give you more information than other types of data.
- You must design investigations that produce repeatable, reproducible and valid results if you are to be believed.
- Be aware that just because two variables are related, does not mean that there is a causal link.
- Hypotheses can lead to predictions and investigations.
- You must make a risk assessment, make a prediction and write a plan in your ISA.

H2

The investigation

Learning objectives

- What is a 'fair test'?
- How is a survey set up?
- What is a 'control' group?
- How are the variables, range and intervals decided on?
- How do we ensure accuracy and precision?
- What causes error and anomalies?

Fair testing

A **fair test** is one in which only the independent variable affects the dependent variable. All other variables are controlled.

This is easy to set up in the laboratory, but almost impossible in fieldwork. Plants and animals do not live in environments that are simple and easy to control. They live complex lives with variables changing constantly.

So how can we set up the fieldwork investigations? The best you can do is to make sure that all of the many variables change in much the same way, except for the one you are investigating. Then at least the plants get the same weather, even if it is constantly changing.

If you are investigating two variables in a large population then you will need to do a survey. Again, it is impossible to control all of the variables. Imagine you were investigating the effect of diet on diabetes. You would have to choose people of the same age and same family history to test. The larger the sample size you test, the more valid your results will be.

Control groups are used in investigations to try to make sure that you are measuring the variable that you intend to measure. When investigating the effects of a new drug, the control group will be given a placebo. The control group think they are taking a drug but the placebo does not contain the drug. This way you can control the variable of 'thinking that the drug is working' and separate out the effect of the actual drug.

Designing an investigation

Accuracy

Your investigation must provide accurate data. Accurate data is essential if your results are going to have any meaning.

How do you know if you have accurate data?

It is very difficult to be certain. Accurate results are very close to the **true** value. It is not always possible to know what that true value is.

- Sometimes you can calculate a theoretical value and check it against the experimental evidence. Close agreement between these two values could indicate accurate data.
- You can draw a graph of your results and see how close each result is to the line of best fit.
- Try repeating your measurements with a different instrument and see if you get the same readings.

How do you get accurate data?

- Using instruments that measure accurately will help.
- The more carefully you use the measuring instruments, the more **accuracy** you will get.

Precision

Your investigation must provide data with sufficient precision. If it doesn't then you will not be able to make a valid conclusion.

How do you get precise and repeatable data?

- You have to repeat your tests as often as necessary to improve repeatability.
- You have to repeat your tests in exactly the same way each time.
- Use measuring instruments that have the appropriate scale divisions needed for a particular investigation. Smaller scale divisions have better resolution.

Making measurements

Using instruments

You cannot expect perfect results. When you choose an instrument you need to know that it will give you the accuracy that you want, i.e. it will give you a true reading.

When you choose an instrument you need to decide how precise you need to be. Some instruments have smaller scale divisions than others. Instruments that measure the same thing can have different sensitivities. The **resolution** of an instrument refers to the smallest change in a value that can be detected. Choosing the wrong scale can cause you to miss important data or make silly conclusions.

You also need to be able to use an instrument properly.

Errors

Even when an instrument is used correctly, the results can still show differences. Results may differ because of a **random error**. This is most likely to be due to a poor measurement being made. It could be due to not carrying out the method consistently.

The error may be a **systematic error**. This means that the method was carried out consistently but an error was being repeated.

Anomalies

Anomalies are results that are clearly out of line. They are not those that are due to the natural variation that you get from any measurement. These should be looked at carefully. There might be a very interesting reason why they are so different. If they are simply due to a random error then they should be ignored.

If anomalies can be identified while you are doing an investigation, then it is best to repeat that part of the investigation. If you find anomalies after you have finished collecting the data for an investigation, then they must be discarded.

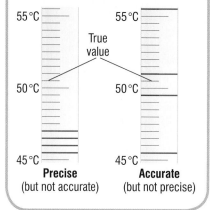

??? Did you know … ?

Imagine measuring the temperature after a set time when a fuel is used to heat a fixed volume of water. Two students repeated this experiment, four times each. Their results are marked on the thermometer scales below:

- A precise set of results is grouped closely together.
- An accurate set of results will have a mean (average) close to the true value.

Precise (but not accurate)   **Accurate** (but not precise)

Key points

- Care must be taken to ensure fair testing.
- You can use a trial run to make sure that you choose the best values for your variables.
- Careful use of the correct equipment can improve accuracy.
- If you repeat your results carefully you can improve precision.
- Results will nearly always vary. Better instruments give more accurate results.
- Resolution in an instrument is the smallest change that it can detect.
- Human error can produce random and systematic errors.
- We must examine anomalies.

H3

Using data

Learning objectives

- What is meant by the 'range' and the 'mean' of a set of data?

- How should data be displayed?

- Which charts and graphs are best to identify patterns in data?

- How are relationships within data identified?

- How do scientists draw valid conclusions from relationships?

- How do I evaluate the reproducibility of an investigation?

Presenting data

Tables

Tables are really good for getting your results down quickly and clearly. You should design your table before you start your investigation.

The range of the data

Pick out the maximum and the minimum values and you have the range. You should always quote these two numbers when asked for a range. For example, the range is between … (the lowest value) and … (the highest value) and don't forget to include the units!

The mean of the data

Add up all of the measurements and divide by how many there are.

Bar charts

If you have a categoric independent variable and a continuous dependent variable then you should use a bar chart.

Line graphs

If you have a continuous independent and a continuous dependent variable then use a line graph.

Scatter grams

These are used in much the same way as a line graph, but you might not expect to be able to draw such a clear line of best fit. For example, if you want to see if lung capacity is related to how long people can hold their breath, you might draw a scatter gram of your results.

Using data to draw conclusions

Identifying patterns and relationships

Now you have a bar chart or a graph of your results you can begin looking for patterns in your results. You must have an open mind at this point.

Firstly, there could still be some anomalous results. You might not have picked these out earlier. How do you spot an anomaly? It must be a significant distance away from the pattern, not just within normal variation.

A line of best fit will help to identify any anomalies at this stage. Ask yourself – do the anomalies represent something important or were they just a mistake?

Secondly, remember a line of best fit can be a straight line or it can be a curve – you have to decide from your results.

The line of best fit will also lead you into thinking what the relationship is between your two variables. You need to consider whether your graph shows a linear relationship. This simply means can you be confident about drawing a straight line of best fit on your graph? If the answer is yes, then is this line positive or negative?

A directly proportional relationship is shown by a positive straight line that goes through the origin (0, 0).

Your results might also show a curved line of best fit. These can be predictable, complex or very complex!

Drawing conclusions

Your graphs are designed to show the relationship between your two chosen variables. You need to consider what that relationship means for your conclusion. You must also take into account the repeatability and the validity of the data you are considering.

You will continue to have an open mind about your conclusion.

You will have made a prediction. This could be supported by your results, it might not be supported, or it could be partly supported. It might suggest some other hypothesis to you.

You must be willing to think carefully about your results. Remember it is quite rare for a set of results to completely support a prediction and be completely repeatable.

Look for possible links between variables. It may be that:

- Changing one has caused the other to change.
- The two are related, but one is not necessarily the cause of the other.

You must decide which is the most likely. Remember a positive relationship does not always mean a causal link between the two variables.

Your conclusion must go no further than the evidence that you have. Any patterns you spot are only strictly valid in the range of values you tested. Further tests are needed to check whether the pattern continues beyond this range.

The purpose of the prediction was to test a hypothesis. The hypothesis can:

- be supported,
- be refuted, or
- lead to another hypothesis.

You have to decide which it is on the evidence available.

Evaluation

If you are still uncertain about a conclusion, it might be down to the repeatability and the validity of the results. You could check these by:

- looking for other similar work on the Internet or from others in your class,
- getting somebody else to redo your investigation,
- trying an alternative method to see if you get the same results.

AQA Examiner's tip

Poor science can often happen if a wrong decision is made here. Newspapers have said that living near electricity sub-stations can cause cancer. All that scientists would say is that there is possibly an association. Getting the correct conclusion is very important.

Key points

- The range states the maximum and the minimum value.
- The mean is the sum of the values divided by how many values there are.
- Tables are best used during an investigation to record results.
- Bar charts are used when you have a categoric independent variable and a continuous dependent variable.
- Line graphs are used to display data that are continuous.
- Drawing lines of best fit help us to study the relationship between variables. The possible relationships are linear, positive and negative; directly proportional; predictable and complex curves.
- Conclusions must go no further than the data available.
- The repeatability, reproducibility and validity of data can be checked by looking at other similar work done by others, perhaps on the internet. It can also be checked by using a different method or by others checking your method.

H4 Scientific evidence and society

Learning objectives

- Is science always presented in a way that takes into account the repeatability, reproducibility and the validity of the evidence?

- What is 'bias'?

- Why is it important to think about who is providing scientific evidence?

- What are the limitations of science?

??? Did you know ... ?

A scientist who rejected the idea of a causal link between smoking and lung cancer was later found to be being paid by a tobacco company.

AQA Examiner's tip

If you are asked about bias in scientific evidence, there are two types:

- The measuring instruments may have introduced a bias because they were not calibrated correctly.

- The scientists themselves may have a biased opinion (e.g. if they are paid by a company to promote their product).

Scientific evidence and society

Now you have reached a conclusion about a piece of scientific research, what comes next? If it is pure research then your fellow scientists will want to look at it very carefully. If it affects the lives of ordinary people then society will also want to examine it closely.

You can help your cause by giving a balanced account of what you have found out. It is much the same as any argument you might have. If you make ridiculous claims then nobody will believe anything you have to say.

Figure 1 Some scientists are paid by companies to do research

Figure 2 Be careful in reaching judgements, think about who is presenting the scientific evidence

Be open and honest. If you only tell part of the story then someone will want to know why! Equally, if somebody is only telling you part of the truth you cannot be confident with anything they say.

You must be on the lookout for people who might be biased when representing scientific evidence. Some scientists are paid by companies to do research. When you are told that a certain product is harmless, check out who is telling you this.

We also have to be very careful in reaching judgements according to who is presenting scientific evidence to us. An example could be when the evidence comes with some political significance. If the evidence might provoke public or political problems then it might be played down. Equally others might want to exaggerate the findings. They might make more of the results than the evidence suggests.

The status of the experimenter may place more, or less, weight on evidence.

The limitations of science

Science can help us in many ways but it cannot supply all the answers. We are still finding out about things and developing our scientific knowledge. For example, the Hubble telescope has helped us to revise our ideas about the beginnings of the universe.

Figure 3 The Hubble space telescope can look deep into space and tell us things about the Universe's beginning from the formations of early galaxies

There are some questions that we cannot answer, maybe because we do not have enough reproducible, repeatable and valid evidence. For example, research into the causes of cancer still needs much work to be done to provide data.

There are some questions that science cannot answer at all. These tend to be questions where beliefs, opinions and ethics are important. For example, science can suggest what the universe was like when it was first formed, but cannot answer the question of why it was formed.

Key points

- Scientific evidence must be presented in a balanced way that points out clearly how repeatable, reproducible and valid the evidence is.

- The evidence must not contain any bias from the experimenter.

- The evidence must be checked to appreciate if there has been any political influence.

- The status of the experimenter can influence the weight placed on the evidence.

- Scientific knowledge can be used to develop technologies.

- People can exploit scientific and technological developments to suit their own purposes.

- The uses of science and technology can raise ethical, social, economic and environmental issues.

- These issues are decided upon by individuals and by society.

- There are many questions left for science to answer.

- Science cannot answer questions that start with 'Should we...?'

Glossary

A

Acceleration Change of velocity per second (in metres per second per second, m/s^2).

Accuracy This tells us how near the true value a measurement is.

Acid A sour substance which can attack metal, clothing or skin. The chemical opposite of an alkali. When dissolved in water, its solution has a pH number less than 7. Acids are proton (H^+ ion) donors.

Activation energy The minimum energy needed to start off a reaction.

Active site The site on an enzyme where the reactants bind.

Activity Number of atoms of a radioactive substance that decay each second.

Aerobic respiration Breaking down food using oxygen to release energy for the cells.

Algal cells The cells of algae, single-celled or simple multicellular organisms, which can photosynthesise but are not plants.

Alkali Its solution has a pH number more than 7.

Allele A version of a particular gene.

Alpha radiation Alpha particles, each composed of two protons and two neutrons, emitted by unstable nuclei.

Alternating current Electric current in a circuit that repeatedly reverses its direction.

Amino acid The building block of protein.

Amylase The enzyme made in the salivary glands and the pancreas which speeds up the breakdown of starch into simple sugars.

Anaerobic respiration Breaking down food without oxygen to release energy for the cells.

Anhydrous Describes a substance that does not contain water.

Anomaly Result that does not match the pattern seen in the other data collected or is well outside the range of other repeat readings. It should be retested and if necessary discarded.

Aqueous solution The mixture made by adding a soluble substance to water.

Asexual budding A form of asexual reproduction where a complete new individual forms as a bud on the parent organism e.g. yeast, hydra.

Atomic number The number of protons (which equals the number of electrons) in an atom. It is sometimes called the proton number.

B

Bacterial colony A population of billions of bacteria grown in culture.

Base The oxide, hydroxide or carbonate of a metal that will react with an acid, forming a salt as one of the products. (If a base dissolves in water it is called an alkali). Bases are proton (H^+ ion) acceptors.

Beta radiation Beta particles which are high-energy electrons created in and emitted from unstable nuclei.

Bile Yellow-green liquid made in the liver and stored in the gall bladder. It is released into the small intestine and emulsifies fats.

Biological detergent Washing detergent that contains enzymes.

Black dwarf A star that has faded out and gone cold.

Black hole An object in space that has so much mass that nothing, not even light, can escape from its gravitational field.

Braking distance The distance travelled by a vehicle during the time its brakes act.

Brine A solution of sodium chloride in water.

C

Cable Two or three insulated wires surrounded by an outer layer of rubber or flexible plastic.

Carbohydrase Enzyme which speeds up the breakdown of carbohydrates.

Carrier Individual who is heterozygous for a faulty allele that causes a genetic disease in the homozygous form.

Catalyst A substance which speeds up a chemical reaction. At the end of the reaction the catalyst remains chemically unchanged.

Cell membrane The membrane around the contents of a cell which controls what moves in and out of the cell.

Cellulose A big carbohydrate molecule which makes up plant and algal cell walls.

Cell wall A rigid structure which surrounds the cells of living organisms apart from animals.

Chain reaction Reactions in which one reaction causes further reactions, which in turn cause further reactions, etc. A nuclear chain reaction occurs when fission neutrons cause further fission, so more fission neutrons are released. These go on to produce further fission.

Charging by friction The process of charging certain insulating materials by rubbing with a dry cloth, causing electrons to transfer between the material and the cloth.

Chlorophyll The green pigment contained in the chloroplasts.

Chloroplast The organelle in which photosynthesis takes place.

Chromatography The process whereby small amounts of dissolved substances are separated by running a solvent along a material such as absorbent paper.

Circuit breaker An electromagnetic switch that opens and cuts the current off if too much current passes through it.

Collision theory An explanation of chemical reactions in terms of reacting particles colliding with sufficient energy for a reaction to take place.

Compound A substance made when two or more elements are chemically bonded together. For example, water (H_2O) is a compound made from hydrogen and oxygen.

Concentration gradient The gradient between an area where a substance is at a high concentration and an area where it is at a low concentration.

Conservation of momentum In a closed system, the total momentum before an event is equal to the total momentum after the event. Momentum is conserved in any collision or explosion provided no external forces act on the objects that collide or explode.

Control rod Metal rod (made of boron or cadmium) used to absorb excess fission neutrons in a nuclear reactor so that only one fission neutron per fission on average goes on to produce further fission.

Coolant Fluid in a sealed circuit pumped through the core of a nuclear reactor to remove energy to a heat exchanger.

Covalent bonding The attraction between two atoms that share one or more pairs of electrons.

Cystic fibrosis A genetic disease that affects the lungs, digestive and reproductive systems. It is inherited through a recessive allele.

Cytoplasm The water-based gel in which the organelles of all living cells are suspended.

D

Deceleration Change of velocity per second when an object slows down.

Delocalised electron Bonding electron that is no longer associated with any one particular atom.

Denatured Change the shape of an enzyme so that it can no longer speed up a reaction.

Differentiated Specialised for a particular function.

Diffusion The net movement of particles of a gas or a solute from an area of high concentration to an area of low concentration (along a concentration gradient).

Digested Broken down into small molecules by the digestive enzymes.

Digestive juices The mixture of enzymes and other chemicals produced by the digestive system.

Digestive system The organ system running from the mouth to the anus where food is digested.

Direct current Electric current in a circuit that is in one direction only.

Directly proportional A graph will show this if the line of best fit is a straight line through the origin.

DNA fingerprint Pattern produced by analysing the DNA which can be used to identify an individual.

Dominant The characteristic that will show up in the offspring even if only one of the alleles is inherited.

Dot and cross diagram A drawing to show the arrangement of the outer shell electrons only of the atoms or ions in a substance.

Drag force A force opposing the motion of an object due to fluid (e.g. air) flowing past the object as it moves.

E

Earthed Connected to the ground by means of a conducting lead or wire.

Elastic A material is elastic if it is able to regain its shape after it has been squashed or stretched.

Elastic potential energy Energy stored in an elastic object when work is done to change its shape.

Electric current Flow of electric charge. The size of an electric current (in amperes, A) is the rate of flow of charge.

Electrolysis The breakdown of a substance containing ions by electricity.

Electrolyte A liquid, containing free-moving ions, that is broken down by electricity in the process of electrolysis.

Electron A tiny particle with a negative charge. Electrons orbit the nucleus in atoms or ions.

Electronic structure A set of numbers to show the arrangement of electrons in their shells (or energy levels) e.g. the electronic structure of a potassium atom is 2, 8, 8, 1.

Electron microscope An instrument used to magnify specimens using a beam of electrons.

Electroplating The process of depositing a thin layer of metal on an object during electrolysis.

Element A substance made up of only one type of atom. An element cannot be broken down chemically into any simpler substance.

Empirical formula The simplest ratio of elements in a compound.

Emulsifies Breaks down into tiny droplets which will form an emulsion.

Endemic When a species evolves in isolation and is found in only one place in the world; it is said to be endemic (particular) to that area.

Endothermic A reaction that *takes in* energy from the surroundings.

Environmental isolation This is when the climate changes in one area where an organism lives but not in others.

Enzyme A protein molecule that acts as biological catalyst.

Epidermal tissue The tissue of the epidermis – the outer layer of an organism.

Epithelial tissue Tissue made up of relatively unspecialised cells which line the tubes and organs of the body.

Error – systematic Cause readings to be spread about some value other than the true value, due to results differing from the true value by a consistent amount each time a measurement is made. Sources of systematic error can include the environment, methods of observation or instruments used. Systematic errors cannot be dealt with by simple repeats. If a systematic error is suspected, the data collection should be repeated using a different technique or a different set of equipment, and the results compared.

Ethanol Chemical found in alcoholic drinks and biofuels such as gasohol, its chemical formula: C_2H_5OH

Exothermic A reaction that *gives out* energy to the surroundings.

Extinction Extinction is the permanent loss of all the members of a species.

F

Fair test A fair test is one in which only the independent variable has been allowed to affect the dependent variable.

Fatty acid Building block of lipids.

Fermentation The reaction in which the enzymes in yeast turn glucose into ethanol and carbon dioxide.

Force A force can change the motion of an object (in newtons, N).

Frequency (of an alternating current) The number of complete cycles an alternating current passes through each second. The unit of frequency is the hertz (Hz).

Fructose syrup A sugar syrup.

Fullerene Form of the element carbon that can form a large cage-like structure, based on hexagonal rings of carbon atoms.

Fuse A fuse contains a thin wire that melts and cuts the current off if too much current passes through it.

G

Gamma radiation Electromagnetic radiation emitted from unstable nuclei in radioactive substances.

Gas chromatography The process of separating the components in a mixture by passing the vapours through a column and detecting them as they leave the column at different times.

Genetic disorder Disease which is inherited.

Genetic material The DNA which carries the instructions for making a new cell or a new individual.

Geographical isolation This is when two populations become physically isolated by a geographical feature.

Giant covalent structure A huge 3-D network of covalently bonded atoms (e.g. the giant lattice of carbon atoms in diamond or graphite).

Giant lattice A huge 3-D network of atoms or ions (e.g. the giant ionic lattice in sodium chloride).

Giant structure See giant lattice.

Glandular tissue The tissue which makes up the glands and secretes chemicals, e.g. enzymes, hormones.

Glucose A simple sugar.

Glycerol Building block of lipids.

Glycogen Carbohydrate store in animals, including the muscles, liver and brain of the human body.

Gradient (of a straight line graph) Change of the quantity plotted on the y-axis divided by the change of the quantity plotted on the x-axis.

Gravitational field strength, g The force of gravity on an object of mass 1 kg (in newtons per kilogram, N/kg).

Gravitational potential energy Energy of an object due to its position in a gravitational field. Near the Earth's surface, change of GPE (in joules, J) = weight (in newtons, N) × vertical distance moved (in metres, m).

H

Half equation An equation that describes reduction (gain of electrons) or oxidation (loss of electrons), such as the reactions that take place at the electrodes during electrolysis. For example: $Na^+ + e^- \rightarrow Na$.

Half-life (of a radioactive isotope) Average time taken for the number of nuclei of the isotope (or mass of the isotope) in a sample to halve.

High mass star A star that has a much greater mass than the Sun.

Hooke's law The extension of a spring is directly proportional to the force applied, provided its limit of proportionality is not exceeded.

Hydrated Describes a substance that contains water in its crystals, e.g. hydrated copper sulfate.

Hydroponics Growing plants in water enriched by mineral ions rather than soil.

Hypothesis A proposal intended to explain certain facts or observations.

I

Inert Unreactive.

Insoluble molecules Molecules which will not dissolve in a particular solvent such as water.

Intermolecular force The attraction between the individual molecules in a covalently bonded substance.

Ion A charged particle produced by the loss or gain of electrons.

Ionic bonding The electrostatic force of attraction between positively and negatively charged ions.

Ionisation Any process in which atoms become charged.

Isomerase An enzyme which converts one form of a molecule into another.

Isotope Atom that has the same number of protons but different number of neutrons, i.e. it has the same atomic number but different mass number.

K

Kidney tubule The structure in the kidney where substances are reabsorbed back into the blood.

Kinetic energy Energy of a moving object due to its motion; kinetic energy (in joules, J) = mass (in kilograms, kg) x (speed)^2 (in m^2/s^2).

L

Lactic acid One product of anaerobic respiration. It builds up in muscles with exercise. Important in yoghurt and cheese making processes.

Light energy Energy in the form of light.

Light microscope An instrument used to magnify specimens using lenses and light.

Limiting factor Factor which limits the rate of a reaction, e.g. temperature, pH, light levels (photosynthesis).

Limit of proportionality The limit for Hooke's law applied to the extension of a stretched spring.

Lipase Enzyme which breaks down fats and oils into fatty acids and glycerol.

Lipid Oil or fat.

Live wire The wire of a mains circuit that has a potential that alternates from positive to negative and back each cycle.

Low mass star A star that has a much smaller mass than the Sun.

M

Macromolecule Giant covalent structure.

Main sequence star The main stage is the life of a star during which it radiates energy because of fusion of hydrogen nuclei in its core.

Mass The quantity of matter in an object; a measure of the difficulty of changing the motion of an object (in kilograms, kg).

Mass number The number of protons plus neutrons in the nucleus of an atom.

Mass spectrometer A machine that can be used to analyse small amounts of a substance to identify it and to find its relative molecular mass.

Mean The arithmetical average of a series of numbers.

Median The middle value in a list of data.

Meiosis The two-stage process of cell division which reduces the chromosome number of the daughter cells. It is involved in making the gametes for sexual reproduction.

Mesophyll tissue The tissue in a green plant where photosynthesis takes place.

Mineral ion Chemical needed in small amounts as part of a balanced diet to keep the body healthy.

Mitochondria The site of aerobic cellular respiration in a cell.

Mitosis Asexual cell division where two identical cells are formed.

Mode The number which occurs most often in a set of data.

Moderator A solid or liquid used in a nuclear reactor to slow fission neutrons down so they can cause further fission.

Mole The amount of substance in the relative atomic or formula mass of a substance in grams.

Molecular formula The chemical formula that shows the actual numbers of atoms in a particular molecule (e.g. C_2H_4).

Molecular ion peak The peak on the mass spectrum of a substance which tells us the relative molecular mass of the substance. The peak is produced by the heaviest positive ion shown on the mass spectrum.

Momentum This equals mass (in kg) × velocity (in m/s). The unit of momentum is the kilogram metre per second (kg m/s).

Multicellular organism An organism which is made up of many different cells which work together. Some of the cells are specialised for different functions in the organism.

Muscular tissue The tissue which makes up the muscles. It can contract and relax.

N

Nanoscience The study of very tiny particles or structures between 1 and 100 nanometres in size – where 1 nanometre = 10.9 metres.

Net movement The overall movement of …

Neutral A solution with a pH value of 7 which is neither acidic nor an alkaline. Alternatively, something that carries no overall electrical charge – neither positively nor negatively charged.

Neutralisation The chemical reaction of an acid with a base in which they cancel each other out, forming a salt and water. If the base is a carbonate or hydrogen carbonate, carbon dioxide is also produced in the reaction.

Neutral wire The wire of a mains circuit that is earthed at the local substation so its potential is close to zero.

Neutron A dense particle found in the nucleus of an atom. It is electrically neutral, carrying no charge.

Neutron star The highly compressed core of a massive star that remains after a supernova explosion.

Nitrate ion Ion which is needed by plants to make proteins.

Nuclear fission The process in which certain nuclei (uranium-235 and plutonium-239) split into two fragments, releasing energy and two or three neutrons as a result.

Nuclear fission reactor A reactor that releases energy as a result of nuclear fission inside it.

Nuclear fusion The process in which small nuclei are forced together so they fuse with each other to form a larger nucleus.

Nucleus (of a cell) An organelle found in many living cells containing the genetic information.

Nucleus (of an atom) The very small and dense central part of an atom which contains protons and neutrons.

O

Ohm's law The current through a resistor at constant temperature is directly proportional to the potential difference across the resistor.

Ohmic conductor A conductor that has a constant resistance and therefore obeys Ohm's law.

Optic nerve The nerve carrying impulses from the retina of the eye to the brain.

Organ A group of different tissues working together to carry out a particular function

Organ system A group of organs working together to carry out a particular function.

Oscilloscope A device used to display the shape of an electrical wave.

Ova The female sex cells, eggs.

Oxidation The reaction when oxygen is added to a substance (or when electrons are lost).

Oxygen debt The extra oxygen that must be taken into the body after exercise has stopped to complete the aerobic respiration of lactic acid.

P

Parallel Components connected in a circuit so that the potential difference is the same across each one.

Percentage yield The actual mass of product collected in a reaction divided by the maximum mass that could have been formed in theory, multiplied by 100.

Permanent vacuole A space in the cytoplasm filled with cell sap which is there all the time.

pH scale A number which shows how strongly acidic or alkaline a solution is. Acids have a pH value of less than 7 (pH 1 is strongly acidic). Alkalis have a pH value above 7 (pH 14 is strongly alkaline). A neutral liquid has a pH value of 7.

Phloem tissue The living transport tissue in plants which carries sugars around the plant.

Planet A large object that moves in an orbit round a star. A planet reflects light from the star and does not produce its own light.

Plasmid Extra circle of DNA found in bacterial cytoplasm.

Plug A plug has an insulated case and is used to connect the cable from an appliance to a socket.

Polydactyly A genetic condition inherited through a dominant allele which results in extra fingers and toes.

Polymer A substance made from very large molecules made up of many repeating units e.g. poly(ethene).

Polytunnel Large greenhouse made of plastic.

Potential difference A measure of the work done or energy transferred to the lamp by each coulomb of charge that passes through it. The unit of potential difference is the volt (V).

Power The energy transformed or transferred per second. The unit of power is the watt (W).

Precipitate An insoluble solid formed by a reaction taking place in solution.

Precision A precise set of repeat readings will be closely grouped together.

Predator Animal which preys on other animals for food.

Protease An enzyme which breaks down proteins.

Protein synthesis The process by which proteins are made on the ribosomes based on information from the genes in the nucleus.

Proton A tiny positive particle found inside the nucleus of an atom.

Protostar The concentration of dust clouds and gas in space that forms a star.

Q

Quadrat A piece of apparatus for sampling organisms in the field.

Quantitative sampling Sampling which records the numbers of organisms rather than just the type.

R

Radiation dose Amount of ionising radiation a person receives.

Random Cannot be predicted and has no recognisable cause.

Range The maximum and minimum values of the independent or dependent variables; important in ensuring that any pattern is detected.

Recessive The characteristic that will show up in the offspring only if both of the alleles are inherited.

Red giant A star that has expanded and cooled, resulting in it becoming red and much larger and cooler than it was before it expanded.

Reduction A reaction in which oxygen is removed (or electrons are gained).

Relative atomic mass, A_r The average mass of the atoms of an element compared with carbon-12 (which is given a mass of exactly 12). The average mass must take into account the proportions of the naturally occurring isotopes of the element.

Relative formula mass, M_r The total of the relative atomic masses, added up in the ratio shown in the chemical formula, of a substance.

Repeatability (of data) We can improve the accuracy of data by repeating measurements and calculating the mean (having re-tested or discarded any anomalous results).

Reproducibility (of data) The consistency of data that is collected when different people carry out the same investigation.

Residual Current Circuit Breaker (RCCB) An RCCB cuts off the current in the live wire when it is different from the current in the neutral wire.

Resistance Ω Resistance (in ohms) = potential difference (in volts, V) ÷ current (in amperes, A).

Resolution This is the smallest change in the quantity being measured (input) of a measuring instrument that gives a perceptible change in the reading.

Respiration The process by which food molecules are broken down to release energy for the cells.

Resultant force The combined effect of the forces acting on an object.

Retention time The time it takes a component in a mixture to pass through the column during gas chromatography.

Reversible reaction A reaction in which the products can re-form the reactants.

Ribosome The site of protein synthesis in a cell.

S

Salivary gland Gland in the mouth which produces saliva containing the enzyme amylase.

Salt A salt is a compound formed when some or all of the hydrogen in an acid is replaced by a metal (or by an ammonium ion). For example, potassium nitrate, KNO_3 (from nitric acid).

Sample size The size of a sample in an investigation.

Series Components connected in a circuit so that the same current that passes through them are in series with each other.

Sex chromosome The chromosome which carries the information about the sex of an individual.

Shape memory alloy Mixture of metals which respond to changes in temperature.

Small intestine The region of the digestive system where most of the digestion of the food takes place.

Socket A mains socket is used to connect the mains plug of a mains appliance to the mains circuit.

Specialised Adapted for a particular function.

Speciation The formation of a new species.

Speed Distance moved ÷ time taken.

State symbol The abbreviations used in balanced symbol equations to show if reactants and products are solid (s), liquid (l), gas (g) or dissolved in water (aq).

Static electricity Charge 'held' by an insulator or an insulated conductor.

Stem cell Undifferentiated cell with the potential to form a wide variety of different cell types.

Stopping distance Thinking distance + braking distance.

Substrate The material or chemical on which an enzyme acts.

Supergiant A massive star that becomes much larger than a giant star when fusion of helium nuclei commences.

Supernova The explosion of a massive star after fusion in its core ceases and the matter surrounding its core collapses on to the core and rebounds.

T

Terminal velocity The velocity reached by an object when the drag force on it is equal and opposite to the force making it move.

Therapeutic cloning Cloning by transferring the nucleus of an adult cell to an empty egg to produce tissues or organs which could be used in medicine.

Thermal decomposition The breakdown of a compound by heat.

Thermosetting polymer Polymer that can form extensive cross-linking between chains, resulting in rigid materials which are heat-resistant.

Thermosoftening polymer Polymer that forms plastics which can be softened by heat, then remoulded into different shapes as they cool down and set.

Thinking distance The distance travelled by the vehicle in the time it takes the driver to react.

Three-pin plug A three-pin plug has a live pin, a neutral pin and an earth pin. The earth pin is used to earth the metal case of an appliance so the case cannot become live.

Time base control An oscilloscope control used to space the waveform out horizontally.

Tissue A group of specialised cells all carrying out the same function.

Transect A measured line or area along which ecological measurements (e.g. quadrats) are made.

Tuber Modified part of a plant which is used to store food in the form of starch.

U

Universal indicator A mixture of indicators which can change through a range of colours depending on the pH of a solution. Its colour is matched to a pH number using a pH scale. It shows how strongly acidic or alkaline liquids and solutions are.

V

Valid Suitability of the investigative procedure to answer the question being asked.

Variable Physical, chemical or biological quantity or characteristic.

Variable – categoric Categoric variables have values that are labels. For example, names of plants or types of material.

Variable – continuous Can have values (called a quantity) that can be given by measurement (e.g. light intensity, flow rate, etc.).

Variable – dependent The variable for which the value is measured for each and every change in the independent variable.

Variable – independent The variable for which values are changed or selected by the investigator.

Variegated Having different colours, e.g. a green and white leaf.

Velocity Speed in a given direction (in metres/second, m/s).

Volt (V) The unit of potential difference, equal to energy transfer per unit charge in joules per coulomb.

W

Weight The force of gravity on an object (in newtons, N).

White dwarf A star that has collapsed from the red giant stage to become much hotter and denser than it was.

Work Energy transferred by a force, given by:

Work done (in joules, J) = force (in newtons, N) × distance moved in the direction of the force (in metres, m).

X

Xylem tissue The non-living transport tissue in plants, which transports water around the plant.

Y

Y-gain control An oscilloscope control used to adjust the height of the waveform.

Yield See Percentage yield.

Index